"The history of Alaska's turn-of-the told a hundred times in a hundred different ways. Brian Shellum's *Buffalo Soldiers in Alaska* shines much-needed light on a part of the story that has received little attention from scholars: the Black soldiers sent to keep order in Skagway and their interactions with white citizens and Alaska Natives and with Canadians on the other side of the border. This important book is a must-read for anyone interested in Alaska history."

—ROSS COEN, editor of *Alaska History*

"Brian Shellum provides a wealth of facts about the lives of the Buffalo Soldiers who served in Alaska. It should be essential reading for anyone interested in the history of African Americans, Alaska, or twentieth-century military history."

—CATHERINE SPUDE, historian, author of *Saloons, Prostitutes, and Temperance in Alaska Territory*

"The author pays particular attention to the Black enlisted men who served in Alaska during the halcyon days of the Klondike gold rush. As such, this well-illustrated and carefully researched study sheds new light on a little-known story in U.S. Army history."

—JOHN P. LANGELLIER, author of *Scouting with the Buffalo Soldiers: Lieutenant Powhatan Clarke, Frederic Remington, and the 10th U.S. Cavalry in the Southwest*

"A thoroughly researched and well-presented account of a little-known episode in Alaskan history. No grand themes, pivotal events, or outsized personalities. The book is a welcome expansion of the story of African Americans in the nation's military."

—TOM PHILLIPS, independent historian, coauthor of *The Black Regulars, 1866–1898*

"Here is an extensively researched and detailed account of a little-known piece of gold rush history. What I particularly enjoyed was reading portions of the narrative that I have investigated myself but from a Canadian perspective. Well worth the read."

—MICHAEL GATES, former Parks Canada curator and author of *Dalton's Gold Rush Trail* and *From the Klondike to Berlin*

"Shellum has added yet another important and crucial volume to his works of untold military history stories by penning this book exploring the lives of the African American soldiers who proudly served on the Alaskan frontier. Readers will gain an appreciation not only for military history but for the way Buffalo Soldiers used baseball to connect with the white citizens of Skagway."

—KREWASKY A. SALTER, executive director of the First Division Museum

BUFFALO SOLDIERS IN ALASKA

Company L, Twenty-Fourth Infantry

BRIAN G. SHELLUM

UNIVERSITY OF NEBRASKA PRESS

Lincoln

Library of Congress Cataloging-in-Publication Data
Names: Shellum, Brian G., author.
Title: Buffalo soldiers in Alaska: Company L, Twenty-
Fourth Infantry / Brian G. Shellum.
Other titles: Company L, Twenty-Fourth Infantry
Description: Lincoln: University of Nebraska Press,
[2021] | Includes bibliographical references and index.
Identifiers: LCCN 2021003600
ISBN 9781496228444 (paperback)
ISBN 9781496228864 (epub)
ISBN 9781496228871 (pdf)
Subjects: LCSH: Skagway (Alaska)—History, Military. |
United States. Army. Infantry Regiment, 24th
(1869–1951). Company L. | African Americans—
Alaska—Skagway—History. | African American
soldiers—History—20th century. | African American
soldiers—Biography. | Alaska—Race relations—
History—20th century. | United States. Army—Civic
action—History—20th century. | Skagway (Alaska)—
Social conditions—20th century. | Skagway (Alaska)—
Biography. | BISAC: HISTORY / United States / State
& Local / West (AK, CA, CO, HI, ID, MT, NV, UT, WY) |
SOCIAL SCIENCE / Ethnic Studies / American / African
American & Black Studies
Classification: LCC F914.S7 S38 2021 | DDC 979.8/2—dc23
LC record available at https://lccn.loc.gov/2021003600

Set in Lyon Text by Laura Buis.

For my sister
Rolynn Anderson

CONTENTS

ILLUSTRATIONS

Following page 66

PREFACE

A conference call planted the seed for this book. Years ago, I participated in a monthly Buffalo Soldier discussion facilitated by National Park Ranger Guy Washington. On one such call more than ten years ago, Tegan Urbanski of the Klondike Gold Rush National Historical Park dialed in, surprising us with the news that a company of Black soldiers from the Twenty-Fourth Infantry had served in Skagway during the Klondike gold rush. She was searching for resources on the Buffalo Soldiers to tell their story to park visitors.

The seed germinated when I arranged a cruise along the Alaskan coast for a group of my West Point classmates in 2018. One of our port calls was Skagway, and I remembered the phone call from Urbanski. So I called Jason Verhaeghe at the Klondike Gold Rush National Historical Park (known by the National Park Service acronym of KLGO) to ask if he wanted me to make a presentation the day I was in port. I did some preliminary research, wrote a paper, gave the talk, and discovered an intriguing story. This book is the fruit of the research conducted in the two years since.

After a preliminary investigation of the resources, I realized I could not build a narrative of the experiences of Company L, Twenty-Fourth Infantry, without visiting Skagway. Now as then, Alaska remains a far-off place unfamiliar to most Americans. Fortunately, I learned from former *Skagway News* editor Jeff Brady about a writer-in-residence program called Alderworks Alaska in Dyea, Alaska. I applied, was accepted, and spent a month in the summer of 2019 researching, writing, and exploring the area around Skagway.

I had the same sense of wonder and excitement as the Buffalo Soldiers surveying the natural beauty of the steep fjords on the ferry trip from Juneau to Skagway. I stepped off the gangplank wharf-side, feeling lost as they had. Likewise, the first night sleeping in a cabin thousands of miles from home felt extraordinarily lonely. The quadruple-wire electric fence that surrounded my compound to discourage grizzly bears added to the anxiety.

I was fortunate to have Jeff Brady, the owner of Skaguay News Depot and Books, as my host at Alderworks. He and his wife, Dorothy, whose great-grandfather was a Faro dealer at the Board of Trade Saloon during the Klondike gold rush, knew all the right people in Skagway.

KLGO was a rich resource of talent and information on the Buffalo Soldiers. Park Ranger Kira Pontius was always at the ready to answer my questions and provide encouragement. Park Historian Karl Gurcke possessed an almost encyclopedic memory of the history and buildings of Skagway, and he took me on a walking tour of the streets the soldiers had occupied. He also created an excellent historic photo essay of the Black regulars in Skagway, which he constantly updates as new discoveries are made. This photo essay was my starting point and handy reference as I wrote the narrative. I supplemented it with trips to the Skagway Public Library to survey issues of the local *Daily Alaskan*, the newspaper published while Company L served in Skagway.

I augmented the information gathered in Skagway with official army records from the National Archives in Washington DC. The War Department's regimental and post returns, filed by Company L monthly, provided important details of the lives and experiences of the officers and soldiers. When cross-referenced with the enlistment records and newspaper stories of events in Skagway, I could piece together a fascinating story of how the officers and enlisted soldiers adapted to life in Alaska. And in one rare case of an officer who served with Company L in Skagway, I found a cache of papers and photos he had passed on to his descendants, documenting his time in Alaska.

This book is a detailed account of the officers and men who served three years in Alaska, from 1899 to 1902. This was a time of change for an army that was transforming from a frontier force to a military establishment fighting to defend an overseas empire in the Pacific.

What I was able to do in this book, more than in my previous manuscripts, was document the lives and experiences of the Black enlisted soldiers in Company L. This is their story.

ACKNOWLEDGMENTS

I owe a great deal of gratitude to my wife, Paula, for offering me the time and encouragement to complete this book. She has ever been my chief advocate and supporter along the way. I am also grateful to my daughter, Kara, and son, Greg, who cheered me on from a distance.

Most of my original source material for this book came from the National Archives and Records Administration (NARA). The most critical documents at NARA consisted of company, regimental, and post returns filed monthly reporting the routine actions of Company L, Twenty-Fourth Infantry. Supplementing these returns were ledgers recording Camp Skagway letters sent and received during the period. And lastly, the Register of Enlistments in the U.S. Army provided critical information on individual soldiers. I used the searchable database of Ancestry.com to locate and view these documents, a far cry from the old days searching the microfilm files at NARA.

Copies of the Alaskan newspapers came from various sources. The Library of Congress has a searchable database of newspapers on its Chronicling America site, where I found many issues of the *Daily Alaskan*, Skagway's daily newspaper. I filled the gaps of missing issues by visiting the Skagway Public Library and the collections of the Klondike Gold Rush National Historical Park in Skagway, Alaska.

Historian Karl Gurcke and Park Ranger Kira Pontius at the KLGO have been my go-to sources for original research materials and advice. The KLGO possesses the most important original source documents and photos from the time Company L served in Alaska. I thank the countless National Park Service employees who plumbed the private and public collections over the years and made my task easier.

Historian Catherine Holder Spude, who wrote *Saloons, Prostitutes, and Temperance in Alaska Territory*, answered countless emails and provided details of the sex and saloon industries in Skagway. Margaret Villarma of the Wrangell Public Library provided copies of the daily newspapers unavailable elsewhere. Benjamin Gilson, a descendant of Isaac Jenks, one of the officers who served in Skagway, shared photos and letters passed to him by his mother and grandmother. Original source documents like this are rare.

I was fortunate to have a group of dedicated readers who worked over my various drafts. Tom Phillips, coauthor of *The Black Regulars, 1866–1898*, spent more time than any other of my readers and reviewed each chapter of my first and second drafts to offer detailed comments and suggestions. He gave me a great deal of good-natured grief along with good advice. My sister, Rolynn Anderson, spent countless hours reviewing the drafts of my books and offering advice. As a former English teacher, she recommended ways to improve my structure and organization. Skagway resident Jeff Brady also read and commented on my first draft while I was still in Alaska. Axel Krigsman, a West Point classmate, also commented on several chapters.

In the peer review process undertaken by the University of Nebraska Press, two readers who specialize in African American and Alaskan history worked over my drafts and provided me with important and insightful comments. Though by publisher policy they remain anonymous, the final product is a much better book because of their time and effort.

I must also thank my copyeditor, who remains anonymous by policy as well. This is my second book with her, and once again, she has saved me from embarrassment and death by a thousand cuts. In addition to finding errors and correcting my grammar, she suggested subtle changes to my text to make my writing sharper.

In addition to those already mentioned, I thank the following organizations for their support: the Alaska State Archives, Charles Young

Buffalo Soldiers National Monument, Elmer E. Rasmuson Library (Fairbanks), Museum of History and Industry (Seattle), Sheldon Museum (Haines), Skagway Museum, Wrangell Museum, and Yukon Archives. Other individuals who assisted and encouraged me along the way include Dean Alexander, Steve Anderson, Paul Berg, Don Burger, Suzanne Christoff, Tracy Churchill, Ross Coen, Cyni Crary, Roger Cunningham, Bonnie Demerjian, Piotr Derengowski, Susannah Dowds, Suzie Eckl, Ward Eldredge, Michael Engelhard, Stephen Gilson, Shelli Gordon, Maura Graziano, Bill Gwaltney, Greg Haitz, Ian Hartman, Bob Hendrickson, Ron Inouye, Shelton Johnson, Cindy Kilpatrick, Joy Kinard, John Langellier, Rosalie L'Ecuyer, Murray Lundberg, Leslie McCartney, Carl Mulvihill, Carolyn Nore, Michael Nore, Alysha Page, George Palmer, Robert Parker, Rik Penn, Antony Powell, Susie Roy, Krewasky Salter, Bryan Saul, Joan Skillbred, Scott Stephenson, Robert Stewart, Floyd Thomas, Gregory Urwin, Curtis Utz, Guy Washington, Karen Winn, Lawrence Young, and Renotta Young.

CHRONOLOGY

1867 U.S. purchases Alaska from Russia for $7.2 million

1868 U.S. Army establishes Fort Wrangel

1887 Captain William Moore homesteads Skagway

1896 August: George Carmack, Keish (Skookum Jim Mason), and Kháa Ghoox (Dawson Charlie) find gold at Rabbit Creek, a tributary of the Klondike River

1897 July: San Francisco and Seattle newspaper headlines report news of Klondike gold discovery

1897 October: Stampeders swell population of Dyea and Skagway to nearly ten thousand each

1898 February: Yukon Relief Expedition arrives in Dyea and Skagway, Alaska

1898 March: Four companies of the Fourteenth U.S. Infantry arrive in Dyea and Skagway

1898 April 25: United States declares war on Spain

1898 May: Fourteenth U.S. Infantry departs, leaving companies at Dyea and Fort Wrangel

1898 August 12: Spanish-American War ends

1898 September: Alaska-Canada Boundary Commission fails to agree on a border

1898 October: Company L, Twenty-Fourth U.S. Infantry, begins organizing

1899 April 5: Company L deploys from Fort Douglas, Utah, to Alaska to replace companies from the Fourteenth Infantry

1899   May 18: Detachment commanded by Lieutenant Isaac C. Jenks arrives at Fort Wrangel, Alaska, aboard ss *Humboldt*

1899   May 20: Company L commanded by Captain Henry W. Hovey arrives in Dyea, Alaska, aboard ss *Humboldt*

1899   July 6: White Pass & Yukon Route completes rail line from Skagway to Bennett City, British Columbia, Canada

1899   July 28: Fire destroys Company L barracks at Dyea and forces Captain Hovey to move to a temporary tent camp in Skagway

1899   September 15: Captain Hovey moves company into leased barracks in the Astoria Hotel

1900   January: U.S. Army creates Department of Alaska

1900   May 13: Detachment under Jenks from Fort Wrangel reunites with Company L in Skagway

1900   May 20: Soldier team plays first baseball game against White Pass railroad team

1900   June: Census records population of Skagway as 2,383

1900   June 28: Skagway becomes the first incorporated city in Alaska

1900   July 29: White Pass & Yukon Route completes rail line from Bennett City to Carcross, Yukon, Canada

1900   October: Company L moves into new barracks built on Sixth Avenue

1901   September 6: Anarchist assassinates President William McKinley

1901   September 18: Theodore Roosevelt assumes presidency

1901   September 24: U.S. Army completes telegraphic line to Skagway

1901   October 13: Great flood ravages Skagway

1902   April 5: First element of 106th Coast Artillery Company arrives in Skagway to replace Company L

1902   May 13: Company L and White Pass teams play last baseball game

1902   May 15: Company L departs Skagway aboard SS *City of Seattle*

1902   May 22: Company L arrives at Fort Missoula, Montana

1903   January 24: Alaska-Canada Boundary Commission settles boundary dispute in favor of United States

BUFFALO SOLDIERS IN ALASKA

PROLOGUE

A Day of Glory in Gay Skagway!
—*DAILY ALASKAN*, July 6, 1901

Independence Day 1901 in Skagway, Alaska boasted fireworks, a parade, music, and sports: a perfect portrait of community at play.

The celebration began at midnight on the third with the rattle of firecrackers mingling with the clatter of gunfire, the sounds not unusual in Skagway, a well-armed town with miners and merchants keen to protect their hard-won Klondike gold. The town gained a reputation as a "hell on earth" during its short existence.[1]

The next day's events began with a morning parade through the dusty streets of Skagway. As with most Independence Day parades, men in uniform played a prominent role in the procession. According to the newspaper, the parade "was led by the colored troops, the attractiveness of the column being enhanced by the cannon and Gatling gun drawn by mule teams."[2]

This reference to "colored troops" is the only mention in the article that the resident soldiers were African American. They were Company L, a unit of Black enlisted soldiers from the Twenty-Fourth U.S. Infantry Regiment, garrisoned in Skagway since 1899.

The Black soldiers did more than march in the parade. Later in the day they competed with the white citizens of Skagway in almost every one of eighteen sporting events. It would be a challenge to find another community in the United States in 1901 where Blacks and whites competed head-to-head in sporting contests on the Fourth of July.[3]

1

More remarkable: this celebration took place in Skagway, a city born in the Klondike gold rush that swelled in population from a handful of men and women in 1897 to ten thousand residents by the end of the next year. A place balanced on the edge of anarchy that had been dominated by the Soapy Smith Gang. Smith, the self-styled captain of his own militia company, rode at the head of the parade during Independence Day in 1898. Four days after the parade, Smith was killed in a shootout with a vigilante committee.

The local newspaper observed, "Of all the sports of the day the baseball game elicited the most frantic interest." Baseball had reached its peak of popularity in the United States and found ardent supporters in Alaska too. The game that day pitted a local club of white railroad workers against a team of Black soldiers.[4]

The "captain of the soldier nine was Corporal Green." His team represented the infantry company backing law and order in the region. On the other side, "Phelps bawled the boys off the bases for the railroaders." The local rail workers played an important role in the community, building and maintaining a railroad that secured the future of the town. The people of Skagway cheered wildly as the soldiers and rail men contested for bragging rights. First prize was a team purse of fifty dollars, second twenty-five dollars: a princely sum for an army private or a track layer.[5]

The teams crossed bats at the baseball grounds near Captain William Moore's sawmill. Beer distributed by the Skagway Brewing Company added to the merriment, and vendors sold ice cream, ice cream soda, lemonade, milk, and juice. The rhythmic chug, rattle, and whistle of the White Pass & Yukon Route steam engine echoed from the tracks bordering the outfield. The smells of cut lumber from the nearby mill and rotting seaweed from the adjacent tidal flats wafted in the wind and mixed with the perspiration of the tightly packed crowd of miners, muleskinners, merchants, laborers, prostitutes, and soldiers. There were no bleachers, so the throng had to jostle for a view of the action.

The game was a hard-fought affair, beginning at 1:00 p.m. and lasting three hours. Two prominent citizens from the town served as umpires.

Ostensibly neutral, but umpires are umpires. They were somewhat acquainted with the modern rules of baseball adopted in 1901 by both the National and American leagues.

Nicknamed the White Pass Boys, the railroaders wore "blue trousers and black shirts and caps, all trimmed in white." The soldiers donned uniforms complete with baseball caps, numbered baseball shirts, knickers, and striped socks. The troops called themselves the Company L team yet were known as the "soldier team" by the locals.[6]

Edward Barry, William C. Blanchard, and Frank Burns, the best hitters, batted first for the White Pass Club; Benjamin Green, William Jennings, and William Sims led off for the soldier team. The two squads battled nine long innings in a high-scoring game. The "men and women shouted their lungs sore" during the competition that day. The contest ended with a railroad team victory by a score of 14–10, and the White Pass team claimed the winning purse.[7]

The atmosphere in 1901 was decidedly different from 1898, with an African American infantry company leading the Independence Day parade and Black soldiers competing with white citizens on the friendly fields of strife. So who were the soldiers participating in the Fourth of July celebration, what brought them to Skagway, and how did they help end the town's "hell on earth" reputation?

1

NORTH TO ALASKA

Colored Troops for Alaska.
—*DAILY ALASKAN*, May 16, 1899

On the first day of April 1899, Colonel Henry B. Freeman, regimental commander of the Twenty-Fourth U.S. Infantry, handed Captain Henry W. Hovey orders reassigning Company L to the Department of the Columbia in the Pacific Northwest. Freeman decided to send Hovey's company, along with three others from the Twenty-Fourth, north on detached duty while the rest of the regiment shipped out to the Philippine Islands. Further, Freeman informed Hovey he would board ships sailing north to occupy two military garrisons on the panhandle of Alaska. Hovey, who had returned to duty with his regiment in Utah after serving the past five years in Vermont, had been in command of his company one week.[1]

Northward Bound

Hovey heard of his new Alaska mission shortly after stepping off a train in Salt Lake City to return to his regiment at nearby Fort Douglas, Utah. He assumed command of Company L on March 24, 1898, after serving five years at Norwich University. While most of the regiment was bound for a brutal guerilla war against Filipino rebels, Company L and the three other companies of the Second Battalion were assigned to the Department of the Columbia. They replaced other units that were also bound for the Philippines.[2]

Most of the Regular Army's active infantry regiments as well as many state volunteer units eventually deployed to the Philippine Islands to fight. Hovey's battalion of four companies journeyed north to Alaska, Montana, and Washington, while the rest of the regiment shipped off to the Philippine Islands. Race had no bearing on the Twenty-Fourth Infantry's serving in the Philippines or in Company L's assignment to Alaska. Company L replaced a white infantry company in Alaska slated to deploy to the Philippine Islands with its regiment. Every regiment in the Regular Army, white and Black, eventually served in the Philippines.[3]

Why did Colonel Freeman choose Company L for this detached service? The most obvious reason was its recent organization.

Company L was one of two companies added to the Twenty-Fourth Infantry after the United States declared war on Spain in April 1898. At that time Congress increased the strength of all Regular Army infantry regiments to bring the companies to a full wartime manning of twelve. Yet the regiment was too busy deploying to fight in Cuba to activate the new units. Companies L and M formed after the war in October 1898 at Fort Douglas, Utah, using officers and soldiers levied from other companies as well as newly arrived recruits.[4]

Colonel Freeman initially took those units he thought most capable for immediate combat operations to the Philippines. These included eight companies with long service in the regiment commanded by the most senior and experienced company commanders. Hovey and the commanders of the other three companies sent north were the most junior captains in the regiment and the most recently assigned to command. Aside from newly formed Companies L and M, Freeman sent Companies B and D north to Washington and Montana. The following year, most of the Second Battalion that initially deployed to the Department of the Columbia joined the regiment in the Philippines. Company L remained in Alaska and was the only unit in the regiment that did not see action in the Philippine War.[5]

On April 5, 1899, Company L boarded trains in nearby Salt Lake City for the trip to the Presidio of San Francisco, California. While the company spent several weeks billeted at this military post awaiting transportation, men became sick or got into trouble. Hovey had to leave five men who were too ill to travel from the military hospital as well as two men in military confinement. Since the Presidio was surrounded by the bars and brothels of San Francisco, there were plenty of opportunities for soldiers to get into trouble.[6]

After the brief stay at the Presidio, the company loaded aboard the U.S. Army transport *McDowell* on May 3 for passage to Oakland and later proceeded by rail to Vancouver Barracks, Washington. Hovey left two more soldiers sick at the hospital at Vancouver Barracks, which was just across the Columbia River from Portland, Oregon. After a short stop, Company L marched to the train depot the evening of May 14 and boarded an overnight train for Seattle. Arriving the next morning, Captain Hovey marched his company to the port in Seattle and camped on the docks for the day.[7]

Hovey loaded his men and equipment onto the commercial steam ship SS *Humboldt* on May 14 at 8:30 in the evening for the passage to Alaska. Four days later, the company touched at Fort Wrangel, Alaska, where Hovey left Lieutenant Isaac C. Jenks, his second in command, with forty-six men to garrison the post. He and the balance of the command steamed north and landed near Dyea, Alaska, on May 20, 1899, replacing a company from the all-white Fourteenth Infantry, which departed immediately aboard the same ship. Hovey and his African American soldiers had traveled more than two thousand miles by train and ship in fifty days.[8]

Before launching into a narrative of Company L's experiences in Alaska, it is important to know something of the background of the two white officers who disembarked SS *Humboldt* to command the detachments at Fort Wrangel and Dyea. More important is an essential understanding of the personal and professional history of the Black sergeants and enlisted soldiers who formed the core of the company. A handful of leaders were veterans with many years of frontier service with the Buffalo Soldiers in the West. The majority were young soldiers in their first or second enlistment in the Black regulars. Alaska would be new to them all.

Captain Henry W. Hovey

The officer assigned to command Company L was Captain Henry Walter Hovey. Born in Vassalboro, Maine, in 1852, Hovey's military roots extended to the Revolutionary War. He studied in Boston and moved to New York City in 1866 where he enlisted in the renowned Seventh Regiment, New York National Guard in 1869. Hovey married Carrie French Tower of Boston in 1878 at Saint Ann's Church in New York City. He continued his service with the New York National Guard until he obtained a commission as a second lieutenant in the Twenty-Fourth Infantry in November 1880. A direct commission for a civilian with National Guard experience was rare and required political connections.[9]

After spending three months en route at Columbus Barracks, Ohio, one of two infantry trainee depots for both white and Black soldiers, Hovey traveled west in command of twenty-seven new African American recruits bound for the Twenty-Fourth Infantry in Indian Territory (later Oklahoma). Hovey reported in March 1881 to his first assignment with Company E, Twenty-Fourth Infantry, at Fort Reno. The regiment guarded thousands of Native Americans held on reservations there—Kiowas, Comanches, Arapahos, and Southern Cheyennes.[10]

He moved with his company to Fort Sill, Indian Territory, in June 1882. Hovey's wife joined him at Fort Sill where their daughter, Clara Drummond, was born in 1882 and son, Bradford Pierce, was born in 1886. He and his family remained at Fort Sill until the regiment moved to Arizona and New Mexico Territory in 1888.[11]

With his promotion to first lieutenant, he transferred to Company A at Fort Bayard, New Mexico Territory. First Lieutenant Hovey remained with Company A, Twenty-Fourth Infantry, at that post from 1888 to 1895. The regiment kept the Apaches on the reservation and guarded them from settler encroachment. During his last year assigned, Hovey served as the post adjutant and post recruiting officer.[12]

Several items of note in Hovey's frontier experience bear on his later service in Alaska. First, Hovey suffered from serious bouts of illness described as "intermittent fever" during his early service. The disease, likely malaria, which was widespread in Indian Territory, took a terrible toll on Native Americans and soldiers. Hovey suffered debilitating outbreaks at least ten times between 1881 and 1895, sick in quarters for weeks or months at a time. During once such illness, he spent six months recuperating on medical leave.[13]

While appointed as regimental adjutant at Fort Bayard, Hovey dealt directly with the regimental commander and staff. He worked closely with Allen Allensworth, the African American regimental chaplain and superintendent of post schools. Hovey and Allensworth arrived at Fort Bayard within days of each other in 1888 and served together at the post until both departed in 1895, so they knew each other well. Allensworth was highly regarded and a vocal proponent of educating Black soldiers.[14]

Finally, the army granted Hovey a home leave of four months in 1895 after fourteen arduous years of frontier duty. Following leave, Hovey reported for duty as professor of military science and tactics at Norwich University in Northfield, Vermont. Such an assignment at a university was common for army officers who had completed five years of service in the field with troops. For Hovey, the assignment also served as a break from active service to recover his health.[15]

Hovey was serving at Norwich University when the Spanish-American War erupted. Promoted to captain on April 26, 1898, the day after Congress declared war on Spain, he wanted to return to his unit for wartime service. However, the War Department directed him to stay at Norwich during the rapid and chaotic deployment of his regiment to Cuba, since the army needed officers at detached duty posts to continue the process of training and fielding the force.[16]

Unable to return to the Twenty-Fourth Infantry in time to see action in Cuba, Hovey was assigned to command nearby Fort Ethan Allen, Vermont, where he helped muster in the First Vermont Volunteers. He remained at Fort Ethan Allen until the end of 1898. In February 1899 the War Department telegraphed Captain Hovey orders to return to Fort Douglas and assume command of the newly formed Company L.[17]

Lieutenant Isaac C. Jenks

First Lieutenant Isaac Coburn Jenks was the only other officer assigned to Company L and the man who commanded the unit between October 1898 and the arrival of Captain Hovey in March 1899. Jenks was born in Dedham, Massachusetts in 1867 and, like Hovey, had ancestors who fought in the American Revolution. After graduating from high school and teaching for two years, Jenks received an appointment to the United States Military Academy at West Point in 1887.[18]

Cadet Isaac "Ikey" Jenks was known by his West Point classmates for his sense of humor and his vibrant tenor voice, having attended the Boston Conservatory of Music. He was also a leader on the baseball team, playing catcher on West Point's first varsity team in 1891. His inability to resist the temptation to pull a practical joke or break out in song resulted in demerits and contributed to his graduating fifth to last in his class. Upon graduation, Jenks was commissioned as a second lieutenant in the Twenty-Fourth Infantry in June 1891.[19]

Jenks was not forced to choose a Black regiment because of poor class standing. Quite the contrary. The four cadets who graduated below him in order of merit selected assignments with white infantry regiments after he picked the Twenty-Fourth. Likely, he could have opted otherwise. Some cadets chose the Black regulars because it was thought they could earn faster promotion there. The Buffalo Soldier regiments earned a credible record during the Indian Wars and experienced higher reenlistment and lower desertion rates than white regiments.[20]

After graduation from West Point, Lieutenant Jenks reported to his first assignment with Company F, Twenty-Fourth Infantry, at Fort Bayard, New Mexico. Fort Bayard was a large post, then accommodating the regimental headquarters, band, and six companies from the Twenty-Fourth Infantry, as well as two troops of the Black Tenth U.S. Cavalry. Jenks and Hovey were both stationed there during the period 1891 to 1895; as two of the ten junior officers on the isolated frontier post, they knew each other and socialized together. Their common New England roots and shared Revolutionary War ancestors might have made it easy for them to get along.[21]

Lieutenant Jenks served with the Twenty-Fourth at Fort Bayard until 1896. This was a period when the regiment's main mission was to keep the Apaches confined to the reservation and to prevent conflict with settlers. The regiment attached him to a troop of the First U.S. Cavalry Regiment escorting the Boundary Commission on the Mexican border from September to November 1892, which earned him the Indian Wars medal.[22]

In late 1892 and early 1893, the notorious Apache Kid, a former Indian Scout who served with the U.S. Army, was terrorizing miners and settlers in the area where Jenks commanded detachments of the Twenty-Fourth Infantry and First Cavalry. He led these small mobile forces on long scouting missions near the Mexican border pursuing hostile parties of Apaches. The Kid, court-martialed and found guilty of mutiny and desertion, was pardoned after serving time at the military prison on Alcatraz. Later rearrested, he escaped a prisoner transfer to Yuma Territorial Prison in 1889 and was never recaptured.[23]

In November 1893 Lieutenant Jenks received orders to report to Willets Point, New York, for instruction in "torpedo service." Willets Point was then the home of the U.S. Army Engineer School of Application, and this assignment was a reward for Jenks's excellent service during his first two years. One might ask what an infantry lieutenant serving in the arid deserts of New Mexico might gain from "submarine mining." Yet he learned valuable engineering skills that he used after his return to Fort Bayard. Jenks also enjoyed the improved living conditions in New York and relished the time catching up with his West Point classmates attending courses there.[24]

After nearly a year of coursework and a month of home leave, Jenks rejoined his regiment at Fort Bayard in November 1894. The regiment appointed him post engineer officer in June 1895 and, in the year that followed, dispatched Jenks leading detachments of infantry and cavalry on several scouting and heliographic missions across New Mexico and Arizona Territory. A heliograph was a signaling device that used mirrors and the sun to relay messages over long distances. Jenks would later put his engineering and heliographic skills to use in Alaska.[25]

Jenks moved with Company G and the Twenty-Fourth to its new regimental home at Fort Douglas, Utah, in October 1896. This was the first time since its creation in 1869 the entire regiment was located together on one post. The pace at the post was quiescent compared to New Mexico, with routine training instead of sporadic skirmishes with Apaches and outlaws. This was a time when the operational mission of the army was changing in the West. With Native Americans settled on reservations, units no longer occupied small, scattered posts. Instead, the army began concentrating troops in the 1890s on larger posts selected for retention, like Fort Douglas. Congress provided appropriations for permanent, comfortable barracks, and with the spread of the railroad and telegraph lines, these forts were no longer isolated.[26]

In June 1897 Isaac Jenks married Alice A. Stevenson, the daughter of the post surgeon, Major Alfred C. Girard. She used the name Alice G. Jenks after her marriage to Jenks. Alice had a daughter named Marion from a previous marriage. After the ceremony in Salt Lake City, Jenks and his family departed on two months of leave to the east coast. He returned to Utah in August 1897 and continued serving in Company G.[27]

Shortly after President William McKinley signed a congressional resolution demanding the Spanish withdraw from Cuba, the Twenty-Fourth Infantry received telegraphic orders to move to Georgia to prepare for deployment to the Caribbean. The army directed all four of the Buffalo Soldier regiments to move to Cuba before the declaration of war on April 25, 1898. Jenks was promoted to first lieutenant, and he served as the regimental commissary officer in addition to his company duties during the move to Cuba. The regiment loaded onto ships in Tampa and disembarked at Siboney, Cuba, in late June 1898.[28]

The regiment joined in the assault on the blockhouse and trenches atop San Juan Hill the first three days of July 1898. Jenks commanded Company G after the company commander, Captain John J. Brereton, was wounded in action on the first day of battle. Company G led the assault, suffering two killed and twelve wounded. In Jenks's own words: "We marched fully a mile in column under heavy fire of small arms, and with shells screeching and bursting around us, stood for about 15 minutes under a deadly fire from the front, flanks, and rear, and then charged forward over a field, open and about one-half mile long, and took Fort San Juan." Jenks was later cited for gallantry during the fighting.[29]

Jenks still commanded Company G when its men served as quarantine guards and nurses in the "yellow fever pest hospital" in Siboney, Cuba, until the end of August. According to Jenks, most of the regiment served as guards, but sixty-five of the men in the regiment volunteered to serve as nurses. The army assigned African American units like the Twenty-Fourth to the fever hospitals in the mistaken notion that Black soldiers possessed an immunity to tropical diseases. Yet they died in the same numbers as white soldiers when exposed to malaria, yellow fever, and other tropical diseases.[30]

Lieutenant Jenks and the regiment redeployed to the United States at the end of August to the quarantine site at Camp Wikoff at Montauk Point, New York. Of the 26 officers and 486 enlisted men who deployed from Fort Douglas in April, only 11 officers and 289 men were fit or alive to make the trip to Montauk Point in August. The regiment lost 12 killed (2 officer and 10 enlisted) and 73 wounded (6 officer and 67 enlisted) in action in Cuba; another 31 men died of disease serving at the fever hospital at Siboney. The army constructed Camp Wikoff to quarantine the 30,000 soldiers returning from Cuba to prevent the spread of yellow fever and other diseases to the general population. After a period of quarantine, during which several more men died, the Twenty-Fourth loaded on trains in late September and disembarked at Fort Douglas the first day of October 1898.[31]

With the hardships of Cuba behind him, Lieutenant Jenks had several reasons to celebrate when he stepped off the train in Salt Lake City. The citizens of Salt Lake City welcomed the regiment as heroes and provided free streetcar rides to transport the soldiers to the post. Jenks had survived combat in Cuba and avoided serious illness during his time commanding troops at the fever hospital in Siboney. The timing of his return home could not have been better, since his wife, Alice, gave birth to their first child, Dorothy Alice, on October 24, 1898.[32]

Sergeant Robert O'Connor

The third important leader assigned to Company L during its formation was Sergeant Robert O'Connor. O'Connor was born in 1872 in Gaston, North Carolina. He was the son of formerly enslaved parents, his father from South Carolina and his mother from North Carolina. Unlike most members of the first generation of Buffalo Soldier noncommissioned officers, O'Connor could read and write. O'Connor grew up in an environment where he was afforded some education amid the Jim Crow laws introduced after Reconstruction. However, he saw few prospects in the South and moved north in search of better opportunities.[33]

Robert O'Connor enlisted in the army in June 1892, in Albany, New York, listing his age as twenty-one and occupation as laborer. The army assigned O'Connor to F Troop, Tenth Cavalry, then stationed at Fort Assiniboine, Montana. The Tenth Cavalry was headquartered at Fort Custer, Montana, with the component troops (cavalry companies were referred to as "troops") spread across Montana, North Dakota, and Kansas. By 1892 the nation had confined the Native Americans of the Great Plains to reservations, so the regiment focused on routine training and long practice marches. The main hazards were boredom, bad food, unforgiving terrain, and brutal winters.[34]

O'Connor served out his first enlistment and was discharged as a private with a good record at Fort Assiniboine in September 1895. He reenlisted two months later in Saint Louis, Missouri, for three years. The recruiting officer, Captain Henry F. Kendall, assigned him to Company C, Twenty-Fourth Infantry, stationed at Fort Huachuca, Arizona Territory. After one year there, he moved north when the regiment shifted its home base to Fort Douglas, Utah, in 1896. During his second enlistment, O'Connor's leadership and experience earned him first the corporal stripes of a squad leader and later the three stripes of a section sergeant.[35]

Sergeant O'Connor led his section in Company C as it deployed from Fort Douglas in April and landed in Cuba in June 1898. He fought at the head of his men in the charge up San Juan Hill to take the trenches and blockhouse held by the Spanish. He survived the action unscathed and, like Lieutenant Jenks, endured the hazardous duty at the fever hospital at Siboney without serious illness.[36]

Upon his return to Fort Douglas in October 1898, the Twenty-Fourth transferred Sergeant O'Connor to Company L as part of the reorganization of the regiment. O'Connor completed his enlistment in November 1898 and was discharged as a "sergeant with an excellent record." He promptly reenlisted the following day and was assigned again to Company L. After his reenlistment, the regiment granted O'Connor a two-month furlough to Charlotte, North Carolina. After his furlough, O'Connor married Louisa Withers in Salt Lake City in April 1899.[37]

O'Connor was a rising star, attested by his promotion to sergeant, accomplishments in Cuba, and reenlistment for a third term. His new wife eventually joined him in Alaska, and he was allotted government-financed family quarters, signaling his value to the command. The regiment also assigned him to Company L, which was badly in need of leadership. Hovey eventually appointed him as his first sergeant in Alaska.

Sergeant James Washington

A fourth key leader and veteran of many years in the Twenty-Fourth Infantry was Sergeant James Washington. Washington was born in May 1862 in Gainesville, Alabama, a small town where Confederate General Nathan Bedford Forrest, one of the future founders of the Ku Klux Klan, surrendered in 1865. Washington's parents, Alex and Maggie Washington, were enslaved, which meant their son James shared that status. He grew up in a setting where he was afforded some education after the Civil War, though he was also exposed to Jim Crow laws and the depredations of the Klan.[38]

He, like Sergeant O'Connor, moved north in search of better opportunities. He lived in Warrenton, Virginia, when he joined the army in nearby Washington DC in August 1886, listing his occupation as laborer. He was twenty-three years old and tall for the time, standing five feet and ten and a half inches. When he enlisted for his first term, the army assigned him to the Twenty-Fifth U.S. Infantry, one of the Buffalo Soldier regiments stationed on the Great Plains. At that time, the Twenty-Fifth had its headquarters and four companies at Fort Snelling, Minnesota, with the remaining companies scattered west through Dakota Territory.[39]

Washington served his first ten years in the army with Company G, Twenty-Fifth Infantry. After his initial training at the recruit depot at Columbus Barracks, Ohio, he reported to his first duty assignment with Company G at Fort Sisseton, Dakota Territory, in December 1886. Fort Sisseton was a small post with just two companies in the eastern part of the territory (now northeastern South Dakota) guarding the easternmost Sioux reservation.[40]

In May 1888 the army relocated the Twenty-Fifth Infantry west to Montana Territory. The headquarters and four companies of the Twenty-Fifth redeployed to Fort Missoula, with the other companies scattered across the territory. Washington moved with Company G when it marched twenty-one miles to the nearest rail junction and boarded trains for the 1,204-mile trip to Fort Missoula. The regimental headquarters and Company G remained at Fort Missoula for the balance of Washington's first enlistment with the Twenty-Fifth.[41]

Washington reenlisted for a second term in August 1891 and stayed at Fort Missoula for the remainder of his service with the Twenty-Fifth Infantry. When his second term of enlistment expired in August 1896, he decided to leave the army. Yet not for long. Five days later he appeared at Fort Sherman, Idaho, about two hundred miles to the northwest, and reenlisted. This time the assignment officer, Lieutenant Daniel Duncan, assigned Washington to the Twenty-Fourth, the other Black infantry regiment in the army, then stationed in New Mexico and Arizona Territory.[42]

The army assigned the ten-year veteran Private Washington to Company G, Twenty-Fourth Infantry in Fort Bayard, New Mexico, in September 1896. With his considerable army experience, he likely caught the eye of Second Lieutenant Jenks, who also served in the company. The following month, Washington moved with the Twenty-Fourth

Infantry when it pulled up stakes and boarded trains for their new home 1,500 miles to the north in Fort Douglas, Utah.[43]

Private Washington settled into garrison life at Fort Douglas and his ability and experience earned him a leadership position. By the time the Twenty-Fourth Infantry deployed to Cuba in April 1898, Washington wore corporal stripes and led a squad of seven privates in Company G.[44]

Corporal Washington was tested in action in Cuba. He charged with Company G in the assault on the blockhouse and trenches atop San Juan Hill, where two company soldiers died and twelve were wounded in action. The two killed included fellow Corporal John R. Miller and Musician George A. Brown. Washington survived and went on to serve with Jenks at the "yellow fever pest hospital" in Siboney, Cuba.[45]

Corporal Washington accompanied the regiment when it redeployed to the United States in August to the quarantine site at Montauk Point. When the Twenty-Fourth disembarked at Fort Douglas the first day of October 1898, Washington was listed as "sick." Yet he had recovered sufficiently to be assigned to the newly formed Company L on October 7, 1898. He was also promoted and wore the three stripes of a sergeant.[46]

Corporal Augustus Snoten

The oldest soldier in Company L was fifty-year-old Corporal Augustus Snoten. Born in 1849 in Sumner County, Tennessee, Snoten lived the first sixteen years of his life in the pre–Civil War South, probably enslaved himself. He celebrated his sixteenth birthday the month Lee surrendered at Appomattox and the Civil War ended. Little is known about his life before he enlisted in the army.[47]

Augustus Snoten, twenty-seven years old, joined the army in April 1876, just two months before Custer was defeated at the Little Big Horn. He and his younger brother, Peter Snoten, walked to the enlistment office in Nashville, Tennessee, and joined the same month. The enlistment officer assigned them both to the Twenty-Fourth Infantry. Both brothers served in the Buffalo Soldier regiments for the next three decades.[48]

After his initial enrollment, Snoten signed the ledger to serve consecutive terms in 1881, 1886, 1891, 1896, and 1899, always on the anniversary of his first enlistment (periods of service were five years until 1896 and three years thereafter). He served his first twenty years in the army assigned to Company C, Twenty-Fourth Infantry. Snoten was what the younger Buffalo Soldiers called "Old Issue," an army slang term for an old soldier who spent his entire life in the army.[49]

Snoten served with the regiment in most of the difficult campaigns against the Kiowas and Comanches in Indian Territory and the Apaches in Arizona Territory. He reenlisted for his second term at Fort Sill, Indian Territory, the same year Captain Hovey arrived there as a new lieutenant. According to his military record, he always ended his enlistments with a character rating of good or very good and did not rise above the rank of private until 1899.[50]

Snoten was still serving with Company C when it deployed to Cuba to fight in the Spanish-American War. He served under Sergeant O'Connor in the charge up San Juan Hill to take the trenches and blockhouse held by the Spanish. He survived the action but was one of six in Company C wounded. After recovering in the hospital, he rejoined the regiment at Fort Douglas and was reassigned to Company L before it deployed to Alaska. He was finally promoted to corporal in Company L.[51]

Musician Edward Bordinghammer

The second-oldest soldier in Company L and the longest-serving veteran of the Buffalo Soldiers was Edward Bordinghammer. Born in Giles County, Tennessee, in 1849, he probably spent his childhood in enslavement. He enlisted in Pulaski, Tennessee, just five years after the end of the Civil War and four years after Blacks were first permitted to enlist in the Regular Army. The recruiting officer assigned the twenty-one-year-old former laborer to Company K, Twenty-Fourth Infantry.[52]

Bordinghammer joined the Twenty-Fourth in the first year of its establishment. The four Buffalo Soldier infantry regiments created by Congress in 1866 were consolidated into two regiments in the army reorganization of 1869; the former Thirty-Eighth and Forty-First Regiments combining to form the new Twenty-Fourth Infantry. Thus,

Bordinghammer was with the regiment from its birth under its first regimental commander, General Ranald S. Mackenzie.[53]

Bordinghammer served with the Twenty-Fourth Infantry for the rest of his military career, signing up for consecutive terms in 1875, 1880, 1885, 1890, 1895, and 1898. He never spent a day as a civilian in that period, always reenlisting the day after his discharge. He, like Snoten, was considered "Old Issue" by the younger Black soldiers.[54]

By the end of his second five-year enlistment Bordinghammer had risen through the ranks to sergeant, a rank he maintained through his first twenty years in Company K, Twenty-Fourth Infantry. He served with the regiment in many of the most difficult campaigns against the Comanches and Kiowas in Texas and the Apaches in Arizona and New Mexico Territory. Sometime after he reenlisted in 1890, he became a field musician and served in that capacity through the rest of his time in the service. Field musicians regulated the day-to-day routine in the army with drums and trumpets. They were also afforded the pay and privileges of noncommissioned officers.[55]

Reassigned to Company E when he reenlisted in 1895, Bordinghammer deployed to Cuba with the company during the Spanish-American War in 1898. He served as a musician during the charge up San Juan Hill, using his army trumpet to relay commands to soldiers who could not hear vocal commands over the din of battle. He survived the action and endured the hazardous duty at the fever hospital at Siboney without serious illness. He was reassigned to Company L as a field musician prior to deployment to Alaska.[56]

Private Benjamin Green

Company L was composed largely of fresh recruits who filled the depleted ranks of the Twenty-Fourth Infantry after its return from Cuba. One such new arrival was Private Benjamin Green, born in 1875 in Piqua, Ohio. Green, a former teamster or muleskinner, had light brown eyes, curly black hair, a dark complexion, and stood six feet tall, a lofty height for any man at that time. When he enlisted for a three-year term in March 1899 in Dayton, Ohio, Second Lieutenant

Henry L. Newbold assigned him to the newly formed Company L, Twenty-Fourth Infantry.[57]

Unlike sergeants O'Connor and Washington, Green was born and raised north of the Mason-Dixon Line. His father hailed from Pittsburgh, Pennsylvania, and his mother Piqua, Ohio. Piqua, thirty miles north of Dayton, had a sizable population of African Americans, many of them descendants of manumitted slaves owned by John Randolph of Virginia. John Randolph was a U.S. congressman and slaveholder who provided in his will for the manumission and resettlement of his slaves in the free state of Ohio. Piqua had also served as an important terminus in the Underground Railroad.[58]

Green had a fine bass voice and, according to one source, had traveled in the United States for several seasons with a "Negro minstrel troupe" before joining the army. Green also had an aptitude for baseball, demonstrated by his later activities in Skagway. By the late 1800s, baseball was an exceedingly popular sport in Ohio, as it was in the entire country. The only two African Americans to play professional baseball in the Major Leagues did so for an Ohio team in the American Association. In 1884 the Toledo Blue Stockings fielded two Black players, Moses Fleetwood Walker and his brother Weldy Walker. But this test in integration was short-lived, and a vote by owners in 1887 excluded Blacks from the Major Leagues.[59]

Benjamin Green did not have far to travel from Piqua to the Columbus Barracks recruit depot. At the time, the U.S. Army trained Black infantry recruits for one to four months at either Columbus Barracks, Ohio, or Davids Island, New York, before sending them to the Buffalo Soldier regiments. It is likely that Green received a short period of instruction at the depot, considering his unit's pending move. Private Green moved to Fort Douglas in April 1899, just in time to join his new company before it deployed northward.[60]

Private Eugene Swanson

Another new soldier assigned to Company L, Private Eugene Swanson, claimed he had been to Alaska before. Swanson, a twenty-six-year-old born in Rockford, Alabama, enlisted in Chattanooga, Tennessee, in April 1899. He listed his occupation as painter, had a light complexion, and at five feet eleven inches was nearly as tall as Green. Private Swanson joined Company L just five days after signing his enlistment papers.[61]

According to his later accounts, Swanson had come to seek a fortune in gold in the Atlin District of British Columbia in 1896, but gave up after a year. He said he then traveled to Seattle, where he enlisted in the Ninth Cavalry, serving with the Buffalo Soldiers in the charge up San Juan Hill during the Spanish-American War. He also claimed that after the Ninth's return from Cuba, he received an early discharge and left the army before Christmas 1898.[62]

Yet there is no record of Swanson joining the army before 1899. It is possible he joined in 1897, fought with the Ninth in Cuba, and received a discharge in December 1898. But if he did so it was under another name. It's conceivable he panned for gold in the Yukon in 1896, since he later showed an uncanny skill at placer mining. Swanson's life before joining Company L in April 1899 remains a bit of a mystery.

Private George L. Wilson

Private George L. Wilson was another young man who enlisted in the Regular Army in the patriotic fervor following the outbreak of the Spanish-American War. Wilson was born in Boston, Massachusetts, in July 1866 to a father born in Scotland and a mother born in Saint John, New Brunswick, Canada. This made him the first generation in his family to be born a U.S. citizen.[63]

When the United States declared war on Spain in 1898, Wilson decided he wanted to be a soldier. He walked to the armory on the corner of Chardon and Green Streets in Boston in May 1898 and joined Company L, Sixth Massachusetts Volunteers. Company L was the only Black military unit remaining in the Massachusetts National Guard and was unique: it was the only African American company in the regiment, and it was led by Black officers. White officers led many of the other African American volunteer units during the Spanish-American War.

The company's attachment to an all-white regiment made it the first Black unit to mobilize for the war.[64]

In July Wilson boarded a ship with the Sixth Massachusetts in Tampa, Florida, and landed in Puerto Rico. With the war over, the unit spent most of its time on patrols and guard duty. Though the regiment did not see any fighting, twenty-five of its men died of disease. The Sixth Massachusetts occupied the island until August and returned home in October to a hero's welcome, one of the few volunteer units to see overseas duty in the short war.[65]

Wilson left Company L on January 21, 1899, when the Sixth Massachusetts mustered out of federal service in Boston. Yet he did not stay a civilian long. On January 27, 1899, Major William Quinton enlisted Wilson into the Regular Army at the Boston recruiting station for a term of three years. The army was anxious to fill the gaps in the Regular Army caused by casualties and disease during the war in Cuba. The army assigned Private Wilson to Company L, Twenty-Fourth Infantry, which was organizing and preparing to move to Alaska.

Other Soldiers

The pattern of returning volunteer soldiers enlisting in the Regular Army after release from federal service was common after the Spanish-American War. Twenty-three of the new privates who joined Company L, Twenty-Fourth Infantry, in early 1899 served in Black volunteer units during the war, constituting about a quarter of its enlisted strength. Either they found military life suited them or they preferred the army to the job options in the civilian community at the time. They represented seven African American volunteer units from a variety of states north and south of the Mason-Dixon Line. Most of these men joined the Regular Army within days of being released from active service in early 1899.

The United States depended on state National Guard organizations to supply the majority of roughly two hundred thousand volunteers for the Spanish-American War effort. By war's end, forty-six states mustered 145 volunteer regiments into federal service, and 8 of these included African American soldiers. Some of these volunteer units, like the Ninth Ohio, Eighth Illinois, Twenty-Third Kansas, and Third North Carolina Volunteer Infantry, were composed entirely of African Americans, including the officers. In the Sixth Virginia Volunteer Infantry, only the commander and a surgeon were white. In the others, like the First Indiana Volunteer Infantry, the senior officers were white while captains, lieutenants, and enlisted men were Black.[66]

In addition to these National Guard units, Congress directed the War Department to enlist ten thousand new volunteers in ten regiments from the southern states "possessing immunity from diseases incident to tropical climates." The army organized four of these regiments as African American Immune volunteers. These Black volunteer regiments were known as "Immunes" because it was mistakenly thought that their African origins and residence in the South would give them immunity from tropical diseases. The Seventh, Eighth, Ninth, and Tenth U.S. Infantry Immune Volunteers (Colored) mustered in the southern states from Virginia to Louisiana from May to July 1898.[67]

Four of the former National Guard enlistees assigned to Company L, Twenty-Fourth Infantry, served with Company L, Sixth Massachusetts Volunteer Infantry. Joining George L. Wilson were William Pate and Edward G. Dewey, both born in 1878 in New Bern, North Carolina. Both Dewey and Pate enlisted on the same day in the same recruiting office in Boston. The other, Elijah H. Knox, was born in New Bedford, Massachusetts, in 1871 and enlisted in early February 1899.[68]

Dewey, Knox, Pate, and Wilson trained at Camp Alger in Virginia near Washington DC the summer of 1898. While at Camp Alger, they had the opportunity to observe Major Charles Young, a West Point graduate and the only serving Black Regular Army officer, who was then commanding the Ninth Ohio Volunteer Infantry. Young, a first lieutenant in the Regular Army, was a volunteer major appointed by the governor of Ohio to command the unit. He was on leave from detached service at Wilberforce University, Ohio, to command the Ninth Ohio.[69]

Five of Major Young's soldiers from the Ninth Ohio were assigned to Company L, Twenty-Fourth Infantry, after the war. The first three, all members of Company B, included Walter Belcher, Fred Joiner, and Benton Trice. All three were from Columbus, Ohio, where the company formed and trained in peacetime. The other two, Thomas Mack and Thomas Martin, lived in Cleveland, which Company D called its home. The Ninth Ohio occupied several east coast camps during training but never deployed overseas.[70]

Next to Ohio, the other state guard unit that provided the most volunteer soldiers to Company L, Twenty-Fourth Infantry, was Indiana. Company A, First Indiana Volunteer Infantry, was inducted into federal service in July 1898 and mustered out in January 1899, having seen no overseas duty. Four soldiers from Company A enlisted in the Regular Army and were assigned to Company L: James M. Banks, Peter Barnett, Orestus Kincaid, and Edgar Merritt. Banks was born in Monroe County, Illinois, and enlisted in Tennessee. Barnett, Kincaid, and Merritt were all from Kentucky and enlisted in Indiana.[71]

One newly enlisted African American soldier assigned to Company L served in a white National Guard unit during the Spanish-American War. Ernest C. Randall, born in 1876 in Worcester, Massachusetts, was a member of Heavy Battery B, First Connecticut Volunteer Artillery. He enlisted in the Connecticut National Guard on May 2, mustered into federal service on May 19, and mustered out on October 27, 1898. The rest of his battery was discharged on December 20, 1898, and there is no record of why he was discharged early.[72]

The balance of the new enlistees with volunteer experience assigned to Company L came from the Immune Regiments. Six new enlistees came from the Eighth U.S. Volunteer and three from the Tenth U.S. Volunteer Infantry. Neither unit saw overseas service. Despite never deploying, the Eighth Immunes lost seventy-three men and the Tenth Immunes fourteen to disease. Disease was by far the biggest killer of American soldiers during the Spanish-American War.[73]

The twenty-three former volunteers from the National Guard and Immunes who enlisted in the army and joined Company L, Twenty-Fourth Infantry, proved a positive addition. They were not green recruits. Rather, they had trained and drilled at camps under officers and noncommissioned officers for more than six months and possessed basic soldiering skills and military experience.

Personnel Organization

Despite the addition of many experienced volunteer recruits, the creation of a new company in the Twenty-Fourth Infantry could not have come at a worse time. In late 1898 the regiment roiled in organizational chaos due to losses and disruptions suffered during the Spanish-American War. In addition to the 12 killed in action, 73 wounded in battle, and 31 who died of diseases in the Siboney fever hospital, more than 100 suffered debilitating illnesses and were left to recover at hospitals in Cuba, Florida, and New York. It took months to sort out losses and gather the sick and wounded. Many never fully recovered and had to be discharged from the army on disability in the months after the war.[74]

On top of the gaps in the ranks caused by combat and disease in the ten companies that fought in Cuba, the regiment had to form two new companies from scratch. Recruiting officers across the country made every effort to enroll soldiers. Among them was the Twenty-Fourth's Black regimental chaplain, Allen Allensworth, who was sent on recruiting service to Louisville, Kentucky, from May through September 1898. Thus, many of the new soldiers assigned to Company L hailed from Kentucky or neighboring Indiana.[75]

Beginning in September 1898, the regiment received 480 new soldiers and assigned them to the ten existing companies. Beginning in October 1898, the regiment established a cadre of officers and non-commissioned officers in Companies L and M and began reassigning privates from other companies to these new units. The privates reassigned to Company L were a mix of soldiers with previous service in the Twenty-Fourth, new enlistees with Spanish-American volunteer service, and new recruits.[76]

The organization and strength of an infantry company in 1898 was straightforward. At full strength, it was authorized 1 captain, 1 first lieutenant, and 1 second lieutenant. Companies routinely served short-handed, with officers on detached duty at service schools (e.g., Jenks at the Engineer School of Application) or on staff positions (e.g., Hovey at Norwich University). In the enlisted ranks, an infantry company had 1 first sergeant, 1 quartermaster sergeant, 4 sergeants, 12 corporals, 2 musicians, 1 artificer (mechanic), 2 cooks, and 84 privates.[77]

The captain commanded the company, assisted by his lieutenants. Among the noncommissioned officers, the first sergeant ran the company for the commander, the quartermaster sergeant kept track of the unit's property, the sergeants led the four sections, and the corporals handled the three squads in each section. In support of the company, musicians regulated the day with trumpet calls, artificers maintained unit equipment, and cooks prepared meals. The infantry privates obeyed orders, endured countless hours of guard, drill, and inspection, and tried to stay out of trouble with their sergeants.

The two assigned cooks deserve special mention since the status of their profession in the U.S. Army had changed. For most of the nineteenth century, cooking duties had been rotated among the soldiers in the company with predictable results. This changed as a lesson learned during the Spanish-American War, where lack of food safety contributed to thousands of deaths from disease. In 1899 Congress authorized two cooks per company: they received training and a sergeants' pay and privileges, which included a stripe on their uniform trouser legs. After 1899 cooks had a profession and soldiers' better food. The Company L cooks carried a copy of the *Manual for Army Cooks*, published in 1896, full of methods and recipes.[78]

By the end of October, Company L had an assigned strength of 2 officers and 104 enlisted men. Lieutenant Jenks commanded the company until Captain Hovey's return from detached service. The enlisted ranks were nearly full strength with 1 first sergeant, 1 quartermaster sergeant, 4 sergeants, 11 corporals, 2 musicians, 1 artificer, 2 cooks, and 84 privates. About half of the 84 privates were newly arrived recruits, the others transferred from other companies in the regiment.[79]

In October 1898 the regiment assigned Sergeant Edward Williams as first sergeant to the company. This was a temporary assignment.

Williams, who had served as the first sergeant of Company C during the Spanish-American War, was hospitalized with an incapacitating illness, and was listed as absent in the hospital from August to October 1898. He was discharged in early November 1898 due to his disabilities. Company L operated without an assigned first sergeant until May 1899 when it arrived in Alaska.[80]

The commander customarily appointed the noncommissioned officers in his company. By army regulation, company noncommissioned officers were appointed "by the regimental commander upon the recommendation of the company commander." However, most companies operated separately, and the company commander made the day-to-day decisions on noncommissioned officer leadership positions. The company commander could make or break a corporal, sergeant, or first sergeant.[81]

The first sergeant ran the day-to-day operations of an infantry company. He and the sergeants and corporals in the company, known collectively as the noncommissioned officers, or noncoms, ultimately shaped the effectiveness of a unit. While Hovey might command the company, as a white commissioned officer, he was separated from his enlisted soldiers by a strict and well-understood social and racial barrier. The first sergeant, on the other hand, came up through the ranks from private to corporal to sergeant and knew the soldiers and their lives intimately.

The reorganization of the existing companies and filling out the new companies continued into the new year. In January 1899 the regiment received another 66 recruits from the replacement depot, 7 of whom went to Company L. In March 1899 another 129 recruits arrived, though none were allocated to Company L. By March 1899 Company L had a present-for-duty strength of 2 officers, 6 sergeants, 12 corporals, 2 musicians, 1 artificer, 2 cooks, and 91 privates. Among the noncommissioned officers were Robert O'Connor, James Washington, Augustus Snoten, and Edward Bordinghammer. More than half of the privates were new recruits, like Benjamin Green, with a leavening of longer-term veterans and soldiers in their second enlistment, like George Wilson.[82]

The Spanish-American War added distant colonies to America's existing territories of Alaska and Hawaii and governing this vast empire would stretch the U.S. Army to its limits. After three decades of duty safeguarding the western frontier, most of the Twenty-Fourth Infantry would find itself defending this new empire in the Philippine War. Only Company L would find its future in Alaska.

One veteran officer and fifteen noncommissioned officers assigned to Company L spent the first weeks of 1899 turning many new recruits into proper soldiers. Captain Hovey and Lieutenant Jenks provided the officer leadership for this company that completed its reorganization by March 1899. Seasoned veteran noncommissioned officers including sergeants O'Connor and Washington drilled newly enlisted soldiers like Private Green and former volunteer soldiers like Private Wilson to prepare them for the challenging 1899 deployment to Alaska. According to the motto of the Twenty-Fourth Infantry Regiment, they were *semper paratus*, which means "always prepared."

2

DYEA BARRACKS

Everything at the camp near Dyea is gone, the town
practically abandoned, and as a point of tactical
necessity, Skagway now alone remains.
—CAPTAIN HENRY W. HOVEY, July 28, 1899

The responsibilities of command weighed on Captain Henry Hovey
after stepping across the gangplank of SS *Humboldt* onto the Dyea
dock on May 20, 1899. He had guided his men more than two thousand miles and nearly twenty degrees latitude north by train and ship
from Utah to Alaska in seven weeks. He left Lieutenant Isaac Jenks
and nearly half of the men of his company at Fort Wrangel, 250 sea
miles to the south. At Dyea, Hovey reported to a commander based
more than one thousand miles south at Vancouver Barracks, Washington. With no telegraphic connection to his headquarters, the only
way to get messages to and from his commander was by ship. Armed
with his orders and twenty years of service in the army, he was very
much on his own.[1]

Dyea

Dyea, located at the mouth of the Taiya River, geographically dominated the northern approaches to the Lynn Canal, the main gateway
to the Yukon. The Lynn Canal is a channel, not a manmade canal.
The canal runs from the northeast where it is plaited by the Chilkat,
Chilkoot, and Taiya Inlets to the Chatham Strait, twenty-two miles
west of Juneau. It is ninety miles long and more than two thousand
feet deep, the deepest fjord in North America.[2]

Dyea initially consisted of a trading post opened by John J. Healy in the mid-1880s on the site of a centuries-old Tlingit village. By the time Healy arrived to establish his post, the Tlingit village was only seasonally occupied. The area around Dyea remained sparsely populated until word of the Klondike gold discoveries reached the United States and shiploads of stampeders began arriving the summer of 1897.[3]

At the height of the gold rush, Dyea had a population of around eight thousand and attracted more stampeders than Skagway through the winter of 1897 and 1898. A twenty-one-year-old writer named Jack London chose Dyea as his destination and set out to climb over the Chilkoot Pass to the Klondike. London spent twenty grueling days carrying his one thousand pounds of equipment up the 3,400-foot Chilkoot, shuttling about one hundred pounds at a time. The North West Mounted Police (NWMP), who manned the border checkpoint, required American miners entering Canada to have a year's supply of provisions to ensure they would not starve in the gold fields.[4]

Like London, few stampeders ever struck it rich in the Klondike. London staked a claim on Henderson Creek seventy miles upriver from Dawson but managed to find only $4.50 in gold dust. By spring, with his gums swelling and bleeding from scurvy, London called it quits and sailed down the Yukon to Saint Michael, Alaska, where he caught a steamer back to San Francisco. Despite his travails, his experiences in the Yukon provided the raw material for his later novels.[5]

By the time Captain Hovey and Company L arrived in Alaska, London was long gone, the Klondike gold rush largely over. During the peak of the gold rush, Dyea offered access to the Chilkoot Trail, while Skagway competed with entrée through the White Pass. As many as thirty thousand stampeders crossed into the Yukon via the Chilkoot Trail, while nearly ten thousand used the White Pass. Supported by three tramways up the pass completed in 1898, the Chilkoot Trail held supremacy until the White Pass & Yukon Route railway was completed through the summit to Bennett City, British Columbia, in July 1899. The shift in prominence to Skagway complicated Hovey's mission since he was in Dyea, which was quickly dying.[6]

Missions

What exactly were Captain Hovey's specific tasks in Alaska? When the regiment was consolidated at Fort Douglas, Utah, the regimental commander met frequently with his three battalion commanders to issue orders, conveyed down the line to four company commanders. Not the case for Captain Hovey: his regimental commander was on a ship headed for the Philippine Islands, and he answered to a battalion commander and the commander of the Department of the Columbia, a thousand miles to the south. Therefore, it was critical for Captain Hovey to understand his mission since he had to carry it to completion himself.

First and foremost, Captain Hovey and Company L occupied a resource-rich and strategically important portion of Alaska to show the American flag and deter the Canadians and British from any military incursion. The area was the center of a boundary dispute between the United States and the United Kingdom, which then controlled Canada's foreign relations. Canada desperately wanted an outlet from the Yukon gold fields to the sea. Dyea and Skagway were the preferred locations since they were only fifteen miles from the provisional Canadian border.[7]

The NWMP sent Superintendent Charles Constantine and Staff Sergeant Charles Brown through Dyea in late June 1894 to "establish sovereignty and determine law enforcement requirements in view of the approaching gold rush." By 1896, fearing his small force of Mounties would be overwhelmed by growing numbers of stampeders, Constantine requested Maxim machine guns to reinforce his small command. Yet the Maxims could not stop the massive influx of thousands of miners through Dyea and the NWMP set up posts on the summits of the Chilkoot and White Passes. What's more, these two passes were also disputed territory, as many Americans believed the border should be fixed at Lake Bennett, twelve miles farther north. To back up the Mounties, Canada dispatched the Yukon Field Force, a two-hundred-man British Army unit, and established Fort Selkirk in Yukon Territory.[8]

Captain Hovey's chief mission centered on the defense of the Lynn Canal from any intrusion by the Canadians. The threat was genuine. The United States and Great Britain nearly fought the so-called Pig War in 1859 over disputed San Juan Island in the Puget Sound northwest of Seattle. In that incident, the United States sent a company of the Ninth U.S. Infantry under the command of then-captain George Pickett to prevent the British from landing on the island. The Canadian governor of Vancouver Island ordered the admiral commanding five British warships and two thousand men to land on the island and engage the U.S. force. Cooler heads prevailed, and negotiations eventually led to a settlement. Yet British and American troops occupied the disputed island jointly for the next twelve years, until the question was finally resolved with the Canadians' departure.[9]

The danger was very real to Captain Hovey, since negotiations to establish the border near Dyea and Skagway remained unresolved. Meetings between the United States and Canada commenced in September 1898 but failed to find a solution agreeable to all parties. Washington went so far as to float an offer to the Canadians for a permanent lease on the port at Haines, Alaska, which Ottawa turned down. When newspapers leaked word of this proposal, Alaskans were furious. Negotiations continued until the Alaska-Canada boundary convention was signed after arbitration in 1903, four years after Hovey arrived in Alaska.[10]

As is always the case in military operations, Captain Hovey had several secondary missions in Alaska. The War Department instructed him to help the civilian authorities in Dyea and Skagway maintain law and order in the region. He was only permitted to do this under the terms of the Posse Comitatus Act of 1878, which allowed military intervention in domestic affairs only when called upon by local government officials such as the district judge or federal marshal. His backup of local officials buttressed his main mission since the Canadians often pointed to the lawlessness in the region as proof of U.S. inability to maintain order.

Hovey was fortunate things had settled down considerably from the period 1897 to 1898 when anarchy reigned the region. Yet even with the peak of the gold rush past, Soapy Smith dead, and the population much reduced, the civilian authorities in the area often called on the army for backup. The mere presence of armed soldiers nearby was deterrent enough to discourage most trouble. Hovey would find himself summoned frequently to support the local federal marshal in carrying out the orders of the district court judge.[11]

Hovey was familiar with another important supporting mission from his service in Arizona and New Mexico Territory: protecting Native Americans. Before the arrival of thousands of stampeders, the Chilkat and Chilkoot clans of the Pacific Northwest Tlingit indigenous peoples lived in the area around Dyea and Skagway. When the initial trickle of miners arrived, the clans tried to control and benefit from the outsiders by charging fees and hiring out as packers. The name Dyea derives from the Tlingit word for "to pack." Yet they were soon overwhelmed by sheer numbers and under threat of losing their lands and lives. So keeping the peace between the Tlingit and the white newcomers grew to be one of Hovey's chief concerns.[12]

The Tlingit experience with the military in three decades of U.S. control of Alaska was brutal and one-sided. The U.S. Army, Navy, and Revenue Service ran the administrative and judicial systems in Alaska for the first few decades of American control. They launched the Schwatka, Abercrombie, and Allen expeditions to map the territory and provide security for white settlers arriving in Alaska. These resulted in skirmishes at Fort Wrangel, Kake, and Angoon, short and violent clashes between Tlingit people and occupiers fueled by cultural misunderstandings and trouble initiated by soldiers. These clashes usually ended with the bombardment of a Native village followed by surrender and retribution. The Tlingit memory of these events impacted Hovey's mission.[13]

Military Continuity

When Company L arrived in Dyea, it replaced the white soldiers of Company B, Fourteenth U.S. Infantry, commanded by Captain Richard T. Yeatman. Captain Yeatman and his fifty-six men had been in Dyea since March 1898. They were the remaining element of a larger force comprising four companies from the Fourteenth Infantry, commanded by Colonel Thomas M. Anderson, that deployed to Alaska beginning in late February 1898. This battalion of infantry had the dual mission of keeping the peace and showing the flag in the region, meant to offset the threat posed to the Lynn Canal by the Canadian Yukon Field Force. They were a follow-up to support the relief expedition that had arrived earlier in the month.[14]

The first major military presence in Dyea had been the Yukon Relief Expedition that commenced arriving in early February 1898. President William McKinley signed a congressional bill authorizing this relief mission after receiving reports that U.S. citizens who had rushed to the Klondike gold fields in Canada were threatened by starvation in winter. The U.S. Army organized the expedition in December 1897 and planned to feed the hungry miners 538 reindeer purchased in Norway and herded by 43 Laplanders, 25 Norwegians, and 10 Finns. The reindeer and their handlers arrived by ship in Haines, Alaska, in February 1898, yet by then the miners were no longer in danger of starving, if they ever were.[15]

The advance party of the Yukon Relief Expedition arrived in Dyea on board ss *George W. Elder* in early February 1898. Sixty-eight enlisted men unloaded 150 tons of supplies at Dyea and established a camp near the Healy and Wilson trading post. The expedition was commanded by Major Louis H. Rucker, Fourth U.S. Cavalry. Rucker, a well-respected cavalry officer, served his first thirty years in the Regular Army with the Black Ninth U.S. Cavalry before transferring to the Fourth in 1897. Additional supplies and equipment arrived in Dyea aboard ss *Oregon* under Captain David L. Brainard two weeks later. The four companies led by Colonel Anderson from the Fourteenth Infantry augmented the contingent in February and March 1898.[16]

In early March 1898, the army pack train arrived to carry the supplies to the hungry miners. Commanding this pack train were First Lieutenants Guy H. Preston and James A. Ryan, Ninth U.S. Cavalry, who had been detached from their regiment in December 1897 to organize the relief mission. Major Rucker knew Preston and Ryan from his service with the Ninth Cavalry and asked them to lead the 22 packers and 101 pack mules. Rucker also asked for the only enlisted muleteers among the 22 packers, 5 African American cavalry troopers from the Ninth Cavalry. These 5 cavalrymen were the first Black soldiers to set foot in Alaska on army orders.[17]

When it became clear that the emergency was over and no U.S. stampeders were in danger of starving, the Yukon Relief Expedition quickly dispersed. The resulting redeployment of army units accelerated with the declaration of war on Spain on April 25, 1898. The army sold the supplies stockpiled in Dyea at auction and the Scandinavian herders drove the surviving 185 reindeer north from Haines to Circle City, Alaska. Most of the army troops boarded steamers bound for Vancouver Barracks to rejoin their units by late April 1898. Colonel Anderson departed with most of the Fourteenth Infantry in May 1898, leaving a residual force of one company in Dyea and another at Fort Wrangel. Captain Hovey and Lieutenant Jenks replaced these two companies when they arrived in Alaska.[18]

Arrival

Who composed Captain Hovey's command? Hovey was the only commissioned officer present at Dyea, though he was assisted by army contract Assistant Surgeon Edward Bailey, who led a small Hospital Corps detachment of three soldiers and one civilian clerk. Dr. Bailey had served with the previous company from the white Fourteenth Infantry and met Hovey dockside when he arrived. Since Company B, Fourteenth Infantry, left on board ss *Humboldt* immediately, Bailey served an important role for Hovey as he struggled to grasp his mission in Dyea. Captain Hovey grew to rely heavily on Dr. Bailey as he provided important continuity between the outgoing company of the Fourteenth Infantry and his own command.[19]

Hovey's first lieutenant, Isaac Jenks, remained on detached duty commanding the forty-six members of Company L at Fort Wrangel for the first year of the deployment. Hovey left Jenks with Sergeant

Washington as his detachment first sergeant. Hovey also left behind one sick soldier at the hospital at Vancouver Barracks, Washington, and five sick in the hospital at the Presidio of San Francisco, California. Moreover, he left a trail of deserters at the ports of call along the route between Fort Douglas and Dyea. It took Hovey several months to clean up this straggle of deserters, most of whom were later jailed and discharged without honor.[20]

The 64 members from his company who landed at Dyea included 4 sergeants, 7 corporals, 1 musician, 2 artificers, 1 cook, and 53 privates. Hovey appointed Sergeant O'Connor as the first sergeant and had 3 sergeants who commanded the sections of approximately 20 men each. Each section was divided into squads, commanded by corporals assigned 7 privates each. A small headquarters detachment included the first sergeant, musician, artificers, cooks, and a couple of other enlisted men assigned special duties.

Hovey relied most heavily on First Sergeant O'Connor to help him run the company and carry out its assigned missions. Hovey would have called him "first sergeant," but the soldiers knew him deferentially as "Top Sergeant" or "Top" in army slang. One of Hovey's educated enlisted soldiers served as his company clerk, and another soldier as his striker (personal orderly). The practice of employing strikers was forbidden by regulation in 1870 but continued anyway. The enlisted men in Company L referred to any soldier who worked for an officer as a "dog-robber."[21]

Hovey's clerk was an extremely busy man as evidenced by the hundreds of handwritten letters contained in the leather-bound volume of "Letters Sent." This ledger contained handwritten copies of all written or printed communications issued by the commander. Before the use of typewriters and carbon copies, correspondence was handwritten by the company clerk and signed by the commander before forwarding. The names of the clerks were not recorded, but the change in handwriting in the leather ledger shows clerks changed periodically.[22]

Captain Hovey's post return lists him as company commander, Camp Dyea commander, District of Lynn Canal commander, disbursing quartermaster, commissary officer, summary court officer, recruiting officer, and signal officer. If First Lieutenant Jenks had been with him in Dyea, Hovey would have unloaded some of these duties on him. Yet only a commissioned officer could be on orders to perform these tasks.[23]

What were these responsibilities and how important were they? Commanding the District of Lynn Canal was his chief responsibility and harkened back to his main mission in Alaska: show the flag and deter the Canadians. He commanded both his company and the post, which included the medical staff and other attached personnel. As disbursing quartermaster he was authorized to expend government funds to house his troops and as commissary officer, to spend money to feed and supply his soldiers. Summary court gave Hovey the power to punish the soldiers for infractions of army regulations. Recruiting allowed him to reenlist soldiers, and signal officer meant he oversaw the unit's communications.[24]

Settling In

Captain Hovey's immediate challenges were to get his soldiers into quarters and assess the mission at hand. The first was easy, since the barracks used by the previous garrison was dockside. Captain Yeatman had moved his company of the Fourteenth Infantry from a tent camp north of Dyea to the Dyea-Klondike Transportation (DKT) Company wharf, about three miles from town in October 1898. After the military occupied the wharf, it was called Camp Dyea, though it was known as "Soldiers Landing" to local civilians. This compound was located on the west side of Taiya Inlet on a steep mountainside connected to Dyea with a three-mile-long wagon road. Since the army had already approved the lease of the dock and buildings, Hovey immediately moved his men into the buildings at the wharf.[25]

Camp Dyea comprised several DKT Company buildings on and near the wharf beginning in 1897 to support its gold rush operations over the Chilkoot Pass. Yet in the intervening year, the competing operation at Skagway had grown in importance. Dyea was slowly turning into a ghost town, so the DKT Company made the buildings available to the army at a reasonable lease price. The camp consisted of a 30-by-100-foot warehouse, a 12-by-20-foot storeroom, a 16-by-24-foot office, and the 30-by-76-foot Coleman Hotel. The hotel served as a barracks for the soldiers, the office as a workplace and quarters for Hovey, and the storeroom and warehouse as space for equipment storage, an arms room, a mess hall, and other necessary purposes.[26]

Dyea controlled the head of the strategically important Lynn Canal, so the army made plans for a permanent military presence in the district. To that end, the army established the boundaries of two pieces of land under the authority of the president of the United States in December 1898, "set apart for future military purposes and proclaimed military reservations." The first was a two-square-mile area that began two hundred yards north of Camp Dyea and fronted on the shore of the Lynn Canal for two miles northward. The army also set aside another parcel that bordered on the Lynn Canal in the vicinity of Haines Mission. The final decision on which parcel to make a permanent military reservation was deferred until Hovey could assess their suitability.[27]

Tweedale Mission

About a month after Captain Hovey and Company L landed at Camp Dyea, Major John Tweedale and Frank B. Bourn paid an official visit to the area. Major Tweedale was the assistant chief of the Record and Pension Office in Washington DC and Bourn was his clerk. Secretary of War Russell A. Alger sent them to Alaska to interview Chilkat chiefs on the Russian presence in Alaska before 1867 to support the U.S. position in the Alaska-Canada boundary dispute. Tweedale and Bourn arrived by steamer from Seattle at the end of June 1899 to commence their investigation, and Hovey supported their mission.[28]

When Tweedale arrived, the district court was in session in nearby Skagway with the judge preparing to adjourn and return to his bench at Sitka, Alaska. The case being heard was of interest to the Chilkat clans, and three of the leaders were in attendance. When the court adjourned, District Judge Charles S. Johnson sent his Tlingit interpreter, George Kostrometinoff, to assist Tweedale. Tweedale obtained the testimony of three Chilkat leaders who were in Skagway the afternoon of his first day ashore and the rest in the days following.[29]

What did the ten Chilkat leaders say? All the Chilkat headmen gave their own family lineages, recounted their recollections of the time under Russian rule, and acknowledged an understanding that they were now wards of the United States. Most importantly for the U.S. position on the boundary dispute, they supported the fact that Russian control had included all their tribal territory and extended to the head of the Lynn Canal. This information was useful to Captain Hovey since it supported his mission and his future dealings with the Chilkats.[30]

The actual transcripts of what the Chilkat elders said must be taken with a grain of salt. Certainly, they conceded they were American wards, but they had no choice for fear of retribution. Their memories of the bombardments of Fort Wrangel, Kake, and Angoon were only thirty years in the past. These transcripts were translated by interpreter Kostrometinoff, transcribed by clerk Bourn, and signed with an X by the Chilkat headmen. Though the content transmitted to Washington supported the American stance in the boundary dispute, it did not contain the actual words or sentiments of the Chilkat leaders.[31]

Tweedale Photos

Major Tweedale brought a camera along on the visit and took photos of the Chilkat headmen for his official report. He also took several snapshots of Company L which reveal a wealth of information about daily life at Camp Dyea. He took several photos on July 3, 1899, of the buildings and camp activities at Soldiers Landing, the only known images of the company in Dyea. Moreover, Tweedale's images have a modern action quality that is lacking in some of the professional photos taken later of Company L.[32]

The photos of the wharf and buildings reveal that the initial quarters occupied by the company were adequate. The 2,280-square-foot Coleman Hotel was new and appeared well built, providing a reasonable barracks for the fifty-four privates in the company. The seven noncommissioned officers occupied a separate space from the enlisted men. Company L designated an orderly room in one of the buildings where the sergeant of the guard stood duty twenty-four hours a day. It also established an arms locker near the orderly room, so weapons had round-the-clock security. Lastly, Dr. Bailey used a building as a hospital space for himself and his three hospital orderlies.[33]

Tweedale's photos also provide some precious information about people not available otherwise. Professional photographers necessarily staged their subjects because of slow shutter speeds and film characteristics, and the resulting images of people tend to be stiff and serious. In Tweedale's photographs, individuals are less stilted, and some even smile. They are also in casual poses, showing individuals talking or relaxing in informal settings.

One Tweedale photograph shows Captain Hovey and Doctor Bailey standing side by side atop the hill overlooking the wharf, near Hovey's office and quarters. Both men are relaxed and smiling, a clue to their good nature and character. Firsthand accounts of both men note they were thoughtful and well liked, both by their soldiers and their peers. Still another Tweedale image shows Captain Hovey standing hatless and grinning in front of his office and quarters next to the ramp leading downward to the wharf.[34]

Only one photograph taken by Tweedale shows a soldier in an informal setting. It shows an unidentified private from Company L standing on a dock littered with lumber getting ready to carry out a task. He is pointing to the left, possibly asking the photographer if he should get out of the way. The image shows the expansive wharf area, an L-shaped shore and office, a tall flagpole, a smaller outbuilding, and the ramp leading to Captain Hovey's office and quarters above the warehouse on the hill.[35]

Uniforms and Equipment

Tweedale's photos of Company L show the uniforms worn by Captain Hovey and his men in Alaska. The soldiers wore the dark blue Pattern 1885 sack coat and the Pattern 1895 forage cap. The noncommissioned officers have a white stripe on their light blue trousers and the corporals and sergeants two and three thin white chevrons or V's on their sleeves, respectively. All wear crossed rifles with 24 above and L below on their caps signifying their branch, regiment, and company. The U.S. Army adopted a khaki cotton field uniform based on a British pattern in 1898, yet these were never worn by members of Company L in Alaska. The blue wool uniform was likely better suited to the cool climate of the north.[36]

The same photo of Company L on the wharf shows the weapons and accoutrements of the enlisted men. Regular Army infantry soldiers were equipped with the American-manufactured U.S. Model 1896 Krag-Jørgensen rifle. The army issued the Twenty-Fourth Infantry these rifles, known as the "Krag," before the Spanish-American War. Company L carried these weapons their entire time in Skagway, since the Krags were not replaced until 1904 with the M1903 Springfield. The Krag fired a rimmed-cartridge .30-caliber bullet known as a .30-40 Krag. The Krags replaced the .45-caliber Springfield Rifles used by the Twenty-Fourth during the Indian Wars.[37]

When in uniform carrying rifles, as in the photo at the Dyea wharf, the enlisted soldiers wore the Pattern 1874 leather belt with Hagner belt plate, McKeever leather cartridge box, and a leather bayonet scabbard. Equipped for field duty as is shown in a later photo of the company, the soldiers wore a brown Pattern 1883 campaign hat, canvas bedroll, canvas haversack, steel bayonet scabbard, and canvas leggings over their boots.[38]

Officers wore slightly dissimilar uniforms and carried different weapons from the enlisted men. In the Camp Dyea photo Captain Hovey wears the 1885-pattern officer's coat with the wider white stripe on his trousers signifying his commissioned rank. He also wears officer shoulder boards with captain's rank on them to signify his commission. The photo is puzzling, since Hovey is carrying a sword and wearing no belt or scabbard. The army issued officers the Colt .38-caliber double-action revolver carried in a leather holster suspended from a leather belt.[39]

Fourth of July

During Tweedale's visit, Skagway invited Captain Hovey to participate in its annual Fourth of July parade. This may have been a strategy by the city fathers of Skagway to show the advantages of the town over Dyea. Whatever the circumstances, Hovey ferried his men by boat the three miles across the Taiya Inlet to Skagway to participate in the parade on July 4, 1899. He likely saw the event as an opportunity to show his soldiers a bit of civilization after spending a month on an isolated wharf more suitable for sailors than foot-soldiers.[40]

Company L's involvement in the 1899 Independence Day parade in Skagway is documented in a series of photos taken by Major Tweedale and a local photographer named Harrie C. Barley. Based on the quality of some of his photos, Tweedale was a proficient photographer and must have had good equipment; at the time most camerawork was done by professionals. It is possible the War Department provided the camera and film to support his mission interviewing the Chilkat chiefs.[41]

Hovey likely traveled to Skagway the day before and camped overnight to be fresh for the parade the following morning. This is evidenced by photos of Company L taken in Skagway on July 4, which show soldiers in clean uniforms, white collars, and white gloves—not what you would expect after hours of travel. In the first of the Tweedale series of Fourth of July photos, Company L is marching north into Skagway on Main or State Street at what seems to be the beginning of the parade. The soldiers marched in the same formation as in the Barley photo taken later, following a civilian drummer striking a beat to keep the men in step. The soldiers appear to be leading the parade, followed by the wagons of the local fire companies with their hose carts and hook and ladder trucks.[42]

Only two of the forty-five men of Company L in the Barley photograph can be positively identified. First Sergeant O'Connor is standing at the front right of the formation, closest to the photographer. He is clearly wearing three chevrons topped with a diamond. The other is the musician standing to the left of the formation with a trumpet in his right hand, trailing the chord that was suspended around his shoulders in an earlier photo. This is the nearly thirty-year-veteran of the Twenty-Fourth Infantry, Musician Edward Bordinghammer.[43]

Captain Hovey's July 1899 post report listed sixty-four enlisted members in his company. He also listed seven on special duty (guard, wood-chopping detail, etc.) and three sick. All but eight privates are in the parade formation as well as most of the noncommissioned officers. Hovey probably brought along a cook to feed the soldiers and a few others to guard the tent camp they set up in Skagway for one or two nights. The balance stayed behind because they were sick or guarding Camp Dyea.[44]

There is no record how long the company stayed in Skagway after the parade. Captain Hovey likely allowed the soldiers some free time to enjoy some of the post-parade activities. The newspaper accounts make no mention of a baseball game as part of the planned events, though such games would be a fixture in future years.

Captain Hovey was happy with his company's visit to Skagway and especially pleased with the reception they received. He wrote a letter on July 6, 1899, to Deputy U.S. Marshal Josias M. Tanner thanking him for the "courtesy and attention shown the men of my Company on July 4, '99 and for your constant attention to their welfare in every respect." Hovey was effusive in his gratitude for Tanner's consideration and thoughtfulness. Both the soldiers and citizens showed their best sides.[45]

Captain Hovey was not present for a momentous occasion for Skagway a few days after the Fourth of July. On July 6, 1899, the last spike was driven by American and Canadian officials to commemorate the completion of the White Pass & Yukon Route between Skagway and Bennett City. The event was attended in Bennett City by representatives of both the Canadian Pacific Railway and the White Pass & Yukon Route. Bennett City lay on the southern shore of Lake Bennett and gave access with steamships through the headwater lakes to the start of the Yukon River near Whitehorse and from there to the interior of the Yukon and Alaska. According to the Skagway *Daily Alaskan*, the completion of the railway made "Skagway the one and only gateway to the wealth-laden vales of the interior."[46]

Company L did not call Camp Dyea home for long. Hovey alerted his superiors of the danger posed by fire to his men in mid-July 1899. He wrote "a few days since, a forest fire was accidentally started about two miles south of here, and only that what little wind there blew from the north, we would have been forced out of here." He quickly made contingency arrangements to transport his soldiers and equipment to safety in case another fire broke out and cut off his land route by the wagon road. Hovey hired a boat and moored it to the wharf as a precaution.[47]

According to company and post returns, on July 28 "at about 8 AM a fire was discovered about 1000 yards north of camp. Upon examination it was found that efforts to extinguish it would be unavailing, and preparations for removal were ordered." Hovey then moved weapons, ammunition, and as much equipment as possible in scows and ferries to the shore west of Dyea a safe distance from the fire. Hovey completed the move by 6:15 p.m. and left a guard of five men. "In about twenty minutes the wind changed, and the fire came down rapidly through the forest, destroying everything in its path, including all buildings occupied by the troops." The guard barely managed to escape the inferno in the boat.[48]

Thanks to Captain Hovey's preparations, there were no serious injuries and no significant loss of equipment. Yet they did not escape totally unscathed. Hovey's special field report the day after the fire listed eight soldiers sick. No soldiers were listed on the sick list in the regular reporting the month before. So at least eight enlisted men were not fit for duty after the escape from Camp Dyea, perhaps from exhaustion or smoke inhalation.[49]

Captain Hovey later investigated the circumstances of the fire and forwarded the findings to the adjutant general in Washington DC, in part to counter an article in the local press that "ascribed the fire to a dissatisfied soldier." He submitted his own affidavit along with statements from one visiting officer and four of his enlisted men. These concluded that the fire began high on the hill above the camp and burned downward toward the wharf. His letter clearly defended the reputation of his company and men.[50]

Since the fire destroyed the wharf, barracks, and other buildings, Hovey had to find a new home. He quickly set up a new tent camp in Skagway on the "west side of town, well located and at a good temporary site." This was just as well since the once thriving town of Dyea was by then dying, with only four families still living there. Hovey had complained to his higher headquarters in Vancouver Barracks that communications were difficult because ships stopped less frequently at Dyea by the summer of 1899.[51]

The completion of the White Pass & Yukon Route through to Bennett City in July 1899 was the final nail in Dyea's coffin. After the fire that burned the DKT Company wharf, the railroad company purchased the aerial tramways over the Chilkoot Trail and shut them down, not wanting the competition. In a few years, Dyea was abandoned, many of the buildings dismantled and moved elsewhere.[52]

Captain Hovey and Company L found themselves back in Skagway little more than three weeks after the Fourth of July parade. They had resided at Camp Dyea since May, slightly longer than two months. The fire had done Hovey a service; he had complained to his headquarters about the deepening isolation of Dyea and the need to find a new home. He got his wish due to a natural disaster, though he certainly would have preferred a bit more time to plan a more methodical move. Fire forced Hovey to move to Skagway and the next phase of his mission.

FORT WRANGEL

A detachment of Co. L, 24th Infantry (colored)
consisting of 49 men under Lieut. I.C. Jenks,
arrived on the *Humboldt* Thursday evening.
—*STIKEEN RIVER JOURNAL*, May 20, 1899

Even before Captain Hovey landed his company in Dyea, Lieutenant Jenks was facing his own set of leadership challenges at Fort Wrangel. Jenks's chain of command ran 250 miles north to Hovey in Dyea, and from there 1,000 miles south to Vancouver Barracks, Washington. Essentially, he had to make the decisions for his detachment alone, based on his official orders and frontier experience from eight years of duty with the Twenty-Fourth Infantry in Arizona and New Mexico Territory. He, like Hovey, was very much on his own.

Fort Wrangel

Fort Wrangel was the oldest U.S. military facility in Alaska and one of its first non–Native American settlements. The community was renamed Wrangell in 1903, but while Lieutenant Jenks was stationed there, the fort and town were known as Fort Wrangel.[1] The post commanded the northern tip of Wrangell Island and guarded the mouth of the expansive Stikine River on the mainland. The area was initially settled by the Stikine Tlingit people who moved to Wrangell Island in prehistoric times. The Tlingit still inhabited the place when the Russian American Company established the first western trading post there in 1834, later renting the compound to the British Hudson Bay Company. Finally, Russia sold Alaska to the United States in 1867 for

$7.2 million, fearing it would soon be seized by the British and cause a war between the two European empires.[2]

Washington initially placed the district (Alaska was not organized as a territory until 1912) under the control of the War Department, with the U.S. Army as the sole authority. The fort was originally built in 1868 and named after Baron Ferdinand von Wrangel, who had been a former governor of Russian Alaska. It covered two acres and included officers' quarters, barracks, hospital, blockhouse, garden, kitchen, and bakery, all surrounded by a stockade. The post was abandoned and reoccupied several times and finally turned over to the Revenue Cutter Service of the Treasury Department to provide law and order in 1877.[3]

Thirty years before Jenks and his detachment arrived, Fort Wrangel was the scene of a U.S. Army bombardment of the Tlingit village nearby. Some of the Tlingit residents who lived near the fort in 1899 likely witnessed that shelling. This incident was a short and violent clash resulting from a misunderstanding and a quarrel initiated by soldiers stationed at the fort.

Accounts differ, yet sources agree that a Christmas Eve argument in 1869, fueled by illegally served liquor, resulted in the killing of a Stikine Tlingit by U.S. soldiers. The father of the victim demanded compensation, according to customs of Tlingit law, and was refused. The father shot and killed a local white trader outside the fort the following morning in an act of retribution.[4]

The army demanded that the Stikine Tlingit perpetrator surrender by noon. When the Tlingit refused, the army commenced shelling the village with cannon fire, resulting in the surrender of the village and the man charged with murder. The Tlingit man was subsequently court-martialed and hanged publicly in front of the garrison, with the body left hanging all day as a warning to the village. A subsequent investigation found the army had neither the legal authority to court-martial a civilian or the jurisdiction to impose the death sentence in Alaska.[5]

Fort Wrangel gained importance serving as an outfitting and transportation hub for three gold rushes: the Stikine gold rush of 1861, the

Cassiar gold rush of 1872, and finally the Klondike gold rush in 1897. The influx of prospectors during the Klondike gold rush brought the army back to Fort Wrangel one last time in May 1898. When gold was discovered in the Klondike, Fort Wrangel initially advertised the Stikine River as the easiest and most well-known route to the gold fields. The shorter overland passes through Dyea and the rail route from Skagway eventually won out, though Fort Wrangel remained an important support base of operations and supply.[6]

At the high point of the Klondike gold rush, Fort Wrangel was one of the largest cities in Alaska. Most of the stores, shops, and bars were false-front buildings crowding both sides of Front Street, which snaked along the waterfront. Wyatt Earp spent ten days filling in as the deputy marshal there on his way to seek his fortune in the Klondike in 1897. The year Wyatt visited, the population peaked at six thousand between March and May 1897, and temporary tent structures covered every inch of available land.[7]

By May 1898, when a company of the Fourteenth Infantry arrived to reoccupy the compound at Fort Wrangel, the population of the town had shrunk to fewer than a thousand. The Klondike gold rush had passed its peak and the declaration of war by the United States on Spain in April 1898 resulted in miners rushing south to volunteer and ships diverting to support the deployment of soldiers to the Philippine Islands. For the third time, Fort Wrangel's population diminished and much of the chaos ceased.[8]

When Jenks arrived in 1899, the city would have appeared much as it did to John Muir, who visited the place several times, describing it as a "rough place." He called it "a lawless draggle of wooden huts and houses, built in crooked lines, wrangling around the boggy shore of the island for a mile or so in the general form of the letter S, without the slightest subordination to the points of the compass or to building laws of any kind." Muir observed that "the fort and about it there were a few good, clean homes, which shone all the more brightly in the somber surroundings."[9]

Settling In

An empty boomtown greeted Lieutenant Jenks when he disembarked his men from ss *Humboldt* at Fort Wrangel at 9:00 p.m. on May 18, 1899. Jenks's detachment replaced Company H of the all-white Fourteenth Infantry Regiment. Captain Eldridge Bogardus, who commanded this company, remained until the return of ss *Humboldt* from Skagway, where it unloaded Captain Hovey and the balance of Company L. This gave him a few days to talk over his mission and share knowledge of the area with Jenks. ss *Humboldt* returned four days later, embarked the white infantry company, and departed south for Seattle.[10]

Jenks and his men must have read the front page of the *Stikeen River Journal* on May 20, two days after landing, that recorded the arrival of Company L under the headline "New Coon in Town." The term "coon" for African Americans was not the only slur used in newspapers in this era, yet it must have reminded the men of Company L what to expect in Alaska. They would face the same racism and bigotry in the north they encountered anywhere in the United States.[11]

The article noted: "A detachment of Co. L, 24th Infantry (colored) consisting of 49 men under Lieut. I.C. Jenks, arrived on the Humboldt Thursday evening." The *Journal* staff artist illustrated the front page of the same edition with a rendering of a bearded white king, representing U.S. Commissioner Fred P. Tustin, derisively known as "King Tustin," surrounded by sixteen minstrel figures in blackface. The citizens detested the federally appointed U.S. commissioner, but the figures around him were clearly an allusion to the minstrel shows of the era, in which white performers acted out offensive stereotypes in black makeup. It is not known whether they represented the newly arrived Black soldiers.[12]

Lieutenant Jenks was the only commissioned officer at Fort Wrangel after the departure of Bogardus, though he was aided by army Acting Assistant Surgeon William M. Hendrickson, who was a civilian contract doctor. Hendrickson, who led a small hospital detachment of three men, provided some continuity between the incoming and outgoing army units. Jenks relied heavily on Hendrickson in the year to come.[13]

Jenks commanded a force of 3 sergeants, 4 corporals, 1 musician, 1 cook, and 37 privates. He also took charge of Hendrickson and his small hospital detachment. A civilian, clerk John Crompton from the U.S. Army Quartermaster Department, assisted him in accounting for the post and property. One of his educated enlisted soldiers served as Jenks's clerk and another as his striker (personal orderly). Lieutenant Jenks was listed in the post return in May 1898 as commanding the District of Wrangel and Post of Fort Wrangel, as well as quartermaster, commissary, recruiting, and summary court officer.[14]

Captain Hovey left Sergeant Washington to serve Jenks as first sergeant at Fort Wrangel, probably because he was the most senior and experienced noncommissioned officer in the company. This choice was predictable since Lieutenant Jenks had served in the same companies with Washington for the past three years in the Twenty-Fourth. They had experienced combat together in Cuba and developed a bond of trust in peacetime and war. This appointment made Washington the first among equals of the three sergeants and the noncommissioned officer in charge at the post.

Jenks immediate tasks upon arrival were quartering his men and assessing his mission. The fort was compact, covering two acres near the waterfront. Jenks initially moved into the large officers' quarters with a veranda while the soldiers occupied the old timbered barracks. Dr. Hendrickson ran the sizable two-story, balconied hospital on post. The cooks prepared meals in the kitchen, baked bread in the bakery, and raised vegetables in the garden. The soldiers manned and maintained the blockhouse where they stored equipment and weapons and guarded a perimeter that no longer had a stockade. The nearby wharf provided Jenks a lifeline to the outside world via the steamships that frequented the port transporting passengers and freight.[15]

First Sergeant Washington used the trumpet of his assigned field musician, Joseph A. Nash, to regulate the rhythm of the daily life of the soldiers at Fort Wrangel. Nash started the day with "Reveille," followed by assembly, surgeons call, and breakfast call. After breakfast there would be familiar calls for reports, roll, guard-mounting, and other details. Nash would signal dinner call at lunchtime, and at the end of the duty day attention, assembly, and retreat. After supper, "Taps" would signal lights out and time for the soldiers to sleep.[16]

As the only assigned field musician, Nash was an important member of the detachment in Wrangel. Nash enlisted in March 1899 but had served during the Spanish-American War as a musician assigned to Company B, Tenth U.S. Infantry Immune Volunteers (Colored). He served with the Tenth Immunes, which never deployed overseas, and enlisted in the Regular Army soon after he was mustered out of the federal service in March 1899.[17]

Other aspects of daily military life at Fort Wrangel also continued. When First Sergeant James Washington and Sergeant Allen Hayes reached the end of their three-year terms of enlistment in September 1899, Jenks discharged them and issued them discharge certificates, with character ratings of "excellent" and "very good," respectively. And as was the custom for senior noncommissioned officers like Hayes and Washington, they each signed enlistment papers the following day for three more years without a break in service.[18]

Other soldiers were not so lucky or chose not to reenlist. Private Charles A. Hayman, a twenty-six-year-old second term soldier from Hamilton, Virginia, was discharged in November 1899 on a certificate of disability. Since Lieutenant Jenks and Dr. Hendrickson judged the disability was incurred in the line of duty, Hayman received an honorable discharge and a character rating of "good."[19]

Mission

Lieutenant Jenks had a mission, like his commander Captain Hovey, to maintain order and provide an army presence in the District of Wrangel. Yet by the time Jenks arrived, the peak of the Klondike gold rush was over and the construction of the railroad from Skagway through the White Pass nearly complete. By then, Fort Wrangel had lost much of its strategic value as the gateway to the Stikine River on the mainland and was of little importance in the Alaska-Canada boundary dispute. Its value rested in its role as a communications hub and link in the tenuous sea transportation chain south to Seattle, since Fort Wrangel, along with Ketchikan one hundred miles to the south, were the southernmost U.S. ports on the panhandle of Alaska.

Shortly after arrival, Jenks helped deal with a group of destitute American miners who had run out of luck prospecting up the Stikine River in Canada. Jenks, along with U.S. Commissioner Fred P. Tustin, Deputy Collector of Customs J. C. Causten, and Deputy U.S. Marshal William D. Grant, requested funds to transport the penurious miners south. After War Department approval, Jenks issued the authorization to pay the Pacific Coast Steamship Company ten dollars per head for ninety-three miners' passage to Seattle. The lieutenant had his men feed and care for the miners, many suffering from frostbite and scurvy, while he interviewed each one to make sure they were "deserving cases." He then shipped them south to Seattle.[20]

What made Jenks's mission more challenging was the diverse population of Fort Wrangel. South of the town stood a sizable Stikine Tlingit village of about thirty-five houses and slightly more than two hundred inhabitants. Many residents of mixed Indian and European ancestry lived in the Tlingit village and in the town proper. A large salmon cannery north of the army compound employed eighty-five Chinese men, who lived as bachelors in a separate neighborhood called Foreign Town. Residents with Scandinavian roots made their living from fishing and shipping, along with others of European ancestry who ran businesses in town. And of course, a trickle of transient stampeders still passed through the town on their way north or south, patronizing the remaining saloons and gambling houses on Front Street.[21]

No Black civilians are known to have resided in Fort Wrangel in 1899, though there had been at least two the year before. Black resident Benjamin Franklin Starkey lived in town with a woman named Minnie Jones the previous summer. Starkey was an old Alaska hand who had come north to seek his fortune in 1897. The *Stikeen River Journal* reported Tim Callahan, the white bartender at the Woodbine Saloon, tried to force his way into Starkey's home one night in August 1898. Starkey "objected and closed the argument with an ax," leaving

Callahan insensible in the alley bleeding from head wounds. A judge determined Starkey was innocent of charges and merely defending his home, but the same month sentenced him to six months in jail at Sitka for selling whiskey to local Native Americans. And one of his partners in this crime was none other than Tim Callahan himself.[22]

Fort Wrangel's rugged and diverse population of about nine hundred made it the fifth largest in Alaska at the time Jenks landed. Plenty of bars, bawdy houses, and gambling halls on Front Street remained to fleece the unwary, an enlisted soldier's paradise. The author of a January 1899 issue of *National Geographic* described the place as having "a score of saloons" where "the most barefaced gambling games and swindling schemes were conducted on every side without concealment." With the fort encircled by the town, it was impossible for Jenks to separate his soldiers from the temptations of Front Street.[23]

Community Outreach

Lieutenant Jenks reached out to engage with the community in the months after his arrival, keen to establish good working relationships with civilian officials to support his mission. He was also eager to show the non-military face of his men to a population that was unaccustomed to the presence of armed Black soldiers living among them. He hoped this outreach would promote understanding and prevent trouble between his men and local citizens.

The *Stikeen River Journal* reported the first fruits of Jenks' efforts in late May 1899. Less than a week after setting foot ashore, the "concert troupe" of Company L put on a show at the Opera House which "was in every respect a grand success." The troupe played to a packed house on Wednesday, May 24, and made the front page of the *Journal* under the headline "A Big Hit."[24]

The *Journal* went so far as to name the core members of the troupe, and praised the work of "Wm. Pate, E.J. Collins, H.V. Jordan, and G.M. Payne," "past-masters of sketch work." The editor singled out stage manager Jordan and judged he had "few equals outside the professional class." The program included "Negro melodies, Song and Dance scenes, a cake walk, and a sparring exhibition by Howard and Pate, followed by a dance for the citizens." The cake walk had its roots in the enslaved culture of the South and was often performed in minstrel shows.[25]

The members of the troupe were a diverse group. Harry V. Jordan, born in Greencastle, Pennsylvania, was a thirty-one-year-old, six-foot-tall former cook who enlisted in Boston, Massachusetts. William Pate, born in New Bern, North Carolina, was a twenty-year-old former volunteer soldier who also enlisted in Boston. Edward J. Collins, a twenty-five-year-old former laborer, was born and enlisted in Piqua, Ohio. George M. Payne, born in Washington DC, was a twenty-eight-year-old former butler who enlisted in Indianapolis. Finally, William Howard, a twenty-six-year-old former laborer, was born and enlisted in Philadelphia. The only common thread of the five, beyond musical talent, was their shared status of being less than four months in the Regular Army.[26]

The *Stikeen River Journal* noted about a week later the Company L "Concert Troupe gave their second entertainment in the Opera House on Monday evening last." The editor of the newspaper noted the presentation was a "decided success," and a "noticeable improvement over the former entertainment, due no doubt to the fact that the boys are benefiting by experience and practice." Clearly Jenks was affording the men time to practice for these performances.[27]

The article provided some specifics of the program, which included "Song and Dance sketch work, a sparring match, and a Cake Walk." The editor gave no other details, except to say that the show was good and the "burlesque on Section 647 by Ben Green in the Cake Walk" was a big hit. Benjamin Green, a twenty-five-year-old former teamster born in Piqua, Ohio, had been in the army less than three months. The report referred to him as Ben Green, implying the reporter's familiarity with the soldier.[28]

Jenks and his men clearly succeeded in these first attempts to connect with and entertain the local population. The report noted there was a "large and appreciative audience and everyone expressed themselves as well pleased." Granted, the people of isolated Fort Wrangel were probably grateful for whatever entertainment they were offered. Yet the reporter mentioned the citizens were pleased to hear future performances were planned and promised to announce them in the newspaper.[29]

A group of distinguished scientists visiting Fort Wrangel missed the soldiers' performance by one night. The same edition of the *Journal* noted the arrival of a large party of noted scientists composing an expedition under noted railroad executive Edward H. Harriman. The list of the two score members of the expedition was a virtual who's-who of the celebrated scientists of the day. Included in the party were photographer Edward C. Curtis, anthropologist George Bird Grinnell, and naturalist John Muir. The expedition chartered the SS *George W. Elder* for the two-month cruise along the Alaskan coast as far as the Aleutian Islands.[30]

Lieutenant Jenks afforded the soldiers another chance to perform during the visit of the Boundary Commission the first day of July 1899. The commission, under Senator Charles W. Fairbanks, steamed into port on board the U.S. Revenue Cutter *McCulloch*. The group traveled north to Alaska to gather information to support the U.S. position on settling the boundary dispute between Alaska and Canada. On the evening of their arrival, Lieutenant Jenks and Dr. Hendrickson visited the ship and brought the "Company Quartette" to entertain the ship's company. There was no report on the reception the group received on board, since the cutter departed early the next morning.[31]

The Company L quartet had yet another opportunity to connect with the citizens of Fort Wrangel during the Fourth of July festivities the day *McCulloch* sailed out of port. The celebration began with the firing of salutes by the soldiers. At 10:00 a.m., the town assembled at the courthouse, followed by an invocation by Reverend Clarence Thwing, oration by Captain T. A. Willson, singing by the children, a concert by the Company L Concert Troupe, a reading of the Declaration of Independence, and singing of "America" by all.[32]

The activities in the afternoon of the Fourth revolved around sporting events. An organization of citizens scheduled twenty-two sports competitions and collected cash prizes for the winners of each event. Two of the contests were opened to the Black soldiers of Company L: the "Colored Gentlemen's Race" and the "Tug of War between Whites, Natives & Col. Men." The two highest purses were for the winners of the tug-of-war, ten dollars, and the "Indian Canoe Race," twenty-five dollars. Either prize was a great deal of money for an army private who collected a base pay of thirteen dollars a month.[33]

The highlight mentioned in the newspaper after the event was the tug-of-war. According to the *Journal*: "The most interesting features were the tug of war which was won by the natives, as against the white and colored contestants; and the Indian canoe race, which was won by the Kake Indians." It appears the Native Americans went home with most of the prize money.[34]

Lieutenant Jenks had to be pleased with the positive impression his men made in Fort Wrangel in the first two months of their residency. The members of the Company L Concert Troupe and quartet received positive reviews in the local newspaper for entertaining the white residents of the town and at least one party of visitors. And the soldiers joined in with the citizens of Fort Wrangel and local Native Americans in the Independence Day celebrations.

Disciplinary Problems

Novelist Rudyard Kipling once commented "single men in barracks don't turn into plaster saints." He made this observation about British regulars, yet it applies to soldiers anywhere. The African American men serving at Fort Wrangel were no exception. Many were in their early twenties, far from home for the first time, and in a place that was strange to them. Most of the men obeyed the rules—two sets since they were answerable to both civil and military authorities. The soldiers conformed to the Articles of War carrying out their official duties in the army, and civil laws when away from the military compound.

If a soldier disobeyed an army regulation or one of the Articles of War, military authorities punished him by court-martial. Lieutenant Jenks could use his summary court-martial authority at Fort Wrangel for relatively minor infractions. In this process, Jenks functioned as the judge and handed out punishment, normally a short period of confinement or extra duty. If the soldier committed a more serious offense or did not consent to summary court-martial, Jenks referred him to a general court-martial, the highest level of military justice. A general court-martial was composed of a judge, prosecutor, defense counsel, and a panel of officers who sat in judgment. All of these were military officers unless the soldier chose his own civilian lawyer. The punishments meted out by a general court-martial were more severe than those for a summary court, including death for certain offenses.[35]

For instance, in late August 1899 a message arrived from the Department of Columbia directing Jenks to send Private Thomas Jones under guard to Vancouver Barracks, Washington, for trial by court-martial. A detachment comprising Corporal Allen McGee, Cook Harry V. Jordan, and Private Charles Fletcher left aboard SS *Dirigo* two days later to escort the prisoner south. It is likely Jordan and Fletcher accompanied because they were witnesses. The three-man escort returned the following month with Jones in tow, acquitted of the charges.[36]

A month later in a different case, the command directed Lieutenant Jenks to send Private Charles S. Johnson under guard to Vancouver Barracks for trial by general court-martial. The charge was "sleeping at post," probably while standing guard duty. Jenks sent Sergeant William Hanson south with Johnson for the legal proceedings, perhaps as both guard and witness to the offense. Sergeant Hanson returned to Fort Wrangel in October while Private Johnson remained in confinement at Vancouver Barracks. A general court-martial found Johnson guilty and sentenced him to dishonorable discharge, forfeiture of all pay, and confinement at hard labor for one month. A dishonorable discharge, referred to as a "bob-tail" in soldier slang, could only be issued to a soldier expressly imposed by general court-martial.[37]

When Jenks referred a soldier to a general court-martial and sent him south to Vancouver Barracks, he lost the services of the soldier and escort for up to a month. He soon learned he could ill afford to waste time and manpower punishing soldiers for minor crimes. Because of the isolation of Fort Wrangel and distance to Vancouver Barracks, he and First Sergeant Washington found ways to enforce discipline locally, because the records show that after September, they shipped no other soldiers south for general court-martial.[38]

When cases did not involve violations of the Articles of War, Jenks worked with local Deputy U.S. Marshal William D. Grant concerning civil infractions of the law by his men. Soldiers tangled with Marshal Grant most commonly after they became drunk in bars, got in fights, and destroyed private property. As a standard practice, when a soldier got in trouble with the civilian authorities, the army turned him over for trial, allowed him to serve his jail term, and discharged him "without honor." This second category of discharge was issued to soldiers serving imprisonment under sentence by a civil court.[39]

On the last day of October 1899, Lieutenant Jenks delivered Private Robert W. Jordan to civil authorities for unspecified charges. This Jordan, not to be confused with Harry V. Jordan, was a twenty-seven-year-old from Nashville, Tennessee, who had enlisted in Dayton, Ohio, in March 1899. Jordan was tried and sentenced to six months in jail and sent to the district prison at Sitka to serve his sentence. Jenks discharged Jordan without honor by direction of the adjutant general in December 1899. Jenks did not have the authority to discharge Jordan himself; rather, he reported the offense to the adjutant general of the U.S. Army, who then ordered the discharge.[40]

In another case, Jenks turned over Musician Robert Harris and Private Fred Joiner to the marshal for trial in November 1899. According to the *Stikeen River Journal*, the two soldiers wandered into the Warwick Saloon on a Wednesday evening in October after they had been "drinking hard all day." They interrupted a game of cribbage being played by two local citizens, and when one of the men, named Mr. Healey, objected, Joiner "made several passes with a razor." Patrons ejected the two soldiers from the saloon and carried the injured Healey to Dr. Hendrickson, the army doctor, who stitched and dressed "a gash six inches long across his abdomen."[41]

The court sentenced Harris to five months imprisonment and Joiner to six months in jail and a hundred-dollar fine, with the sentence served in Sitka. Harris was a thirty-year-old second-term soldier from Cincinnati, Ohio, and Joiner a twenty-three-year-old former volunteer soldier from South Carolina. Jenks discharged both Harris and Joiner without honor by direction of the adjutant general a month later. In all these cases of civil confinement, Jenks forwarded a certificate noting a discharge "without honor" to prison officials to be given to the ex-soldier upon release.[42]

Also, in November, Jenks reported Private Huston Shannon absent without leave, referred to as "French leave," after he failed to return from two months of furlough. That month Private Shannon, a twenty-four-year-old former waiter from Bowling Green, Kentucky, turned himself in to authorities in San Francisco and was furnished transportation north to Fort Wrangel. He jumped ship in Portland, Oregon, and was apprehended by the civilian authorities there at the end of November. Shannon remained in the hands of civil authorities and was discharged without honor in February 1900.[43]

Lieutenant Jenks's disciplinary issues continued in the new year. Jenks reported Cook Ike Holloway "absent in the hands of the civil authorities" for unspecified charges at the end of February 1900. Holloway was a twenty-four-year-old former painter and carpenter from Columbus, Alabama. First Sergeant Washington had to find others with cooking skills to replace Holloway, who was discharged without honor in April.[44]

Likewise, in April 1900, the civil authorities at Fort Wrangel sentenced Private David McIntyre to five months imprisonment in Sitka "for selling an Indian whiskey." The sale of alcohol to the local Tlingit people was prohibited by both army regulation and federal law. McIntyre was a twenty-year-old from Cambridge, Massachusetts, who listed his former occupation as barber, so the soldiers likely lost their post barber. McIntyre was discharged by the army without honor in May.[45]

And finally, in April 1900, Jenks reported Private Emery Collier was sentenced to fifty days in jail for assault. Since Collier was sentenced in a civilian court, he must have had an altercation with a local citizen. Collier was a twenty-one-year-old who enlisted in March 1899 in Dayton, Ohio. He listed his former occupation as cook, so his loss probably added to First Sergeant Washington's food-preparation problems at Fort Wrangel. The army ordered Collier discharged in May 1900 without honor.[46]

In all, Lieutenant Jenks lost seven of thirty-eight privates after prosecution for civil or military violations of the law. He sacked a musician, a cook, and nearly one out of five of his privates in less than one year. Jenks had barely enough men to carry out the normal functions of maintaining Fort Wrangel and his missions. Instead of upholding law and order, his men added to the chaos.

The blame cannot be placed solely on the leadership of Lieutenant Jenks and First Sergeant Washington, especially considering their later success in Skagway. The surfeit of disciplinary problems probably had more to do with the isolation of the detachment, proximity to the temptations of Front Street, and strangeness of Fort Wrangel to the Black soldiers, many of whom were young and naive. The only members of Jenks command who stayed out of trouble belonged to the hospital detachment.

Hospital Staff

While his youngest soldiers presented leadership challenges for Jenks, his more experienced hospital staff stayed out of trouble while providing good medical care to the men. They must have done their job well because there were no reports of serious illness or death during their stint at Fort Wrangel. Jenks listed two men sick in May 1899, the month they arrived, yet there was not another man noted on the sick list the entire year the detachment occupied the post. This was a remarkable record, considering the unhygienic conditions in the town at the time, with scarce fresh water and no central sewage system.⁴⁷

The man responsible for keeping the unit healthy was Acting Assistant Surgeon William Hendrickson, the contract physician who ran the hospital. He was one of thousands hired to make up for the shortage of commissioned medical doctors to staff army facilities. During the frontier period, these acting assistant surgeons were neither commissioned nor enlisted, never promoted, and habitually underappreciated. One author compared their status to that of "the mule, without pride of ancestry or hope of posterity, neither horse nor ass, unloved and unlovely, the recipient of contumelious language, the Army's standby in time of trouble."⁴⁸

Until 1898 contract surgeons did not wear military uniforms. That changed after the army hired more than 650 civilian surgeons to handle the heavy workload during the Spanish-American War. During the war, the U.S. Army learned important lessons about the causes of vector-borne diseases and the effects of high-velocity bullets. They also earned a new appreciation for the importance of good medical personnel. After the war, the army awarded contract surgeons recognition by allowing them to wear uniforms with the rank of first lieutenant and medical insignia in silver with the letters CS for "contract surgeon." Jenks and the soldiers treated Dr. Hendrickson with the customs and courtesies of an officer at Fort Wrangel.⁴⁹

The enlisted members of the staff administered the hospital for Hendrickson, led by a hospital steward, considered a noncommissioned officer equivalent in rank to an ordinance sergeant. Hospital Steward George Arnold was the workhorse of the clinic, serving as the druggist or chemist who worked in the dispensary, as well as hospital administrator and clerk. Arnold served out his term of service in January 1900 and reenlisted for another three years. The three privates working for Arnold at the hospital served as orderlies, attendants, nurses, and performed other essential jobs. Hospital Corps enlisted soldiers earned more money than their enlisted counterparts in the infantry.⁵⁰

Until January 1900, the hospital staff comprising the steward and three privates assigned to the hospital at Fort Wrangel were all white. However, in January 1900 special orders arrived transferring Private Robert Grant, formally a Black infantryman in Company L, to the Hospital Corps. The Hospital Corps was the only branch in the army that was fully integrated at the time. Grant was a twenty-two-year-old former sailor from Philadelphia who had enlisted in December 1898. Grant, like all members of the Hospital Corps, had to serve a minimum of one year in the army and pass a rigorous test before transferring to the branch.[51]

Distaff Side

One last component of the small military community at Fort Wrangel was the distaff. The old army term commonly used for the wives and children of the officers and noncommissioned officers was the "distaff side." This expression comes from the old English word for a bunch of flax or the staff of a weapon. The families embodied the opposite end of the sharp point of the spear.[52]

The distaff served a particularly important function in the army, whether living side by side with the men in peacetime or residing at home during war. The wives and families provided human companionship and support for their husbands and fathers in an otherwise solitary profession of men. This was especially important to the officers, who did not socialize or fraternize with the noncommissioned officers or privates. The divides of rank, class, and race combined with adherence to the customs of the service kept officers and enlisted men separate during off-duty hours.[53]

When stationed on frontier posts and overseas, the army allowed officers and some noncommissioned officers to bring along their wives and children if conditions permitted. Lieutenant Jenks brought his wife and children to Fort Wrangel once the unit was established in quarters. Isaac Jenks had married Alice Girard Stevenson in 1897 while he was stationed at Fort Douglas, Utah. Alice was no stranger to hardship posts; she was born at Fort Duncan, Texas, in 1872, the daughter of an army surgeon.[54]

Alice joined Isaac Jenks at Fort Wrangel in June 1899 with their one-year-old daughter, Dorothy. Jenks's ten-year-old stepdaughter, Marion, arrived two months later. The family did not stay in the officers' quarters in the compound of Fort Wrangel long. At some point they leased a house in the city and joined the social life of the professional class in the city.[55]

Alice's mother visited Fort Wrangel in October 1899. Her mother was Anne R. Girard, wife of Major Alfred C. Girard, then the surgeon commanding the U.S. Army General Hospital at the Presidio of San Francisco, California. Girard was familiar with isolated military facilities since she had served with her husband on frontier posts in the west. Yet even to her, Fort Wrangel must have seemed strange with its mix of American stampeders, Black soldiers, Stikine Tlingit, and Chinese cannery workers.[56]

Initially, no noncommissioned officers' wives accompanied their husbands to Fort Wrangel. That changed after First Sergeant James Washington completed his third term of enlistment the first day of September 1899 and reenlisted for another three-year term the following day. Jenks granted Washington a furlough to travel to Seattle to marry his fiancée, Alice Cooper, in September 1899. It was his first marriage and her second. They must have met while he was stationed at Fort Douglas, since she listed Salt Lake City, Utah, as her residence. Alice was born in Nashville, Tennessee, and was thirty years old. She sailed with Washington on his return and brought a one-year-old daughter named Maggie. Jenks granted Washington permission to bring her to Fort Wrangel, where they set up housekeeping as the only Black family in the city.[57]

The distaff was small at Fort Wrangel since the detachment was not large. It must have been exceedingly lonely for Alice Washington, since she was the only Black female resident of the city. Noncommissioned officers' wives often served as laundresses for the soldiers and did other extra jobs to supplement their husbands' income. There is no record of what Alice did in her free time other than care for her daughter.[58]

Life for the other Alice, Alice Jenks, was easier since she was white. She and Lieutenant Jenks were active in the social circle at Fort Wrangel. Isaac Jenks was known for his fine baritone voice, and a West Point classmate insisted he missed a career with the Metropolitan Opera. He used this talent to his advantage among the influential citizens in the city. He sang at an April 1900 party hosted by steamship agent John F. Collins and his wife, Lula, an accomplished pianist. The newspaper called the event "the most select and elegant ever given in Wrangel."[59]

Chain of Command

In his official duties, Lieutenant Jenks was challenged by a complicated chain of command, since he reported to two superiors. As a detached member of Company L, Jenks reported routine actions monthly and serious incidents to Hovey. As the commander of the post at Fort Wrangel and the District of Wrangel, he answered to the headquarters of the Department of the Columbia. In this capacity, Jenks filed a monthly post return as the commander of Fort Wrangel to Vancouver Barracks, Washington.[60]

Jenks's higher headquarters, the Department of the Columbia, took its name from the Columbia River, the largest waterway in the Pacific Northwest. The department controlled army units spread throughout Washington, Oregon, Idaho, Montana, and Alaska. Railroads and telegraph lines facilitated communications between posts on the Columbia Basin, yet ship-borne communications were the only connection with units like the Company L detachment at Fort Wrangel.

Because of the difficulties controlling this far-flung department, President William McKinley created a separate military Department of Alaska in January 1900, to be headquartered at Fort Saint Michael, Alaska. The department, temporarily headquartered in Seattle, embraced the following posts: Circle City, Fort Davis at Cape Nome, Fort Egbert at Eagle, Fort Gibbon at Tanana, Valdez, Rampart City, Fort Saint Michael, Fort Wrangel, and Skagway. The entire organization comprised 37 officers and 1,088 enlisted men in 1900.[61]

The commander of this far-flung department was Brigadier General George M. Randall. He was serving in Cuba when appointed as the commander of the Department of Alaska. Randall assumed authority directing the military forces in Alaska on the first day of February 1900.[62]

Soon after arriving in Seattle in March 1900, General Randall realized how difficult it would be to control his scattered Alaskan command. Ships carried messages to and from the isolated stations since there were no telegraph communications with his posts in Alaska. And ice blocked the far northern outposts like Fort Saint Michael, the planned site for his headquarters, for much of the winter. Soon after assuming authority, Randall sailed north to personally assess the situation of his widely dispersed command.

General Randall's first stop on his tour of Alaska was Fort Wrangel. On April 11, 1900, Lieutenant Jenks greeted Randall, his military aide First Lieutenant Howard R. Hickok, and his chief surgeon, Major Rudolph G. Ebert, after they landed at the wharf. The ship did not remain at Fort Wrangel long, since it had other stops to make—just long enough for Randall to make a quick tour of the post and discuss the situation with Jenks.[63]

Randall had by then decided to reunite Company L at a permanent base in Skagway, which had become the gateway to the Yukon. General Randall was aware of the disciplinary difficulties at Fort Wrangel based on Jenks's monthly post returns. The detachment was simply too small to function effectively in a place like Fort Wrangel.

Not long after General Randall visited, he ordered Lieutenant Jenks to abandon Fort Wrangel and move his detachment to Skagway. The order reached Jenks early in May and directed him to leave Fort Wrangel on May 12, 1900, barely a month after Randall's visit.[64]

Lieutenant Jenks filed his final post return the day he departed. He left civilian clerk John Crompton from the Quartermaster Department in charge of accounting for the post and property. Since his detachment was the last army unit to occupy Fort Wrangel, thereafter, it remained U.S. government property, serving as federal government offices, schools, and other public functions.[65]

When Lieutenant Jenks boarded ss *Humboldt* for the trip north to Skagway, the surgeon and thirty-nine enlisted men went with him. The group included thirty-four enlisted men from Company L, four from the hospital detachment, and one white soldier from the Seventh U.S. Infantry, recently released from prison in Sitka.[66]

When Lieutenant Jenks and his detachment of soldiers from Company L steamed north to Skagway in May 1900, the era of U.S. Army occupation of Fort Wrangel that began in 1868 ended. The place had been first occupied by the Stikine Tlingit in prehistoric times, the Russian American Company beginning in 1832, and the British Hudson Bay Company after 1840. It served as an outfitting hub for three gold rushes yet lost its importance after the construction of the White Pass & Yukon Route railroad in Skagway.

Jenks was probably relieved to be free of his independent command and anxious to rejoin Hovey and the rest of the company. He never had enough soldiers to properly operate a military outpost, especially one that had lost its strategic value. In Skagway he would share the leadership burden with Captain Hovey and have twice the noncommissioned officers and soldiers to face the challenges ahead.

1. This Alaska and Klondike Gold Region map from 1899 shows the routes from Portland and Seattle to Fort Wrangel, Skagway, and Dyea, as well as to Saint Michael, which served as the headquarters for the army's Department of Alaska. It also illustrates the Klondike gold region that straddles the Alaska-Canada border south of Dawson. (Courtesy of Murray Lundberg)

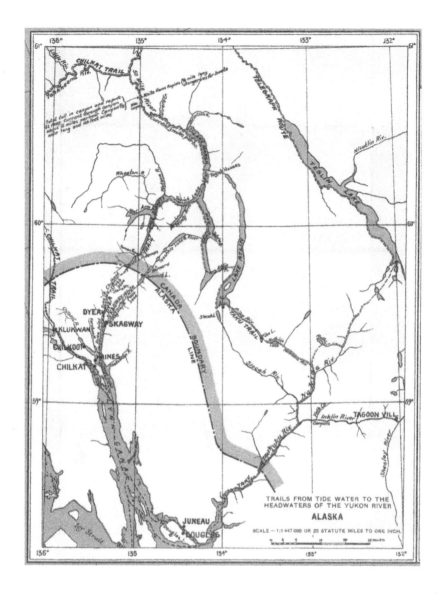

2. Dyea and Skagway dominated the northern approaches to the Lynn Canal, the main gateway to the Yukon. The Lynn Canal is a channel, not a manmade canal, and runs south toward Juneau. It is ninety miles long and more than two thousand feet deep, the deepest fjord in North America. (Courtesy of Murray Lundberg)

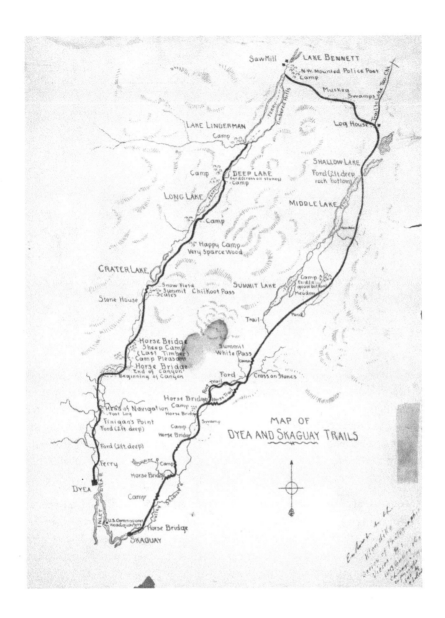

3. This map of the Chilkoot Trail from Dyea and the White Pass Trail from Skagway to Lake Bennett was published in the *Seattle Post-Intelligencer* in 1897. The White Pass & Yukon Route railroad, completed in 1900, ran roughly along the path of the trail between Skagway and Lake Bennett. (Alaska and Polar Regions Collections, UAF-1975-01-56, Archives, University of Alaska–Fairbanks)

4. *Above*: Company L boarded ss *Humboldt* on May 15, 1899, in Seattle, Washington, for the trip to Alaska. The ship touched briefly at Fort Wrangel three days later to disembark Lieutenant Isaac Jenks with a detachment to garrison the post. Captain Henry Hovey and the balance of the company continued northward, arriving at Soldiers Landing in Dyea on May 20, 1899. (Yukon Archives, H. C. Barley fonds, 82/298, #5166)

5. *Opposite top*: Captain Hovey inspects his soldiers at Camp Dyea before visiting Skagway for the Fourth of July parade in 1899. The soldiers wore the dark blue Pattern 1892 sack coat and the Pattern 1895 forage cap. The officers and noncommissioned officers have a white stripe on their light blue trousers, and the noncommissioned officers wear white chevrons or V's on their sleeves. The men carry the U.S. Model 1896 Krag-Jørgensen rifle. (Alaska State Library, William Norton Photo Collection, ASL-P266-868)

6. *Opposite bottom*: This view of Camp Dyea shows the expansive wharf area, an L-shaped warehouse, a tall flagpole, a smaller outbuilding, and the ramp leading to Captain Henry Hovey's office and quarters above the warehouse on the hill. A private from Company L stands on a wharf littered with lumber. (Alaska State Library, Frank B. Bourn Collection, ASL-P99-160)

7. *Above*: Captain Henry Hovey (*far left*) and Dr. Edward Bailey (*far right*) greet Major John Tweedale and his party at Soldiers Landing in July 1899. Frank Bourn, Tweedale's clerk, stands next to Bailey. Tweedale must have taken the photo, as he is not shown. Myra Tweedale and Dolly Bourn, who were sisters, are probably the women in dark coats, and Bailey's wife, Florence, one of the two younger women in the center. (Alaska State Library, Frank B. Bourn Collection, ASL-P99-203)

8. *Opposite top*: Captain Henry Hovey (*left*) and Dr. Edward Bailey stand side by side atop the hill overlooking the wharf at Soldiers Landing. Both men are relaxed and smiling, a clue to their good nature and character. Firsthand accounts of both men agree they were thoughtful and well-liked men, both by their soldiers and their peers. (Alaska State Library, Frank B. Bourn Collection, ASL-P99-85)

9. *Opposite bottom*: Company L traveled by boat from Dyea to march in the Skagway Fourth of July parade in 1899. Here the company marches north on Main Street behind a civilian drummer. The soldiers appear to be leading the parade, followed by the wagons of the local fire companies with hose and ladder trucks. (Alaska State Library, Frank B. Bourn Collection, ASL-P99-168)

474   COLORED INFANTRY U.S.A. SKAGWAY JULY 4 99   H.C.BARLEY.

10. *Opposite top*: Forty-five enlisted soldiers appear in this Fourth of July 1899 photo of Company L on Fifth Avenue. This includes one first sergeant (three chevrons topped by a diamond on the sleeve) and one sergeant (three chevrons) in front of the formation. Five squad leaders or corporals (two chevrons) march in the left of the formation in charge of two ranks of seven privates each. Corporals march to the rear of the righthand file and another to the left of the formation calling cadence to keep the soldiers in step. Finally, a musician stands to the left of the formation with his bugle. The company stands at attention with rifles at order arms. (Alaska State Library, Paul Sinic Photo Collection, ASL-P75-144)

11. *Opposite bottom*: A wagon loaded with children dressed for the Fourth of July parade rides into Skagway. Among the children is a Black child who is standing next to a Black man watching Company L on Fifth Avenue in figure 10. The white children with white decorations on their shoulders also appear in the parade photo. (Alaska State Library, Frank B. Bourn Collection, ASL-P99-169)

12. *Above*: The wharf at Fort Wrangel provided Lieutenant Isaac Jenks a lifeline to the outside world via the steamships that frequented the port transporting passengers and freight. His soldiers occupied the buildings of the fort surrounding the flagpole. View from the wharf, 1890s. (Michael Nore Collection)

GOVERNMENT BUILDINGS, WRANGELL, ALASKA.

13. *Above*: This 1908 postcard of Fort Wrangel shows the officers' quarters (*left*), barracks behind the flagpole, and two-story hospital (*right*). The stockade surrounding the fort was gone by the time Lieutenant Jenks and Company L arrived in May 1899. (Author's collection)

14. *Opposite top*: First Lieutenant Isaac Jenks commanded the detachment of Company L at Fort Wrangel for the first year of its deployment to Alaska. Jenks and his detachment rejoined Company L at Skagway in May 1900. (Isaac C. Jenks Collection, Hanover, New Hampshire)

15. *Opposite bottom*: Four wharfs on the southern waterfront served as Skagway's lifeline to the outside world. They were long to allow ships to dock in deep water beyond the mudflats that lined the seashore. The oldest was Moore's Wharf (*right*), which connected to a spur of the White Pass & Yukon Route railroad delivering freight directly to ships. (National Park Service, Klondike Gold Rush National Historical Park, KLGO 55931b)

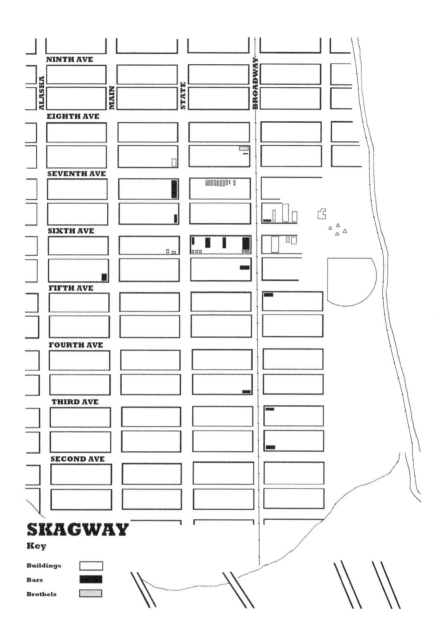

SKAGWAY

Key

Buildings

Bars

Brothels

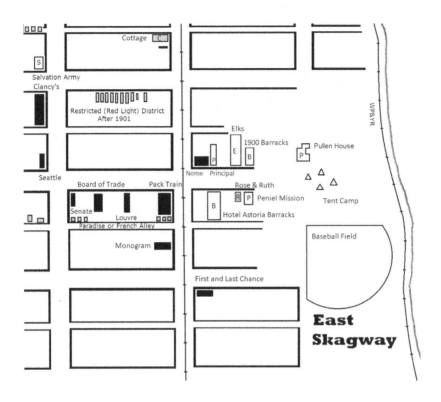

16. *Opposite*: Planners laid out Skagway in an orderly grid pattern with streets running north–south and avenues running east–west. Alleys ran between the avenues. The town was hemmed in by the sea to the south and by mountains to the north, east, and west. The White Pass & Yukon Route rail lines ran down the middle of Broadway for passengers and to Moore's Wharf in the southeast for freight. (Map by author)

17. *Above*: This map of central Skagway shows the soldier barracks, bars, brothels, baseball field, and other places important in the lives of the soldiers of Company L. (Map by author)

U.S. Colored Soldiers.   Ford.

U.S. Colored Soldiers.   Ford

18. *Opposite top*: The soldiers of Company L assemble in formation in front of a tent camp on the east side of Skagway the summer of 1899. First Sergeant Robert O'Connor is standing in front of the formation with his back to the camera, reading orders to the soldiers. One sergeant and a musician stand to the left and five corporals in the front rank with their squads of privates. (Sheldon Museum and Cultural Center, 2012.015.0009)

19. *Opposite bottom*: The soldiers of Company L move to carry out tasks after release from formation at the tent camp in Skagway. The three stripes and diamond on the sleeve of First Sergeant Robert O'Connor (*fifth from left*) are clearly visible, as are the other noncommissioned officers' stripes. The white soldier wearing a campaign hat looking at the camera (*right*) may be one of the hospital staff. (Alaska State Library, Paul Sinic Photo Collection, ASL-P75-013)

20. *Above*: Cooks and soldiers prepare three halibuts near the kitchen of the Astoria Hotel barracks in 1900. The soldier (*right*) with the knife and stripes on his pants is likely one of the assigned cooks, Elijah Lee or Jacob A. Pon. This view shows the alleyway behind the barracks between Sixth and Fifth Avenues, facing west toward Broadway. (Alaska State Library, William Norton Photo Collection, ASL-P266-867)

21. *Opposite top*: Citizens and soldiers wait for the finish of a race on Sixth Avenue during the Fourth of July festivities in 1900. Several uniformed soldiers gather in the street (*center*), and three stand on the boardwalk in front of the Hotel Mondamin. The corporal with his hand on his right hip closest to the photographer stands near three Black women. (Yukon Archives, Anton Vogee fonds, 82/271, #228)

22. *Opposite bottom*: Citizens and soldiers watch the boys' footrace during the Fourth of July festivities in 1900. No fewer than twenty-five uniformed Black soldiers stand interspersed and cheering with the white citizens of Skagway, watching the competition. The soldiers laugh, cheer, and clap side by side with the residents. (Yukon Archives, Anton Vogee fonds, 82/271, #229)

23. *Above*: Company L cooks and soldiers prepare Christmas dinner in 1900. Only two cooks were assigned to Company L, and preparing meals for one hundred men was beyond their ability. So the company rotated soldiers on special duty through the kitchen to assist the cooks, especially during holiday events. The soldier with a stripe on his pants (*left*) is likely one of the assigned cooks, Elijah Lee or Jacob A. Pon. (Yukon Archives, H. C. Barley fonds, 82/298, #5087)

24. *Above*: First Sergeant James Washington (with stripes on his sleeve) and cooks prepare tables for Christmas dinner in 1900. The soldier in the white jacket, a uniform piece worn by cooks, is probably one of the two assigned cooks. Tablecloths, plates, silverware, glasses, and napkins are set for the soldiers to enjoy turkey, apples, nuts, cinnamon rolls, pies, and cakes. (Yukon Archives, H. C. Barley fonds, 82/298, #5086)

25. *Opposite top*: Company L stands in formation on Sixth Avenue in front of the Astoria Hotel barracks. Corporals (two chevrons on the sleeve) stand in the front rank with their squads of privates arrayed between and behind them. The trees at the end of Sixth Avenue are the site of the tent camp the soldiers first occupied when they moved to Skagway. (Courtesy of Karl Gurcke)

26. *Opposite bottom*: Company L stands in full campaign gear on Sixth Avenue in front of the Astoria Hotel barracks. Equipped for field duty, the soldiers wear a brown Pattern 1883 campaign hat, canvas bedroll, canvas haversack, steel bayonet scabbard, and canvas leggings over boots. A roving guard with his shouldered rifle can be seen on the sidewalk behind the formation. The brothel run by Rose Arnold and Ruth Brown was in one of the buildings next to the barracks. (Library and Archives Canada / Ernest F. Keir fonds, c-63099)

27. *Opposite top*: Patrons drink in the Nome Saloon, located on Sixth Avenue across the street from the Astoria Hotel barracks. The Nome changed owners and was renamed the Commerce Saloon in September 1900. Among the customers sitting at the bar are at least one, and perhaps several Black men, indicating the Nome was one of the bars in Skagway that welcomed Blacks. The woman in a hat seated near the wall (*left*) worked at the bar as a dance girl or prostitute. (Alaska State Library, Paul Sincic Collection, ASL-P75-040)

28. *Opposite bottom*: Advertisement for the Principal Barbershop on Sixth Avenue across from the Astoria Hotel barracks, December 1900. The white, mustached officer (*left*) is likely Second Lieutenant Edward Rains, one of the three officers stationed in Skagway at the time. He is wearing officers' trousers with a stripe, and his uniform jacket and hat hang on a hook behind him. (Alaska State Library, Paul Sinic Photo Collection, ASL-P75-22)

29. *Above*: A white child holds hands with Black child, Skagway. Several Black children from the families of noncommissioned officers lived in Skagway from 1900 to 1902. (National Park Service, Klondike Gold Rush National Historical Park, KLGO-32333)

30. *Above*: A Black boy plays with a white boy in front of advertisements for local establishments in Skagway. The two are on a boardwalk walking on what appear to be improvised stilts made of cans held by strings. (Courtesy of Karl Gurcke)

31. *Opposite top*: Lieutenant Isaac Jenks (*far left*) stands with two Black soldiers and two white citizens on a hunting trip to Warm Pass in September 1901. All five carry Winchester hunting rifles and pose with three mountain goats, two ptarmigans, and a woodchuck. (Alaska State Library, William Norton Photo Collection, ASL-P266-868)

32. *Opposite bottom*: Men dine at a social session at the Elks Hall in Skagway in October 1901. Captain Henry Hovey sits near the head of the table in uniform and has a pair of glasses tucked in his left breast pocket. (Alaska State Library, Paul Sincic Collection, ASL-P75-041)

FIRST MORNING IN CAMP AT WARM FALLS SEPT 15 1901.

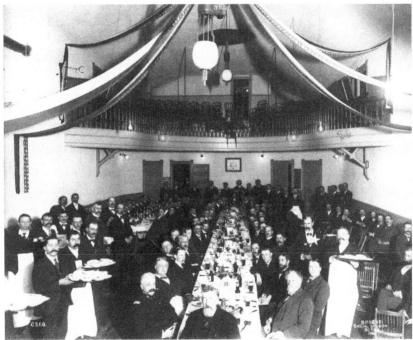

33. *Above*: Dr. Edward Bailey (*left*) poses with a citizen of Skagway in 1901. Bailey wears the dark blue Pattern 1895 officers' coat and the Pattern 1895 officers' cap with a Maltese Cross on his collar indicating his medical branch. His uniform is trim, and he carries a more military bearing than in figure 8, where he appeared in ill-fitting khakis. (Courtesy of Karl Gurcke)

34. *Opposite left*: The soldiers of Company L staged a minstrel show at the Elks Hall next to the soldier barracks in August 1901. The production featured songs, dancing, and a cake walk, and was accompanied by a local white orchestra. The Magnolia Four was a soldier minstrel group that entertained the soldiers and the community in Skagway. (*Daily Alaskan*, August 19, 1901)

35. *Opposite right*: A professional minstrel company traveled to Skagway in September 1901 and staged *A Trip to Coon Town* at the Elks Hall. This play by Bob Cole was the first full-length Broadway musical comedy written, directed, performed, and produced exclusively by African Americans. Members of Company L participated in the show. (*Daily Alaskan*, September 27, 1901)

Magnolia Four

Minstrels

AT ELKS HALL, AUG. 20

Members Co. L, 24th Infantry

True Southern

DANCES

AND

SONGS

A Rare Treat

Admission, 50c & 75c
Reserv

"Coon, Coon, Coon, I wish my color would fade."

A Trip to

Coon Town

The greatest Ragtime production of the Day By An

All

Colored Company

Clean and up-to-date Negro Comedy. Supported by some of the Leading Talent of the Colored Race.

Strictly First-Class

This company is under the direction of Geo. H. Williams, and are going to make a tour through Alaska, supported by 12 first-class artists.

A Big Three Act Production Taken From True Life

1st Act. Coon Town Society.
2d Act. A Race Track Scene In Memphis.
3d Act. Celebration Day In Coon Town. Between the acts there will be a number of clever specialties, including

A Cake Walk Carnival

and the Famous Standard Quartet.

ELKS HALL

Saturday, Sept. 28

SEATS FOR SALE AT Kelly's Drug Store and at Bitter's News Stand in Postoffice.

GENERAL ADMISSION

Adults 75c.   Children 50c.

Reserved Seats $1.00

36. *Opposite top*: The baseball team of the Third Battalion, Twenty-Fourth Infantry, sits for a photograph sometime after 1902, possibly at Fort Missoula, Montana. The Company L baseball team wore uniforms like this during games against the railroad team in Skagway from 1900 to 1902. (Muller, *The Twenty-Fourth Infantry*)

37. *Opposite bottom*: The White Pass baseball team posed for this photo in 1903. Employees of the White Pass & Yukon Route railroad organized a team that played against the Company L soldier team from 1900 to 1902. The two seated players in the front are balancing what is probably the Kirmse Cup on their knees. Top row (*left to right*): Daniels, Knott, Mark Phelps, Alex Blanchard, Billy Blackmore. Second row: Tom Barry, Clarence Olsen, Manager G. Murry Woodburn, Lee Gault. Bottom row: Eddie Taleen, Dugan Barry. (Skagway Museum, George and Edna Rapuzzi Collection 0892, Rasmuson Foundation)

38. *Above*: The grateful citizens of Skagway hold a farewell banquet for Captain Henry Hovey at the Pullen House in May 1902. Hovey (*left*) stands behind the seated guests. Lieutenant Edward Rains is probably the other mustached man in uniform standing behind the seated guests on the left. (Alaska and Polar Regions Collections, UAF-1976-35-22, Archives, University of Alaska–Fairbanks)

H.C. BARLEY.

39. *Opposite top*: Company L boarded SS *City of Seattle* at Moore's Wharf on May 15, 1902, en route to its new home in Fort Missoula, Montana, after serving in Skagway three years. Moore's Wharf connected to the White Pass & Yukon Route with a rail spur. (Yukon Archives, H. C. Barley fonds, 82/298, #5091)

40. *Opposite bottom*: This bird's-eye view of Skagway in 1903 was taken from the mountains east of the city. The crowd in the center of the image is standing on the baseball field, with people seated in the bleachers. The large, dark two-story building behind the crowd in the center is the Astoria Hotel soldier barracks on Sixth Avenue. The white two-story building to the right is the newer soldier barracks, built in 1900. The ornate false-front building next to the 1900 barracks is the Elks Hall, where the Magnolia Four performed in 1901. (Museum of History and Industry, Seattle)

41. *Above*: The White Pass & Yukon Route employed Benjamin Starkey as the day porter at the Broadway Depot in Skagway, shown here warming by the stove. He was an old Alaska hand, having lived at Fort Wrangel in 1898. "Old Ben Starkey," as he was known, worked for the railroad for more than a year and retired shortly after Company L departed Skagway in May 1902. (Skagway Museum, Lester Moyer Collection 02.210, Edith Lee)

42. Eugene Swanson served as a corporal with Company L at Skagway from 1899 until he ended his service honorably in 1902. He married a member of the Black community in Skagway and sought his fortune in the goldfields of Alaska. He did quite well in the mining business and died in Fairbanks in 1942 at the age of seventy-eight, having lived in Alaska for more than forty years. (*Fairbanks Daily News-Miner*, March 7, 1942)

SKAGWAY BARRACKS

The colored troops may have fought bravely, but they
are the most peaceful people we have here in Skagway.
There are no ruffians or drunks among them. Wait
till two or three companies of white boys arrive and
then you can see a commotion every day or two.

—*DOUGLAS ISLAND NEWS*, January 3, 1900

Once Captain Hovey and First Sergeant O'Connor moved their men
from Dyea Barracks to Camp Skagway, they quickly came to understand the lesson Lieutenant Jenks and First Sergeant Washington
learned after their arrival at Fort Wrangel. At the Soldiers Landing
wharf barracks, the company was isolated from civilian society, three
miles by road from Dyea and by sea from Skagway. Company L's leaders found it easier to keep soldiers out of trouble when they were far
from the temptations of town. However, the new camp in Skagway
was just a short walk from sixteen saloons and several bawdy houses.
Hovey and O'Connor would shortly have their hands full with disciplinary problems.

Skagway

The town was only three years old, but Hovey's first task was to understand its complex history. The site was homesteaded in 1887 by Captain
William Moore, who earned his title piloting ships along the coastal
waters of Canada and Alaska. With the help of his son, Benjamin, Captain Moore expanded the settlement with a cabin, sawmill, and wharf
in the late 1890s, hoping that the coming gold rush would make him

rich. The area remained sparsely populated until word of the Klondike gold discoveries reached Seattle and San Francisco in July 1897. Then the rush was on, and Skagway's life as a city began.[1]

The first shipload of prospectors landed at Skagway within weeks of the news of the strike, and by October 1897 the town had grown into a sprawling settlement of ten thousand people. The city boasted a planned grid of streets, frame buildings, stores, hotels, saloons, gambling houses, dance halls, and a bustling red-light district. The gold rush peaked in 1898, before the start of the Spanish-American War, and Skagway's population dropped to about three thousand by the time Company L arrived in 1899.[2]

Along with a calmer, smaller population, Hovey and his men benefited from the end of Soapy Smith's influence in the town. Jefferson Randolph Smith, alias Soapy Smith, was a confidence man who formed a close-knit, disciplined gang of shills and thieves to create a small criminal empire in Skagway. Soapy operated Jeff Smith's Parlor in Skagway, where he held court and ran all sorts of con games, card tricks, and sleights of hand. With so much gold flowing through the town, Smith grew wealthy enough to put the local deputy U.S. marshal and other officials on the payroll to turn the other cheek.[3]

Soapy's criminal empire ended in a dramatic shootout with a vigilante committee just four days after the Independence Day celebration of 1898, one in which Smith rode at the head of his own "Skagway Military Company" as grand marshal. On July 8, 1898, after three of his men stole three thousand dollars in gold dust and nuggets from a Klondiker named John D. Stewart, the town reacted swiftly. A gunfight at the Skagway wharf between Smith and vigilante committee guards John Landers, Jesse Murphy, Frank H. Reid, and Josias M. Tanner brought the villain down. Smith died on the spot from a bullet through the heart, and Reid died twelve days later. The committee quickly rounded up his gang for trial, and the Soapy Smith era ended.[4]

Skagway might have become a ghost town like Dyea if not for the construction of the White Pass & Yukon Route, which began in 1898.

This was the first railroad in Alaska and provided freight, mail, and passenger service to the Yukon. The initial line from Skagway to Bennett City in Canada was completed on July 6, 1899, just three weeks before Hovey and Company L arrived in Skagway.[5]

At the end of July 1899 when Company L established its tent camp, Skagway was still one of the largest cities in the District of Alaska. It boasted an impressive array of services including a bank, 2 breweries, 5 churches, an electric light company, 3 fire companies, 3 hospitals, 18 hotels, 3 newspapers, 4 schools, 11 restaurants, 16 saloons, a theater, 4 wharfs, a water company, and 4 U.S. government agencies (U.S. Customs, U.S. Commissioner, U.S. Army, and U.S. Post Office).[6]

Permanent Barracks

After the Dyea wharf burned in July 1899, Hovey moved his men to a temporary tent camp near Skagway. Hovey described it as being on the "west side of town, well located and on a good temporary site." Later, he shifted the company bivouac to a more suitable site on a tract on the east side of town that belonged to Captain Moore, the original settler of Skagway. This new camp occupied an open field north of the Moore house, at the end of Sixth Avenue east of Broadway.[7]

The Company L camp comprised about fifteen tents in an open field. Ten were Sibley tents, which could comfortably hold a dozen men. Most of these housed a squad of eight soldiers: one corporal and seven privates. There were also smaller tents and at least one large command tent where Captain Hovey slept and had his headquarters. The sergeants in the company would normally have shared a Sibley tent separate from the rest of the men in the company. Additionally, two small wooden prefabricated buildings probably contained the kitchen and arms room.[8]

With winter approaching, Captain Hovey decided it prudent to move his men out of the tent camp, so in mid-September 1899, after a month and a half under canvas, Company L moved into the leased Astoria Hotel on Sixth Avenue. The Astoria, built in early 1898, stood at 236 Sixth Avenue just east of Broadway, not far from the tent encampment.

It was a two-story false-front structure, measuring twenty-five by one hundred feet, which according to an advertisement had steam heat, electric lights, electric call bells, bathrooms, and hot and cold water. An ad called it the "Finest Hotel in Alaska" with a "First-Class Bar and Club Rooms." With the gold rush over, the Astoria was available for lease to the army at a reasonable price.[9]

The new accommodations must have felt luxurious to the soldiers after two months at the wharf hotel and seven weeks in tents. The chief quartermaster of the Department of the Columbia described the Astoria as well constructed with the upper floors piped for steam heat, though the building needed an additional boiler. The rent for the building was $175 a month from A. H. Davis, "exclusive of steam boilers and such other slight repairs to make them fit for occupancy by troops." These repairs, approved by the quartermaster, included the cost to connect the Astoria to the city water mains and the installation of plumbing and bathtubs. With no central sewage in Skagway, Hovey had a "dry earth closet" built, which had to be emptied daily by a "scavenger," whose job was emptying human excrement from privies and cesspits.[10]

Hovey later requested emergency funding for sewer repairs and upgrades, noting the "problem of disposing of soiled water had been a very serious one." He tried cesspools, but these backed up at high tide. He then had a two-inch drainpipe laid 225 feet to a nearby creek, which also backed up and filled in under the barracks. Finally, Hovey buried four-inch clay tiling to dispose of liquid waste from the barracks that flowed to nearby streams and into the ocean.[11]

Hovey worried about fires in Skagway and took active measures to prevent them. He positioned fire buckets and water barrels in all rented government buildings and purchased two hundred feet of canvas and rubber hose, a nozzle, and couplings to hook to the town fire hydrants. This supplemented the two hose carts and hook and ladder truck manned by the Skagway volunteer fire companies. Hovey's concern prompted him to volunteer the use of his soldiers to help the city in case of fire. The company's twenty-four-hour roving security guard, who patrolled the company buildings, served an important role in reporting fires, especially at night when the town slept.[12]

One good example of the utility of this fire guard occurred at 5:00 one morning in February 1900. Three women who lived at the west end of Sixth Avenue near the soldier barracks were involved in a domestic dispute when a lamp overturned, and a fire started. The soldier on patrol "noticed the flames or heard the cries and sounded the alarm. The military firefighters turned out promptly and quenched the flames ere they had done more damage than the burning of a rug, a few wall decorations, and some bed clothing."[13]

The lease of the Astoria included two small gable-roofed wooden buildings behind the hotel, which improved the company's fire protection. One was used as a kitchen and the other for coal storage. Kitchens used ovens that burned wood and coal, a fire hazard in a town constructed of wood. Wooden buildings in this era often had kitchens built in structures separate from the living spaces due to the danger of fire.[14]

To solve a third problem, lack of storage and office space, Hovey rented a building for eighty dollars a month from P. W. Snyder. This building, about two blocks from the barracks, was always occupied or kept under guard. Hovey kept an office there.[15]

And finally, to house a medical facility to care for his men, Hovey rented the old Pacific & Arctic Railway & Navigation Company building for use as a hospital. Like the building used for office and storage, this structure was several blocks from the barracks. The roving sentinel also had to keep this building under guard, though one of the hospital staff was on duty to care for patients.[16]

Military sentries or patrols visited the separate buildings at twenty-minute intervals at night to provide security and guard against fires. As an additional measure, Hovey had phones installed that connected to the city phone system, though not to the outside world. In addition to the phone in Captain Hovey's office, there was one at the army hospital, one at the headquarters, and one at the barracks.[17]

No matter how hard Hovey worked to ensure comfort, safety, and security, the Astoria was not an ideal barracks for a company of infantry. The individual rooms were not suitable for the enlisted men, who were normally quartered together in larger rooms for ease of control and discipline. Squads or sections normally slept in large open bays where they could be inspected and roused quickly in case of emergency, for guard duty, or for morning reveille formation. Yet the main drawback of the Astoria was its proximity to the saloons, gambling halls, and bawdy houses surrounding the barracks. These establishments were too tempting for soldiers with few other options and their pockets lined with money each payday.

Color Line

White Americans carried their racist values with them to Alaska. Consequently, some of the businesses in Skagway refused to serve Black soldiers, money in their pockets or not. Certain saloons in Skagway introduced rules excluding the African American infantrymen from their establishments. This was illustrated in a newspaper article published just days after the arrival of Company L in the city, which noted: "The negro soldiers in Skagway are kicking because some of the saloons in that town draw a color line."[18]

By 1899 sixteen saloons remained in Skagway. According to historian Catherine Holder Spude, each had "become something like a club house to its own clique of customers." For instance, "the Board of Trade fancied itself as a gentleman's club and was more likely to draw in businessmen, the Mascot and Idaho saloons were solidly working class, and the Last Chance catered to a somewhat more eclectic and (perhaps in the eyes of the local residents) less savory crowd."[19]

The owners of the saloons and bars of Skagway who survived the end of the gold rush were keen to stay in business. Selling liquor in the District of Alaska was made illegal in 1897, so saloon owners lined up to pay the fine of $100 to the district court each year to stay in business. This ended in March 1899, when Congress enacted legislation that imposed a requirement for a liquor license fee of $1,500 a year in Alaska. The temperance movement wanted an outright ban on liquor and the high license fee was a compromise. This drove Skagway's number of saloons in 1899 from one hundred to sixteen, all owned by the wealthy and powerful in Skagway. And Skagway viewed the liquor license fee as a financial boon since it paid for the town's public schools.[20]

The owners of the remaining saloons in Skagway accommodated their day-to-day customers to stay in business. If the regulars of an establishment "objected to the proprietor about catering to men outside their chosen cohort, the proprietor might well refuse to serve some men," according to Spude. This was not fair to the men of Company L, but it was a business reality in Skagway.[21]

Some of the sixteen saloons in Skagway allowed African American soldiers entry to spend their money. The soldiers were paid once a month and the business owners of the town were anxious to separate the men from their cash, no matter the color of their skin. Skagway was not so prosperous that its business community could ignore the opportunity, especially with the ever-shrinking population in 1899. Gold is gold; gold can sometimes trump prejudice.

Payday

Captain Hovey paid the soldiers of Company L once a month. Most of the privates did their duty with little complaint and looked forward to the monthly muster for pay, though the sum was far from princely, as low as a private's base pay of thirteen dollars in cash. Still, a Black private earned the same as a white private, something unheard of elsewhere in society. Noncommissioned officers earned slightly more each month, with the first sergeant collecting twenty-five dollars, sergeants eighteen dollars, and corporals fifteen dollars. And longer-serving soldiers earned additional pay for consecutive years served after their initial enlistment.[22]

Payday each month for Company L was a significant occasion in Skagway since it brought money to town. Skagway's landlords and merchants were delighted at the money flowing to their bank accounts from the coffers of the U.S. government, affectionately known as "Uncle

Samuel." The newspaper sometimes reported the arrival of the payroll in Skagway to alert businessmen.[23]

The man who least enjoyed payday each month was Captain Hovey. Nearly half of all correspondence he sent out in the first six months at Skagway Barracks was to the chief paymaster of the Department of the Columbia. Rarely did Hovey enjoy a payday without problems.[24]

Hovey's difficulties with the distribution of pay, fraught with complications to begin with, was exacerbated by the remoteness of Skagway. The chief paymaster sent Hovey the monthly wages by ship from Portland on the last day of the month, and the money arrived in Skagway weeks later. For instance, Captain Hovey acknowledged receipt of the payroll for July on August 19, 1899. After paying the men he sent a letter to the paymaster certifying the transactions. He also enclosed a slip signed by each soldier acknowledging they had been paid.[25]

The payday routine had not changed over the years. Each enlisted soldier waited his turn, knocked on the door for the command to enter, marched smartly to Captain Hovey's desk, snapped to attention, saluted, reported with rank and name, and waited patiently for his cash. After stiffly counting his money and signing his receipt, the soldier saluted again, executed an about-face, and marched out of the room. Dr. Bailey looked on from a nearby desk as a witness, and an armed guard stood outside the office for security. Hovey was also armed with his army-issue .38-caliber revolver.[26]

It was a rare payday that Captain Hovey did not report a discrepancy to the chief paymaster. Each of the roughly seventy officers, soldiers, and civilians assigned to Skagway Barracks received an individual envelope containing the pay due with the total written on the outside. Hovey had Dr. Bailey double-check the rolls and verify the cash in the envelopes each payday. This system invited human error. For instance, Hovey reported in August 1899 the envelope for Sergeant Henry Robinson, marked $26.60 on the outside, contained only $26.10 when opened. So Sergeant Robinson and Captain Hovey signed and returned a certificate noting the shortage of fifty cents to the chief paymaster. Robinson received an envelope with his fifty cents the following month.[27]

At other times money arrived for soldiers no longer in Skagway. When Hovey acknowledged the August 1899 payroll in September, he returned the envelope intended for Corporal Walter J. Whited since he had already been discharged at the end of his enlistment. In October 1899 he returned the envelopes with the September pay of privates John Graves and Frank Jenkins, both in the hands of civil authorities serving sentences. He also returned the pay envelope of Private Walter M. McMurry, who had deserted.[28]

Hovey's payday headaches worsened in December 1899. The November pay arrived on December 20 and was locked as always in a safe at the office of the Alaska Pacific Express Company, which handled the shipment of the payroll. When Hovey tried to retrieve the money, the safe would not open. Efforts to open the safe were futile, and it was sent south to Seattle in early January 1900 to be unlocked. The Express Company finally opened the safe, shipped the money back, and Hovey paid the men their November and December pay on January 21, 1900. The members of Company L were by necessity frugal in their Christmas celebrations that year.[29]

One more factor added to Captain Hovey's payday troubles. After being paid each month, some of the soldiers visited the motley collection of saloons, gambling halls, and bawdy houses located a short walk from the barracks. Soldiers being soldiers, some got into trouble.

Disciplinary Problems

Captain Hovey and First Sergeant O'Connor spent a good amount of time in Skagway dealing with disciplinary issues, some old and quite a few new. In August 1899 Private Harry Stewart rejoined the company after being released from hospitalization and confinement at the Presidio of San Francisco, California. Hovey left Stewart at the hospital in Presidio in May when the company was en route to Alaska. Once Stewart recovered, he did something to warrant military confinement from June to July 1899. After his release from detention, the army shipped him north to Alaska.[30]

Another soldier who was left behind at the Presidio of San Francisco, Private James Rare, was apprehended in August 1899 by authorities in Juneau on his way north to join Company L. He committed a crime in Juneau and was sentenced to twenty-five days in prison. After serving his sentence and returning to Skagway, Hovey issued him a discharge without honor in October 1899 under the authority of the adjutant general of the army.[31]

By October 1899 Hovey listed five of his men in confinement. Some of these were soldiers held by the civilian authorities, yet most were confined by the company to Skagway Barracks. Local confinement for the soldiers meant they were either confined to their rooms or to a provisional jail at the barracks under guard. Hovey could punish soldiers with confinement under his summary court-martial authority.[32]

In another case, Captain Hovey reported the desertion of Private Walter McMurry in October 1899. McMurry, who had enlisted in February 1899 in Evansville, Indiana, was just eighteen years old, having previously served with the First Indiana Volunteers during the Spanish-American War. Hovey detailed the circumstances of his desertion as follows: "This man had connected himself with a house of prostitution near the barracks and was there without my knowledge at various times performing different kinds of service for them. I expected it and was waiting for proof of his action when he became aware of it and left with women running the house who went to Dawson, NWT [Northwest Territory]. He has been on sick report a good deal and was in general a worthless man to the company."[33]

Hovey also reported the case of another badly behaving soldier, Private John Graves, in October 1899. Graves, a twenty-five-year-old first-term soldier from Pittsburgh, Pennsylvania, was arrested by the local marshal for "entering a house to obtain money through threats of violence" and for entering another house, drawing his bayonet, and threatening to kill First Sergeant Robert O'Connor. Hovey planned to charge Graves with being drunk on guard, abandoning his post, and "concealing his bayonet with the avowed purpose of doing the First Sergeant bodily harm." The civilian court saved Hovey the trouble and sentenced Graves to six months at Sitka.[34]

As if Captain Hovey did not have enough disciplinary issues with his own men, he had to deal with soldiers from other units. In October 1899 Private George W. Wood, a white trooper from Company A, First U.S. Cavalry Regiment, surrendered from desertion. Wood had been on furlough for twenty days from his unit stationed at Fort Huachuca, Arizona Territory, and deserted in January 1898. How he reached Skagway is a mystery, but the gold rush was probably a factor. Captain Hovey tried Wood by summary court-martial in December and held him in confinement, awaiting instructions from the Adjutant General's Office.[35]

In another case, Captain Hovey was summoned to Juneau in November 1899 as a "witness before civil court." This was likely in connection with the arrest and confinement of ex-soldier James Rare, who Hovey had discharged without honor in October. Rare assaulted a Native American with a pistol, was arrested, charged, and jailed. Because there was no other commissioned officer in Skagway, Hovey put Dr. Bailey in temporary command of the post during the period he was absent.[36]

In December 1899 the *Daily Alaskan* reported a case of a white Skagway resident getting into a fight with a soldier from Company L. According to the newspaper: "Dick Case, the pugilist, and one of the colored soldiers got into an altercation last night at Clancy's Theater, which resulted in Captain Hovey promptly cancelling all passes and recalling all of the soldiers not on duty to the barracks." There were no civil charges filed as a result of the fight.[37]

This may seem like an overreaction on Hovey's part, yet he was keen to keep good relations with the citizens of Skagway. Withdrawing the privileges of all the soldiers put pressure on individuals to behave themselves or risk the wrath of their fellows. It is also likely that the soldier who caused the trouble received some private boxing instruction from the sergeants behind the barracks, which was common practice at the time.

The soldier got into trouble at Clancy's Theater, one of the places that welcomed Captain Hovey's soldiers. The term "theater" does not do justice to the variety of services offered by this business. Established by Frank Clancy in 1897, it was a place a soldier "could find drink, gambling tables, dancing, vaudeville shows, music and upstairs rooms with willing women to offer all sorts of delightful sensations." If he wanted, the soldier could go far on his monthly pay of thirteen dollars, with ten-cent beer, twenty-five-cent whiskey, nickel cigars, quarter dances, and a two-dollar session with a prostitute.[38]

According to the *Daily Alaskan*, Clancy's gambling houses were "cosmopolitan. Nobody is barred. White men, Colored men, Chinese, Japanese, and Indians jostle one another at the tables where the Blackjack dealers sit and fill the air with profanity, foul tobacco smoke, and fouler conversation."[39]

Though we do not know if it occurred at Clancy's, there was at least one other case of note involving a white citizen assaulting an African American in Skagway. The *Daily Alaskan* informed readers in December 1899 that among prisoners being transported was "E.C. Barheight, formerly of Skagway, sentenced for a year at Sitka for assaulting a negro here." There were no other details in the article on whether this was an African American soldier or a civilian.[40]

By January 1900 orders from the Adjutant General's Office directed Hovey to discharge without honor the following individuals from Company L serving civil sentences: privates James Rare, Frank Jenkins, John Graves, Robert Harris, and Fred Joiner (Harris and Joiner were at Fort Wrangel). Hovey was also directed to discharge Private George Wood from the First Cavalry Regiment. This cleared the backlog of punishments and discharges, and in each of the following months Hovey averaged just one soldier in local confinement at Skagway Barracks.[41]

The *Daily Alaskan* noted at least one incident of violence within the Black community. In February 1900 the newspaper reported, "Looney Moore, who was arrested a week ago and sentenced to three months' imprisonment for assault on a negro woman of the city, was sent on the *Cottage City* to Sitka, there to serve his time." The article provided no additional information about the identity of the African American woman. The name of the Black soldier from Company L was Loney Moore, not "Looney" as the newspaper printed. This might have been a typo, yet more likely an example of the *Daily Alaskan*'s habit of indulging in amusement at the expense of the soldiers in Skagway.[42]

Loney Moore was a thirty-year-old career private from Penola, Virginia, on his fourth enlistment. He had served on and off in the Regular Army since enlisting in 1890, never rising above the rank of private. He fought in Cuba and was wounded in the charge up San Juan Hill. Hovey discharged Loney without honor in May 1900 under orders from the adjutant general. Moore was released from Sitka after serving his sentence, committed another misdemeanor, and was arrested and thrown into prison again.[43]

The punishments meted out to soldiers found guilty of offenses varied. The soldiers convicted in civilian courts were generally discharged without honor while they served in prison. The army's standard punishment for desertion at the time was trial by court-martial, confinement for three months, and a dishonorable discharge. For those found guilty of minor military offenses, Hovey handed out punishment after a summary court-martial, and the offender served his term of confinement or extra duty supervised by the sergeants of the company.

Every soldier when discharged had to be provided a discharge certificate. As a post commander, Hovey had a stack of blank forms for this purpose. He issued discharges marked "honorably" to those who ended their terms as such, with character ratings of excellent, very good, good, fair, or not good. He issued discharges marked "without honor" to those soldiers who were in prison under sentence of a civil court, upon approval of the adjutant general of the U.S. Army. A "dishonorable discharge" could only be given to a soldier expressly imposed by sentence, normally by general court-martial. Soldiers referred to a dishonorable discharge or a discharge without honor as a "bob-tail" and to the process as being "bob-tailed."[44]

The soldiers discharged from Company L for disciplinary reasons found themselves in a pickle. A soldier separated from the service, except by way of punishment for an offense, was granted travel pay to return to the place of his enlistment, presumably near his home. The African American soldiers discharged from Company L after serving sentences in Sitka found themselves with only one option: leave by the first ship for the closest U.S. state or forfeit the privilege of being sent there at the expense of the U.S. Army.[45]

It is likely that most former soldiers released from Sitka took advantage of the travel allowance to sail to Seattle. Especially in winter. Otherwise, they would be left penniless in Alaska with nothing more than the civilian clothes on their backs. Ex-soldiers were not allowed to wear their army uniforms after a discharge without honor, and one set of civilian clothing was purchased for them if they did not own one.[46]

Inspector General Visit

The main staff component concerned with monitoring the disciplinary system in the army was the inspector general's office. Captain Herbert E. Tutherly served as the Department of Alaska inspector general, and he periodically inspected the units to check on their discipline, along with morale and training. Captain Tutherly and the other department inspector generals submitted their reports to the inspector general of the U.S. Army at the War Department in Washington DC. The inspector general, who consolidated these reports, used them to guide War Department policy. Brigadier General Joseph C. Breckinridge Sr., the U.S. Army inspector general, visited Skagway in October 1899.[47]

Captain Hovey had to have been concerned with the prospect of the visit of General Breckinridge. Then as now, official visits by the inspector general, known as the IG, made any commanding officer apprehensive. An unsatisfactory rating in any IG inspection could lead to a commander losing his job. Just a month and a half before Breckinridge's visit, Hovey had moved into the Astoria Hotel, which was still under renovation and located literally across the street from several saloons and bawdy houses. Hovey also had a long list of disciplinary issues involving his soldiers.

Captain Hovey need not have worried about the visit. According to historian Joseph Whitehorne, General Breckinridge had a reputation as an untiring traveler, visiting every post in the West as the inspector general, as well as overseas posts in Cuba and China. In addition to discipline, he was especially interested in the welfare of soldiers, care of the sick, and the efficacy of military training. It is likely Captain Hovey raised the issue with General Breckinridge of his soldiers' lack of proper clothing to face the rigors of the cold climate in Alaska.[48]

Winter in Alaska

The first winter in Skagway must have come as a rude shock to the members of Company L. Many of the soldiers hailed from southern states and may never have seen snow or experienced temperatures below freezing. The average low in Skagway, Alaska, is eighteen degrees Fahrenheit and the average snowfall more than fourteen inches in January. The lowest temperature recorded was negative twenty-four degrees Fahrenheit. Skagway is famous for high winds, and its name derived from the Tlingit word meaning "where the water bunches up," referring to the white caps seen in the northern Lynn Canal. The wind chill could be deadly in wintertime.[49]

The soldiers of Company L sent to Alaska did not have adequate military clothing the first winter. Captain Hovey complained of the lack of suitable uniforms issued to his men in correspondence to his superiors at Vancouver Barracks. Records show he purchased extra cold-weather gear for his soldiers locally to take them through the first winter in Skagway. Hovey also allowed his men great latitude in wearing non-uniform items during the cold, wet winters.[50]

In February 1900 the secretary of war added the following to the clothing issued to enlisted men serving in Alaska: "1 southwester hat, 1 fur cap, 1 pair fur gauntlets, 1 mackinaw overcoat, 1 oilskin coat, 1 pair oilskin trousers, 1 pair buckskin gloves, 1 pair buckskin mittens, 1 pair moccasins, 1 pair German [wool] socks, 1 pair shoe pacs [a type of waterproof cold-weather boot], and one sweater." The uniform allowance for soldiers serving in Alaska was increased by thirty dollars a year to pay for these additional items. The new directive took effect in April 1900, so the soldiers in Skagway did not benefit from this change during their first winter in Alaska.[51]

The *Daily Alaskan* reported under a headline on December 20, 1899, the "Heaviest Local Snow Storm Ever Known Now Raging." The three-day snowstorm was the heaviest on record in Skagway, with an average depth of two feet. In the mountain passes traversed by the White Pass & Yukon Route above Skagway the depth was three to eight feet. A rotary plow pushed by two locomotive engines became stuck at White Pass and was buried by an avalanche. The train following the plow with twenty passengers was stuck in the pass for four days.[52]

The snow did not prevent the members of Company L from celebrating Christmas. The married officers and noncommissioned officers could spend time with their families in Skagway during this holiday. The single soldiers had to celebrate together, many of them the first time away from home. The *Daily Alaskan* noted the day after Christmas 1899: "The observances yesterday included . . . a big dinner in the United States Barracks for the soldier boys."[53]

The heavy snow and cold temperatures did not keep the soldiers from completing their required training. A week after the record-breaking snowstorm hit, the *Daily Alaskan* carried an article titled "Learning to Signal." According to the story, the soldiers were "learning the army signal code and will soon begin practice of signaling with signal lanterns, several of which were received last week." The article noted the code was the same one Captain Hovey had employed in New Mexico and Arizona Territory using heliographs. Ten words a minute was the maximum rate for accuracy, and Hovey claimed his Black troops were more adept than white soldiers. Hovey planned to test the signal lanterns in the hills around Skagway, though at present the men "during the inclement weather practice within doors."[54]

Signal instruction was only one of the areas the noncommissioned officers taught in winter to round out the military education of soldiers. Training would have included a good deal of marching in various formations and firing practice, as well as inspections of rifles, equipment, and uniforms. Instruction began each morning at 6:00 a.m. when the bugler sounded "Reveille" and ended each night when "Taps" closed the duty day. Education also included instruction in essential tasks such as first aid, map-reading, and field sanitation.[55]

It was common practice for a company to have a drill or training room in the barracks, used for instruction that was best done indoors or for employment during inclement weather. The training room was set up as a study area with the company manuals for tactics and operations and training supervised by the training noncommissioned officer. This drill room was used extensively in the winter months.

Distaff Side

The Company L distaff, the wives and children, likewise weathered their first winter in Skagway as they settled into some measure of normalcy living in Skagway. Life in Alaska must have been as strange to them as it was to their husbands. One officer, several noncommissioned officers, and one civilian clerk brought their families with them to live in the military community in Skagway. These families lived in homes leased by the army on Fourth and Sixth Avenues.[56]

Surgeon Edward Bailey had his wife, Florence, and nine-year-old son, Mark, with him in May 1899, when Company L arrived at the wharf barracks near Dyea. Bailey's family likely lived in Dyea until the fire at the wharf forced the company to move. After the transfer to Skagway, Edward and Florence joined the social life and mingled with the professional class in the city.[57]

Captain Hovey's family did not accompany him to Alaska. His wife, Carrie French Tower, and two children, thirteen-year-old Bradford and seventeen-year-old Clara, remained in Northfield, Vermont—where Hovey had been assigned to Norwich University from 1895 to 1899—perhaps due to educational necessities, leaving Hovey to serve out his tour in Alaska as a geographical bachelor.[58]

A white civilian army clerk from the U.S. Army Quartermaster Department also served in Camp Skagway. Charles Clarkson, who was born in Hampshire, England, in 1863 and later became a naturalized U.S.

citizen, kept track of government property at the post. His wife, Mary, and son, Fred, who was born in Skagway in January 1900, added to the small army distaff community. Clarkson, like Bailey, lived in quarters with his family rented at government expense. He was paid a salary of nine hundred dollars annually. Clarkson was an old hand in the army, having served three three-year enlistments in the infantry and earning a promotion to sergeant with an excellent service record.[59]

The African American military community in Skagway was initially small yet would see growth in the years to follow. Two of the Black non-commissioned officers of Company L brought their wives and families to live with them in Skagway. Louisa or "Sussie" Withers O'Connor, wife of First Sergeant Robert O'Connor, and Sarah M. Robinson, wife of Sergeant Henry Robinson, lived with their husbands in quarters leased by the army in town.[60]

Sussie O'Connor, as the wife of First Sergeant O'Connor, headed the small African American distaff community in Skagway. Sussie Withers married Robert O'Connor shortly before their departure for Alaska from Salt Lake City, Utah. She was thirty-two years old, born in Louisville, Kentucky, in 1867, and had lived previously in Paris, Kentucky, and Emporia, Kansas.[61]

Sarah Robinson, the wife of Sergeant Henry Robinson, assisted Sussie in supporting the African American distaff in Skagway. Sarah M. Clemmens married Henry C. Robinson in Salt Lake City, Utah, on September 30, 1898. Sarah was the same age as Sussie, thirty-two, and born in Kansas City, Missouri in 1867. She worked as a hospital matron at the Camp Skagway army hospital, earning $120 annually to supplement her husband's income. Sergeant Robinson earned $26.60 a month at the time, making his annual income approximately $320.[62]

Army Hospital

The small army hospital run by Dr. Edward Bailey at Camp Skagway guaranteed the soldiers health care by a trained army doctor. Free medical treatment was an important benefit to soldiers at a time when such care was unavailable to many Americans. And doubly true for

African Americans who lived at the bottom of the social ladder at the turn of the century.

Bailey and his staff worked closely with Skagway's three other hospitals and ten physicians. Skagway had a facility called the Bishop Rowe Hospital to serve its citizens as well as a small Red Cross hospital. A railroad hospital in town provided medical care to the men who constructed and maintained the White Pass & Yukon Route railroad. In fact, the clinic run by Bailey on Seventh and Broadway was in an old building previously used by the railroad.[63]

What composed the Camp Skagway hospital? Acting Assistant Surgeon Bailey led the small staff. Baily was a fully trained and experienced doctor, one of hundreds of contract surgeons employed by the army at a salary of $150 a month. He had been assigned to Dyea and Skagway since December 1897, so there was nothing temporary about his service. The word "assistant" was inaccurate since he was the only doctor at the hospital. It was a term used much like the university faculty title of "assistant professor," implying only lack of tenure or in his case lack of commission. Moreover, the officers and men of Company L treated Bailey with the customs and courtesies due a commissioned first lieutenant. The soldiers would have referred to Dr. Bailey as "sawbones" in the army slang of that time.[64]

Acting Hospital Steward Gabriel Cushman was Dr. Bailey's righthand man at Skagway. Listing Saint Joseph, Missouri ,as his home, Cushman was born in Grodno, Russia, in 1873 and came to the United States in 1891. Naturalized in 1900, he was Jewish and listed his occupation as a druggist when he enlisted in the army in 1895. The army assigned Cushman to the Hospital Corps with Fort Snelling, Minnesota, and Fort Keough, Montana, as his first duty assignments. Those were posts occupied at the time by the Black Twenty-Fifth U.S. Infantry, making Skagway his third time serving with the Buffalo Soldiers.[65]

Cushman was assigned to the Hospital Corps based on his experience as a druggist. After his basic service in the Hospital Corps as a private, he took a test encompassing care of the sick, ward management, minor surgery, first aid, and elementary hygiene. Once promoted, he worked one year as an acting hospital steward, followed by another examination. Cushman had by early 1900 served five years in the army and was working toward his promotion to full hospital steward. Cushman was popular with the soldiers of Company L, who referred to the steward as "pills" in common army usage.[66]

In addition to Cushman, Camp Skagway was authorized three Hospital Corps privates to assist Bailey. Unmarried enlisted men who had served at least one year were eligible to request a transfer to the Hospital Corps as privates, where they received training in nursing, first aid, cooking, pharmaceuticals, clerical work, and the care of animals. Of the three, Private Charles R. Oakford served as a nurse, Private Henry G. Kane as a cook, and Private Henry Sterly as an orderly. Sterly was born in Germany and had become a naturalized citizen like Cushman.[67]

As hospital matron, Sarah Robinson played an important role in the efficient operation of the clinic, serving as the senior nurse assisting Bailey and Cushman. The army employment of hospital matrons dated to the Revolutionary War. During the Spanish-American War, the army hired more than 1,500 contract nurses to care for the wounded. This led to the founding of the Army Nurse Corps in 1901. Since Robinson was listed in the official army pay records as a hospital matron, she served in a precursor role to the nurse corps. She was the only person of color working in the clinic.[68]

Dr. Bailey and his staff treated the sicknesses and injuries of the men at Skagway Barracks. If they encountered a problem they could not handle locally, they sent the man south to the larger hospital at Vancouver Barracks, Washington. For example, in February 1900, on Bailey's advice, Hovey sent Private John Kimball to Vancouver Barracks for medical treatment. Kimball, a former confectioner from Atlanta, Georgia, returned two months later to full duty at Skagway and served out his enlistment.[69]

If a soldier was not capable of performing his military duties because of medical issues, Bailey recommended a discharge. Captain Hovey approved a "discharge on Surgeons Certificate of Disability" in December 1899 for Private Ellis Hunter. Bailey treated Hunter and issued the certificate of disability based on his diagnosis of "injury to left knee caused by an accident and for syphilitic rheumatism, neither of them contracted in the line of duty."[70]

Doctor Bailey's most important job was to guarantee the soldiers of the company were fit for duty. At an isolated post like Camp Skagway, good medical care was critical to mission success. Hovey needed as many men as possible present for duty each day to carry out its primary mission of maintaining a military presence in this strategically important section of Alaska.

Permanent Post

The big news in Skagway in early 1900 was Captain Hovey's recommendation the army establish a military fort at Skagway. The local newspaper mentioned Hovey's report in the New Year's Day edition of 1900. According to the article, Hovey recommended the permanent post "would include all buildings and shops necessary for the accommodation of a command of 120 men."[71]

Under the headline "Big War Works for Skagway," the story detailed the planned expenditure of twenty-five thousand dollars to construct a permanent base at Skagway. Captain Hovey refused to release details in "accordance with the strict business custom of the war department." Yet Hovey did mention he had requested the immediate transfer of Jenks and his men from Fort Wrangel to Skagway. Hovey noted that Skagway was the "tactical point of this region" and that troops "could easily be placed on the heights above Smugglers Cove, between Skagway and Dyea, and from that vantage ground, should it be found necessary, pour a destructive fire from big guns into an enemy in Dyea or Skagway."

Though the citizens favored the idea of a permanent military establishment in Skagway, many were not happy that Hovey recommended a site west of the city on the other side of the Skagway River. Landowners and landlords were keen to make money by selling or leasing property to the army in or near the city. They reacted quickly with an offer that might keep the army in town. A day after the big news broke in the *Daily Alaskan*, an article reported: "The citizens of Skagway have at last agreed among themselves and bought an army post site. The purchase price, $500, will be raised by popular subscription."[72]

Command Visit

On April 11, 1900, the new head of the Department of Alaska, Brigadier General George M. Randall, his military aide, First Lieutenant Howard R. Hickok, and his chief surgeon, Major Rudolf G. Ebert, visited Skagway. Randall, who had just assumed command of the Department of Alaska, was making his initial tour of his units and posts. His visit to Skagway followed on the heels of his stop to see Lieutenant Jenks at Fort Wrangel. Skagway was an important stop for Randall since it was the largest post in the department in terms of soldiers assigned and money spent.[73]

The most important topic of discussion during Randall's visit concerned the continued military presence in Skagway. Hovey thought Skagway was the appropriate place to build the post, though there were problems finding enough land inside or outside the city for an adequate site. He reminded Randall that there was also an option to locate the new post at nearby Haines Mission, where land for the reservation was set aside in December 1898 by the War Department.[74]

General Randall's visit galvanized the leaders in Skagway to redouble efforts to convince the army to build the post in Skagway proper, and not across the river as Hovey had recommended. A committee formed to work with property owners of an area of northern Skagway to purchase land for the reservation. They wanted the post in town to profit from land sales. They also realized the soldiers "being on guard all night, gave a great deal of fire protection, and their complete organization enabled them to get to a fire quickly."[75]

In connection with this plan to build a permanent post at Skagway, General Randall discussed his decision to have Lieutenant Jenks rejoin Captain Hovey from Fort Wrangel. Skagway had clearly won the competition as the gateway to the Yukon with the completion of the White Pass & Yukon Route railway to Bennett in July 1899. Randall also understood the challenges of operating two separate posts at Fort Wrangel and Camp Skagway with too few officers, noncommissioned officers, and soldiers.[76]

General Randall's visit was short. He had other posts to visit and the steamer had other stops to make. Not long after his visit, he sent orders to Lieutenant Jenks to abandon Fort Wrangel and reunite with Hovey in Skagway.[77]

After the Dyea wharf barracks burned in late July, Captain Hovey billeted his company in a tent camp on the east side of Skagway. As winter approached, he moved his soldiers into more permanent leased buildings in the town and took steps to improve the living conditions of his men. He and First Sergeant O'Connor then settled into a routine of carrying out their mission while maintaining training and discipline, a real challenge because of the company's proximity to the temptations of the town.

Both Captain Hovey and Lieutenant Jenks struggled to accomplish too many tasks with too few soldiers in the first year of deployment at Fort Wrangel, Dyea, and Skagway. The order from General Randall to reunite the two detachments in Skagway was a relief to Hovey and Jenks. They confronted a new year of change and challenges with a combined force of twice the officers, noncommissioned officers, and soldiers to carry out the tasks ahead.

5

COMPANY REUNITED

Last Saturday evening the S.S. *Humboldt* landed at the
Douglas wharf and was met by an unusually large crowd
of sightseers. And they were rewarded by hearing some
fine quartet music rendered by the colored soldiers from
Wrangel, who were onboard the boat bound for Skagway.

—*DOUGLAS ISLAND NEWS*, May 16, 1900

The Skagway garrison swelled considerably when General Randall
ordered Lieutenant Jenks and his men to abandon Fort Wrangel and
rejoin Company L. SS *Humboldt* transported the detachment 250
miles north to arrive in Skagway on May 13, 1900. After operating as
two separate units for a year, the reinforced garrison now comprised
two officers and nearly one hundred enlisted men. The consolidation
improved Captain Hovey's ability to carry out his military and diplomatic missions in Alaska.[1]

Consolidation

The arrival of Lieutenant Jenks and his 34 soldiers almost doubled
the garrison in Skagway. The company now included 2 officers, 6 sergeants, 12 corporals, 2 musicians, 1 artificer, 2 cooks, and 66 privates.
Also, 2 army assistant surgeons, 8 hospital corpsmen, a civilian clerk,
a hospital matron, and a deserter from the Seventh Infantry whom
Jenks brought from Fort Wrangel. All were Black, save the officers,
clerk, deserter, and 7 of the 8 hospital corpsmen.[2]

Hovey's increase in manpower created some logistical challenges,
since he had to feed, quarter, and supply more soldiers. In the past ten

months Captain Hovey had been forced out of his Dyea wharf barracks by fire, lived in two different temporary tent camps in Skagway, and finally moved into the Astoria Hotel. With the arrival of the Fort Wrangel detachment, Hovey needed more space for the additional soldiers, officers, and family members.

To house the reunited company, Hovey signed a lease with contractor Philip W. Snyder to construct a purpose-built barracks on Sixth Street across from the Astoria. Snyder began work on the two-and-a-half-story, twenty-five-by-fifty-foot building in early October 1900, and the soldiers moved in the following month. It was a plain yet functional building, with a door and four windows on the front, two per floor, and eight windows, four per floor, on each side. A rear stairwell connected the two stories and the two long floors were undivided and lined with rows of bunks. It was an ideal barracks for an infantry company and must have pleased the sergeants as much as it was disliked by the soldiers for lack of privacy.[3]

The new barracks was not large enough to answer all the needs of the company, so Hovey retained the old Astoria Hotel for unaccompanied noncommissioned officers, office space, a mess hall, and other needs. He also rented several other smaller buildings for himself, the married officers, and some of the married noncommissioned officers and their wives. Hovey, acting as company quartermaster, disbursed thirty-five thousand dollars on rent for the buildings in Skagway in 1900, which was about a third of that expended for rent in the Department of Alaska for the year. Since Hovey's buildings were all leased, some enterprising businesspeople in Skagway pocketed a pot of Uncle Samuel's gold that year.[4]

One of Captain Hovey's subsequent actions was to reassign some of his extra duties to Lieutenant Jenks. Effective May 1900, Jenks assumed responsibility as post adjutant, recruiting officer, ordinance officer, signal officer, and summary court officer. This was nothing new to him since he bore these same responsibilities at Fort Wrangel. On the regimental roster, Jenks also filled the billet as the adjutant of the Second Battalion, Twenty-Fourth Infantry. This last assignment had more to do with where Jenks was carried on the books and aligned with his approaching promotion to captain. It also vacated the first lieutenant position in the company and opened it for replacement.[5]

Soon after the detachment arrived, Sergeant Washington assumed the duties of first sergeant for Company L. According to army regulations, "The captain will select the first sergeant from the sergeants of his company and may return him to the grade of sergeant without reference to higher authority." Since Washington had acted as the first sergeant of the detachment at Fort Wrangel, he simply assumed those duties of the reunited company in Skagway. Sergeant Washington was ten years older and had been in the army six years longer than O'Connor.[6]

The consolidation resulted in other changes in the enlisted ranks of the infantry company at Camp Skagway. O'Connor became a section sergeant, taking his place among the other three. Hovey appointed new corporals at the recommendation of his sergeants to replace those who ended their enlistments. The section sergeants moved privates where necessary to bring undermanned squads up to strength. And of course, the cooks, musicians, artificers, and clerks merged and adjusted their duties and living arrangements.

The consolidation of the garrison also forced some changes in the hospital staff. Captain Hovey had worked with Dr. Bailey for a year and was happy with his abilities and their working relationship. What is more, Bailey signed a new contract for another term, which was forwarded to the surgeon general of the U.S. Army in April 1900. When Hovey learned that Dr. Hendrickson was coming to Skagway from Fort Wrangel, he alerted the Department of Alaska that he needed only one doctor and preferred to retain Bailey. So Bailey stayed, and Hendrickson boarded a steamer for a new assignment in San Francisco at the end of May 1900.[7]

One additional leadership change occurred among the members of the combined hospital staff. Bailey did not need two hospital stewards in Skagway, so he had to choose between George Arnold, who came from Fort Wrangel, and Gabriel Cushman. Though Arnold was senior to Cushman, Bailey chose the man he had served with for the past two years in Alaska. So Cushman remained, and Arnold shipped out for a new assignment at Vancouver Barracks in May 1900. The army appointed acting hospital steward Gabriel Cushman full hospital steward the following month, making him a noncommissioned officer.[8]

Cushman was apparently well liked in Skagway, since the *Daily Alaskan* published the news of his promotion in a prominent newspaper article. Under the banner "Receives New Stripes," the piece noted that Cushman had been promoted to "the highest rank conferred in the hospital corps." It mentioned he had recently traveled "to Seattle to undergo an examination and his new stripes the result." As a hospital steward, he wore on his arm above the elbow three bars and an arc of one bar in emerald green cloth, enclosing a red cross. The article also added that Cushman was "popular with both officers and men."[9]

The reunification of the company resulted in a slight increase in the military family members living in Skagway. Captain Hovey, Dr. Bailey, and Florence Bailey welcomed Lieutenant Jenks and Alice Jenks to the small officer distaff community. Likewise, Sergeant O'Connor, Sussie O'Connor, Sergeant Robinson, and Sarah Robinson welcomed Sergeant Washington and Alice Washington to the Black military community in Skagway. Hovey leased housing for both new families.

Despite the reintegration of the company, Hovey reported to the Department of Alaska that he needed ten new recruits to bring his company to its full authorized strength. He had lost several soldiers who completed their enlistments and others to disciplinary issues. Three soldiers of the company who were absent in the hands of the civilian authorities in Sitka were discharged without honor in May 1900: privates Loney Moore, David McIntyre, and Emery Collier. This cleared Captain Hovey's disciplinary backlog and he listed only one soldier in local confinement in the barracks in his May 1900 post return.[10]

Football

The consolidation of the company provided the non-martial advantage of manpower for sports teams. The first Skagway newspaper reference to sports relating to the soldiers involved football. An early May 1900 edition carried the headline "SOLDIERS AT FOOTBALL. Will Shortly Have a New Ball and Large Ground." The article reported the soldiers played evening games between picked teams of African American soldiers near the barracks.[11]

The army in 1900 had no formal off-duty physical training or testing program as it did in later years, yet its enlisted soldiers played sports and held competitions at every opportunity. Before the company moved to Alaska from Utah, the regiment had encouraged the fielding of both company and regimental teams at Fort Douglas, sometimes playing local white teams from Salt Lake City. Soldiers enjoyed individual and team sports, encouraged by officers who used company funds combined with individual donations to purchase uniforms and equipment.[12]

Captain Hovey and Lieutenant Jenks encouraged sports to maintain soldier fitness, encourage teamwork, and fight boredom. Hovey sent for a "Rugby ball" and had his men fill in a ditch and grade an area "from Broadway right on to the Moore lot" to make it safe for the soldiers and protect his barracks windows from errant balls. Captain Hovey was pleased with the reaction of the residents of Skagway, keen to show the locals the non-military face of his men. Lieutenant Jenks was familiar with the game, since he watched the first Army-Navy football game played at West Point as a cadet on November 29, 1890.[13]

The soldiers played football games among themselves rather than against the citizens of Skagway. Hovey used such contests between his soldiers as physical training to keep them fit and to break the monotony of routine camp life in Alaska. It would be the more civil game of baseball that would bring the Black soldiers and the white residents of Skagway onto what General Douglas MacArthur called "the friendly fields of strife."[14]

Baseball

On Saturday May 19, 1900, the *Daily Alaskan* carried a story headlined "THREE BALL TEAMS HAVE ORGANIZED. The Soldiers, the Railroaders, and the Skagway Juniors. BIG GAME TOMORROW."

The soldiers, like the railroad men and the citizens of Skagway, came from all parts of the country. They brought their love of baseball to Skagway along with the urge to compete against others in the sport. And since the soldier team was Black, their competition against the white teams of Skagway generated added interest.[15]

The soldiers were eager to play baseball and had the support of their leadership. The sport found an active supporter in Lieutenant Jenks, who played catcher and lettered on West Point's first varsity baseball team. He would not have participated in the game as a player, since he was an officer and had to distance himself from his enlisted soldiers, yet he would have encouraged Captain Hovey to allow the team time to practice, facilitate games with the Skagway teams, and guide the team from a discrete distance.[16]

It was no accident that the first newspaper reference to the Company L soldier team came a week after the arrival of the detachment from Fort Wrangel. First, Jenks would have supported the fielding of a team after he landed in Skagway. Second, the company had twice the talent to draw upon with the doubling of the enlisted ranks. Also, by chance or design, Lieutenant Jenks had among his Fort Wrangel detachment some of the best baseball players in the company. And finally, it was spring in Skagway and time to play ball.

The Saturday article noted:

Skagway has taken up the great American game of baseball with the true American spirit, and three crack teams have been formed and are in training. They promise to furnish a great deal of sport before the summer closes.

The United States soldiers stationed at the local post have organized a team, all colored boys; the railroad men and other hardy fellows have combined and gotten up a nine known as the Skagway Baseball Club, and the youths have organized a team dubbed the Skagway Juniors.

All three organizations have been practicing several weeks. Their practice grounds are chiefly on the long, sloping, hard beach in front of the city in the big vacant lot at the east end of Fourth avenue.[17]

Since water and mountains hemmed Skagway on all sides, finding a suitable baseball field was a challenge. One of the few open tracts of land suitable lay on the east side of Skagway, where the company pitched its tent camp after the Dyea fire. The area was flat, mostly dry, and not obstructed by trees or buildings. By the spring and summer of 1900, teams were practicing and competing on a provisional baseball diamond in this area near Captain Moore's sawmill.

Decisions about when to play baseball came next. Sundays seem to have been the prime game day: the soldiers were off duty, the railroad men did not have to work, and the local civilians could attend. Playing baseball on Sunday was improper to some on religious grounds. Many professional baseball teams still refused to host games on Sunday due to blue laws, and Pennsylvania did not pass legislation allowing such games until 1933.[18]

Who filled out the rosters? The local newspaper mentioned only the names of the white players. The Skagway team captain and catcher was John Phelps, who worked as a messenger on the International Flyer of the White Pass & Yukon Route. Other members included: "Randall, pitcher; McGrath, first base; Kenny, second base, W. Cleveland, third base; Barry, shortstop; T. Cleveland, center field; Durgin [Dugin], right field; Tharlson, left field; Van Zant, substitute."[19]

Both the soldier and Skagway teams wore uniforms. The Skagway Baseball Club wore "blue trousers and black shirts and caps, all trimmed in white." The Company L team brought uniforms, bats, balls, and gloves with them as part of their unit equipment or personal possessions. A photo of the Company L team members taken a few years later shows the soldiers in pin-striped shirts with 24 and L enclosed by a diamond, matching knickers, striped socks, cleats, and baseball caps emblazoned with the letter L.[20]

The soldier and citizen teams crossed bats in their first game on Sunday, May 20, 1900. The Company L team won a close contest with the "railroad men" by a score of 16–15. The score indicated good hitting and bad fielding by both teams, perhaps a reflection of a lack of practice. The article noted the "attendance was large, and a great deal of interest was taken." Skagwayans welcomed the diversion.[21]

Though both teams played well, they were not treated equally in the newspaper, reflecting a journalistic bias by John W. Troy, the editor of the paper. The newspaper failed to list the names of the soldiers, although it recorded those of the railroad team. In addition, the *Daily Alaskan* always relegated reports to a few lines on an inside page when the soldiers won but gave the railroad team headlines when it prevailed.[22]

Another example of bias appeared on Tuesday, June 5, 1900, under the title "Soldiers Won the Ball Game." It noted: "The baseball contest on Sunday between the soldiers and the Skagwayans resulted in a victory for the warriors by the score of 13–9. On account of rain the game was called at the end of the fifth inning." The article ran as a short piece on an inside page, again showing a journalistic preference.[23]

The win by the Black soldier team likely challenged the white concept of racial superiority of the Skagwayans. It was one thing for the African American company to be stationed in town to protect the area from Canadian incursion. That was their mission. And it was another for the soldiers to protect white citizens from the Tlingit. That was their job. Yet for the Black players to beat the white nine at the great American game of baseball was quite different.

The soldiers won all the initial contests between the two teams because the headline a month later in the *Daily Alaskan* boasted: "SKAGWAYANS VICTORS, Win Their First Ball Game from Colored Players." The article noted that the game on Sunday June 17 ended with a Skagway Baseball Club win, thanks to some newly recruited talent, especially the way "E. T. Pope, the genial agent for the *City of Seattle*, covered third base." It also mentioned the "pitching of Moody and the batting of McDonald" as noteworthy and credited the play of those three "new additions" for the win. The article mentioned no other players on either team except Pope, Moody, and McDonald.[24]

The article suggested the Skagway team sought outside talent after its initial losses to the soldier nine in May and June 1900. It noted that "Pope had played one season with the Tacoma team in the Northwest League." The Tacoma Daisies played in the professional Pacific Northwest League from 1890 to 1892. The newspaper also gave interesting details of the game, reporting "Skagway went to pieces in the third inning, and by a series of inexcusable errors, permitted the colored boys to get in six runs." Yet the Skagway team "redeemed themselves in the next inning, getting seven runs by timely batting." In that inning, "McDonald made the only home run of the game." The contest ended in a 14–11 Skagway win.[25]

The game resulted in at least one casualty. A newspaper piece reported: "Frank Peterson a member of the firm of H.O. Peterson, while watching a base ball game at Skagway on the 17th inst., was struck in the groin by a foul ball and seriously injured, being rendered unconscious for several hours." No backstops or fences protected unwary spectators like the unfortunate Peterson.[26]

A commentary published three days after the game added an important postscript to the Skagway victory. Under the headline "Soldier Ball Tossers," the *Daily Alaskan* noted the names "of the U.S. Army baseball team of Skagway here given for the first time." The names of the African American players were "Gant, catcher; Oby, pitcher; Green, first; Jennings, second; Johnson, third; Sims, short; Banks, left; Bracy, center; Mack, right; Dewey, managing captain, on the bench." Did the soldier team have to be defeated before the Black players could be named?[27]

Troy's listing of the soldiers is noteworthy. The white press in this era rarely noted the names of Black people in general reporting. The only exception, and the *Daily Alaskan* was no different, was when the paper related crimes or misbehavior. Nearly all other references to Company L in the *Daily Alaskan* noted the surnames of the white officers only, while the Black soldiers remained anonymous. In this case, the reporter likely had to walk over to the Black coach, ask him for names, and jot them down in his notebook.

Army enlistment records provide details of the soldiers to flesh out the newspaper story. Corporal Edward G. Dewey, the manager of the team, was a twenty-two-year-old former railroad dispatcher from Worchester, Massachusetts, and the only noncommissioned officer on the team. He had first served in the army with the Sixth Massachusetts Volunteers during the Spanish-American War. The rest were privates: Frank Gant, thirty-three, a laborer from Washington DC; John W. Oby, twenty-four, a barber from Pittsburgh, Pennsylvania; Benjamin Green, twenty-four, a teamster from Dayton, Ohio; William Jennings, thirty-two, a laborer from Princeton, New Jersey; Ernest L. Johnson, twenty-eight, a butcher from Baltimore, Maryland: William Sims, twenty-two, a former Tenth U.S. Volunteer Infantry soldier; James M. Banks, twenty-one, a laborer from Carlinville, Illinois; George Bracy, twenty-two, a train expressman from Columbia, South Carolina; and William Mack, twenty-two, a former Tenth U.S. Volunteer Infantry soldier.[28]

Despite the lack of detailed coverage in the newspaper, the teams almost certainly played other games the summer of 1900. Though not deemed sufficiently newsworthy to justify coverage of all the games the summer of 1900, the contests would become a bigger story in the years to come. Baseball served as a means of introduction for the citizens of Skagway to the soldiers of the company, evidenced by the newspaper description of the team evolving from the anonymous "colored boys" in May to players with real names in June.

Census of 1900

Just a few weeks after the baseball season opened in Skagway, the United States Census Bureau completed the country's thirteenth decennial census.[29] In addition to the forty-six states and the District of Columbia, the bureau counted the populations in the U.S. District of Alaska and the territories of Arizona, Hawaii, and New Mexico. The resident population of the United States in 1900 was 92,228,496, while that of all of Alaska was 64,356. Skagway first appeared in the 1900 census as the second-largest city in Alaska with 2,383 people, of which the vast majority were white. Outside of the 94 African American soldiers and family members, who were enumerated separately, there were 108 Tlingit people, 14 Japanese, 4 people of mixed race, and 2 Black civilians.[30]

Census takers enumerated the U.S. Census of 1900 in Skagway between March 13 and 31, 1900. They compiled a special count of the military community in Skagway on June 1, 1900. Both provide a detailed picture of Company L and Skagway, Alaska.[31]

Skagway was unique in the makeup of its population. There were three men for every woman and five single men for every single woman. Many married males, such as Captain Hovey, left their wives at home when they came to Alaska, fearing the hazards of life in Alaska for their families. Children composed only 19 percent of Skagway's population, compared to 36 in the rest of the United States. This made Skagway a community of adult, unmarried or unaccompanied males, driven by its history as a gold-rush boomtown. This in part led to a thriving business of public drinking establishments and prostitution that impacted the lives of the soldiers stationed in Skagway.[32]

Census takers counted two of the officers and some of the soldiers in Skagway twice. The 1900 census listed Lieutenant Jenks and the thirty-four soldiers of Company L, the hospital detachment, and their family members as living at Fort Wrangel when they tallied the count there between April 5 and 9, 1900. They counted them again when the census was recorded of the military community of Skagway on June 1, 1900. So at least forty-six members of the military and their family members were counted twice in Alaska.[33]

Despite this error, the census offers a valuable snapshot of the military community in Skagway. Skagway Barracks on June 1 totaled 108, comprising 91 from Company L, Twenty-Fourth Infantry, 8 from the Hospital Corps, 1 deserter from Company F, Seventh Infantry, and 8 family members. The officers and men of the company listed twenty-two different states and one British territory as home. Slightly more than half of the Black enlisted soldiers listed home states south of the Mason-Dixon Line, with the northern state of Pennsylvania having the most at 11. Under the category of place of birth, the southern states had an even larger majority, with Virginia having the greatest number at 14.[34]

The soldiers in the company ranged in age from twenty to fifty-one, and several were born into enslavement in the South. Captain Hovey was forty-seven and Lieutenant Jenks thirty-three years old. The average age of the six sergeants was thirty-six years. Sergeant O'Connor, twenty-seven years old, was the youngest of the six while Sergeant William Hanson, a section sergeant, was oldest at forty-seven. The average age of the corporals was twenty-nine, with the old man of Company L, Corporal Augustus Snoten, still serving at the ripe old age of fifty-one. Three of the sergeants, James Washington, Henry Robinson, and Allen Hayes, and two of the corporals, Allen McGee and Augustus Snoten, were born in southern states while slavery was still practiced. One of the musicians, Edward Bordinghammer, was the second-oldest man in the company at forty-eight and born in the pre–Civil War South. The average age of the infantry privates in the company was twenty-five, with the youngest soldier twenty and the oldest thirty-six years old.[35]

The 1900 census also noted the education and marital status of the Black soldiers. Of the sergeants, only Henry Robinson, Robert O'Connor, and James Washington were married and had their families living with them in Skagway. Sergeant Allen Hayes and Corporal Augustus Snoten were married yet unaccompanied by their wives at the time of the census. All the other enlisted soldiers were listed as single. It is noteworthy that every enlisted soldier in the company could read and write, a significant contrast to an earlier generation of Buffalo Soldiers.[36]

Apart from the two officers, all the members of the company were recorded as Black (B), a total of eighty-nine. One soldier in the hospital staff, Robert Grant, was also Black. There were four Black family members listed, including Sussie O'Connor, Sarah Robinson, and Alice Washington and her daughter, Maggie.[37]

Who were the other two African Americans cited by census officials in their official count of Skagway? In the March tally, there were two residents listed as Black who were not part of the military community:

Charles Munson, a laborer born in Alabama, and Phil Brown, a cook born in Jamaica. Brown was aboard the steamer *City of Seattle*, so it is likely he was employed on the ship. The crewmembers aboard the ships in port on the day of the count were included in the tally. Charles Munson listed his home city as Cripple Creek, Colorado, and previous occupation as barber, so it is possible he served in that capacity for the Black soldiers in Skagway.[38]

The Buffalo Soldier community in Skagway would grow in the years to come. First, some of the soldiers who completed their enlistments and separated from the company chose to stay on in Skagway to take up civilian jobs. In addition to serving as a barber, an ex-soldier might remain in Skagway to shine shoes or provide other services the soldiers were willing to pay for. And though none were yet enumerated in the 1900 census, Black laundresses as well as Black prostitutes followed the Buffalo Soldiers wherever they were assigned on the U.S. frontier. Skagway would have been no different.

Horton Murders

The census taken during the summer of 1900 was conducted amid renewed tension between the white citizens of Skagway and the local Tlingit. One of Hovey's important missions in this region of Alaska was keeping the peace between the white newcomers and the Native Americans who had lived in the area for generations. Company L stood at the ready to support local law enforcement should the situation get out of hand and the local judge ask for support. This was the first of many occasions Hovey would have his men at a high state of readiness.

The cause for the tension was a murder. Jim Hanson, a twenty-three-year-old Sitka resident and Chilkat Tlingit, confessed to killing a Skagway couple named Bert and Florence Horton in October 1899. Hanson made the confession at the urging of a Salvation Army preacher's wife during a March 1900 revival in Skagway and led the authorities to where the bodies were buried. U.S. Commissioner Charles Sehlbrede and Deputy Marshal Josias Tanner asked Captain Hovey to detail a security force of soldiers to go with them to retrieve the bodies. Hovey directed Sergeant Robert O'Connor to accompany the party with a squad of soldiers, including Corporal Lafayette Coats and Privates Walter Belcher, Leonard Watkins, George Wilson, and Ellis Turner. They steamed to the location by boat on March 15, 1900, and returned with the bodies the same day.[39]

The murder trial of Hanson and twelve Tlingit co-conspirators in June 1900 won headlines across the United States. The June census counted Hanson and his accused accomplices in the Skagway jail under the protection of Deputy U.S. Marshal Tanner. District Judge Melville Brown and the grand jury heard the case in the Elks Hall on Sixth Avenue, across the street from the Astoria barracks of Company L. The presence of the soldiers so near the court provided an extra layer of security, and the usual roving guards at night added protection when the town slept.[40]

Hundreds of Tlingit people gathered in Skagway to witness the trial, which put local law enforcement officials on guard. After a short proceeding that featured Hanson's admission of the crime and plea of guilty, a jury found Hanson and several of the twelve co-conspirators guilty. Each Tlingit was informed of the case against him through interpreter Edward Armstrong. The entire case turned on Hanson's vivid confession and the fact that he showed the authorities where to find the bodies.[41]

Judge Melville Brown sentenced Jim Hanson on June 27, 1900, to hang in Sitka and set a September execution date. However, he recommended mercy by the president, who had the power to commute the sentence to life in prison. Salvation Army representatives lobbied President William McKinley, who eventually commuted Hanson's sentence to life. Five of the other defendants were also found guilty. Under the charge of murder in the second degree, the judge sentenced Jim Williams and Kitchikoo to fifty years, Day Kauteen to thirty years, Jack Lain to twenty-two years, and Mark Clanet to twenty years of "penal servitude" at the federal prison at McNeil Island, Washington.[42]

Captain Hovey made no mention of the trial of Jim Hanson in his monthly return. The nature of Hanson's confession and the handling of the trial by Deputy Marshal Tanner and District Judge Brown made active U.S. Army involvement unnecessary. The Tlingit took no action that would invite another bombardment and certain retribution. Hovey's only mention of the Horton murders came in a report warning his superiors of possible trouble between the Tlingit and whites over fishing rights.[43]

Skagway Incorporated

A day after the Hanson sentencing, Skagway incorporated on June 28, 1900, the first city to do so in Alaska. It had a population of 2,383 people according to the 1900 census, second only to Juneau in Alaska at that time. This achievement distanced it from its boomtown beginnings and legitimized its future. The move also made Skagway more appealing as a site for a permanent military base.[44]

The process for incorporation in Skagway was complicated by the fact that Alaska was still a district. Skagway elected its first city council in 1898, though this government technically had no mandate. The real authority in Skagway rested with the U.S. district commissioner, Charles A. Sehlbrede, and his appointed federal deputy marshal, Josias M. "Si" Tanner. After Congress passed a municipal incorporation act for Alaska in 1900, the citizens of Skagway had local attorney John G. Price prepare a petition for District Judge Melville C. Brown to incorporate. Judge Brown accepted and filed the petition on June 21, 1900.[45]

Balloting and election of the city council was held on June 28, 1900, at City Hall, a one-room log cabin on Fifth Avenue, a block away from the soldier barracks. Citizens overwhelmingly approved with a 246–60 vote. Only men who owned property could take part, so the turnout was light. Judge Brown signed the order to incorporate Skagway the following day. The seven members chosen by voters for the city council were E. O. Sylvester, William L. Green, Lee Guthrie, Edgar R. Peoples, Laramie Mayer, John Hislop, and John L. Laumeister.[46]

The councilmen selected John Hislop, chief engineer of the White Pass & Yukon Route, as the first mayor. All the other members were prominent businessmen in the town who had been active in Skagway since the early days of the gold rush. Sylvester owned and operated

Sylvester Wharf; Green was a merchant; Guthrie ran the Board of Trade Saloon and owned real estate; Peoples was a furniture manufacturer and undertaker; Mayer was a merchant; and Laumeister ran a meat market. So the prominent businesses in Skagway were well represented.[47]

The real power behind the mayor and city council was the editor of the *Daily Alaskan*, John W. Troy, who would later become governor of Alaska. John Weir Troy worked as a Seattle newspaper reporter in Olympia, Washington, before joining the gold rush to Skagway in 1897. Troy became editor of the *Daily Alaskan* in 1898 after his predecessor, J. Allen Hornsby, was forced out of town in the wake of the Soapy Smith shooting.[48]

The *Daily Alaskan* was owned by George W. DeSucca, yet as editor, Troy used his writing talents to influence the opinions of the citizens of Skagway. Among other things, his coverage of Black soldiers was biased and often racist. He was also an outspoken booster of Skagway and won the support of middle-class businessmen in the city. His coverage of the 1900 Fourth of July celebration serves as a good example of this boosterism.[49]

Fourth of July

Independence Day was celebrated in Skagway on July 4, 1900, under starkly different circumstances from previous years. In the first chaotic commemoration in 1898, Soapy Smith had ridden at the head of his Skagway Military Company as one of four parade marshals. The Fourth of July in 1899 witnessed the first appearance of the Black soldiers, when they traveled from Dyea Barracks to march in the parade as guests. The year 1900 was the first in which Company L participated as active members of the Skagway community.

The *Daily Alaskan* detailed the elaborate preparations for the celebration of Independence Day 1900, which centered mainly on twenty-six sporting events. It noted almost apologetically that "many of the usual features of a Fourth of July celebration were omitted." There was no parade featuring the Black soldiers as in the previous year, which must have disappointed Hovey. The focus of the "jolliest Fourth of July that Skagway has yet had the pleasure of celebrating" was on sports. The celebration committee of the chamber of commerce raised money to finance prizes for the competitions planned for that Wednesday. Skagway insured the streets were raked clean, and the Skagway Baseball Club leveled and improved the playing field on the east side of the city.[50]

Skagway clearly considered the soldiers of Company L as part of the community since it reported, "All the contests were between local people except the baseball game, and that proved an easy victory over Bennett. The score was 28 to 8." Why the Skagway nine played against the Canadians from Bennett instead of the soldier team is a mystery. Perhaps they wanted an easy victory rather than risk another in their minds embarrassing loss to the African American players on the Fourth of July.[51]

Yet the citizens of Skagway invited Captain Hovey and the soldiers to participate for prizes in some of the sports. There was a hose and cart race for the fire companies, rifle shooting, bicycle races, long jump, fifty-yard dash for girls, hundred-yard dash for boys, hundred-yard dash for soldiers, hundred-yard dash for citizens, three-legged race, sack race, high jump, bucket race, barrel race, tug-of-war, greased pole climbing, horse race, fat men's race, and several others. Private William H. White won the hundred-yard dash for soldiers and collected the ten-dollar prize; Corporal George M. Payne collected five dollars for second place. Only in the tug-of-war did the African Americans compete against a team of white railroaders. The ten Black soldiers won and collected the prize of thirty dollars. Captain Hovey, wanting badly to win, was seen on Monday before the contest drilling his tug-of-war team by "placing against ten men selected, fourteen other soldiers for them to pull against."[52]

News coverage of the Fourth of July confirms that the citizens of Skagway considered the soldiers of Company L a part of the community in 1900. The only known photos of this celebration show no fewer than twenty-five uniformed Black soldiers interspersed and cheering with the white citizens of Skagway, watching the completion of the young boys' footrace. The soldiers stand, laugh, and clap side by side with the residents. This points to a form of recognition if not total acceptance.

The Fourth also boasted social events. The city organized a dance at the armory during the afternoon and there was a fireman's ball in the evening. Captain Hovey, Lieutenant Jenks, Alice Jenks, Dr. Bailey, and Florence Bailey would have been invited to these social affairs, though we do not know if they attended. Because of the social and racial norms of the day, the African American soldiers would not have been invited to these communal gatherings, nor would the Native Americans, Japanese, or other minority residents of Skagway.[53]

Canadian Diplomacy

Captain Hovey and Lieutenant Jenks busied themselves with diplomacy and escort work involving their British and Canadian counterparts in the days and months after the Fourth of July. An important part of their mission in Skagway was to show the flag, literally and figuratively, and protect the area from incursion. Both the soldiers and citizens were well aware of ongoing negotiations to fix the boundary between Alaska and Canada around Skagway, a topic frequently reported in the newspaper.

Captain Hovey asked the U.S. Army Department of Alaska to expend funds to maintain a flag on the border with Canada at the White Pass railroad crossing. He noted that the North West Mounted Police hoisted and maintained a British flag daily on the Canadian side of the border. The citizens of Skagway and the White Pass & Yukon Route railway flew an American flag on the U.S. side of the border point intermittently, but Hovey wanted an official flag maintained regularly at the summit by U.S. customs officials. He aimed to have the colors greet Americans returning to U.S. territory so they could, in his words, "take off their hats and cheer the flag with tears rolling down their cheeks." Such was Hovey's patriotic fervor.[54]

The day after Independence Day, Captain Hovey reported the passage of British troops through the port of Skagway. He informed Washington that six officers and eighty British soldiers arrived on July 2 and departed on the steamer *Amur* at 1:00 a.m. the morning of July 4, 1900. Hovey stated that he "went up the road to meet them and extended every courtesy," so they must have arrived by train to board an outbound ship. The incongruity of the presence of British troops on the Fourth of July could not have been lost on Hovey.[55]

The *Daily Alaskan* reported the arrival of the British soldiers on the front page of its July 3, 1900, morning edition, noting the arrival of the "Yukon field force" at 11:10 p.m. in Skagway. According to the report: "the red-coated soldiers were drawn up before the depot and were put through a few evolutions before being marched uptown and sent to their quarters." It noted that Captain Hovey and Dr. Bailey showed every "American courtesy" to the commander, Lieutenant Colonel G. D. R. Hemming, and adjutant, Captain Thacker. It also noted there "were several ladies in the party and to the comfort of these the American officers gave particular attention."[56]

Just weeks after the passage of the British troops, Captain Hovey attended the last spike ceremony at Caribou Crossing, now known as Carcross, Canada. On Sunday July 29, 1900, Samuel H. Graves, the first president of the White Pass & Yukon Route, assisted other officials and railroad employees in driving the golden spike that connected the line from Skagway to Whitehorse. They were met by Canadian officials who were equally excited about the rail connection that would allow them access to the port in Skagway.[57]

A crowd of about two thousand was on hand to see the ceremony, more than half of them railroad employees who had toiled for a year to complete the last tract of rails in Canada. Graves and White Pass & Yukon Route General Manager Erasmus C. Hawkins met Canadians including railroad contractor Michael J. Heney and Inspector Philip C. H. Primrose and Dr. L. A. Pare of the Northwest Mounted Police. Captain Hovey, also attending, was asked by Graves to give the golden spike the first blow. To Hovey's embarrassment and to the amusement of the railroad men, he took a great swing and completely missed the spike. The onlookers howled. The men who followed Hovey were more careful, though the soft golden spike was bent sideways and dilapidated when the ceremony was complete.[58]

Railroad builder Mike Heney, who had first conceived the idea of the rail line, pried the gold spike out and pocketed it as a souvenir. Heney had convinced skeptical London investor Sir Thomas Tancred to finance the project after a chance meeting in Skagway. Heney had famously bragged: "Give me enough dynamite and snooze, and I'll build you a railroad to hell." The $10 million railroad construction project was the product of British financing, American engineering, and Canadian contracting. Laying 110 miles of track, the first 20 miles from Skagway at sea level to the summit at 3,000 feet, took three years, employed thirty-five thousand workers (two thousand at any one time), and cost the lives of thirty-five men.[59]

After the spike ceremony, the first train from Caribou Crossing proceeded to Skagway, making it the first through-train on the White Pass & Yukon Route. The engine, called the *Australian*, pulled the initial train of dignitaries first to the railroad camp a mile below for a banquet. After dinner, the train continued down the grade to Skagway where it arrived at the station after midnight early Monday morning.[60]

On the heels of the golden spike ceremony, Captain Hovey departed on detached service to Porcupine City northwest of Skagway, the first week in August, and to Whitehorse, Yukon Territory, ten days later. He was coordinating operations with his NWMP counterparts to regulate the flow of gold prospectors between Skagway and the Yukon, as well as the passage of Canadian civilian and military personnel, who were unpopular with American citizens. Hovey was also trying to prevent trouble resulting from the provisional boundary agreement between American miners and Canadian officials around the mining camp at Porcupine.[61]

Hovey had just boarded the morning train for Whitehorse when Company L welcomed the highest-ranking visitor of its entire three-year stay in Skagway. Because Hovey was away in Canada, Lieutenant Jenks handled the first part of the official visit. On August 10, 1900, Gilbert John Elliot-Murray-Kynynmound, Fourth Earl of Minto, the governor general of Canada, arrived with his wife, Lady Mary Caroline Grey, and three aides, aboard the Canadian revenue cutter *Quadra*. Lord Minto was a British aristocrat and politician who served as governor general of Canada from 1898 to 1904. The governor general was the federal viceregal representative of Britain's Queen Victoria and carried out her constitutional and ceremonial duties in Canada.[62]

Lieutenant Jenks greeted the party at the wharf. "The company was turned out in heavy marching order, and every civility and courtesy in our power shown him. An escort was tendered him to the Summit, but according to the uncertainty of his departure was not accepted." Lieutenant Jenks also showed Minto through the company barracks. After his visit in Skagway, the earl continued his journey to Dawson on the Yukon River in Canada.[63]

According to the *Daily Alaskan*, Lord Minto only stayed the day in Skagway, departing at 2:00 p.m. on a special train put at his disposal by the White Pass & Yukon Route. Railroad president Graves made a hurried trip to Skagway from Whitehorse the evening before to accompany the governor general.[64]

Captain Hovey had returned from his trip to the interior when Lord Minto completed his visit and returned to Skagway for departure. Hovey's report to the Department of Alaska observed: "On the 23th of August, being appraised of his return from Dawson, I proceeded to the summit of the White Pass with the officers of the command and an escort of nineteen men, received him in due form, and escorted him to the wharf at Skagway, where he was again properly saluted, after which he embarked on the steamer. He expressed himself as being much pleased by the courtesy extended."[65]

Lord Minto reported he was happy with the treatment he received in Skagway. He had specifically requested an official reception by the U.S. Army troops stationed there. According to Lord Minto, his "reception proved a great success." He also noted that he "and the American Commanding Officer in charge of the honour guard remained fast friends long after the tour."[66]

New Officer

Just a few days after Lord Minto's visit, Captain Hovey welcomed a new officer. Second Lieutenant Edward L. Rains joined the garrison in late August, filling the vacant junior officer position in the company. At full strength, the army allocated three officers to an infantry company: a captain, a first lieutenant, and a second lieutenant. Rarely did an infantry company at the time have its full complement of three officers.[67]

Lieutenant Rains had come up from the ranks, having joined as an enlisted soldier in April 1898 at the onset of the Spanish-American War. Rains was born in Tennessee in 1877. He was the eldest son of James K. Rains, who inherited a 260-acre farm outside Nashville from his father, a former slaveholder. Before enlisting, the younger Rains graduated from Montgomery Bell Academy and passed the state examinations in pharmacy at Vanderbilt University, both in Nashville. He enlisted as Edward Lee Rains, though he was born Edwin Lee Rains—not the last time in his life he would change his name.[68]

Rains sailed in January 1899 to the Philippine Islands and served as a hospital corpsman before taking ill with fever. In July 1899 Rains was evacuated to San Francisco and later convalesced at the army general hospital in Hot Springs, Arkansas. After his time at Hot Springs, the army granted him home leave to complete his recovery.[69]

Upon finishing the requisite two-year term as an enlistee, Rains passed the officers commissioning examination at Fort Baker, California, and received his commission as a new second lieutenant or "shave-tail" in late July 1900. Captain Hovey was likely pleased to have a third officer in the company, especially with the pending promotion and reassignment of Lieutenant Jenks. Jenks was also happy as he was no longer the "goat" or junior officer on post.[70]

There were only three paths to a commission as an officer in the Regular Army. The main source of commissioned officers was the United States Military Academy at West Point, the track taken by Lieutenant Jenks. The other was a direct commission based on a political appointment as with Captain Hovey, who had served as an officer in the New

York National Guard. The last route was reserved for enlisted soldiers who had served at least two years, were recommended by their officers, and passed written, oral, and physical examinations.

The U.S. Army in 1900 was transitioning from a frontier constabulary force to an "Army of Empire" under the leadership of Secretary of War Elihu Root, who served in that capacity from 1899 to 1903. The Spanish-American War and the empire it created caused Root to expand the Regular Army from twenty-seven thousand men and two thousand officers in the 1890s to one of ninety thousand men and four thousand officers by 1913. Part of this expansion included commissioning hundreds of officers from the enlisted ranks, and Lieutenant Rains was one of this cohort.[71]

Law Enforcement

One of Lieutenant Rains's first assignments involved law enforcement, according to Hovey's September 1900 post return. Hovey wrote: "The U.S. Court called upon the military forces to protect U.S. Marshals in enforcing a decree of the court. Two NCOs and 20 privates were furnished. They proceeded to Moore's dock, protected the U.S. Marshals, and returned to the barracks. The presence of troops was all that was necessary." The size of the force chosen by Hovey, a section commanded by a section sergeant, was appropriate to the task at hand.[72]

In this case, the court needed soldiers to protect law officials after sailors deserted from the steamer *South Portland*, en route from Seattle to Nome. The deserters were arrested by the deputy U.S. marshal in Skagway, tried for mutiny, and jailed. When the marshal tried to put them back on *South Portland*, the sailors refused to board, and local longshoremen gathered on the wharf to prevent him from carrying out his duty. The U.S. commissioner in Skagway called for military support, and the soldiers held the crowd back while the marshal put the sailors back on the ship. The incident was over in ninety minutes, and the ship steamed away without incident with a full crew.[73]

John Troy, the editor of the *Daily Alaskan*, saw the event in a more dramatic light. He wrote "seven sailors who were arrested Saturday for attempted desertion from the *South Portland* were forced aboard the ship at the point of the bayonet." When two deputies tried to put the men aboard the ship, the seven refused, encouraged by a crowd of longshoremen. U.S. Commissioner Judge Charles Sehlbrede called on the army for support. According to the account, "Lieutenant Rains with a sergeant and twenty-two privates with arms loaded with ball cartridges and bayonets marched double quick to the scene of the trouble." This of course drew a crowd of several hundred spectators.[74]

"The soldiers," Troy continued, "led by Lieut. Rains were lined up on the wharf and given an order to charge bayonets which was executed with dispatch, the sailors being surrounded in an instant with a semi-circular wall of cold steel." The sailors resisted, Rains threatened them with a "clubbing," and deciding "disagreement was the better part of valor the sailors submitted and were somewhat unceremoniously hustled aboard the ship." The ship sailed, and at least one of the twelve lawyers in town promised a lawsuit. But the citizens of the city had "nothing but commendation for the orderly manner in which Lieut. Rains handled the task." Not surprisingly, there was no mention of Black soldiers forcing white sailors against their will.[75]

Lieutenant Jenks dealt with this issue since Captain Hovey was absent, anchored at the time in the bay on board the U.S. revenue cutter *Parry* in consultation with Alaska district governor John G. Brady and U.S. District Court judge Melville C. Brown. The three discussed "important matters pertaining to this section of Alaska." Hovey did not notice the disturbance on the wharf, but by the time he returned to shore and *Parry* sailed away, the emergency was over.[76]

Jenks understood army regulations put strict limits on the employment of military troops in the enforcement of U.S. laws. According to Article 52 of the *Regulations for the Army of the United States*: "It is unlawful to employ any part of the Army of the United States as a posse comitatus or otherwise, for the purpose of executing laws, except in such cases and under such circumstances as such employment of said force may be expressly authorized by the Constitution or by act of Congress." Jenks had to be very sure of his mandate to assist the civil authorities in this case.[77]

Opportunely, Hovey left instructions with his officers "to act quickly in support of the authorities" in such a case if he was away. He cited his "instructions to protect life and property, and the Statute 5299" in support of civil authorities. Statute 5299 was part of a body of federal law involving civil rights enforcement codified in 1874 Revised Statutes, originally passed in 1872 as part of the Ku Klux Klan Act. Revised Statute 5299 "could be invoked by the federal executive without a state's request of approval, if its civil and military authorities were unable or unwilling to act on their own, or they, themselves, opposed the execution of federal laws or acted to repress the civil rights of individuals." It was particularly ironic having Black soldiers enforce this statute against white sailors and longshoremen.[78]

Comparing the accounts of Hovey and Troy reveal a great deal. Hovey's report in his monthly return and letter to General Randall were short and precise. He mentioned the request by the U.S. commissioner, the dispatch of two noncommissioned officers and twenty privates, and noted the mere presence of the troops was enough to defuse the situation. Hovey did not even mention the role of Lieutenant Rains. Troy on the other hand emphasized Rains's leadership, the presence of loaded weapons and fixed bayonets, and the threat of a "clubbing." He gave all the credit to the gallant leadership of the white officer, while Hovey praised the Black soldiers. This contrast says much about Hovey's tolerance and Troy's bias.

Not long after the mutiny, Hovey faced an incident where he could not find an appropriate legal basis for action. In October 1900 he asked the U.S. Army adjutant general for guidance on handling a smallpox epidemic. Smallpox had broken out near Dawson in Canada, and the area had been placed under strict quarantine. Hovey noted, "there is no statute that I can find which empowers civil authorities or myself to stop people from crossing the summit of White Pass or for tying up the railroad at that point, should such action be demanded by the spread of the disease, and the consequent danger to this post." In the end, smallpox did not spread to Skagway, yet it showed Hovey struggled with the limits of his authorities and complexity of his mission.[79]

Disciplinary Matters

Captain Hovey had several other disciplinary and legal issues to deal with in the fall of 1900. The first involved the same type of rifle used so effectively to force the sailors back on the boat and perhaps prevent a riot among the longshoremen. The other was an incident where those same rifles were used to quell a riot caused by his own men.

The newspaper reported the first event in an article titled "Uncle Sam's Rifle." Apparently, while Lieutenant Jenks was posted to Fort Wrangel, a man stole one of the detachment's Krag-Jørgensen rifles. It is also possible the theft occurred during the move from Fort Wrangel to Skagway in May 1900. The loss of a weapon in a military unit was a profoundly serious affair and must have reflected badly on Lieutenant Jenks.[80]

In late September 1900 Lieutenant Jenks returned from Fort Wrangel, where he had been attending a court case against a civilian named M. E. Smith. The court charged Smith with possession of the stolen U.S. Army rifle, which he claimed to have purchased. There was some doubt about his story since he was also accused on another charge of housebreaking and "stealing a suit of clothes and some nuggets," for which he was sentenced to two years in prison. Smith surrendered the rifle, and Jenks was happy to return with the army Krag-Jørgensen to close the embarrassing episode.[81]

Closer to home, Captain Hovey reported privates Harry Andrews, Harry V. Jordan, and George M. Payne in the hands of civilian authorities and serving a three-month sentence "for riot." The incident occurred on October 8, 1900, when "four colored soldiers were arrested in Skagway . . . for rioting." In legal terms, a riot is a type of civil disorder resulting in a public disturbance against authority, property, or people.[82]

Who were these rioting soldiers? Harry Andrews was a thirty-year-old former laborer from Philadelphia; Harry Jordan was a thirty-two-year-old former cook from Boston; and George Payne was a twenty-seven-year-old former butler from Indianapolis. All three were privates, on their first enlistment, and a bit older than average for a private in Company L.[83]

As usual, Troy at the *Daily Alaskan* furnished colorful details of the disturbance. Under a banner of "Soldiers Attempted to Bulldoze Saloon Keepers and Are Arrested," the editor detailed an attempt by a group of soldiers to challenge the "color line" imposed by certain establishments. He noted:

> Some of the colored soldiers took possession of Sixth Avenue yesterday morning and produced a small-sized riot. They had been drinking and the special mark of their disfavor were the saloons which refused to permit colored people to patronize the bar. There were four of them in the gang and they entered both the Board of Trade and the Senate saloons and attempted to force the barkeepers to furnish them drinks. They were armed with clubs and threatened to use them. A corporal and a squad of soldiers placed them under arrest. They were afterwards turned over to the civil authorities and they will be complained against today for riot.[84]

The soldiers singled out the Board of Trade and Senate saloons for their "special mark of disfavor" because they enforced a "color line" near the barracks at Sixth Avenue and Broadway. It must have galled these men to face this insult so close to the barracks every day. Company L handled the disturbance themselves, quickly dispatching the corporal of the guard with a force to arrest the soldiers.[85]

Several days later the *Daily Alaskan* reported the U.S. commissioner found three of the soldiers guilty. It noted, "Privates Payne, Jordan, and Andrews were tried before Judge Sehlbrede yesterday morning and found guilty of rioting. Each was sentenced to three months in the Sitka jail. A writ of habeas corpus was served out yesterday in the district court. It will be heard at two o'clock today. E.M. Barnes represents the soldiers." This was essentially an appeal by the soldiers' lawyer, E. M. Barnes, to the higher court, which ultimately failed. The three soldiers were shipped off to prison, and Captain Hovey later discharged them without honor.[86]

The newspaper made no mention of the fourth soldier, so he must have avoided civil justice. It is possible the fourth soldier had second thoughts and left the scene of the riot and warned the company of the disturbance. Captain Hovey had two men listed in confinement in October, so he may have handled the fourth soldier with a summary court-martial and local punishment.[87]

Captain Hovey was content to let the civilian authorities handle cases involving soldier crimes in Skagway. Since civil courts had jurisdiction for crimes not committed on military property, he willingly turned over the soldiers to the deputy marshal in town for trial and punishment by the U.S. commissioner or district judge. If Hovey charged his soldiers by general court-martial for an offense, he would have to send the soldier by boat escorted by a noncommissioned officer to Vancouver Barracks for trial. The result would have been similar to that of the civilian court: the soldier found guilty, sentenced to jail time, and then discharged dishonorably. Employing the civilian judicial system saved time, conserved manpower, and assuaged local officials.

Native Americans

Captain Hovey dispatched Lieutenant Rains on his second operational assignment across the Lynn Canal to Haines Mission. He directed Rains to lead a detachment on October 11, 1900, to support the local marshal protecting residents there from the Tlingit. Captain Hovey's written instructions to Rains noted: "You will proceed tonight upon the steamer *Ruth* with one sergeant, two corporals, and twelve privates . . . to Haines Mission, Alaska, and there go into camp as close to the houses as possible, and practicable for the purpose of protecting the people there from intoxicated or turbulent Indians." This body of soldiers comprised a section, commanded by a sergeant who led two platoons, each led by a corporal.[88]

The civil authorities requested army support because the Tlingit were planning a potlatch, a gift-giving feast, at Klukwan, up the Chilkat River from Haines Mission. This seemed innocent enough, though Hovey warned Rains that "quantities of whiskey have already been introduced." A special deputy marshal accompanied the army detachment, and Hovey directed Rains to follow the deputy's lead in "carrying out the orders of the District Court of the United States."[89]

Once again, Editor Troy gave an alarmist and biased account of the event. Under the headline "Haines Riot" he noted: "The Chilkat Indians developed symptoms of rioting at Haines Monday, and troops have been ordered to the scene of the disturbances. Reports from the town down the canal are to the effect that the noble proteges of Alaska's distinguished executive have been indulging in too much whiskey and their exhilaration found vent in going about town knocking on doors and windows. Several rows are said to have taken place among the Indians." The article featured Lieutenant Rains again, as with the mutinous sailors, as the gallant white officer leading soldiers.[90]

Troy used the term "riot" in connection with this event as he did in describing the four soldiers two days earlier who tried to force the proprietors at the Board of Trade to serve them drinks. In Troy's eyes, it appeared the term riot was reserved for incidents involving African Americans and Native Americans. How "knocking on doors and windows" can be considered a riot is inexplicable. He did not use the word "riot" in connection with the longshoremen preventing the mutinous sailors back aboard the *South Portland*, even though that incident was far more serious.

On October 20, 1900, Hovey sent new instructions via the steamer *Alert* for Rains to move his detachment from Haines Mission to Pyramid Harbor. The "crisis" had ended when the production of illegal whiskey or "hootch" by white citizens near Haines seeking to profit from illegal sales was halted by the marshal. Rains was to take his men in the steamer *Alert* to Pyramid Harbor, where the detachment was quartered in Jack Dalton's warehouse, much warmer accommodations than the tents they had used at Haines Mission. It was closer to Klukwan, should they be called on to move there, but farther away from Skagway.[91]

Alert, the steamer that transported Rains's detachment to Pyramid Harbor, was later called away and communications with the troops severed. Rains was left isolated with only a small sailboat used by the detachment. Hovey hired a small commercial steamer for daily runs to Pyramid Harbor to carry messages and supplies.[92]

Reports finally reached Skagway that the presence of troops was no longer needed with the Tlingit potlatch over. There was never any trouble at Klukwan, and Hovey's responses were measured and appropriate to the situation. Moreover, the Black regulars of the company performed their peacekeeping mission as trained, reliable, and well-disciplined soldiers.[93]

When Hovey directed Rains to bring the detachment back to Skagway in the rented steamer, the trouble on the return trip reflected the danger of sea travel on the Lynn Canal. The steamer carrying the men encountered rough weather and the crossing, which should have taken four hours, took eleven. The company's towed sailboat swamped and sank, and efforts to recover it failed. As a result of this event, Hovey recommended a U.S. Customs Service revenue cutter be stationed at Skagway to ease future transportation and communications at sea.[94]

Year-End Replacements

Clearly, Captain Hovey needed a full-strength company to carry out missions like the ones involving the mutinous sailors or the Tlingit potlatch, and to that end, he requested replacements. In late fall 1900, the company received twenty new recruits, bringing the enlisted strength up to one hundred men. For some of these young African American men, many from the South, the first winter in Skagway must have been a bracing experience.[95]

Hovey required these new recruits because of desertions and other personnel losses. Privates Loney Moore, David McIntyre, and Emery Collier were tried and discharged for desertion in May after being released by civilian authorities. Also, in October, Private William White was dropped from the rolls after deserting and two other privates were discharged for disability. Privates Harry Andrews, Harry Jordan, Frank

Gant, and George Payne, who were in the hands of civilian authorities, were discharged without honor between November 1900 and January 1901. The company lost another half-dozen privates and sergeants at the expiration of their service.[96]

One such loss to the company was a reason to reflect and celebrate. In August 1900 Musician Edward Bordinghammer, at forty-eight years old the second-oldest man in the company, retired from the army after three decades in uniform. According to army regulations, an enlisted man could apply to retire after thirty years in the U.S. Army. Upon retirement, Bordinghammer received "thereafter seventy-five per centum of the pay and allowances of the rank upon which he was retired."[97]

Born in the enslaved South, Bordinghammer first enlisted in Tennessee five years after the end of the Civil War and four years after Blacks were permitted to enlist in the Regular Army. He had first served in the Twenty-Fourth as an infantryman, rising to the rank of sergeant by the end of his second five-year term, a rank he maintained through his first twenty years. Sometime after he reenlisted in 1890, he became an army musician and served in that capacity through the rest of his time in the service.[98]

Captain Hovey also reported several losses to his company due to death and disability in the fall of 1900. Private Ellis Turner died in October 1900 in the hospital at Vancouver Barracks of pulmonary tuberculosis in the upper lobe of the right lung. Turner had been evacuated to Vancouver Barracks for medical treatment in September 1900. Privates Elijah H. Knox and Henry C. Martin were discharged in late October 1900 on certificates of disability, Martin on account of acute keralites of the left eye and inherited syphilis, and Knox for epilepsy.[99]

With Company L reunited in Skagway, Captain Hovey and his men had a better chance of carrying out their complicated and sometimes confounding mission in Alaska. The addition of a new officer and an infusion of new recruits made up for the shortages caused by desertions, departures, and death. Yet challenges remained in balancing the missions of showing the flag, conducting diplomacy, enforcing the law, and dealing with the local Tlingit people, not to mention getting along with the citizens of Skagway.

By the end of 1900, Hovey and Jenks once again had a company at full strength to focus on mission success. The officers, noncommissioned officers, and soldiers had more than a year of service in Alaska under their belts, and the knowledge gleaned from their experiences was the best preparation for the days ahead. More educated than the first generation of the Buffalo Soldiers, the men were better prepared for the challenges of the new year. And baseball, among other things, would help the Black servicemen grow more accepted by the white citizens of Skagway.

SETTLING IN

The soldiers and the Skagway Baseball Club will cross
bats on the Fourth Street diamond Sunday afternoon.
—*DAILY ALASKAN*, May 19, 1901

Captain Hovey and the men of Company L entered 1901 benefiting
from eighteen months of diplomacy, law enforcement, and working
with the people of Alaska and Canada. They accomplished this while
maintaining training to be prepared for overseas deployment, possibly rejoining the regiment in the Philippine Islands. Thus far, they had
succeeded in carrying out a complex and sometimes confusing mission.
The new year would see additional challenges as well as a renewed
focus on finding a permanent home for the U.S. Army in Skagway.

Diplomacy

Captain Hovey engaged with American and Canadian officials early
in 1901 on several sensitive diplomatic issues. In the first, Hovey sent
a February 1901 letter to the adjutant general of the U.S. Army about a
potentially explosive situation involving American miners on Glacier
Creek, north of Porcupine City, about twenty miles west of Skagway. As
Hovey described the situation, a strip of land had been transferred to
Great Britain under the provision of a modus vivendi agreement with
the United States. Since the American miners were unaware of this,
they filed their mining claims with the U.S. authorities rather than the
Canadians. The Canadians were threatening to invalidate these claims.[1]

The provisions of the modus vivendi between the United States and
Great Britain, signed in October 1899, had been printed in full in the

Daily Alaskan in 1900. Yet the temporary diplomatic agreement was anything but easy to enforce on the ground, especially in the mining camp of Porcupine, where gold had recently been discovered. In order to know where the temporary boundary ran, a miner had to have a British map sheet and an American map sheet and know where the line ran along the trails between the Klehini River, the Chilkat River, and Porcupine Creek. This was no trivial task with ardent American gold diggers involved.[2]

Hovey warned his superiors that the feeling among the American miners was strong and that trouble might result if their claims were invalidated by the Canadians. He cautioned that if "ordered away, they are likely to refuse, and if the Mounted Police attempt to remove them by force, this action is likely to be met by force." He noted that in the past year, hostile acts by American miners against British representatives had been prevented twice, once by Hovey himself and once by men acting under Hovey's advice. Moreover, the area was so remote that Hovey might not be able to intervene in time on the next occasion. He was concerned the miners would not yield without a fight and that events would move so rapidly that the two governments would find themselves in a diplomatic crisis before he could intervene.[3]

In a related issue, Hovey voiced his concern about a rumor a nearby port was "to be given up to Great Britain in connection with the Clayton-Bulwer Treaty and the Nicaragua Bill." The idea had been floated to grant Great Britain and Canada a long-term lease on a port providing them an outlet to the sea. The British wanted Pyramid Harbor near Haines as an outlet for Canada, which would be their compensation for allowing the United States to build a canal in Nicaragua. Hovey worried that his company would be "bottled up" in Skagway if Pyramid Harbor was given up to the British. To Hovey's relief, the British did not push this effort since they were preoccupied fighting the Second Boer War in South Africa until 1902.[4]

Another troubling diplomatic incident with the British occurred in Skagway in June 1901 and reflected the depth of anti-Canadian feeling in the region. A man tore down the British flag flying over the new Canadian Customs office in Skagway the first day it was raised there. He cut the lanyard ropes and tore the flag from the flagpole, finally "kicking it unceremoniously into a convenient corner." When Canadian Chief Customs Inspector I. W. Busby rushed out and asked the man his name, he coolly handed him a business card imprinted with: "George M. Miller, Attorney at Law, Eugene, Oregon." Miller shortly thereafter shipped out to Porcupine City, presumably to seek his fortune in gold.[5]

The *Daily Alaskan* front-page coverage, under the headline "FLAG DOWN," explained the case resulted from a misunderstanding. Miller thought he tore down the British national flag. Yet as Busby explained in an interview, the flag raised was the Canadian Customs ensign. This so-called red ensign had a Union Jack in the upper left-hand quarter and a "Crown in the fly" on a red background. Busby had discussed the appropriateness of flying this flag with Skagway authorities in the days prior, and all agreed that it was allowed by international customs and courtesies.[6]

Yet there was more to the story, according to the *Daily Alaskan*. The piece noted, "The statements made on the street yesterday that the flag was raised to accustom Americans to it to prepare them for the final surrender of this country to England was, no doubt, inspired by the belief that the flag taken down was the English Emblem. It was not. It was a customs flag only." Skagwayans were clearly still worried about the threat of British annexation.[7]

The Canadian authorities were naturally outraged at the incident and made an official complaint through their ambassador in Washington DC. With Hovey absent at the time, Jenks had to deal with this matter. He promptly informed Washington and warned "the affair may seem trivial, in itself, yet the sentiment in this town is very strongly against the raising of any English flag." Jenks asked his superiors for instructions on how to deal with future incidents, which he noted were "not unlikely."[8]

Jenks also wrote a letter responding to an official protest sent to him by Busby. In it, he extended his "deep regrets for the outrage to your official flag." He noted he had personally investigated the affair and informed Busby that a formal complaint had been made against Miller. He promised action, and Miller was eventually arrested and charged by the civil authorities with destruction of property.[9]

Permanent Post

To maintain a military presence in the region, Captain Hovey spent a great deal of time talking with local officials to secure a permanent reservation in Skagway. Thus far, the deliberations about securing the land for a fixed military establishment had proven nearly as complex as Hovey's diplomatic mission. Yet by 1901 it seemed the last obstacles to acquiring the land to be used as a military post near Skagway had been overcome.

In January 1901 Captain Hovey forwarded a letter to the U.S. Army with the "plat of the proposed military reservation, together with the field notes of the survey." Hovey suggested a "small rectangle facing on the river" west of Skagway as the future site of the army post. The projected parcel was sixteen acres of land above the flood plain separated from the city by the Skagway River. He noted the delay in submitting the final papers were due to "the seemingly unsurmountable obstacle of obtaining the land on the river as an outlet for the post." This last problem had delayed the process for more than a year. When the owner of the property dragged his feet, Hovey "read him the riot act."[10]

There is no record that an army engineer officer ever visited Skagway to assist in planning the layout of the new post. This duty fell to Lieutenant Jenks, since he had attended the U.S. Army Engineer School of Application seven years earlier and served as the post engineer officer at Fort Bayard, New Mexico, in 1895. Jenks's alma mater, West Point, was still the premier engineering school in the country. While Jenks dealt with the technical issues, Hovey negotiated with citizens and city leaders of Skagway on securing the purchase of the land.

In a competing bid, Juneau, Alaska, submitted an offer to Hovey to host a permanent military post as an alternative to Skagway. In response, Hovey asked the Chamber of Commerce of Juneau to send their proposal directly to the War Department in Washington DC. Among Juneau's advantages were central location, good harbor, superior access, better prospects, and available land for the post. Despite all these, Hovey remained a supporter of the choice of Skagway.[11]

With the decision of the permanent post unresolved, the company remained quartered in buildings clustered in eastern Skagway. As an incentive to remain, the owner of the new barracks built in 1900 offered to build a 25-by-170-foot addition to the existing two-story frame building. Yet the company still did not have enough room to give up the dilapidated Astoria Hotel and billet all the enlisted men in one place. The landlord also agreed to build for lease a small building nearby as a guardhouse, an adjoining structure for storage and office space, and a new set of officers' quarters. Moreover, he agreed to add a second story to an existing double set of officers' quarters to be used as a new hospital.[12]

As an added advantage, the barracks, storehouse, offices, and officers' quarters would be immediately adjoining, so one roving sentinel could guard them all. And the new hospital, which replaced the old rundown Pacific & Arctic Railway & Navigation Company building, was only one structure away. This would combine nearly the entire post together in an area of town that was in the least danger of fire. Only the post commander's quarters and the stable and wagon shed were located elsewhere.[13]

Despite all these advantages, Hovey considered the location west of the city the best choice for a permanent reservation. A military post scattered among buildings in the middle of a city, just a stone's throw from bars and brothels, was never more than a temporary solution. No incentive the city fathers of Skagway could offer would change Hovey's mind.

Technology

Technology reared its problematic head for Captain Hovey beginning in 1901. About that time, the captain accepted delivery of a brand-new typewriter, a new technological advance of the time. Some of his reports began appearing as typed letters on white paper with a carbon copy in early 1901. Hovey's memos were certainly easier to read, though the typed page proved a pale reflection of the beautiful cursive handwriting of his clerks over the past two years.

Hovey did not yet enjoy modern communications aside from telephone connections within Skagway. He continued to depend on messages sent and received via ships plying the coastal waters between Skagway and Seattle. The only exception was the occasional telegram, received in a roundabout way, via Canada. The U.S. Army occasionally sent telegrams overland through Canada to Captain Hovey, which were then delivered by hand the remaining distance from the Canadian border via the railroad. Yet most routine messages took a week or more to reach their destination via steamer from Seattle.

The White Pass & Yukon Route had a telegraph line between their offices in Skagway and Bennett. Canadian Dominion lines stretched from Bennett to Dawson and Atlin, another set of lines linked Tagish through Atlin, all connected with the Canadian Pacific system. Yet Hovey could not send his official military communications via lines that would certainly be read by the Canadian authorities.[14]

Something a bit more ominous arrived in Skagway at about the same time as the typewriter. Captain Hovey accepted delivery of a Gatling gun in September 1900 for use "in case of war or riot to maintain the dignity of Uncle Sam," as reported by the *Daily Alaskan*. Invented by Richard J. Gatling in 1862, this weapon saw occasional use by Union forces during the Civil War yet was not officially accepted for use by the U.S. Army until 1866. An early form of rotary cannon and forerunner of the modern machine gun, it could fire four hundred rounds per minute and have a devastating effect on an enemy.[15]

Colt upgraded the Gatling for the U.S. Army in 1895 and 1900, so Skagway Barracks likely received the newer model. The upgraded system fired the same smokeless .30-40 Krag round used by the soldiers of the company. The number of barrels were increased to ten, and the weapon could fire as many as eight hundred to nine hundred rounds per minute. These newer models were mounted on a field carriage and pulled by the mules of Company L. The army provided no special training to the soldiers in the company since the weapon had been in use for many years. And the company artificer supervised the maintenance of the gun as well as the field carriage.[16]

Why would Captain Hovey need a Gatling gun in Alaska? That question is perhaps best answered by examining the places it was employed during this period. Lieutenant Jenks had observed the weapon's effectiveness during the assault on San Juan Hill during the Spanish-American War, where it wreaked terrible carnage on the Spanish troops. The weapon might have been intended as a deterrent aimed at the Mounted Police and military forces in Canada, who were equipped with their own machine guns. The NWMP set up Maxim machine guns in the Chilkoot and White Passes in 1898 to control the massive influx of miners into Canada.[17]

Gatling guns developed more sobering uses. European colonial powers used these weapons most successfully in defeating indigenous fighters who mounted mass assaults in Asia and Africa. Perhaps the army believed their presence might deter trouble with the Tlingit. Gatling guns were also used to intimidate crowds, and U.S. and state governments used the army frequently in this period as an instrument to break up labor strikes. Whatever the reason, Hovey had his Gatling, which to him was just another piece of equipment to clean, maintain, and guard.[18]

In addition to the Gatling, the army also shipped a cannon to Company L in Skagway. Both the cannon and Gatling gun sat next to the Astoria Hotel barracks on Sixth Avenue at the ready. Skagwayans enjoyed the evening firings of the cannon when a company trumpeter played "Taps" and soldiers solemnly lowered the Stars and Stripes at the end of each duty day. The people voiced their disappointment when Hovey had to temporarily end this daily routine when he ran out of gunpowder in December 1900.[19]

Death, Sickness, and Psychosis

To man his crew-served cannon and Gatling, Hovey needed soldiers, and he lost several in early 1901 to disease and death. The first, Private Esaw Simmons, died in March 1901 of acute influenza at the army hospital in Skagway. Simmons, twenty-two, who listed Indianapolis,

Indiana, as his home of record, was born in Dugan County, North Carolina. He served in the Eighth U.S. Volunteer Infantry during the Spanish-American War. When the unit mustered out of the federal service in March 1899, Simmons enlisted a few days later at Camp Thomas, Georgia and was assigned to Company L.[20]

For Simmons and all soldiers who died on active duty, the army paid for a military funeral or for his body to be sent home for burial. Captain Hovey shipped the body of Simmons south for burial on SS *Humboldt*, the same ship on which the soldier had arrived two years earlier. The *Seattle Star* noted in March 1901 that "*Humboldt* had on board the bodies of the infant son of Mr. and Mrs. E.R. Peoples of Skagway, and of Esau [Esaw] Simmons, a soldier." Edgar E. Peoples was a member of the city council and the only undertaker in Skagway, so he likely prepared both bodies for transport.[21]

Another soldier's illness and subsequent death was more complicated for Hovey. In late March 1901, the captain asked the adjutant general for permission to send Private Oscar D. Henry to Fort Bayard, New Mexico, for medical treatment. Fort Bayard housed the army general hospital dedicated to the care and treatment of tuberculous officers and soldiers. Henry was a twenty-nine-year-old laborer from Ridgedale, Tennessee, who had enlisted in the army in March 1899. According to Hovey's letter, Henry's condition was "such as to require his immediate transfer from this climate in order to save his life." Dr. Bailey endorsed the request.[22]

The adjutant general approved the application and Hovey shipped Henry south. The treatment was unsuccessful, and Henry died in early May 1901 of pulmonary tuberculosis. The army determined that the death was incurred in the line of duty, and he was buried with full military honors at Fort Bayard. Henry, like the other soldiers of the company, received better medical treatment and death benefits than those available to most Black Americans.[23]

Captain Hovey and Dr. Bailey also dealt with a mentally ill soldier at Camp Skagway in March 1901. Hovey sent Private Webster Altmann, escorted by First Sergeant James Washington, to Washington DC for "insane treatment." The two departed Skagway in late March and arrived in Washington DC the first day of April. There Altmann was accepted as a patient at the Government Hospital for the Insane, which also had a separate U.S. Army general hospital for that purpose.[24]

Altmann was a twenty-three-year-old former laborer from New York City who enlisted in February 1899 and joined the company shortly before it deployed to Alaska. His treatment was presumably successful, and the army discharged him in April 1901 with a disability and a character rating of "good." Altmann returned to New York City and resumed a normal life, eventually marrying twice.[25]

Though he was not sick, dead, or mentally ill, First Sergeant Washington, Altmann's escort, requested and received permission to remain on furlough in Washington DC for thirty days. Though born in Gainesville, Alabama, Washington enlisted in the army in 1886 in Washington DC and listed his home as Warrenton, Virginia. He had been stationed in Montana, Utah, and Alaska in his career and had probably never been home on leave. He was back in Skagway by mid-May to resume his duties with the company.[26]

Officer Lyceums

The army instituted several measures to improve the training and professionalism of the U.S. officer corps before the turn of the century. In addition to the promotion examinations and officer efficiency reports, the army established the School of Application for infantry and cavalry at Fort Leavenworth in 1881. And since not all officers could attend this school, it extended the improvement of the army's educational system to the field by instituting intensive training sessions called lyceums in 1891.[27]

During these lyceums, officers at all posts having troops of the line (infantry, cavalry, and artillery) prepared papers and took part in discussions on professional topics at regular assemblies. Captain Hovey served as the president of the lyceum and the instructor for these mandatory sessions for the four-man officer cadre in Skagway. Afterward, he sent the papers to the Department of Alaska for review.[28]

The papers and sessions reflected on the professionalism of the officer. And not always positively. On at least one occasion, Captain Hovey directed Lieutenant Rains to explain, in writing, the cause of his lateness for the lyceum in February 1901.[29]

Captain Hovey sent his annual report on officer lyceums at Camp Skagway to the adjutant general of the Department of Alaska in September 1901. He noted the lyceum met twice each week from early December 1900 to late March 1901. Captain Hovey scheduled the sessions for Tuesday and Thursday of each week, and each featured recitations and discussions. This was presumably done during the cold winter months when outdoor activity was limited.[30]

Hovey covered the following subjects during the instructions that season: drill regulations, military field engineering, military law, security and information, and organization and tactics. He devoted two sessions to sanitary subjects for which no papers were prepared but which were fully discussed by Dr. Bailey. Jenks presented an essay he wrote in March 1901 titled "Notes on the Siege of Ladysmith," which took place during the Second Boer War in South Africa. Lieutenant Rains gave an essay the same month titled "Notes on the Medical Department, U.S. Army, in the Philippine Islands," based on his personal experience. The captain forwarded these last two papers to headquarters for evaluation.[31]

Promotion and Temporary Command

Lieutenant Jenks celebrated his promotion to captain on April 4, 1901, signaling changes to come. According to tradition Captain Hovey, as the senior officer, would have affixed the new rank insignia to one of Jenks's shoulders, while Mrs. Jenks placed the other on the opposite shoulder. Lieutenant Rains, as the post adjutant, read the orders. Captain Hovey, Lieutenant Rains, and Dr. Bailey, the only officers present, celebrated the event with their wives and wetted down Jenks's new captain's bars, nicknamed "railroad tracks" for their resemblance to two wooden ties crossed by two iron rails. Once promoted, Jenks could not remain in Skagway long.[32]

Promotion to captain was a watershed event for Jenks in a Regular Army that featured a tortuously slow promotion system based purely on seniority within the regiment. Army reforms in the 1890s introduced examinations for promotions below the grade of major as well as efficiency reports, which improved the quality of the officer corps. And the expansion of the army after the Spanish-American War sped the rate of promotion. Yet Jenks spent seven years as a second lieutenant and three years as a first lieutenant before his elevation to captain. So Jenks's promotion was an occasion to celebrate.[33]

Events caused Captain Jenks to stay in Skagway longer than planned. Captain Hovey became ill in May 1901 and was unable to carry out his duties. Records show Hovey was absent on sick leave in Seattle between May and October 1901. The nature of his illness is unknown yet must have been serious to necessitate his evacuation to a hospital in Seattle and sick leave for five months. His condition may have been connected to his bouts of malaria while stationed on the frontier. With Hovey away on sick leave, Captain Jenks was left with the task of commanding the company and post in Skagway.[34]

One of Captain Jenks's first official duties was to help Skagway celebrate Memorial Day in May 1901. An article ran in the *Daily Alaskan* providing details of the event, noting, "Those who wore the blue will beautify graves of comrades." The Civil War had ended thirty-six years earlier, so the youngest veterans of that conflict were approaching sixty years old. According to the report, the "Sunday preceding the 30th of May is always set apart for the religious portions of the services in memory of the honored dead."[35]

A full reconciliation between North and South was not yet complete, so the official commemoration was reserved for the Union dead. The article mentioned at least four Union Army veterans living in Skagway at the time. There was no reference in the article to accommodations for the Confederate dead or Southerners who lived in Skagway.[36]

Captain Jenks volunteered an honor guard for the ceremony. The paper noted, "Through the kindness of Capt. Jenks a detail of Company L in charge of a noncommissioned officer will escort the old soldiers to the cemetery and fire an army salute over the graves of the comrades." It is noteworthy that African American soldiers, referred to in the article as "the Nation's Defenders," provided a color guard to honor those who fought to free the enslaved people of the South. Among those they freed were the parents of the soldiers themselves.[37]

A week after the Memorial Day celebration, Jenks received a surprise visit by the Department of Alaska inspector general, Captain Herbert E. Tutherly. The IG arrived aboard *City of Seattle* unannounced, as was customary. He inspected the barracks and hospital and turned out the company for drill and inspection. According to the *Daily Alaskan*: "The boys were not informed in advance nor given time for preparation. They simply had to go through their drills as they happened to be able."[38]

The people of Skagway found the whole process very entertaining. Tutherly directed the soldiers to drill in front of the barracks and pitch their tents. "A large crowd of civilians gathered to watch the work, and it was exceedingly interesting to the greater number to see how the boys form their little camp in such quick order as they do. Later the men went through evolutions on the beach at the foot of Broadway." Tutherly later reported to Washington that the company "had reached a high degree of efficiency" and passed the inspection.[39]

Baseball

The baseball season opened in Skagway the same weekend as Memorial Day. An article ran in the *Daily Alaskan* on May 24, 1901, under the title "THE GREAT AMERICAN GAME." It noted that activity in baseball circles was increasing, and it saw "no reason why the people should not be afforded the opportunity of witnessing some lively exhibitions of the national game." The article proposed the formation of a regular league and games with nearby towns.[40]

Unlike the previous year, the soldier team played the first recorded game of the 1901 season in Canada. According to the *Douglas Island News*: "The most exciting game of baseball in the Northwest took place in Whitehorse, Y.T. [Yukon Territory], May 24th, between the U.S. soldiers' club of Skagway and the Northwest Mounted Police club of Whitehorse." The soldiers won the game by a score of 6–5 before a crowd that might have included American prospectors living in the Yukon.[41]

The road game to Whitehorse in Canada was a significant undertaking. Whitehorse is more than one hundred miles north of Skagway as the crow flies, which in 1900 would have taken a full day of travel. Thanks to the completion of the connection to Carcross the previous year, the soldier team could take the train the entire 110 miles to Whitehorse.

Uncharacteristically, Jenks made no mention of the game in the official record; he did not mention the visit across the border in official letters or in his monthly post return. The teams played the game on a Friday, which was a normal day of military duty. Perhaps Jenks considered the game an informal extension of the U.S. Army's diplomatic mission in Alaska. Call it baseball diplomacy.

Skagway cheered on the first recorded contest of the season on Sunday, May 26, hard on the heels of the Whitehorse trip. The game was "between picked teams of the W.P.E.C. [White Pass & Yukon Employees Club] and the soldier boys." The newspaper noted considerable interest in the game because the teams were composed of the best players in the city. The result of that game was reported in the *Douglas Island News*: "The soldiers recently took the railroad men into camp by a score of 7 to 6."[42]

Skagway witnessed a proliferation of baseball teams and games the summer of 1901, though the newspaper record of the games is scant. The *Daily Alaskan* reported in mid-June: "The Skagway Junior Baseball Team defeated the junior team of the soldiers Sunday by a score of 19 to 14. The Skagway Seniors went down to defeat before the first team of soldiers." This indicates there were two teams playing for the soldiers, as well as a pair playing for Skagway. Both had enough players to field first- and second-string teams.[43]

The *Daily Alaskan* noted: "While other sports have many admirers base ball has the call upon the people and still remains the great American sport." The reporter hoped that the game would be one of the chief attractions of the coming Fourth of July celebrations. He also proposed an invitation be extended to the Whitehorse team "to play a return game here with the soldier boys on Independence Day." There were even suggestions, tongue-in-cheek, that the border issue be resolved by a game between the Buffalo Soldiers and Mounties, winner take all.[44]

Fourth of July

Skagway celebrated the Fourth of July 1901 in a big way, and Captain Jenks was pleased to take part in the festivities. The city invited the soldiers to add a military flavor to the festivities as they had in 1899. The soldiers provided a marching unit complete with blue uniforms, white gloves, and rifles with fixed bayonets. The marching was "led by the colored troops, the attractiveness of the column being enhanced by the cannon and Gatling gun drawn by the mule teams."[45]

After the parade at 8:30 a.m., the soldiers of the company performed a "Sham Battle" on the waterfront. According to the *Daily Alaskan*: "The sham battle was a noisy affair and looked very much like war. Sergeant O'Conner's force defended themselves gallantly down at the mouth of the creek, but the dashing onslaught of Lieutenant Rains' command seemed to be too much for them, and they gave themselves over cannon and all."[46]

The army never undertook a major demonstration like this without a rehearsal. A week before the Fourth, two hundred Skagwayans witnessed a "bloodless battle in which the boys in blue proved 'Foeman worthy of their steel.'" The *Daily Alaskan* reported: "After a short but decisive battle the command under Lieutenant Rains captured Sergeant O'Connor's squad, guns and all, and the white flag of truce was all that was left of that body, but the colored troops fought nobly." The piece noted: "It was realistic in tactics and recalled to mind the bloody days of '61–65," a reference to the Civil War.[47]

After lunch on the Fourth, the soldiers played a baseball game against the best side from Skagway. According to the *Daily Alaskan*, men, women, and children "shouted their lungs sore." Calling the contest were umpires W. Davis and Thomas Berry. The captain of the "soldier nine" was Corporal Green, and "Phelps bawled the boys off the bases for the railroaders." The railroad team won by a score of 14–10. This game must have been the source of a great deal of celebration in Skagway, and Troy gave it prominent coverage in the newspaper.[48]

The railroad team members were listed in the newspaper with names and positions in the order they batted: Edward Barry at shortstop, William C. Blanchard in center field, Frank Burns in right field, Van Brocklin at first base, George B. Daniels in left field, Frank B. McDonald at second base, John C. Phelps catching, Edward J. Tholin pitching, and Clarence Olsen at third base. All were White Pass & Yukon employees except McDonald and Burns. The only holdovers from the team named in May 1900 were Phelps and Barry.[49]

The soldier side was also listed in the order they batted: Benjamin Green at first base, William Jennings at second, William Sims at shortstop, William Freeman pitching, John W. Oby at third, Ernest L. Johnson catching, Thomas Morton in left field, William Pate in center field, and William Rollins in right field. The five players who carried over from the 1900 team were described in detail in the previous chapter: Green, Jennings, Sims, Oby, and Johnson. All five of these men played the infield in 1901, considered the skill positions in baseball. Benjamin Green had been promoted to corporal and was now the player-captain of the soldier team.[50]

Of the four new players on the soldier team, one played pitcher and the other three were outfielders, the latter usually recruited for their ability at batting. All of the new players were privates: Thomas Morton, thirty-two, a former laborer from Bourbon County, Kentucky; William Pate, twenty-three, a former coachman and soldier in the Sixth Massachusetts Volunteer Infantry; William Freeman, twenty-four, a former laborer from Madison, Georgia; and William Rollins, thirty-one, a former soldier who enlisted after completing his first term with the Twenty-Fourth Infantry. Rollins completed his enlistment with Company B, Twenty-Fourth Infantry, in the Philippines, returned to the states, spent six months as a civilian, and then enlisted in Portland, Oregon with Company L. As in the previous year, the new players were from across the country and quite a bit older than the average soldier in the company.[51]

There were several players from the previous year who were no longer on the team. Corporal Edward Dewey, the captain of the team the previous year, was still in Skagway but no longer with the team. He may have been sick, as Captain Hovey sent him to the Army and Navy General Hospital, Hot Springs, Arkansas to recover from an illness in December 1901. Of the non-players from the previous year, Frank Gant was serving a three-month sentence in Sitka for selling whiskey to a Tlingit, while James Banks, George Bracy, and William Mack were still with the company but had been replaced. William Mack may have also been too sick to play, as Captain Hovey evacuated him to Fort Bayard, New Mexico, for treatment, and he died of pulmonary tuberculosis on November 5, 1901.[52]

After the game, there were fourteen sports competitions, some for citizens, some open to soldiers and citizens, and others just for soldiers, such as the "220-yard Dash for Soldiers." Nelson Casselle won the soldier 220-yard dash, followed by Reid W. Davis and baseball outfielder William Rollins. It is remarkable that some of the competitions pitted white Skagwayans against Black soldiers. For instance, soldier and baseball player William Rollins won the high jump, with a citizen named Felix Estrade placing second. Rollins also won the broad jump, with fellow soldier Casselle placing second. Civilian A. E. Kimball won the "Rifle Contest, Range 100-Yards."[53]

According to the *Daily Alaskan*, the most laughable event was the horse race. The contest was held between a "soldier on a measly little cayuse and a citizen on a dray horse." "Cayuse" was an archaic term for a feral or low-quality horse, and a dray was a draft horse used to pull a wagon. The spectators laughed as "the cayuse turned tail and ran away from the goal while the dray horse bucked off his rider." The riders were not named.[54]

The year 1901 was the first that Company L was stationed at full strength in Skagway, Alaska. Captain Hovey and newly promoted Captain Jenks continued their challenging diplomatic and presence missions in the disputed borderland of the panhandle of Alaska. They also took significant steps toward creating a permanent post in the region by adding temporary structures in town and planning a military reservation on the outskirts.

Most though not all of Skagway had come to know the officers and men of the unit and appreciated their contributions to the city. Though not welcome at certain bars in town, the Black soldiers had provided honor guards, defended the citizens, guarded against fires, played baseball against white citizens, and competed against Skagwayans in sports competitions on Independence Day. By all appearances, the residents recognized and accepted the important role the Black soldiers played in the community.

7

COMMAND CHANGE

It is reasonable to believe that the present perfect
security to life and property in this city is in a great
measure due to the presence of the colored troops.

—*DAILY ALASKAN*, July 24, 1901

The summer of 1901 marked the end of the second year Company L lived
and served in Alaska. In the wake of the season's baseball games and
the joint celebration of Independence Day, Captain Jenks, filling in for
Hovey, had to be pleased that his men were recognized by the citizens of
the town as contributing members of the community. The months ahead
would provide more evidence of the soldiers' importance to Skagway.

Black Community

The longer Company L remained in Skagway, the larger the Black community grew. In addition to the wives and families of Robert O'Connor,
James Washington, and Henry Robinson, at least one other noncommissioned officer's wife moved to Skagway. Sergeant Herbert Williams,
a twenty-five-year-old from Columbus, Ohio, was joined by his wife
in 1901. Sergeant Williams reenlisted in February 1901 for a second
term, so perhaps Hovey granted him sponsorship as an incentive to
sign up for an additional term. Sergeant Williams and his wife took
a short furlough from Skagway after his reenlistment before joining
the Black military community in Skagway.[1]

That Captain Hovey officially sponsored four noncommissioned
officers and their wives in Skagway may not have been a coincidence.
Before 1881 regulations permitted company commanders to allow four

wives who worked as laundresses to accompany the unit wherever it was stationed. The laundresses were paid a fixed fee for laundry services and allowed to draw army rations. By 1901 this had changed, and in Skagway the laundry was done by local civilians. Yet the old allowance of four laundresses might have shifted to the custom of sponsoring the same number of noncommissioned officers' wives.

Two other noncommissioned officer wives eventually joined the Black military community in Skagway, though it is not clear whether they were sponsored. Corporal Snoten's wife, Cora, née Smith, lived with him there as early as 1901. Their son, William W. Snoten, was born in Skagway in February 1902. Sergeant Allen Hayes also had his wife with him in Skagway; she was mentioned as a participant in a social event in August 1901.[2]

Aside from those noncommissioned officer families, other African American civilians resided in Skagway. Some of these were residents attracted to the jobs and opportunities created by the presence of one hundred soldiers. Some former soldiers also stayed on after ending their terms in the U.S. Army. And two men of color were already present in Skagway when recorders enumerated the 1900 census.[3]

Wherever the U.S. Army assigned African American soldiers, Black women established themselves as laundresses for the men. The army issued soldiers uniforms, coats, and other clothing items, but it was up to the individual to keep them clean and ironed. If the soldier chose not to do this himself, the job was done by washerwomen. These women also performed other services to make money, sometimes moonlighting as prostitutes.

Accounts of the Black laundresses in Skagway are scant. Yet the newspaper reported that one of these women got into trouble in July 1901. According to the article, Reena Gamon, "a colored washerwoman whose principal patrons are the soldiers of Co. L[,] was found guilty of petit larceny by a jury in the commissioner's court yesterday."[4]

The story of the trial reveals important details of the Black community in Skagway. Gamon lived near an unoccupied cabin owned by Captain Marsh, from which she was accused of stealing articles of small value from time to time. A jury of six men found her guilty in the commissioner's court. Gamon's attorney, E. M. Barnes, caused amusement during the proceedings, since he quarreled with the witnesses, jury, judge, prosecuting attorney, and finally with his own client, who challenged his "thorough knowledge of the law." Judge Sehlbrede gave Gamon the minimum fine of twenty-five dollars, plus costs. According to the report, the courtroom was full, "as nearly every colored resident was present at some time during the day."[5]

In addition to Black laundresses, Black barbers always followed Buffalo Soldiers to new posts. The noncommissioned officers enforced army regulations requiring the soldiers keep their hair neatly trimmed, so barbers were necessary. At least one of the privates in the company, John Oby, who pitched on the baseball team in 1900, listed his previous civilian occupation as barber. He may have cut the hair of some of the privates in the company. Yet most of the soldiers visited a competent barber on a regular basis.

One or two Black barbers probably served the military community in Skagway, though there is little record to prove this. Charles Munson, an African American civilian residing in Skagway during the 1900 census, could have worked as one of those barbers. Though he listed his Skagway occupation as laborer, he had previously worked in Cripple Creek, Colorado, as a barber. He might have operated a small shop on Sixth Avenue that catered to the soldiers of Company L.

It is also possible that Munson or some other Black barber worked part time in the Principal Barbershop on Sixth Avenue opposite the Astoria Hotel barracks. A February 1900 advertisement in the *Daily Alaskan* noted, "First class bath for 25 cents. The Principal, opposite U.S. Barracks." Another advertisement appeared with a photo taken in December 1900 of an army officer sitting in a barber chair getting a haircut. The officer is not identified but is likely Lieutenant Rains. The officers and soldiers probably favored the Principal because of its location close to the barracks.[6]

A newspaper story mentioned a Black man named Walter Smith who worked in a Skagway barber shop. Smith was a suspect in the theft of some valuables belonging to Private Thomas Mozeak in June 1901. Mozeak offered Smith five dollars if he returned the items, and under pressure Smith identified Private Thomas Williams as the thief. This reference to Smith as a "colored man who works in a barber shop" is the only solid proof Skagway had such an operation serving Black soldiers.[7]

The thief was Private Thomas Williams, a twenty-three-year-old former bricklayer who was born in the British island colony of Barbados. Under questioning by Skagway's Marshal J. W. Snook, Smith identified Williams, who was then convicted of larceny by Judge Sehlbrede and sentenced to three months in Sitka. The army directed Captain Hovey to discharge Williams without honor the following month.[8]

Black Prostitutes

Black members of the civilian community also committed crimes that made newspaper headlines. In June 1900 Green Johnson, an African American man, was arrested for assaulting a Black woman in Skagway. The article described him as "a man of considerable color and muscle" and promised the case would be "rich and racy," since the woman was of "rather shady color and character."[9]

Judge Sehlbrede heard the case before a jury of six men the next day in the commissioner's court. After hearing the testimony of witnesses and pleas of counsels, the jury deadlocked at four for acquittal and two for conviction. The defendant, Viola Smith, caught the first boat out of town with her partner, Helen, fearing she would be prosecuted for "smoking opium and being a common nuisance." According to the report, she had opened a "house of the demimonde stripe," become jealous of "her sisters in sin," and "squealed on them" for selling liquor without a license. Johnson's assault of her was a consequence of her actions, according to the article. Both Smith and her partner must have been Black prostitutes catering to the soldiers.[10]

Daily Alaskan editor John Troy was uncharacteristically crass in his use of language in this case. While Company L was stationed in Skagway and Captain Hovey tended to good relations with City Hall, Troy usually steered clear of vulgar references to African Americans. Yet when he reported on the case two days later explaining a further delay in the proceedings, he referred to the situation as a regular "nigger in the woodpile" affair, where "one is afraid and the other dare not." Sehlbrede eventually dismissed the case for lack of a prosecuting witness.[11]

With Viola and Helen out of business, Skagway became a more lucrative market for two Black prostitutes who ran a bawdy house on Sixth Avenue. Rose Arnold and Ruth Brown set up shop some time after the arrival of the Buffalo Soldiers in Alaska. They moved their operations from Dawson City, Yukon, and catered to the African American soldiers and the small Black community in Skagway, which locals referred to as the "colored colony."[12]

By the time Rose and Ruth arrived, the powerful men who ran Skagway had come to a "gentleman's agreement" on the issue of prostitution. City Hall tolerated the second-oldest profession, occasionally arresting and fining the women but never moving to put them out of business. The bawdy houses were a necessary evil, and so long as they set up shop on Seventh Avenue in the restricted district, they were condoned. When the authorities arrested and prosecuted prostitutes, the chief booster of the city, *Daily Alaskan* editor John Troy, generally did not print their names or details of court appearances. This kept the white citizens out of trouble with their wives at home.[13]

When Rose Arnold and Ruth Brown set up their establishment on Sixth Avenue, City Hall took notice. It was admittedly a great business location, across the street from one barracks and next door to the other. The location raised two serious issues. First, it was not on Seventh Avenue, and second, it was next door to the Peniel Mission, whose mostly women missionaries aimed to evangelize in Skagway. This was a problem for City Hall and would eventually lead to trouble for the two African American prostitutes.

One other known crime committed in late 1901 involved a Black civilian assaulting a white citizen at the Last Chance Saloon. Jerry Moore, described as a "frenzied negro," assaulted Richard Ryan with a knife. According to the *Daily Alaskan*, Moore was intoxicated, vituperative, and wielding a knife, so the bartender threw him out. Moore returned with a vengeance, cutting Ryan's coat to ribbons, until the defender hit him over the head with a stove poker. Moore later pleaded guilty to assault with a deadly weapon and was sentenced to a fifty-dollar fine and a thirty-day stint in the Skagway jail.[14]

Officers and Society

At the other end of the social spectrum from the Black community stood the powerful men who ran Skagway. Officers were considered gentlemen; they and their wives were automatically included in the upper strata of society. The officers socialized with the people they worked with professionally each day: the wealthy and powerful men who insured the city ran efficiently and to their liking. All the army officers in Skagway were active members of society.

Captain Hovey acted the role of the military doyen in Skagway. He spent his days in discussions with powerful public officials like the governor of Alaska, district judge, deputy U.S. marshal, mayor of Skagway, and his military counterparts on the Canadian side of the border. The absence of his wife, Carrie, in Skagway was a limitation, for Hovey since she would have played an important role leading the small military community, but this role was carried out instead by other officers' wives.

Hovey became an integral part of the social fabric of the professional class in the city, a communicant at the Methodist Episcopal church and active member of the local Military Order of the Loyal Legion. He was also a Mason, Shriner, and member of the Elks, all very active in Skagway, as well as a frequent guest for dinner and parties at the homes of the most influential families in Skagway.[15]

The Arctic Brotherhood initiated Captain Hovey into membership, and he attended meetings at their intricately decorated hall on Broadway. Gold-seekers had founded this fraternal organization in February 1899 and established its first lodge at Skagway Camp No. 1. Eventually, the brotherhood established thirty-two "camps" throughout Alaska and the Yukon Territory in Canada. The organization's membership included the most influential men in Skagway and served as an informal power center. Hovey's social position was such that the brother-hood elected him leader with the title Arctic Chief No. 1.[16]

Captain Jenks was Hovey's second in command as well as the deputy "military mayor" of Skagway. Jenks stepped in during natural disasters and diplomatic visits while Hovey was away. Jenks was senior and experienced enough to fill in for Hovey smoothly, having served the same role at Fort Wrangel for a year. He was also active in the Elks and the Presbyterian church and was an avid hunter.[17]

The only known photo of Lieutenant Jenks in Alaska shows him on a hunting trip posing with two white citizens and two Black soldiers in mid-September 1901. The photo was taken at Warm Pass near White Pass and shows five men with three mountain goats they had gutted and hung on poles. It is noteworthy that all five men are armed with what appear to be Winchester rifles, and the two Black soldiers appear to be posing as hunters, not cooks. The photo, marked Case and Draper, was likely taken by one of those two men, William Case or Horace H. Draper, who ran a photo studio in Skagway.

A newspaper article later in September reported another hunting trip taken by Jenks. The story noted: "Capt. Jenks, Capt. Snyder, Vice-President Newell, and Supt. Rogers spent several days this week in the neighborhood of Marsh Lake [Canada], hunting ptarmigan and wild cats. They brought back well filled sacks of the former." The men Jenks hunted with reflected his social circle. Captain Philip W. Snyder commanded the local militia company in Skagway, and Ashby B. Newell was vice president and James P. Rogers superintendent of the White Pass & Yukon Route.[18]

Jenks possessed talents beyond those he developed as an army offi-cer. Jenks had trained at the Boston Conservatory of Music and was a tenor soloist and leader of the cadet choir at West Point. In Skagway he sang with a local group called the White Pass Quartet. A large audi-ence attended "The Event of the Season" at the Elks Hall in July 1901 to hear "Captain Jenks and the White Pass Quartet." He also sang as a soloist at the Presbyterian church in Skagway.[19]

Jenks's wife, Alice, played an active role in women's social circles in Skagway, as she had at Fort Wrangel. Yet she had two-year-old Dorothy and eleven-year-old Marion to care for, so she had to limit her social life. Alice was an active member of Saint Savior's Episcopal Church and served as the president of the Ladies Guild. Her daughter, Marion, was the president of the sewing circle organized from the "little misses." Both Alice and Isaac were frequent guests and hosts at parties and dinners held by high society in Skagway.[20]

Dr. Bailey was also active in social circles, supplemented by connections with the other medical doctors in the region. No stranger to serving isolated communities, Bailey and his family had lived in China, where he served as a missionary physician for the American Baptist Mission in the provinces of Guangdong, Guangxi, and Fujian prior to his service in Alaska. Bailey's wife, Florence, and three-year-old son, Mark, had been in Alaska longer than any of the others in the military community.[21]

Bailey cared for the civilian injured in addition to his soldier charges, further endearing him to the people of Skagway. The newspaper reported in December 1901 he set the broken leg of a hospital orderly who slipped while moving equipment out of the old hospital on Fourth Avenue and was recovering at the new hospital on Fifth Avenue. Less than a week later the principal of the Skagway schools, Miss Harriet E. McCarroll, fell on the sidewalk on the corner of Broadway and Fifth Avenue, and Dr. Bailey treated her fractured wrist.[22]

Bailey worked with other doctors and hospitals in the town to improve medical care. He ran a charity sale at Behrends' Dry Goods Store in May 1901, with 15 percent of the receipts going to benefit the Bishop Rowe Hospital in Skagway. The sale was staffed by twenty local women.[23]

Bailey was also socially active in Skagway and served as the recorder of the Arctic Brotherhood. He and his wife hosted many parties at their quarters on Sixth Avenue, not far from the barracks. He was fond of playing cards and loved to attend card parties. Edward and Florence had an interest in the natural attractions of Alaska, visiting the Muir Glacier in September 1901.[24]

After his arrival in 1900, Lieutenant Rains joined the officers in Skagway's social circle. Rains arrived a bachelor yet did not remain so long. Just six months after arrival, he married Ella Burns Hayes, the daughter of a businessman from Orillia, Washington. They eventually occupied a house that was relocated from Broadway and Eighth to the Moore tract near the barracks. Edward and Ella were fond of dancing and hosted frequent parties. Ella was an active member of the ladies' guild at Saint Savior's Episcopal Church.[25]

Rains, like Jenks, was an avid hunter and spent time tracking game with local citizens in the mountains and rivers around Skagway. Lieutenant Rains took two African American soldiers on a hunting trip to "act as camp cooks" in late September 1901 with four civilians. The army allowed officers to take "hunting leave," and it was not unusual for them to bring enlisted soldiers along as helpers. The party hunted around Sheep Camp on the Chilkoot Trail.[26]

Lieutenant Rains was evidently not happy with his assignment to the Twenty-Fourth Infantry. He had no choice with his initial posting after passing the commissioning examination; the army assigned newly commissioned "rankers" wherever they were needed. Yet by 1901 he was actively seeking reassignment outside of the Twenty-Fourth. In July 1901 Captain Jenks forwarded a request from Rains to the adjutant general of the U.S. Army for a transfer to the artillery. There were no Black soldiers in the artillery. He was eventually successful in transferring out of the Twenty-Fourth, but not until after his departure from Skagway.[27]

Native Americans

Before his departure on sick leave, Captain Hovey was called to Sitka and Juneau on "public business" concerning relations with the local Tlingit, among other things. He noted in a letter to the Department of Alaska that it was "necessary that I should see the governor, who is at Sitka, and then proceed to Juneau, where the other officials are now located." The post return reflected his absence on detached service in Sitka and Juneau for two weeks in February 1901.[28]

The issue with the Tlingit concerned a plan to start running a steamboat to transport miners up the Chilkat River near Haines Mission.

The steamboat would make it easier for miners to reach the goldfields around Porcupine City; however, this route passed through Tlingit land. Hovey wanted to work out an arrangement with civil officials to hold army troops in reserve and force the civil authorities "to handle the situation without calling on the military."[29]

With Hovey away on sick leave, Jenks had to deal with potential trouble involving the Tlingit in July and August 1901 around Haines Mission. As Hovey anticipated, authorities were not prepared to handle the situation with the steamboat transporting miners up the Chilkat River through Tlingit lands and requested army help. Jenks sent Sergeant Henry Robinson and a section of twelve enlisted men in two squads to Haines Mission in July 1901 to "prevent trouble between Indians and citizens." They camped in tents at Haines for most of the month of July. Jenks replaced this force with a squad under Corporal Thomas Martin with eight privates in late July, and they stayed about two more weeks to prevent any trouble at Haines Mission.[30]

It is unlikely there was ever any real threat at Haines to civilians. During the first two years Company L was stationed in Skagway, there were no serious incidents involving the Tlingit in the area. The Tlingit for the most part stayed within the confines of what the United States and Canada considered their domain, an area much reduced from their traditional lands by U.S. and Canadian authorities. The only official complaints from the Tlingit concerned their fishing rights and the illegal encroachment of white fishermen and canneries on their fishing grounds.

Blackface in Alaska

When the soldiers were not actively occupied with mission-related tasks, they sought opportunities to entertain themselves and others. The Magnolia Four comprised a group of soldier-singers in Company L who found an outlet for their talent in Alaska. The leader of this group was Corporal Benjamin Green, the captain and first baseman of the soldier team. The other three core members were Corporal James Banks, Corporal William Freeman, and Private William Pate; Green and Pate performed in similar shows at Fort Wrangel. The four sang as a quartet to entertain the soldiers as well as the white residents of Skagway, often performing minstrel shows. And Lieutenant Jenks, who sang in his own quartet, supported the efforts of the Magnolia Four, just as he did baseball.

There were at least three Black minstrel shows in Skagway the summer of 1901. The first featured a joint production by the Magnolia Four and a visiting acting group, the second presented a show sponsored by the Magnolia Four with performers from Company L, and the third showcased a professional acting troop touring the coast of Alaska. Minstrel shows featuring white actors donning blackface and depicting "the genre's derogatory stereotypes of black life" were all the rage in America in the nineteenth century. By the late 1800s, Black actors began appearing in minstrel shows as well. The trio of performances drew large crowds in Skagway, where good entertainment was in short supply.[31]

The first minstrel show was a joint production staged in July 1901 at the auditorium of McCabe College and sponsored by the Ladies Auxiliary of the YMCA. It was touted as the first appearance of the jubilee concert company and featured the Georgia Anniversary Jubilee Singers. The newspaper noted the company had been traveling widely in the western states for the last two years. The Magnolia Four joined the Jubilee Singers in putting on the production, the first mention of the soldier-singing group from Company L in the *Daily Alaskan*.[32]

The joint troupe presented the jubilee concert in two parts. The first consisted of visiting singers and soldiers from Company L singing in choruses, solos, duets, and quartets. Soldiers Edward Collins, Nelson Casselle, Benjamin Green, and David Caughman sang solos. Jubilee company singers included Dora Clark, George H. Williams, and quartets by the Troubadour Four. Notably, the program and names of all the African American soldiers and jubilee company members were printed in the newspaper on the Skagway society page (appendix C).[33]

The second part of the show was a mix of solos, duets, quartets, and sketches. Soldier William Pate and civilian George H. Williams sang and performed the first sketch, company-member Fran Poole crooned a solo, the Magnolia Four intoned a duet, George H. Williams sang a solo, and finally soldier William Freeman and Fran Poole performed a character song and sketch. The show ended with a full, combined chorus.[34]

A newspaper review after the performance at McCabe College boasted that an audience of more than three hundred enjoyed the show. The article praised the "colored Magnolia Four from the barracks" for arranging the presentation. The Ladies Auxiliary, who sponsored the show, received 50 percent of the ticket proceeds, a net of seventy-five dollars, which helped them pay off most of the one hundred dollars they had pledged to lifting the debt of the YMCA.[35]

This first recorded stage production with soldier participation is significant for several reasons. First, the performance was sponsored by the YMCA, which had Black and white members and tolerated no color line. The show attracted a large, mixed audience to its performance. Second, it was sponsored by the Ladies Auxiliary of the YMCA, an active white women's group in town. And finally, this first production focused more on singing African American spirituals and less on acting out the offensive stereotypes of Black enslavement.[36]

The second production featured the soldiers staging their own show in August 1901 at the Elks Hall next to the new barracks. The *Daily Alaskan* gave prominent coverage headlining a "SPIRITED COON SHOW," featuring "The Magnolia Four, with Auxiliary Local Talent." The performance was supported by Skagway's Harper's orchestra and Mrs. A. H. McKay. Professor Harper's orchestra played often for dances and McKay was the socially active wife of the White Pass & Yukon Route traffic manager. According to the article, the Magnolia Four had performed at white venues, and those groups felt obliged to return the favor, indicating a reciprocal relationship with citizen organizations in Skagway.[37]

The *Daily Alaskan* printed the extensive program of the show in its entirety and ran ads promoting the show for a week (appendix C). The company hosted a dress rehearsal the night before the event and promised "a show that will cast in the shade any minstrel performance that has ever been placed before an Alaskan audience." The performance promised "buck dancing, cake walks, melodies, and sonorous choruses." And quite unusual for the time, the soldier actors and singers were accompanied by a local white orchestra and supported by local white citizens.[38]

At least eleven soldiers sang, danced, or acted in the production: corporals James Banks, William Freeman, Benjamin Green, and Charlie White; privates Edward Collins, Nelson Casselle, David Caughman, Robert Grant, William Pate, Frank Watson; and Musician Edward Williams. Other soldiers likely supported the program behind the scenes. The first part of the show involved the playing of "The Stars and Stripes Forever," some chorus numbers, a dance, and several solo performances by Pate, Collins, Banks, Green, White, Williams, and Casselle, in that order.[39]

The second part of the show featured soldiers and several Black women from Skagway in a stage performance. The play depicted an old plantation scene where an old slave escapes his owner, returns, and finds his children grown. Green played Old Ephe the slave and Pate and Banks his two sons. Freeman, a Black soldier, played the role of Mr. Stevenson, the white planter. Black women played the other three roles on stage: Mrs. Thomas as Ephe's wife, Mrs. Hayes as Stevenson's niece, and Mrs. Amelia Beckwith as Stevenson's daughter. All the Black actors would have worn blackface, but the article does not describe how the Black actors and actresses made themselves up to play white roles.[40]

The third part of the performance began with a comic duet, a solo, and a cakewalk. The cakewalk had its roots in the enslaved culture of the South and was often performed in minstrel shows. Corporal Banks led the cakewalk followed by five dancing couples: Corporal Green and Amelia Beckwith, Mr. and Mrs. Williams, Private Pate and Mrs. Hayes, Private Watson and Mrs. Thompson, and Corporal White and Mrs. Sussie O'Connor. The show ended with several songs and "Clog and Buck Dancing."[41]

The last two parts of the program provide clues to the identities and roles of some of the Black women who lived in the African American community in Skagway. At least one and perhaps two of the noncommissioned officers' wives took part. Sergeant O'Connor's wife, Sussie, was one of the cakewalk dancers. Mrs. Hayes was likely the wife of Sergeant Allen Hayes, who was listed in the 1900 census as married. Mr. and Mrs. Williams must have been a married civilian couple who resided in the Black neighborhood. The rest of the women, named Thomas, Thompson, and Beckwith, were Black women who lived and worked in Skagway, perhaps as laundresses. At least one of these women, Amelia Beckwith, married Corporal Eugene Swanson in 1902, when he completed his army service.[42]

A newspaper article the following day gave the show rave reviews. At the Elks Hall, "Every seat was occupied, and standing room was at a premium. The show was in every way better than anything that has ever been furnished by professionals in Alaska." Lieutenant Rains was thanked for his efforts, likely because he was an Elks member and facilitated the show. And Private Pate and Mrs. Hayes were singled out as "the shining lights of the cakewalk."[43]

A third minstrel show came to Skagway the following month. In mid-September 1901, the *Daily Alaskan* featured an article headlined "A Trip to Coon Town" and called it the "greatest Ragtime production of the Day." Unlike the soldier performance, the company that visited Skagway, under the direction of George H. Williams, was a professional acting troupe. The article noted Williams owned the rights to stage the play on the Pacific coast and reported that the "All Colored Company" produced "Clean and up-to-date Negro Comedy, Supported by some of the Leading Talent of the Colored Race."[44]

A Trip to Coon Town by Bob Cole was the first full-length Broadway musical comedy written, directed, performed, and produced exclusively by African Americans. It premiered in 1898 and ran in New York City for nearly twenty-five years. Cole's musical perpetuated many offensive stereotypes of Blacks, yet his efforts eventually led to productions that explored African themes and characters and sought to liberate Black musicals from white misconceptions. So Black musical comedy was in its early phase when it visited Skagway in 1901.[45]

An article the following day noted that the initial date for the show had been shifted due to scheduling issues. The production was booked to perform in Juneau, Douglas, Ketchikan, Fort Wrangel, and Sitka, so distances between venues and boat timetables forced the change. The article also noted, "A number of the best talent of Company L will also take part in the show, which promises to be something out of the ordinary."[46]

After another date change, A Trip to Coon Town finally played at the Elks Hall in Skagway at the end of September, though not as intended. The performance was spoiled by the "avariciousness or cussedness" of three of the lead performers, who made exorbitant wage demands at the last minute on director Williams, who then fired them. Williams offered to refund the ticket price to the audience, yet the people of Skagway refused, and the show went on without the main actors. The members of Company L who participated in the show, likely the same men who took the stage a month earlier, must have shared Williams's disappointment. Though judged a failure financially, the newspaper reported that the actors "acquitted themselves very creditably."[47]

New President

The reason for the second postponement of A Trip to Coon Town was the death of a president. William McKinley, the president who had led the nation to victory in the Spanish-American War, was shot in the abdomen by anarchist assassin Leon Czolgosz on September 6 and died of his wounds on September 14, 1901. The news of his death arrived in Skagway several days later and headlined the front page on September 18, 1901, followed by a period of mourning.[48]

McKinley was the last president who served in the Civil War and the only one who began his service as a private in the army. He served from 1861 until the end of the war with the Twenty-Third Ohio Volunteer Infantry, seeing action at Antietam and the Shenandoah Valley and earning a brevet commission as major. After the war McKinley returned to his home state to study law and entered politics, serving as governor of Ohio and as president of the United States beginning in 1897.[49]

African Americans voted for McKinley, hoping his Republican Party would appoint Blacks to government posts and take steps to end the lynching of Blacks. McKinley lost the support of some Blacks during his first term because of his silence on racial violence and promotion of reconciliation with the South. Yet he retained the support of Booker T. Washington and other key Black leaders, who continued to vote for the Republican Party. McKinley won a landslide reelection and was inaugurated for a second term in 1901, appointing Theodore Roosevelt as his vice president.[50]

Many Black Americans found President Theodore Roosevelt, McKinley's successor, more to their liking. A month after he took office, he invited Booker T. Washington to the White House for dinner, the first African American to be so honored. His effort to reach out to the leader of the African American community sparked protest and bitter criticism by many whites, especially in the South.

Roosevelt was known to Captain Jenks and some of the old veterans of Company L, since he fought with them in Cuba during the Spanish-American War at the head of the First U.S. Volunteer Cavalry. Yet some Black leaders felt Roosevelt owed them an apology for his disparaging remarks in a *Scribner's Magazine* article about the actions of some of the Buffalo Soldiers during the charge up San Juan Hill. In that article, he had accused the African American infantrymen of being unreliable without their white officers.[51]

Telegraphic Connection

Shortly after the inauguration of President Roosevelt, Skagway was connected by telegraph with the outside world. For the first two years in Skagway, Company L depended on messages carried by ships south to Seattle for retransmission to Washington DC. Beginning in September 1901, all this changed.

Congress appropriated funds for the extension of military telegraph and cable lines to Alaska in May 1900. As a result, the army sent Signal Corps officers and soldiers to various stations in Alaska to complete the work, including Skagway. The Signal Corps built more than twelve telegraph stations and laid 336 miles of line and cable to connect Alaska with the outside world. They also worked with Canadian authorities to extend the existing lines in that country to connect to the Alaskan system.[52]

Starting September 24, 1901, telegraphic communications opened between Skagway and Fort Egbert on the Upper Yukon River via the United States military and Canadian land lines. On that date, telegraph operators exchanged messages between the commanding officers of Fort Egbert, Skagway, and military authorities in Washington DC.[53]

As part of this project, the commanding general of the Department of Alaska also recommended an underwater cable be laid between Skagway and Juneau, Alaska. This enabled communications between Juneau and Camp Skagway, and from there to Washington DC. Signal Corps Major William A. Glassford was in Skagway supervising the work. The contractor completed this work on August 23, 1901, and the U.S. Army formally accepted the system after thirty days of successful operations.[54]

Along with the telegraph, there was one arrival of note at the end of August 1901 that signaled military permanence in Skagway. Commissary Sergeant August Luttge arrived at Camp Skagway to assist the commissary officer in the discharge of his duties. President McKinley, so recently assassinated, had begun his military service as a nineteen-year-old commissary sergeant with the Twenty-Third Ohio Volunteer Infantry during the Civil War.[55]

Commissary Sergeant August Luttge was a forty-year-old former sergeant in the Sixth U.S. Cavalry and first sergeant in the Fourteenth U.S. Infantry. Born in Germany, he enlisted in Seattle, Washington, in 1894, and after serving the requisite five years of service, was appointed a post commissary sergeant. Luttge, who was white, was assigned as part of the garrison at Camp Skagway and not to Company L.[56]

Captain Jenks stayed on in temporary command at Camp Skagway until Hovey returned and resumed command on October 17, 1901. Yet Jenks did not ship out in time to miss the historic flood of October 1901, his final crisis while commanding Company L.[57]

On October 13, 1901, the *Daily Alaskan* carried the headline "Skagway Experiences Flood. Maddened River Torrents Rush Out of Their Banks. Bridges Wash Away. Railroad Tied Up. Houses Are Inundated. Many Narrow Escapes." Captain Jenks and thirty men deployed in two wagons to reinforce an exposed riverbank and rescue people from homes threatened by the surge. The newspaper credited the soldiers with saving lives and property since they provided an immediate and organized response to this first great natural disaster in the recorded history of Skagway. The post return noted the company was "instrumental in saving considerable property during a flood, besides aiding the railroad line in getting U.S. mails through otherwise impossible" conditions.[58]

Fire was also a real danger to the residents of Skagway, as the soldiers learned the hard way during the blaze that destroyed their first home in Dyea. The buildings in the town were built entirely of timber and heated by wood-burning stoves, prone to catch fire. Since Camp Skagway shared the danger of a conflagration spreading in the town, Company L offered the use of soldiers in case of fire. The company turned out in mass to fight a fire when the alarm sounded, supplementing the local fire companies.[59]

One of the justifications for co-locating the barracks, storehouse, offices, and officer's quarters was for fire protection. One sentinel could keep the entire complex under watch for smoke and flames. Captain Jenks noted in a letter in May 1901 that fire was an ever-present danger, especially in the winter when a strong north wind blew. The location of the buildings occupied by the company in the northeastern corner of downtown was "the least liable of any point in the town to be swept by fire in case of conflagration."[60]

By 1901 Company L had developed such a close working relationship with the fire companies in Skagway that when one of the respected old firemen died, the soldiers participated in the funeral procession. After the funeral service of Robert M. Parkin, the deceased firefighter was placed upon a bier on a hose cart covered with an American flag. The fire department turned out in full force and uniform as a cortege, preceded by the draped colors of Company L and three army buglers. As they moved down Broadway past the barracks, "the colored troops stood at attention, with uncovered heads, and fell in at the rear of the procession when it had passed." The firemen and soldiers escorted the bier to the cemetery and attended final services at the grave.[61]

Jenks's Departure

Just before the great flood of October, the army sent Jenks orders to leave Skagway and report to a new assignment. He had served in Alaska for more than two years, directed the detachment at Fort Wrangel for a year, and commanded the garrison at Skagway nearly six months in the absence of Hovey, one of the most remote and lonely commands in the U.S. Army at the time.[62]

In the weeks before his departure, his many friends in Skagway celebrated his service to the community. In early October the *Daily Alaskan* reported under the headline "GIVE HIM A BANQUET" a stag dinner held at the Pack Train Restaurant in his honor. Ten of his best friends hosted the affair and "sipped to the success and good health of the popular officer."[63]

The venue for this stag dinner and the men who attended reflected the standing of Jenks. The Pack Train Restaurant was an institution in Skagway. Anton Stanish and Louis Ceovich established the restaurant in 1897, naming it after the pack trains that were the main means of transportation for miners before the appearance of the railroad. While other such establishments opened, closed, or traded hands, "the Pack Train remained, thrived, and became a fixture and a landmark." It remained in the same modest building for more than a dozen years, where Big Louie was the cook and Little Tony manned the counter.[64]

On the evening before the great flood of October 12, Isaac and Alice Jenks hosted a card party at their home with nine other couples one last time. This was another set of men and their wives with whom the Jenks socialized and played cards. Only Edward Bailey belonged to both groups of well-wishers, so he and Florence were likely closest to Isaac and Alice.[65]

Isaac, Alice, and Marion and Dorothy Jenks boarded a steamer for Seattle on October 30, 1901. He did not rejoin the regiment in the Philippines, since it was soon due to rotate back to the United States. Instead, the Twenty-Fourth Infantry sent him to command the Provisional Company at Angel Island, California, the station where the regiment sent soldiers from the Philippines to be discharged from the army. He remained there until the regiment returned to the United States the following year.[66]

By the summer and fall of 1901, the citizens of Skagway had grown to know the officers and men of the company. The white officers continued to mingle in upper social circles while the soldiers interacted with the growing African American community in the city. Over time, connections between some of the white citizens and Black soldiers expanded to something approaching acceptance.

The officers and soldiers of Skagway Barracks prevented trouble between whites and Tlingit, fought floods, improved medical services, connected Skagway with the outside world, and entertained the community. The talents of the Magnolia Four supplemented the connections created earlier by baseball and helped promote linkages between the Black soldiers and the white citizens of Skagway.

CHALLENGES

The general appearance and behavior of the officers and men
at the time of my visit evinced an excellent discipline, although
conditions were unfavorable thereto, the company having
been surrounded by saloons and demoralizing influences.

—GENERAL GEORGE M. RANDALL, 1902

Matters altered considerably for Captain Hovey and Company L by the last quarter of 1901 in Skagway. With Jenks gone, Hovey depended heavily on inexperienced Second Lieutenant Rains to run the company. Hovey still had Dr. Bailey and most of his original team of senior non-commissioned officers, and these veteran soldiers bore the lion's share of the leadership challenges. He needed these leaders, since many of the soldiers in the company were nearing completion of their three-year terms in Alaska.

Command Visit

Hovey witnessed army organizational changes in 1901 that directly affected the mission of his company. The army decided to eliminate the separate Department of Alaska and combine it again under the Department of the Columbia. Brigadier General George M. Randall realized the impracticality of commanding the department from the isolated post at Fort Saint Michael in the far north of Alaska. His recommendation to shift the headquarters south was approved by the War Department and he moved his headquarters to Vancouver Barracks, Washington, in late October 1901. He sailed out of Fort Saint Michael before winter closed the northern port to sea travel.[1]

On his way south to occupy his new headquarters, General Randall once again visited and inspected the command in Skagway, arriving on board the U.S. Army transport *Seward* in mid-October. He brought with him his entire staff, six officers in all. The short stop in Skagway allowed them time for an inspection of the barracks, hospital, and other company accommodations.[2]

Randall granted an interview with the *Daily Alaskan* and "expressed himself as being emphatically in favor of establishing in Skagway an army post." Randall had a long meeting with Captain Hovey, and each agreed Skagway was the logical choice for a military reservation from the strategic and logistical point of view. This was good news to the mayor and citizens of Skagway, who were keen to keep the troops to maintain security and support the local economy.[3]

Randall's summary of the situation he found in Skagway in his official report noted: "The company at Skagway has been quartered in rented buildings in the town for nearly three years. The buildings now occupied are the best available, but not suited for the purpose of a garrison. . . . The general appearance and behavior of the officers and men at the time of my visit evinced an excellent discipline, although conditions were unfavorable thereto, the company having been surrounded by saloons and demoralizing influences. This post is regarded as an important one, and I earnestly recommend the construction of permanent barracks and quarters at the earliest practical date."[4]

Randall's visit occurred at a challenging time for Hovey. The great flood of October had hit the town a week before. Moreover, Hovey had returned from six months of sick leave just two days prior to the visit. Thus, the fact that General Randall and his staff found "excellent discipline" in the appearance and behavior of the company is a tribute to Captain Jenks, who had commanded the post since May.[5]

Intoxicating Liquors

General Randall mentioned in his annual report the impact of a recent order by the War Department to control "intoxicating liquors" and forbid the consumption of alcohol on military posts. Alcohol consumption and drunkenness had long been an issue in the army, and commanders experimented with ways of managing this problem. Some commanders created post canteens or exchanges where they offered food, beer, and wine in a controlled atmosphere, encouraging men to spend their money and leisure time on post and stay out of trouble with the locals. Yet these canteens were a mixed success, and men always found other ways to obtain alcohol and get in trouble.[6]

Captain Hovey did not mention a post canteen or exchange at Skagway in his official correspondence or monthly post returns. If he had one, he would have closed it as a result of the new War Department policy. He wrote to the adjutant general, Department of Columbia: "I have the honor to inform you that there was no exchange at this camp for the period ending December 31, 1901."[7]

As General Randall mentioned in his report, the soldiers had ample opportunity to acquire alcohol within blocks of their barracks on Sixth Avenue. This despite the fact the number of saloons fell from one hundred to just sixteen at about the time the company moved to Skagway. Unhappily for Hovey, twelve of those sixteen were within five hundred feet of the soldier barracks.[8]

The issue of alcohol, where it was obtained, and its effect on his Black infantrymen was an especially vexing problem for Captain Hovey. Poet John Dryden penned, "Drinking is the soldier's pleasure," but it also sharpened his inclination to argue and fight. Adding racism to the equation compounded the trouble. Prejudice existed in Skagway, since the residents carried their bigotry with them to Alaska. Yet the records show few incidents involving soldiers being punished for drunk and disorderly conduct, which was probably attributable to the good leadership of the officers and noncommissioned officers of the company.

At least one incident involving soldiers and alcohol made front-page headlines the month of General Randall's visit. The *Daily Alaskan*, under the headline "SOLDIER THREW ROCKS," told of privates Julius Hutson and Marion Bullitte, who argued over a game of blackjack and got into a fight late one night at the Last Chance Saloon. Hutson, a former farmer from Kentucky, wisely beat a hasty retreat from the place. He paused on the street long enough to hurl two rocks through the door of the saloon, "barely missing some of his comrades." No damage was done, and Hutson was hustled back to the barracks by soldiers "where he might have time to reflect upon his sudden tendency toward artillery practice."[9]

Bullitte, a former cook from Kentucky, was not so lucky. He remained at the Last Chance, caused more trouble, and was arrested. The newspaper reported the next day the U.S. commissioner sentenced him to six months at Sitka and a fine of one hundred dollars, so he must have done some serious damage to people and property. If he failed to pay the fine, he would have to "bask fifty days longer in jail."[10]

Two weeks after the brawl, the newspaper related a front-page story about Bullitte's sea transit to Sitka under the title "HIS LAST LITTLE JOKE." While under way, the captain of the ship asked the soldier to "favor them with some music, as he was a fine singer and played the banjo." He did so for a while, but then quit, and refused an encore. He gave this excuse: "I wish to save all my vocal powers as it will doubtless be so quiet at [Sitka Prison] that to hear even my own voice will give me joy."[11]

Bawdy Houses

Only one incident made headlines in Skagway involving a Black soldier, a white prostitute, and disorderly behavior. Alcohol contributed. Private Robert Grant was refused services in April 1901 by Marie Melgrim, a white woman in one of the bawdy houses on Seventh Avenue. According to the newspaper, Grant retaliated by throwing a stone through the window of the front door of Melgrim's establishment. Rocks seemed to be the weapon of choice for the soldiers in Skagway. Grant promptly turned himself in to Deputy Marshal Snook and was arrested, tried by the U.S. commissioner, and sentenced to three months confinement in Sitka.[12]

The *Daily Alaskan* had some fun with the account of the incident, titling the story the "Costly Rock." The article was one of the few times editor John Troy used the name of a prostitute in the newspaper, likely because a Black soldier was charged and not a white citizen or the white woman. Calling Melgrim "Sweet Marie," the report called the rock a murderous-looking affair when it was shown at the hearing. The report also noted Private Grant showed up at Snook's office acting "as if he had been in a mix-up with John Barleycorn," a period phrase for whiskey.[13]

That the *Daily Alaskan* mentioned the names of Grant and Melgrim is noteworthy, since the gentlemen's agreement in Skagway normally precluded publicity about prostitutes. The newspaper solely publicized disturbances involving prostitutes when they implicated African Americans or Native Americans. This was like the exclusive use of the term "riots" when they involved the Black soldiers or the Tlingit.

The only other time a newspaper editor mentioned the name of a prostitute and her customer was in January 1899. The article appeared in January 1899 under the headline "Perforated Siwash," using the derogatory word for a Native American derived from the French *sauvage*. The story detailed how "soiled dove" Jessie Rounds shot and killed a half-Tlingit man named George Johnson in White Pass City, a rough tent camp twelve miles north of Skagway. Rounds, fellow prostitute May Bark, and blacksmith Patrick Murphy, who supplied the gun, were sent to jail in Sitka. They languished there five months before the authorities acquitted them of murder. As was the case with Grant, the reporter "left it to the reader to explain why a prostitute would reject a customer because of his race."[14]

Grant was a twenty-four-year-old former sailor from Philadelphia on his initial enlistment in the army, yet not his first in the U.S. military. He enlisted as an ordinary seaman in June 1898 and served on several navy ships during the Spanish-American War. The navy gave Grant an honorable discharge in October 1898, at the end of the war. He reenlisted in the navy two days after his discharge, deserted after two months, and joined the army three days after jumping ship. Military law barred the enrollment of deserters, but the enlistment officer did not know Grant was AWOL from the navy.[15]

Though assigned to Hovey's command, Grant was not a member of Company L. He came to Alaska as an infantry soldier assigned to the company and later transferred to the Hospital Corps. A soldier had to serve a minimum of one year of competent service and pass a rigorous test before such a transfer, so Grant must have shown initial promise.[16]

After release from prison in June, Grant returned to Skagway to resume his duties at the hospital. Yet old habits sometimes die hard, and Grant absconded in September, one of a select group to desert from both the army and navy.[17]

Captain Hovey dealt with at least one other soldier involved with prostitution who did not make the local paper. Before Private Walter McMurry's desertion in October 1899 (described earlier), McMurry had, according to Hovey, "connected himself with a house of prostitution near the barracks" and performed "various different kinds of service for them." He deserted and traveled with the proprietor of the house to Dawson, Canada. Since both Rose Arnold and Ruth Brown, the two Black prostitutes on Sixth Avenue, had worked in Dawson before coming to Skagway, there may have been a connection between them.[18]

The bawdy houses like that of Marie Melgrim on Seventh Avenue formed the core of what Skagway called the "sporting world" or the demimonde. Some rented rooms in the upper floors of saloons to ply their trade. The proprietors of these establishments maintained their ignorance of what happened in the privacy of the women's room, hoping to avoid being charged with operating a house of prostitution. Other prostitutes worked out of small one-room cribs on Seventh Avenue or the adjoining alleys.[19]

Religion and Education

Company L had no chaplain on staff to offset the temptations posed by the bawdy houses of Skagway. The Buffalo Soldier regiments were the only Regular Army units assigned regimental chaplains, also referred to as "Holy Joes." Yet Captain Allen Allensworth, the regimental chaplain, was with the Twenty-Fourth in the Philippines, and Camp Skagway too small to warrant a post chaplain.[20]

The Baptist church in Skagway provided religious services for the Black soldiers of the company who wished to attend church each Sunday. The church also hosted a "colored" Sunday school group, which served a double purpose. It first provided a religious education and promoted learning through reading and discussing the Bible. The *Daily Alaskan* noted: "The colored Sunday school at the Baptist church is a new feature and has had a good and zealous attendance from the start." It also served an important social function, giving the soldiers a safe place to gather outside of the restrictive bounds of the military.[21]

Skagway's Young Men's Christian Association (YMCA) also served as a place where the Black soldiers could learn and socialize. Captain Hovey received guidance from the Adjutant General's Office in Washington supporting the work of the YMCA and encouraging commanders to make their services available to soldiers. Secretary of War Elihu Root officially granted the International Committee of the YMCA permission to "establish their work among the Regular Army and volunteer soldiers at the various posts and camps of the Army." He directed commanders to facilitate the YMCA's efforts "to provide helpful social and unsectarian religious influences."[22]

Skagway's YMCA opened its doors to the Black soldiers of the company, setting aside two evenings a week for them, Tuesday and Friday, for class work and recreation. The YMCA director also set aside evenings of the week for other groups, with separate nights for women. The branch in Skagway had a total membership of about three hundred, of which thirty were Black soldiers. It offered athletic amenities such as a gymnasium, basketball court, and baths, as well as a library, reading room, and classrooms spread over several buildings in town.[23]

According to the *Daily Alaskan*, Corporal James Reed was invited to speak at one "of the businessmen's lectures at the Y.M.C.A. hall." The article noted Reed would discuss "the progress of the negro race, a subject of which he has made a special study." A report the following day noted under the headline "Full House Greets Mr. Reed" that "the talk in itself was entertaining and instructive, and Mr. Reed, in a scholarly handling of the subject, reflected credit upon the people of whom he spoke, and of whom he is one of the most advanced types."[24]

That Corporal Reed was invited to speak to white businessmen in Skagway is remarkable on its face. The newspaper coverage before and after Reed's talk make this event even more extraordinary. The reporter provided Reed's rank of corporal as well as his full name of James Edward Bell Reed. The glowing review in the Saturday edition is noteworthy, though the reporter seemed to qualify Reed's performance by commenting that the soldier was "one of the most advanced types." James Reed was a thirty-one-year-old former printer from Charleston, Ohio, on his first enlistment in the army. Perhaps his background as a printer impressed the reporter as much as his "scholarly handling of the subject."[25]

Not everyone in Skagway was happy about the presence of Black soldiers at the YMCA. It was one of the few unsegregated institutions in the United States in this era. One woman was quoted in the newspaper saying, "I do not care to go where I must meet colored men. I have Southern blood, it is true, but I have the greatest respect for a colored person in his proper place." The same woman complained that she objected to seeing a Black soldier playing on a basketball team with white men from Skagway. When some members requested that YMCA secretary W. A. Reid exclude the soldiers from the club, he responded that the "Young Men's Christian Association knows no color line. It stands for young men regardless of nationality the world over."[26]

The reporter used his own biased views to skew the argument. The headline of the story was "LINE DRAWN," even though the opposite was true. Under the headline appeared the bold headings "Objections Arise to Colored Men in YMCA" and "WITHDRAWALS MADE," followed by "Some of the Members of the Association Displeased with the Fact Sons of Ham Are Permitted in the Organization." One had to read quite far into the article to find that Reid recognized no color line and that only seven of three hundred members withdrew their memberships because of the issue.[27]

The *Daily Alaskan* coverage recounted the Black soldiers' reaction to the controversy:

The colored members themselves seem to take different views on the matter. Several of them were asked yesterday if they knew about the affair. All said they had heard nothing up to that time of any of the whites having withdrawn and knew of none of the soldiers having drawn out or expressed any intention or desire to do so. One of the colored men stated he would keep his membership and intended to stay in regardless of what were the likes and dislikes of the white members. Three other soldiers took another view of the matter. They wanted to withdraw. One appeared at the secretary's office last evening to ask for withdrawal of his name. He stated he was not going to remain where he was not wanted and where someone might object to his presence and insult him. He thought there were other places he could find suitable society.[28]

To the credit of the *Daily Alaskan*, it ceased publishing the comments of citizens who wrote letters to the editor complaining about the Black soldiers being members at the YMCA. The editor noted: "The *Daily Alaskan* cannot afford to sacrifice valuable news for communications on questions already shifted to a matter of personal opinions."[29]

The newspaper coverage of Reed's speech and the "color line" at the YMCA provide some important insights into the state of race relations in Skagway at the time. There was still a clear color line in Skagway among the citizens and businesses, with the YMCA and Baptist church proving the exceptions. In a case by case basis, the white residents might praise an exception to the rule, as in the case of Corporal Reed. Yet most still considered the soldiers "colored men" or the "sons of Ham," a term used for Blacks at the time referring to the descendants of Noah's second son. Collectively, the white Skagwayans treated the African American soldiers as a separate class of people.

Shooting Competition

To demonstrate another aspect of his soldiers, their shooting skills, Captain Hovey agreed to let Lieutenant Rains organize a shooting contest with local Skagwayans. The *Daily Alaskan* suggested, as in baseball, that one team might be formed among the citizens to compete against another of soldiers. Both parties agreed to a range placed on the beach where a hundred-yard distance might be achieved.[30]

Under normal training conditions, the soldiers of Company L competed for marksmanship and sharpshooter badges and pins. If a soldier could hit a target eight times out of ten at six hundred yards, he earned a marksmanship award that he could wear on his uniform. If he hit a target eight times out of ten at one thousand yards, he won the more coveted Sharpshooter Award. During training in Skagway, the company was forced to fire at targets of two hundred and three hundred yards only, for lack of a longer range.[31]

The soldiers fired the modern Springfield Model 1896 Krag-Jørgensen bolt-action rifle. It was the first .30-caliber rifle employed by the army, and the first to use smokeless powder in a rimmed centerfire cartridge. A .30-caliber firearm has a barrel diameter of roughly .30 inches or 7.62 millimeters. It fired a pointed cartridge, which increased its range, accuracy, and velocity, loaded into a five-round magazine.[32]

In October 1901 the Skagway Rifle Club beat a picked team of soldiers and "won the championship." Under a headline of "BLAZED AWAY FIERCELY," the *Daily Alaskan* noted that the "team from Company L were handily beaten," despite the unfavorable weather. The winner won a "handsome silver loving cup lined with gold, which was offered as a prize by P.E. Kern, a local Skagway jeweler."[33]

The newspaper article provided the names of the contestants of both teams. The Company L team included Lieutenant Edward Rains, Sergeant William Hanson, Musician John W. Oby, Private James H. Ballard, Private William Fox, and Private James C. Matthews. Lieutenant Rains competed in this event as the team captain. Customarily an officer would not have participated with enlisted men in such a competition, though exceptions might have been made for a necessary military skill such as marksmanship. The civilian captain of the team, J. W. Snook, was the deputy marshal in town and likely a good shot.[34]

Klondike Matter

In a matter more consequential to Hovey, the *New York Times* reported in November 1901 a troubling occurrence under the front-page headline "Yukon Miners Want a Free Government." It described a "huge conspiracy existing in Dawson and ramifying to Skagway, Victoria, Vancouver, and Seattle for the overthrow of the local government of the Klondike and the establishing of a republic, with Dawson as its capital." The story first broke in the *San Francisco Call* on November 17, 1901, speculating that prominent residents of Skagway were ringleaders, weapons had been smuggled in over the railroads, and five thousand miners awaited the call to arms.[35]

Several newspapers also recounted a midnight conference on the plot held in Skagway on November 5, 1901, between Inspector James Corrigan of the North West Mounted Police, Judge Melville C. Brown of the U.S. District Court, Deputy U.S. Marshal James M. Shoup, U.S. District Attorney Robert A. Frederick, and Captain Hovey. Reportedly, it was the seventh such meeting held on the issue. Despite the tabloid account, no evidence exists these meetings ever occurred. Subsequent reporting indicated this intrigue was much ado about nothing.[36]

The conspiracy theory had its root in a kernel of truth, even though it never proved a serious threat. In September 1901 the NWMP discovered a group of American miners, calling themselves the Order of the Midnight Sun, plotting to take over the Yukon. Many of the order were also members of the Arctic Brotherhood. Canadian authorities launched a full investigation, but concluded the conspiracy was "too much of a bubble to be taken seriously." Yet the new superintendent of the NWMP detachment in Whitehorse, Z. T. Wood, sent a letter to Captain Hovey in mid-October 1901 telling him about the plot.[37]

The Canadians were concerned enough about the affair to send two NWMP officers to Skagway to investigate. Superintendent Philip C. H. Primrose and Detective J. H. Seely boarded the train to Skagway on Sunday, October 20, 1901, and drank heavily en route. Troy had great fun with the result under the front-page headline "PRIMROSE IN DIS-

GRACE," noting the two having "several glasses of Canadian hootch abroad, proceeded to sample some of the real stuff." After arrival in Skagway, the two visited several bars, pausing at the house of an American officer to insult his wife. Seely at some point retired to his hotel, but Primrose continued to drink. Finally, at 3:00 a.m. Monday morning, a night watchman arrested Primrose "splashing around in the mud near the Peerless Theatre," and locked him in jail. Primrose was quoted in the newspaper as yelling, "To hell with the night watchman, to hell with the American people, and to hell with the American flag."[38]

Deputy U.S. Marshal Snook released Primrose the following morning, after he pleaded guilty in court to being drunk and disorderly and paid a ten-dollar fine. He quickly departed for Ottawa, while Seely remained in Skagway to meet with Captain Hovey. Hovey assured Seely that he "would prevent any organized body of men going into Yukon Territory." He also informed Seely that once told of the conspiracy, he had warned members of the order "he would not permit any such organization to exist in Skagway." He had admonished the mayor of Skagway, an alleged supporter of the order, and informed Seely that Fred J. Clark, a ringleader of the conspiracy, had just departed for Seattle. Seely then shipped out to Seattle in pursuit of Clark.[39]

Hovey made no official mention of the meetings or the event in his monthly post returns for October 1901. The matter certainly affected his chief mission in Alaska, maintaining the status quo on the border until an agreement was signed by the United States and Great Britain. He likely conducted his own investigation, concluded there was no serious threat, and handled the matter locally. Since he was a member of the Arctic Brotherhood and many members of that organization were also in the order, he was in a unique position to intercede in the affair.[40]

The *Daily Alaskan* downplayed the rumors and devoted a short article to the plot on December 3, 1901. The newspaper noted: "No one will take the conspiracy story seriously. Residents of Skagway must have heard of the plotting had there been any movement looking to the overthrow of the government. . . . No, the story was made out of whole cloth and should not be given the slightest degree of credence."[41]

The matter did raise the interest of the army Department of the Columbia headquarters at Vancouver Barracks, Washington. General Randall sent an urgent letter to Hovey in early December 1901 with questions concerning the "Klondike" matter. Hovey assured him "there is no cause for anxiety, there is no chance for trouble, and if ever there was anything to do, so far as action from Skagway was concerned, it is absolutely all over." It sounds like there was indeed something to the Klondike matter, yet it never had a serious chance of getting off the ground.[42]

Departures

The end of 1901 and beginning of 1902 witnessed scores of personnel losses due to attrition in Company L. Captain Hovey knew these losses were coming, since the company formed in early 1899 largely with new recruits who enlisted for three years, meaning their contract obligations ended by early 1902. Hovey watched helplessly as the men of his command approached the end of their terms, hoping some would reenlist and remain in Alaska.

As a recruiting officer, Hovey had the authority to reenlist any of his soldiers for another three-year term if they were "able-bodied, free from disease, of good character, and temperate habits." As an incentive to reenlist, the army offered soldiers reenlistment pay if they served continuously longer than five years, regardless of rank. A soldier received two dollars per month more after his second consecutive enlistment and, thereafter, another dollar for each additional consecutive reenlistment term. A soldier had to reenlist for another term within three months of his previous discharge to qualify for this continuous service pay.[43]

When Sergeant O'Connor completed his enlistment and was discharged in November 1901, Captain Hovey rated his character as "good." O'Connor reenlisted for another three-year term the following day. For a career sergeant and former first sergeant, "good" was not a satisfactory rating by any measure. Recall that O'Connor completed his previous enlistment shortly after the regiment returned from victory in Cuba and was given a character rating of "excellent." Something had happened during the first year in Alaska for Hovey to lose his high regard for O'Connor.[44]

Hovey discharged Sergeant William Hanson at the end of his service in December 1901, giving him a character rating of "excellent," and he reenlisted for another term. In December the company also lost three privates, of whom only one, Private Robert Cotton, reenlisted. One soldier who did not reenlist was James Reed, who had spoken so eloquently at the YMCA the previous year. Hovey granted furloughs to both Hanson and Cotton, and they eventually returned to Skagway. As post commander, he was authorized to grant his soldiers furloughs of up to twenty days; longer furloughs required department commander approval.[45]

Amid the departures, the soldiers celebrated New Year's Eve. The *Daily Alaskan* reported: "Corporal Benjamin Green, as master of ceremonies, presided over a spirited dance last night, attended by the gay spirits of Company L. The function occurred in Anderson's hall and was a full blown and complete affair from grand march to cakewalk." Green, the master of ceremonies, was also close to departure.[46]

The soldiers held a dance again in January to celebrate the expiring enlistment terms of some of their fellows. The dance, held again at Anderson's hall, featured the "entire colored colony of Skagway." The event was quite a success with the ladies "radiant in party dresses, and they were gallantly swung to the best dance music that Skagway could afford."[47]

The tempo of exits quickened by early 1902. In January the company lost a corporal and seven privates at the expiration of their service. Not all these soldiers abandoned the army. Four of them chose to leave Alaska, return to their homes for a short visit, and then reenlist later. For example, both privates Doc L. Harrill and Landon Jackson traveled to Tennessee at army expense, spent a month as civilians, and enlisted again to be assigned to the Twenty-Fifth Infantry. To them, this was like a vacation with travel expenses paid by the army. Soldiers know the rules and use them to their advantage.[48]

At least one soldier who departed in January ended his enlistment and remained in Alaska: George L. Wilson. Wilson was a thirty-six-year-old former laborer from Boston who had served in the volunteers during the Spanish-American War. He may have stayed in Skagway for a time, but he eventually sought his fortune in the gold fields elsewhere in Alaska.

In February 1902 departures surged with the loss of four noncommissioned officers and sixteen privates. Quartermaster Sergeant Charles Reed and corporals Thomas Martin, Herbert Williams, and Edgar Merritt all reached the end of their enlistment terms. Of these, only Williams enlisted again in Alaska, though Martin and Merritt rejoined again later in the United States. Sergeant Reed returned home to Pittsburgh, lived as a civilian two and a half months, and signed up to be assigned to Company L again, retaining his reenlistment pay. None of the privates enlisted again in Alaska, though six later rejoined the army after returning home.[49]

One of the soldiers who enlisted for another term, Corporal Herbert Williams, must have been well liked in Skagway. The *Daily Alaskan* noted in the "Personal Mention" section: "Herbert Williams, the colored soldier, and family, left on the *Cottage City*." Hovey's regimental return acknowledged the corporal was granted a month-long furlough beginning February 19, 1902, a bonus for his reenlistment. Williams returned to duty with the company the following month.[50]

A flood of soldiers departed in March 1902, representing the loss of nearly a third of the enlisted strength. Captain Hovey discharged sergeants Orestus J. Kincaid and Allen McGee, as well as corporals Charles J. White, Benjamin Green, and James M. Banks. Of these, only Sergeant McGee reenlisted in Alaska. Benjamin Green, the former player-coach of the baseball team and leader of the Magnolia Four, chose to remain and eventually moved to the interior of Alaska.[51]

Also reaching the end of their terms in March 1902 were cooks Elijah Lee and Jacob A. Pon, musicians Joseph A. Nash and John W. Oby, and artificer John E. Davis. Only the two cooks and artificer reenlisted and stayed in Skagway. Moreover, twenty-four privates reached the end of their terms, and only two reenlisted again and remained in Skagway. Ten more men left Alaska and later enlisted for another army term in the States. One private, John A. Perkins, lingered in Skagway and joined the Black community.[52]

In April, the month before Company L shipped out, only two additional soldiers reached the end of their enlistment terms. Corporal Augustus Snoten, the oldest man in the company, ended his term and reenlisted. He had been in the army continuously for twenty-six years since first enlisting in 1876. The other was Corporal Eugene Swanson, who chose to stay in Alaska. Swanson married an African American widow named Amelia Beckwith from Skagway and, like Wilson and Green, moved elsewhere in Alaska.[53]

For these African American soldiers who left the army honorably after one term, a discharge paper with an officers' character rating of excellent, very good, or good was a particularly important document. By assessing the soldiers' character, the officer was vouching for his service, conduct, and behavior. In an era when few Blacks had paper records, this was an exceedingly valuable credential when seeking post-army civilian employment or a government job. Captain Charles Young, Ninth U.S. Cavalry, the senior of three serving Black Regular Army officers at the time, recounted how precious his father's Civil War discharge certificate was to him. It was the only written record of performance he was given in his lifetime, and for many of the former soldiers who served in Skagway, their discharge certificate held similar value.

To most privates in Company L, army service was a temporary occupation, not a career. Despite this, these short-term soldiers learned some valuable lessons in their brief time in the service. A few learned or honed skills that might be valuable later in civilian life. Yet the most important virtues they took home were the essential soldierly traits of good order and military discipline. These translated into respect for authority, personal pride, neatness, and responsibility, all skills useful out of uniform.

There were other losses in the company due to sickness and death. Private William Mack died at Fort Bayard, New Mexico, in November 1901 of pulmonary tuberculosis. Mack had been sent to the hospital at Fort Bayard in October 1901 for treatment. Private Arthur Wheeler died in Skagway in December 1901 of typhoid fever. Corporal Edward G. Dewey received orders in December 1901 to proceed to the Army and Navy General Hospital in Hot Springs, Arkansas, for treatment. This facility specialized in the treatment of rheumatism, arthritis, lumbago, and dysentery in soldiers. Dewey was discharged with a surgeon's certificate of disability in March 1902.[54]

Shortfalls also resulted from soldiers who committed crimes and were sentenced to prison. Private John M. Kirk was assigned to Company L in May 1901 yet never joined the company. He was convicted of a general court-martial en route and served his sentence at Vancouver Barracks. Private Thomas Williams had been convicted by the civil authorities in Skagway of larceny, sent to prison in Sitka in June 1901, and discharged without honor in July 1901. And the March 1902 post return listed Henry Johnston as "absent in the hands of civil authority." Captain Hovey had to carry these men on his books until they were officially discharged by the army.[55]

All these losses combined to reduce the company to approximately half its authorized strength. In March 1902 Hovey listed as present for duty 3 officers, 1 commissary sergeant, 6 hospital corpsmen, 8 sergeants, 7 corporals, 1 musician, 1 artificer, 26 privates, and 2 cooks. The company had deployed three years earlier to Alaska with a total of 91 infantry privates. Without replacements, Hovey was perilously close to being unable to carry out his mission.[56]

Hovey requested thirty "Colored" recruits be sent to Skagway to replace his losses. The Department of the Columbia turned down his request: "In view of the fact that Company L, 24th Infantry, will be returned from Alaska in a short time, it is not the intention of the Department Commander to send more recruits to Skagway." This was the first official notice to Captain Hovey of the company's pending departure.[57]

Captain Hovey ended his second full year in Alaska facing several challenges. Despite the good discipline and welcome contributions of Black soldiers who served honorably, Skagway exhibited the era's persistent racism. While certain institutions such as the YMCA and the Baptist church embraced the African American soldiers, the citizens of Skagway maintained a clear color line.

The months leading to the first quarter of 1902 witnessed significant command changes for the officers and soldiers of the company. Hovey and his men struggled to carry out their missions despite personnel losses due to expiring enlistment terms, disciplinary issues, sickness, and death, while their time in Alaska was rapidly approaching a close.

DEPARTURE

> When the *Seattle* whistled yesterday evening the
> men of Company L were taken to the freight spur of
> Moore's wharf in heavy marching order and as soon
> as the passengers landed were marched aboard.
> —*DAILY ALASKAN*, May 16, 1902

The U.S. Army rotated its troops regularly among its scattered forts across the country and throughout the world at the turn of the twentieth century. In the absence of a war or other crisis, this change occurred every three years. The army did this to keep the regiments from home-steading and spread the burden of garrisoning hardship posts overseas or on the western frontier. Most of the Twenty-Fourth Infantry, less Company L, had been posted to the Philippine Islands since the summer of 1899 and was due for rotation back to the United States in June 1902. The company's time to rejoin the regiment had come.[1]

Replacements

The first week of April 1902, two officers and fifty enlisted men arrived in Skagway by steamer to begin the process of replacing Company L. The two officers, First Lieutenant Louis S. Chappelear and Second Lieutenant Earnest S. Wheeler, commanded a mixed detachment of white artillerymen from the Thirty-Second and 106th Companies, Coast Artillery Corps. Despite the name, the new soldiers brought no heavy artillery with them. They were the precursor force sent to Skagway to replace the Buffalo Soldiers and begin building a permanent base.[2]

The U.S. Army Coast Artillery Corps was responsible for the coastal and harbor defense of the United States and its new territories. It was a new branch, formed in 1901 when army leaders realized the need for heavy fixed artillery. The Thirty-Second and 106th Companies were 2 of the 126 new numbered companies of the Coast Artillery Corps created just one year earlier. These Coast Artillery Corps companies freed up line units like Company L for other contingencies, such as garrisoning interior posts or fighting overseas.[3]

Captain Hovey remained in command of the army garrison after the arrival of the two officers and fifty artillerymen, awaiting official orders on the reassignment of his company. Where Hovey billeted the newly arrived white artillerymen is unknown. He certainly had plenty of barracks space since his company had shrunk to less than half its original authorized strength. Yet housing white and Black soldiers together would have posed some logistical problems. Hovey likely solved this by keeping his men in the newer barracks on the north side of Sixth Avenue and temporarily billeting the white artillerymen across the street in the old Hotel Astoria barracks. It is also possible the newly arrived troops camped in tents, as Company L had done three years earlier.[4]

The Department of the Columbia informed Hovey at the end of April that his company would be relieved by the 106th Company, Coast Artillery Corps. A week later Hovey got word that the commander and balance of the 106th Company would arrive at Camp Skagway on May 15, 1902. On this date Captain Hovey would officially relinquish command of Camp Skagway and depart with his company.[5]

Baseball

The railroad, firemen, and soldier teams were already organizing for the baseball season when the artillerymen arrived. Because of the pending departure of Company L, there may have been some urgency to getting the 1902 season underway. Both the Skagway and soldier teams hoped to squeeze in another series of games before departure.[6]

In mid-April, a news article reported a membership meeting of the White Pass & Yukon Employees Club to organize a baseball team. Players voiced great enthusiasm for the season and elected E. A. Murphy as manager and Clarence Olsen as captain of the team. The article noted "very promising material" for a winning baseball team and also promised that equipment and uniforms would be "sent for on the first boat."[7]

The White Pass team planned to begin practice as soon as the playing field was ready and intended to challenge teams "from Seattle to Dawson." A tentative list of prospective players included: Charles De Succa, Clarence Olsen, Mark Phelps, Edward Tholin, Ed Barry, Lee Gault, and George B. Daniels. Olsen, Phelps, Tholin, and Barry played on the White Pass team in years past. They also hoped to have one of their best players, Van Brocklin, "back from the south" before the season opener.[8]

Later in April, the *Daily Alaskan* ran a story under the title "Men and Boys Are Throwing the Sphere," celebrating the arrival of the baseball season in Skagway. The piece mentioned the "railroad boys'" practice the day prior and the first game played between the newsboy and the schoolboy teams. The schoolboys won the game 26–17 in an offensive slugfest.[9]

The members of the Skagway Fire Department had their own organizational meeting in late April 1902 to prepare for the coming baseball season. They elected Harry St. Clair as manager and H. D. Kirmse as captain. The article noted they would have uniforms made and would commence practice in a few days. The firemen lagged the White Pass team in their preparations for the season and did not complete arrangements before the departure of the soldiers in May 1902.[10]

The newspaper did not report on the organizational activities of the soldier team. The soldier nine had lost many of their best players between January and March, when many of the Buffalo Soldiers completed their three-year enlistments and departed. Past team captain and first baseman Green, shortstop Sims, second baseman Jennings, third baseman Oby, and outfielders Pate, Morton, Bracy, and Mack no longer served in the company, so the soldier team had to field at least eight new players.

The *Daily Alaskan* reported two baseball milestones in 1902. First, organizers planned to improve the old ball grounds near the sawmill and build a proper stadium, complete with grandstand and wire netting. Second, avid fan H. D. Kirmse purchased a silver cup for the winner of the three teams competing for the 1902 championship. This came to be called the Kirmse Cup.[11]

A subsequent article focused on improvements to the ballfield under the headline "WILL FIX GROUNDS." The piece noted the "fans of Skagway will have their diamond on the baseball grounds well-arranged before the end of the week." U.S. Commissioner J. J. Rogers, another baseball fan, offered to donate "cinders for the runs between the bases" so the playing field would be in condition for teams to practice the following week.[12]

The soldiers assisted the citizens of Skagway in preparing the ballfield for the coming season. The newspaper mentioned in late April: "The baseball fans were out with the military mules clearing the ball grounds yesterday." Company L had eight draft mules used to pull the unit's assigned wagons, cannon, and Gatling gun. The article also reported the first game of the season would "probably be played Sunday."[13]

Company L's team beat a "mixed nine of Firemen and White Pass boys," on Sunday, May 4, 1902, the first game of the season. This all-star team picked from the best firemen and railroad players in town served as a practice game for the Kirmse Cup series. The newspaper did not elaborate on a score or the names of players.[14]

Ugly Incident

The same weekend of the first baseball game, two white soldiers of the newly arrived Thirty-Second Company got into an altercation with a former Black soldier in Skagway. Private Edward G. Davidson and another white artilleryman were walking past the rear of the Commerce Saloon on Broadway, not far from the barracks, when a white woman asked them to protect her from John A. Perkins, a man who had been discharged from Company L two months earlier. She was likely an employee of one of the bawdy houses in town, as no "respectable" woman would have been by herself at night in an alley behind a saloon. Perkins made a lunge at Davidson with a razor, cutting him from behind the left ear down under his chin, nearly severing his jugular vein.[15]

The *Daily Alaskan* printed the essence of the story several days after the incident, yet there was more to the episode. Private Davidson and another member of the Thirty-Second Company, Private Henry A. Hansen, had summary court-martial charges proffered against them by First Lieutenant Chappelear on May 5, 1902. This was likely the result of their part in the altercation with Perkins, so they were clearly not blameless in the affair. Private Davidson proved anything but a model soldier; he deserted in 1904 and was apprehended and dishonorably discharged in 1905.[16]

Perkins was a twenty-four-year-old former laborer from Buckingham County, Virginia, who enlisted in the army in Philadelphia in 1899. He was one of the fifty-six privates to end his enlistment in early 1902, separating on March 15. When soldiers left the army, commanders noted an assessment of the soldier's character, ranging between not good, good, very good, and excellent. This rating was sent to the War Department and noted in the soldier's enlistment record. Perkins was the only private separating in early 1902 rated by Captain Hovey as "not good" and therefore not eligible to reenlist. Perkins chose to stay after he severed his ties with the army and joined the small Black community in Skagway.[17]

Private Perkins had been a troublemaker for Captain Hovey and Company L from the beginning. He and Private Harry Stewart had gone AWOL on the trip north to Alaska, earning Perkins two months in confinement at the Presidio of San Francisco from May to July 1899. After joining the company in Skagway in August 1899, he continued to be a problem-soldier until he left the army in March 1902.[18]

A week after the slashing incident, Perkins was fined five hundred dollars and sentenced to six months in jail in Sitka. U.S. Commissioner J. J. Rogers conducted the trial instead of the district judge in the interest of time and availability of witnesses. The court extended the sentence to fourteen months in default of the fine payment. By the time Perkins was released from prison, the company had been gone from Alaska for more than a year.[19]

Kirmse Cup

A week before the company's departure, the *Daily Alaskan* reported: "The members of the White Pass baseball nine are out practicing every night and expect to put up a strong game next Sunday." Two days later the paper noted that the "first baseball game of the series that will decide the championship of Skagway and entail the possession of the Kirmse trophy will be played on the baseball grounds Sunday between the White Pass boys and the soldiers." The game was scheduled for 2:30 p.m. on May 11, 1902.[20]

In preparation for the game, the firemen and railroad workers erected a grandstand and planned to charge twenty-five cents for admission, with the proceeds used to maintain the field and pay for equipment. Another piece ran the following morning encouraging fans to get out and "root" during the "hot game between the railroad and soldier nines." The contest had come a long way from its humble beginnings three years earlier.[21]

Details of the game played on Sunday appeared in the *Daily Alaskan* when newsboys hawked the next morning edition on Tuesday, May 13; no paper was printed Monday. On the fourth page under the headline "WHITE PASS BOYS LOSE FIRST GAME," the article recorded the soldiers trounced the railroad team by a score of 10-0. The story blamed the loss on "lack of practice and inability to find the sphere for safe hits." Despite this, the reporter found the game "one of the most interesting played on the local diamond."[22]

The White Pass team "practically lost the game" in the first innings due to bad pitching by Clarence Olsen. In the first two innings he failed to strike a man out, hit two batters, and walked two more. The soldiers managed to score five runs in those first two innings, after which "the White Pass boys seemed to lose heart." The railroad team failed to get hits, though their fielding was "brilliant at times."[23]

Olsen covered third base well after he was replaced as pitcher by Eddie Tholin in the third inning. John Phelps also played well as did much of the White Pass team on defense. These were the only railroad team players mentioned, who, according to the account, "played hard." The article chocked up the loss to "lack of teamwork." The newspaper was always quick to find excuses for the White Pass team and rarely found positive things to say about the soldier team.[24]

According to the report, the railroad nine was "unable to find Whirlwind Freeman for safe hits." The soldier team appeared to have some talented new players from the replacements who arrived since the past baseball season. The article opined: "Several of the soldier players are not new to the game and the new men, the third baseman, nicknamed 'Red Stockings' and the shortstop, in base running, showed that they had been on the diamond many times before." The implication was clear: the soldiers had some unfair advantage.[25]

William Freeman, who pitched for the soldier team against Skagway during the 1901 series, seemed to be the only holdover from the former Company L nine. Red Stockings at third base was William Fox, who had replaced William Sims from the previous year. The shortstop, who played well, was Thomas Kennedy, mentioned in a later article at that position. Unlike the previous two seasons, when the Daily Alaskan showed a familiarity with the soldiers on the team, only three members were mentioned by name. Perhaps the new players were not yet familiar to the editor of the paper.[26]

One of the new players, William "Red Stockings" Fox, was a thirty-seven-year-old career soldier born in Richmond, Virginia. Fox, who enlisted in 1884 in Louisville, Kentucky, had served eighteen years with the Twenty-Fourth Infantry as an infantry private and wagoner. Fox left the army in September 1900 and, after spending six months as a civilian, reenlisted and was assigned to Company L, arriving in Skagway in late April, just in time for the 1902 baseball season.[27]

The only other new player mentioned was shortstop Thomas Kennedy. He was a twenty-six-year-old former volunteer soldier born in Stanford, Kentucky. He had served previously with Company D, Forty-

Ninth U.S. Volunteer Infantry. The Forty-Ninth was one of two African American volunteer regiments organized for service in the Philippine War. Unlike the Buffalo Soldier regiments, the Forty-Ninth was led by Black company grade officers (lieutenants and captains). Kennedy was discharged in June 1901, enlisted in the regulars in July 1901, and was assigned to Company L, Twenty-Fourth Infantry. Kennedy had arrived in August, too late to play in the 1901 baseball season.[28]

The last paragraph about the Sunday game noted a controversy concerning the umpire. According to the story: "Lieut. Rains was umpire to the sixth inning when the White Pass boys protested against his rulings, and he gave way to 'Slim' Keating, a professional, who gave satisfaction." For an officer to act as an umpire in a game involving soldiers was not unusual. Yet an officer challenged for his fairness was remarkable. This served as yet another excuse for the loss.[29]

A front-page story in the same Tuesday newspaper announced the arrival of the twelve-inch-tall sterling silver Kirmse Cup on board the *Topeka*. The article indicated three teams would be vying for the trophy: the "Firemen, White Pass Club, and Soldiers."[30]

The *Daily Alaskan* edition on Wednesday, May 14, reported a White Pass Club victory in a return game on Tuesday. It noted "the score of 8 to 3 tells part of the story of the ball game yesterday." The piece described an exciting game: "Both nines put on their baseball clothes ready for business and both eager to win the game." Yet the White Pass team played a better game, with a combination of good hitting, pitching, and fielding. The article observed that the soldiers "placed one or two new men, which perhaps weakened their Sunday team somewhat."[31]

The Wednesday commentary on the game mentioned some of the White Pass team standouts. Slim Keating played first base, and Ed Tholin at pitcher "shook the glass out of his arm and the soldiers were unable to make safe hits." John Phelps was a standout batter, as were George Daniels, Edward Barry, and Clarence Olsen. The editor asserted, "all the members of the nine seemed to have taken a good dose of baseball elixir." The White Pass defense was stingy, and the "bags were guarded as never before." Phelps, Tholin, Barry, and Olsen were all veterans of the White Pass team from the previous year.[32]

For the Company L team, William Fox, a new member of the team, "pitched a good game." The White Pass team was able to get hits off his pitching, but "his work was stiff." Thomas Kennedy, the other new infielder, also played well and "pulled the balls off the bat in his usual clever manner." Yet the Black regulars "met their Waterloo" in hitting and base running. Soldier-manager William Freeman pitched the last two innings of the game and allowed White Pass to score three more runs, sealing their fate.[33]

Tuesday after the game, Company L team manager Freeman issued a public challenge for a third game on Wednesday "in order to play the tie off." He even offered to put up fifty dollars on the game. The White Pass Boys were unable to accept the challenge, as they were all scheduled to work. The White Pass & Yukon Route railroad managers had already given them one day off to play the Tuesday game. The article reported that the "two games will therefore go down as an even break between the soldiers and the White Pass nines." There was no time for another game since the company was scheduled to ship out on Thursday.[34]

Sendoff

A week before, Captain Hovey had notified the mayor and city council of the company's planned departure on May 15, 1902. Though both Hovey and the citizens of Skagway knew the company was leaving, this was the first official announcement of the exact date of departure. The *Daily Alaskan* gave the news front-page coverage, which set off a flurry of departure activities.[35]

In the week before departure, the newspaper lamented the loss of Captain Hovey and celebrated his contributions to Skagway. He was given lifetime membership to the Elks Club and the Arctic Brotherhood, and speeches dedicated to him were published in the paper. Captain Hovey was the "guest of honor at a charming little dinner given by Mr.

and Mrs. A.H. Brackett." Other articles mention the departure of the white officers and their wives, touted as "society favorites."[36]

The Pullen House hosted a lavish banquet in Hovey's honor attended by all the notable citizens of Skagway. The speech by city attorney R. W. Jennings, detailing what Skagwayans valued most about Hovey and the company's presence in Alaska, appeared in the *Daily Alaskan* the week of departure (appendix D).[37]

Jennings first detailed the primitive and dangerous conditions in Skagway when the Buffalo Soldiers arrived in 1899. He marveled at the way Hovey strove from the very beginning to "thoroughly understand the situation and to meet its wants." Jennings noted the absence of government, lack of law enforcement and fire protection, deficiencies of the courts, and dangers from "lawless characters" and "Indians." The very presence of Hovey and his men "exercised a wholesome restraining influence," prevented "concerted action on the part of the natives," and guaranteed "the process of the courts." Jennings spent a great deal of time thanking the soldiers for standing fire guard "on the darkest and coldest and wildest nights."[38]

The city attorney then praised Hovey's efforts to establish a permanent post in Skagway, always mindful of the best interests of the city. He was especially appreciative of the way Hovey made himself a citizen of Skagway and "entered actively into the personal, social, and business life of the city." And Hovey did this without wrapping himself in a "mantle of exclusiveness" or showing "an air of conscious superiority." On the contrary, he became part of the community through encouraging sports, joining lodges, and passing the hat around church. He observed of Hovey: "Though kind, you were not soft; though friendly, you were not familiar; though powerful, you were not officious."[39]

Jennings applauded Hovey for wielding his military powers cautiously and only when requested by the civil authorities. He praised the conduct of the Black soldiers of Company L, who were inspired by Hovey's example. He noted if a soldier violated laws "he was promptly and without cavil handed over to the civil authorities, to be dealt with as the statute requires." He commended Captain Jenks, Lieutenant

Rains, and Dr. Bailey, who ably assisted Hovey. Jennings concluded by wishing Hovey and the Buffalo Soldiers good fortune at their next assignment.[40]

On May 15, the night before his scheduled departure, a committee of businessmen presented Captain Hovey with a farewell gift. The presentation, made by J. H. Kelly, "the popular steamboat man," was a purse containing $315. The money was given "because the committee had been unable to find anything that was entirely satisfactory as a present." Hovey was taken by surprise at the gift and responded: "For the first time in my life I have nothing to say, I can say nothing." No record exists of what Hovey did with the money, but he likely turned it over to the army to steer clear of violating gift regulations.[41]

Departure

Captain Charles P. Summerall arrived as scheduled on May 15, 1902, with the remaining seventy enlisted men of his company to assume command of Camp Skagway. He commanded the 106th Company of the Coast Artillery Corps assisted by First Lieutenant Chappelear. Lieutenant Wheeler departed the same day north with his men from the Thirty-Second Company for their posting to Fort Liscum, Alaska. Dr. Bailey and his hospital detachment of eight stayed on to provide continuity, as they had three years earlier when Company L arrived. Also remaining at Camp Skagway were Commissary Sergeant Luttge and civilian clerk Charles Clarkson.[42]

Captain Hovey, Lieutenant Rains, First Sergeant Washington, Sergeant O'Connor, and the forty remaining enlisted members of the company steamed south out of Skagway aboard SS *City of Seattle* on May 15, en route to their new home at Fort Missoula, Montana. There they would rejoin the Twenty-Fourth Infantry for the first time in more than three years.[43]

On the day following their departure, the *Daily Alaskan* headlined "Skagway Bids Army Officers a Final Farewell." The reporter observed, "All night long the palatial *City of Seattle* was the scene of a brilliant reception." And finally, "Skagway bid Capt. Hovey, Lieut. Rains, and

Mrs. Rains a final goodbye last night on board the *City of Seattle* before the splendid Pacific Coast flier left the moorings at Moore's warf." When the throng bid their farewells to Captain Hovey, "there were tears in the old warrior's eyes."

The paper made no mention of a similar parting that must have occurred between the departing African American soldiers and the remaining members of the Black community in Skagway. A short article relegated to page 4 noted, "When the *Seattle* whistled yesterday evening the men of Company L were taken to the freight spur of Moore's wharf in heavy marching order and as soon as the passengers landed were marched aboard." Skagway feted the officers with a farewell reception on the upper decks of the steamboat while the Black soldiers boarded unceremoniously via the freight entrance.[44]

With their departure in May 1902, the officers and men of Company L closed out three years of service in Alaska. Captain Hovey, First Sergeant Washington, and the soldiers of the company had reason to be proud of their achievements in Skagway. The company had helped end lawlessness, backed the civil authorities, exercised restraint, and guarded against fire and flood. Because of this and three seasons of baseball, the African American soldiers became familiar if not totally accepted members of the community.[45]

AFTERMATH

One thing can be said of Capt. Summerall's boys,
they did not chew the rag or kick at decisions, as
was so common with the colored soldiers' nine.

—*DAILY ALASKAN*, May 27, 1902

What was the legacy of the three years Company L spent in Skagway and how well did the officers and men accomplish their assigned missions in Alaska? On a personal level, did the time stationed in the north mark the officers and men of the company and did their service impact the citizens of Skagway? And finally, how long did the Black community in Skagway last and did it leave a long-term trace?

Safeguarding Skagway

Captain Hovey's chief mission centered on the defense of Skagway and the Lynn Canal from any incursion by the Canadians. The Buffalo Soldiers succeeded in the mission of guarding the flag in this strategic and resource-rich corner of Alaska. During Company L's three-year watch in Dyea and Skagway, there were no serious incidents involving American and Canadian citizens or officials. Captain Hovey maintained an active liaison with his Canadian counterparts, facilitated a successful visit by the governor general of Canada, and did not let volatile situations like the British flag incident in Skagway or the mining claims issue in Porcupine get out of hand. And Captain Jenks extended a sort of baseball diplomacy in arranging to play a challenge game against the Mounted Police in Whitehorse.

As a result, amity was maintained until the Alaska-Canada Boundary Commission settled the dispute in January 1903, just eight months after the company left Skagway. Three Americans, two Canadians, and one British member decided in binding arbitration to favor the U.S. position. The Canadians were furious at the settlement and refused to sign the agreement. The accord resulted in Skagway and Haines remaining U.S. cities and the White Pass enduring as the northeastern border of Alaska's Panhandle.[1]

Hovey's secondary mission in Alaska was to assist the civilian authorities in maintaining law and order. This supported his main mission since the Canadian authorities pointed to the lawlessness in Skagway as proof of the inability of the United States to maintain order in the region. Hovey was fortunate that Skagway had settled down considerably from the earlier gold rush period of Soapy Smith, and his company was called upon to assist the local authorities less often.

Even so, Hovey and the African American soldiers showed a combination of strength, diplomacy, and restraint when coming to aid the local authorities on several occasions. The company needed just two sergeants and twenty privates to protect U.S. marshals enforcing the U.S. District Court order to return mutinous sailors to their ship. Captains Hovey and Jenks used a similar commonsense approach when asked by local law enforcement officials to prevent conflict between the Tlingit and American citizens. Good leadership, measured response, and well-trained soldiers on the scene averted any significant trouble.

Implicit in the company's mission in Skagway was the protection of the lives and property of citizens. Captain Jenks accomplished this most conspicuously during the great flood of October 1901, when he directed his soldiers to shore up sandbags and rescue Skagwayans from raging floodwaters. Soldiers and sentries also provided a life-saving service as fire guards at night while Skagway slept.

Baseball

Skagway felt the loss of the Black soldiers of Company L in baseball. Wittingly or not, the soldiers of the company had used baseball to connect with the Skagwayans. In three seasons of baseball, the African

American soldiers of Company L had transformed from faceless "colored" soldiers to men with names and personalities who contributed to the community. The people acquired this understanding through reading about baseball in the newspaper and watching the games directly.

The Kirmse Cup championship continued after the departure of the Buffalo Soldiers of Company L, yet without the same enthusiasm of previous years. The series continued when the railroad boys played the firemen on May 18, 1902. The White Pass team crushed the firemen by a score of 22–1.[2]

A new team entered the competition for the Kirmse Cup after the departure of the Company L nine. The *Daily Alaskan* noted on May 24, 1902, the White Pass Boys would cross bats with the new soldier team from the 106th Company on Sunday afternoon. Appropriately, they were referred to simply as the "soldier team," whether Black or white.[3]

The newspaper reported the result of Sunday's game on the front page on May 27, 1902. The White Pass team had played a road trip against Whitehorse the previous day, so they were tired. Yet they "gingered up like professionals and played great ball." White Pass beat the soldiers by a score of 13–4, and the report noted the soldier nine lacked teamwork and batting skills. Next time White Pass played the artillery soldiers in early June the score was more lopsided: 34–7 in favor of the railroaders.[4]

The newspaper aimed at least one snub at the departed Company L team. The slight came at the very end of the report on the early June game against the artillery soldiers. The newspaper noted: "One thing can be said of Capt. Summerall's boys, they did not chew the rag or kick at decisions, as was so common with the colored soldiers' nine. The white boys go at it in a sportsman like manner."[5]

This sounds a bit like sour grapes on the part of the editor of the *Daily Alaskan*. He and the citizens of Skagway were perhaps still embarrassed at the 10–0 drubbing the White Pass team suffered at the hands of the Buffalo Soldiers in the first game of the series less than a month earlier. The White Pass victory by 8–3 in the second game did not quite answer. The Black soldiers of the Company L

team were tough competitors. Their daily lives growing up in a prejudiced America taught them they should take every advantage to
come out as winners. To do otherwise in the Jim Crow South could
cost a Black man dearly.[6]

Despite the White Pass team's dominance over the hapless firemen and
inept artillery teams, the Kirmse Cup could never be won as originally
envisioned. The Kirmse Cup was born in three years of tough competition
between the railroad team and the Buffalo Soldiers. The White Pass and
Company L nines split the 1902 series and never broke the tie. Perhaps
this was a fitting end to the contest fought so fiercely over three years.

It was not long after the departure of Company L that the *Daily Alaskan* resumed using the standard derogatory stereotypes and invented
dialect commonly used in the American press at the time. In July 1902
the paper printed the following version of how a local baseball game
between two white teams was described by "an ex-colored soldier":
"De hottest game of baseball dat was ever played in de limits of old
Skagway. Why the steamboat fellas jus put it all over dem guys from
the railroad, and Lordy knows where dat score would have stood if
the steamboat fellas hadn't quit."[7]

So long as the Black soldiers of Company L lived among them, the
white citizens of Skagway were reminded every day, perhaps grudgingly, of their value to the community. Once they were gone, it was
easy for Skagwayans to fall back on the negative stereotypes of the day.
Soon, the recollections of the Buffalo Soldiers faded from memory
and the pervasive racism that permeated American society returned
to Skagway. Perhaps it never left, just went quiet.

On an individual level, something may have survived. Perhaps individual White Pass players like John Phelps and Clarence Olsen remembered the hard-fought games against Black soldiers such as Benjamin
Green or William Fox. They also lived through the great flood of October 1901 and fought fires side by side with the Buffalo Soldiers. They
laughed and cheered together during the Fourth of July horse race
and tug-of-war. The results of these kinds of personal interactions
are hard to quantify.

For three years, the African American soldiers lived, served, and played among the citizens of Skagway. The soldiers were marked by their time in Alaska just as the citizens of Skagway were marked by their passing. It changed them both, at least for a time.

Black Community

The former soldiers and Black civilians who remained in Skagway after the departure of Company L did not stay long. Most, if not all, had scratched out a living serving the Black soldier community as barbers, shoeshines, laundresses, and prostitutes, among other odd jobs. And business dried up when the company departed by steamboat in May 1902.

Soldiers who made the choice to stay in Skagway beyond their enlistments found themselves in a predicament. The army paid for transportation to the soldier's initial place of enlistment upon discharge. If the soldier declined and settled in Skagway, the army had no further obligation. And those soldiers with jail sentences and dishonorable discharges had a one-time option of transportation to the nearest U.S. state port of entry, normally Seattle, upon release. If they decided to stay in Alaska, they were on their own, and it was a long and costly trip back to the States.

The Black community left small trace of their experiences in Skagway after the departure of Company L. What little exists came in the form of reporting in the *Daily Alaskan* about members of the community, some positive and some negative. The newspaper accounts give a glimpse of the experiences of Black community members in a Skagway devoid of African American soldiers.

The first report of a soldier remaining in Skagway appeared in the *Daily Alaskan* a day after the Buffalo Soldiers shipped out of Skagway. Under the heading "Another Wedding Yesterday," the newspaper informed readers ex-soldier Joseph A. Nash and "Miss Helen L. Obery were married at the home of the bride on Fourth Avenue by Rev. G. S. Clevenger," the pastor at the Baptist church. The report described Nash as the "late bugler for Company L" and noted he planned to remain in Skagway.[8]

This account is important for several reasons. First, the coverage is a positive news item noting an event to celebrate. Nash was a thirty-one-year-old from London, Ohio, who was a volunteer soldier during the Spanish-American War prior to his three-year enlistment with Company L. An army musician, he had entertained the citizens of Skagway playing his trumpet for daily military calls and special musical events. The story also provides the name of another member of the Black civilian community, Helen Obery, who owned or rented a house on Fourth Avenue. And finally, "another wedding," implies other marriages preceded that of Nash, perhaps involving other Black former soldiers.[9]

A month after Nash's wedding, the *Daily Alaskan* reported the retirement of faithful "Old Ben Starkey, the colored day porter at the depot." The White Pass & Yukon Route lost one of its most trusted and familiar faces with the departure of Starkey, according to the piece. He had worked for the railroad more than a year and had to quit because an illness had "fastened its hold upon him." He planned to leave Skagway for the south within the week for his health.[10]

Benjamin Starkey was an old hand in Alaska and tougher than his portrayal in the *Daily Alaskan* indicates. He had lived with a woman named Minnie Jones in August 1898 at Fort Wrangel when white resident Tim Callahan tried to force his way into the couple's home while drunk. After Callahan forced the door past Minnie, Ben took an ax and "let fly at [Callahan's] face, which landed square, and also laid [Callahan] out for repairs." A judge determined Starkey was merely defending his home and no charges were filed, showing a Black man could get a fair trial against a white man in Alaska.[11]

Again, this account represented positive news of a well-liked African American man who was part of the Black community in Skagway for more than a year. A photo was taken of Starkey sitting by the stove warming himself in the main depot where he worked. The article noted the White Pass & Yukon Route would replace him with a "Mr. Frasier, of Chicago." The piece does not specify whether Starkey's replacement was also African American, but this position was often reserved for Black men.[12]

On the seedier side of town, two ex-soldiers and a Black prostitute were accused of a suspected crime two months after the departure of Company L. An article reported on the front page that Deputy Marshal Snook arrested Ernest C. Morris, a "Negro ex-soldier" on suspicion of robbing the Mug Restaurant in mid-July 1901. The arrest and subsequent trial provide a window into other members of the Black community in Skagway at the time.[13]

According to the initial report, Morris was followed to a house of ill repute by two witnesses and later arrested by Snook. At the time of his apprehension, Morris was allegedly in possession of a "lot of silver," which corresponded to the $24.75 taken from the restaurant. Snook likewise arrested George Thornell, also an ex-soldier, who lived in an adjoining shack. Both were found fully clothed in bed. Morris was arrested for the theft and Thornell for vagrancy, pending an investigation. The two lived on Seventh Avenue in the restricted district designated for prostitutes in Skagway.[14]

These two ex-soldiers had not been civilians long. Morris was a twenty-eight-year-old former volunteer soldier and hostler from Cairo, Illinois, and Thornell a twenty-six-year-old former laborer from Salisbury, Virginia. Both enlisted in the army in 1899 and joined Company L shortly before it deployed to Skagway. Thornell ended his enlistment in February 1902 with a good character rating and Morris a month later with an excellent assessment. Both, it seems, ended up living and working amid the bawdy houses on Seventh Avenue.[15]

Front-page headlines the next day gave further details of the arrest and investigation. Morris was bound over by Commissioner Rogers to await the action of a grand jury. Rogers set bail at five hundred dollars, which Morris could not pay, so he stayed in jail. Snook made a further arrest in connection with the theft the next day, apprehending Peggy Moore, described as a "colored woman of the half world." The reporter noted that this made "the third of the gang to be bagged, all colored."[16]

After examination, Snook and Rogers determined that the only charge possible against Moore was vagrancy. She pled guilty and was fined fifty dollars and costs. Moore "at first determined to served time in jail but after two or three hours in the bastille, repented and paid up." The legal definition of vagrancy in the city ordinances included being an "inmate of a house of ill-fame." Vagrancy was the charge, but her actual offense was being a prostitute. After paying her fine, Moore announced her intention to leave town.[17]

The newspaper noted that after an investigation, Thornell was likewise charged with vagrancy, even though he had a home. He too was fined fifty dollars and costs. Vagrancy was the formal charge, but being Black and involved with a prostitute was his real offense. Thornell, unlike Moore, did not have the cash to pay the fine, so he served in jail while he worked off the fine on the courthouse grounds at two dollars per day. Presumably, he left Skagway as soon as he worked off the fine and found passage south.[18]

The legal proceedings against Morris were more complicated and dragged on for months. While the ex-soldier sat in jail, the investigation continued and another suspected theft at the Delmonico was added to the charges. A grand jury returned the indictment against Morris among three other cases on October 10, 1902.[19]

The grand jury acquitted Morris of "stealing the cash register from the Mug." According to an article, Morris's defense was handled by court-appointed attorney John G. Held. No details were given, but the former soldier must have been well represented by counsel and received a fair trial. Or perhaps the case against him was thin from the start. Morris, like Moore and Thornell, likely left town at the first opportunity.[20]

The grand jury heard three other cases beside the one against Morris that week. The first, which preceded that of the ex-soldier, was against Frankie Belmont, for "keeping and maintaining a house of prostitution." The two cases scheduled to follow Morris's were the trials of "Omote, the Jap," and "Blind Isaac, Chilkoot Indian." The order of these grand jury trials revealed the bottom rungs of the social order of that time in Alaska: white madam, Black ex-soldier, Japanese cannery worker, and Native American, in that order.[21]

The trial of Frankie Belmont is significant because she, like Black prostitutes Rose Arnold and Ruth Brown, operated outside the restricted district on Seventh Avenue designated for "those who work behind scarlet curtains." Frankie operated a house called the Cottage on

Broadway, just north of Seventh Avenue. The Cottage was a traditional brothel with several working prostitutes and a madam, owner Frankie Belmont.[22]

By operating a house of prostitution outside the designated area on Seventh Avenue, Belmont earned the wrath of the city council. Aside from operating a brothel, she also served alcohol without paying the $1,500 annual license fee. The influential businessmen of Skagway, "who would have liked to keep the scarlet women confined within a narrower prism," were angered by Belmont's refusal to play by their rules. So the indictment the week of Morris's trial was the culmination of City Hall's efforts to shut her down.[23]

After the grand jury indicted Frankie Belmont, District Judge Brown lectured her in court and fined her $250, whereupon she "sank into a chair in fainting condition." After the verdict, she quarreled at the Cottage with her sister Ollie, who struck Belmont in the head with a wine bottle, causing an ugly gash requiring stitches. Two weeks after the indictment, Belmont sold a quarter interest in the Cottage, possibly to raise money for the fine. Frankie Belmont put the Cottage up for sale the following April. Again, the authorities got what they wanted.[24]

Rose Arnold and Ruth Brown lasted a bit longer than Frankie Belmont. The two Black prostitutes remained in Skagway a few years after Company L's departure, finding fewer customers in the shrinking Black community. City Hall and the Peniel Mission wanted them out of business on Sixth Avenue across from the barracks, so their days were numbered.

In 1905 Magistrate Si Tanner, the former deputy federal marshal, cracked down on Arnold and Brown. Though prostitution was still tolerated in town, it was highly regulated. Each quarter the women of the bawdy houses pled guilty and paid a fine of twenty dollars and court fees to remain in business. If they operated within the established limits of the restricted district on Seventh Avenue, Skagway officially condoned their existence.[25]

In January 1905 Arnold and Brown challenged Judge Tanner and pled not guilty of "being an inmate of a house of ill repute." Only two prostitutes had tried this before, and initially it worked. A jury acquitted Rose Arnold, and Ruth Brown tied up the courts for days fighting the charges of "keeping a house of ill repute in connection with Rose Arnold." Brown was also reluctantly cleared of the charges.[26]

It took two more arrests and two more acquittals before Judge Tanner obtained the conviction "on the charge of being an inmate of a disorderly house." Rose Arnold and Ruth Brown paid the fines, packed up, and departed for Juneau in February 1905. City Hall won and the newspaper printed their names in the paper one last time, mocking that they were "now Juneauites."[27]

Skagway's Black community did not last much longer than Arnold and Brown. The former Black soldiers who chose to stay in Skagway after the end of their enlistments probably took the first opportunity to catch a steamer south to Juneau. Others shipped out to other locales in Alaska or Canada. By 1910 the sole Black resident of Skagway was a seventy-two-year-old widow working as a cook.[28]

The officers and men of Company L accomplished their mission in Alaska, preserving law and order in Skagway and maintaining the frontier status quo until the final border convention was signed in 1903. Because of this, the Black soldiers earned the grudging regard of the citizens of Skagway, who grew to respect their military professionalism and upstanding behavior. The people also greatly appreciated the efforts of the African American soldiers to keep the city from burning to the ground or washing away in a flood.

However, these sentiments faded once the Black soldiers left town and were replaced by white soldiers. Shortly after their departure, Skagwayans fell back on the negative stereotypes and racism of the era. Soon, the recollections of the baseball games, minstrel shows, and Fourth of July celebrations faded from memory, and the quiescent racism of Skagway resumed. This made Skagway an unwelcome place for the Black community, which disappeared as quickly as it arose.

POSTSCRIPT

E.E. Swanson, who has lived at Rampart for many
years and all told has been in Alaska 41 years, came
to Fairbanks for a few days to transact business.
—*FAIRBANKS DAILY NEWS-MINER*, June 12, 1939

What happened to the officers and soldiers after their departure from
Skagway? Did they acquire skills or learn lessons in the north that
benefited them personally or professionally? Although it is more difficult to track the lives of the enlisted soldiers, some conclusions can
be drawn about the officers. And even with the enlisted soldiers, a
few general deductions can be made and the lives of a few men who
remained in Alaska examined. For a fortunate few, gold was still to
be found in Alaska.[1]

Officers

Four officers who led the African American soldiers in Skagway were
the key to mission success. Captain Hovey, the "old man" of Company
L, was especially suited by experience and temperament to lead the
enterprise. He was ably assisted by First Lieutenant Jenks, who initially led the separate command at Fort Wrangel. They joined forces in
Skagway, where newly promoted Captain Jenks stepped in to assume
command for an ailing Hovey. After Jenks departed in 1901, Second
Lieutenant Rains assisted Hovey as his deputy, though his inexpe-
rience and lineage showed at times. And reliable Dr. Bailey ran the
army hospital, treated the soldiers of the company, and cared for the
citizens of Skagway.

Captain Henry Hovey held a unique position as the first real "military mayor" during a formative time in Skagway's history. Over his three-year stay, he became an integral part of the social fabric of the professional class in the city. He used his special social status to even the playing field for what could have been a challenging mission, thus making the task of his Black soldiers easier. He was an extremely effective representative in Skagway for the U.S. Army and initiated the plan for a permanent post called Fort William H. Seward near Haines Mission, which opened in 1904.[2]

Hovey served with the Twenty-Fourth Infantry for the rest of his time in the military. In August 1902, as Company L settled into its new station at Fort Missoula, Montana, Hovey moved to a tour teaching military science and tactics again at Norwich University in Northfield, Vermont. There he rejoined his wife and two children, who he had not seen for more than three years while in Alaska.[3]

The army promoted Hovey to major in 1903 by seniority in the regiment, and he returned to the Twenty-Fourth Infantry to serve on its second tour in the Philippines. He commanded the battalion at Cebu, Department of Visayas, and led the regiment for a short period at Camp Bumpus in Tacloban, Leyte, since he was the senior officer present. After Hovey retired on disability in 1907, he moved to his home in Northfield, Vermont, where he died suddenly of a heart attack a year later. He was fifty-six years old and had served twenty-seven years with the Buffalo Soldiers of the Twenty-Fourth.[4]

Captain Isaac Jenks likewise grew professionally and personally during his time in Alaska. His confidence grew during his year-long independent command at Fort Wrangel. He was the man who saved citizens and property during the great flood of October 1901 and led the company during Hovey's extended sick leave. His athletic talents and singing ability added value to the lives of his soldiers and to the cultural life of Skagway.

After Skagway, Jenks had a long military career, serving with the Twenty-Fourth Infantry as a company commander and regimental quartermaster after its return from the Philippines. He served with the Twenty-Fourth on its second posting to the Philippines and was promoted to major in 1913. Around the time he was promoted, one of the old enlisted veterans of Skagway, Samuel Cropper, came to work for Jenks as a cook after retiring from the army.[5]

Promoted to lieutenant colonel and colonel in 1917, Jenks assumed challenging assignments outside the Twenty-Fourth during World War I. He commanded the 317th Supply Trains supporting the Black Ninety-Second Division in the Meuse-Argonne Offensive. After the war he attended the Army War College and served in several high-level staff positions. He died on active duty in 1931 at the age of sixty-three after forty years of service in the army, the first twenty-two with the Buffalo Soldiers of the Twenty-Fourth.[6]

Dr. Edward Bailey did not stay in Skagway long after the departure of Company L in May 1902. He requested a leave of absence of one month, which was endorsed by Captain Hovey. Hovey's endorsement noted: "Contract Surgeon Bailey's services here, have been greater than his professional record indicates." Hovey noted that Bailey had been indispensable in several emergencies and stepped in and acted as a line officer on several occasions. Bailey had been continuously on duty in Dyea and Skagway from December 1897 without a break.[7]

Baily's initial leave request was denied because the army could not find a contract surgeon to temporarily replace him. The doctor was finally granted leave beginning in mid-June 1902 for one month, after which he reported to Vancouver Barracks for orders. His replacement at Skagway, contract surgeon Jesse P. Truax, arrived there the day Bailey departed on leave.[8]

Bailey remained a contract surgeon and later served as a first lieutenant in the new Medical Reserve Corps. He was assigned to various posts in the State of Washington until he resigned from the U.S. Army in September 1912. He moved to Seattle, Washington, with his wife and eventually retired from medical practice. The army had benefited from his skill as a physician and surgeon for fifteen years. He died in 1927 at the age of sixty-six in Seattle.[9]

Lieutenant Edward Rains, who spent two years with the company in Alaska, made the missteps expected of any new second lieutenant in Skagway. Captain Hovey depended on Rains as the only other line officer in the company after the departure of Jenks. Yet after he left Alaska his record was checkered.

Rains moved with Company L to its new home at Fort Missoula, Montana. After promotion to first lieutenant in 1903, he obtained a transfer to the all-white Twentieth U.S. Infantry Regiment. This was not uncommon in the army at the time when promotions were slow and a white officer wanted to be transferred out of a Black regiment.

While assigned on recruiting duty in Rhode Island for the Twentieth Infantry in 1908, Lieutenant Rains was investigated for duplicating his pay accounts. Before he could be charged and answer the specifications, he disappeared. It was exceedingly rare for an officer to go absent without leave. The army dropped him from the rolls as a deserter in 1909. This ended Rains's military service as an officer, which had begun with his time in Skagway.[10]

This ex-officer reappeared as L. Edward Rains in the 1920 census as a coal mine superintendent in Utah with a new wife and child. He later resurfaced as Edward Lee Rains in Omaha, Nebraska, as a druggist and as Edwin Lee Rains in Salt Lake City, Utah, as a car salesman, both times with new wives. He died in Salt Lake City in 1924 at the age of forty-seven, leaving a trail of ex-wives and children in his wake.[11]

Noncommissioned Officers

The noncommissioned officers of Company L had the greatest impact on the day-to-day lives of their soldiers and proved the key to success in Skagway. A private might see his company commander once a day at morning formation, from afar. Yet he would see his first sergeant, section sergeant, or corporal nearly every minute of the day and, if necessary, in his face.

Sergeant James Washington enjoyed continued success after leaving Skagway. When his three-year term ended at Fort Missoula, Montana, in 1902, he was no longer listed as the first sergeant, yet his character was rated as excellent. He was later reassigned to Company C, Twenty-Fourth Infantry, where he ended his enlistment in 1905 as a corporal with an excellent rating. He served two more enlistments and retired in 1911 as the first sergeant of Company C, Twenty-Fourth Infantry at Madison Barracks, New York, with an excellent character rating after twenty-five years of service in the army.[12]

Sergeant Robinson, whose wife, Sarah, was employed as a hospital matron at the army hospital in Skagway, enjoyed more success as a noncommissioned officer after leaving Alaska. By the time he completed his term in 1903, he was the first sergeant of Company L. By the end of his next enlistment in 1905 he was listed as a sergeant with an excellent character rating. Sometime after he signed up for another term in 1905, he was appointed first sergeant of Company L again and remained in that position until he retired at Fort McDowell, California, in 1912. He had served twenty-six years in the army, twenty years as a noncommissioned officer, and most of the last ten years as the first sergeant of Company L.[13]

Sergeant Robert O'Connor did not enjoy the same success as Washington and Robinson after his departure from Alaska. He was busted to private in 1902 with Company L at Fort Missoula, Montana. He left the army when his three-year term expired in 1904 but reenlisted a month later and was assigned to Company F, Twenty-Fourth Infantry. Discharged a year later at Fort Assiniboine, Montana, as a corporal, he reenlisted again for another three-year term. Finally, Private O'Connor was given a general court-martial and dishonorable discharge in 1907 at Camp Bumpus, Philippine Islands, with an aptitude rating of "not hail and fit." Somewhere along the way his wife left him.[14]

Robert O'Connor next appeared in the official record as an inmate at the Stockton State Hospital in San Joaquin, California. He was committed in November 1910 under a judge's order. O'Connor was listed as thirty-eight years old, single, and a laborer. He had suffered attacks of epilepsy for a week and was "violent, restless, and dangerous." The attending physician noted that O'Connor "states that enemies are injecting electricity and poisonous acids in his system." The diagnosis of insanity was later revised to alcoholism, and he was discharged in February 1911 after recovering. The records are silent on what happened thereafter.[15]

In addition to those three noncommissioned officers, several others experienced successful careers in the army after leaving Skagway. Three, sergeants Hanson, Hayes, and Snoten, later served as color sergeants, positions of honor for senior noncommissioned officers on the regimental staff. Two, sergeants Hanson and Reed, subsequently served as quartermaster sergeants in Company L, Twenty-Fourth Infantry. Finally, Reed served his last tour in the army as the first sergeant for Company L for three years during its deployment to the Philippines. They all enjoyed full and successful careers, eventually retiring and collecting pensions.

Privates

Many privates who served with the company in Skagway had productive army careers in the years after leaving Alaska—so many, in fact, that one might conclude the company's service in the north served as a training ground for future noncommissioned officers. The combination of positive leadership, challenging mission, and confidence-building isolation might have had a formative influence on many of the young soldiers in Skagway.

Of the 117 privates who served in Skagway between 1899 and 1902, 42 went on to reenlist and serve one or more subsequent periods in the army, and many later served in leadership positions. This 36 percent reenlistment rate was above average at the time, possibly a reflection of the privates' positive experiences serving in Skagway on their first or second enlistment in the army.

The high reenlistment rate must be balanced against the fifteen privates either discharged without honor or dropped from the rolls after deserting while posted at Fort Wrangel or Skagway. This 13 percent is also slightly higher than the army average at the time and reflects the isolation of Alaska and the proximity of what General Randall called "demoralizing influences." The challenges of serving in Skagway induced borderline or substandard soldiers to desert or misbehave more readily than elsewhere.

Of the privates who lived up to the challenge and reenlisted, sixteen later served as noncommissioned officers and another five in the Hospital Corps. Three of those sixteen future noncommissioned officers were later selected by their company commanders as first sergeants, and one was chosen by the regimental commander to be a battalion sergeant major, the top noncommissioned officer rank. And most remarkable, two later earned commissions as officers.

The three future first sergeants included Robert Cotton, Junius Dawson, and William Fox (aka Red Stockings of the 1902 soldier team). All three served in succession as first sergeant of Company L, Twenty-Fourth Infantry, between 1908 and 1913. All enjoyed long, successful careers and collected pensions. For three privates with service in Skagway to become future top sergeants in Company L is quite extraordinary.[16]

The army awarded officer commissions to two enlisted members who served in Skagway. With the expansion of the army during World War I, the U.S. Army began commissioning Black officers in 1917 to lead the Black regiments being readied for service in Europe. The Black officers trained at the Fort Des Moines Provisional Army Officer Training School in Iowa. About 1,200 men attended the camp, comprising noncommissioned officers from the four Buffalo Soldier regiments and civilians. Of those, 639 graduated and received commissions as captains, first lieutenants, or second lieutenants.[17]

Landon Jackson, a former waiter born in Raising Fawn, Georgia, enlisted in January 1899 and joined Company L shortly before deployment to Alaska. He served as a private and noncommissioned officer for eighteen years in the Twenty-Fourth and Twenty-Fifth. After he was selected for and completed the Fort Des Moines Officer Training School, he was commissioned a first lieutenant in the Regular Army in October 1917. The army assigned Jackson to Camp Grant, Illinois, during the war. He retired from the army in 1924 after twenty-five years.[18]

Chester Sanders, a former Spanish-American War volunteer born in Carrollton, Kentucky, enlisted in March 1899 and joined Company

L en route to Alaska. He served as a private and sergeant for nineteen years in the Twenty-Fourth Infantry. In 1908 he was appointed a battalion staff noncommissioned officer and later sergeant major, the highest such enlisted rank. After completion of the Fort Des Moines Officer Training School, he was made a captain in the Officer Reserve Corps and was assigned to the 370th Infantry. Captain Sanders fought with the Seventy-Third French Division in Europe and was decorated for bravery while commanding Company F, 370th Infantry in combat. He retired from the army at Camp Meade, Maryland, in 1920 after serving twenty-two years.[19]

Ex-Soldiers in Alaska

Some Black soldiers stayed in Alaska after their military service to seek their fortunes after desertion, discharge, or the end of their enlistments. The records show only six soldiers who remained for any lengthy period in Alaska, though there were probably others.

Juneau served as the destination for the initial group of three soldiers, about one hundred sea miles south of Skagway and the first major port-of-call in that direction. For the soldiers who stayed in Skagway, this city was the logical destination on their route southward. And for those being discharged from prison at Sitka, Juneau was their initial stop after release.

The first of these ex-soldiers was John A. Perkins, who ended his enlistment in March 1902 and was jailed two months later for cutting a white artillery soldier from ear to chin. Upon his release from prison the summer of 1903, he stayed in Alaska. He might have had no option since he was penniless and discharged from the army. In 1910 Perkins lived in Juneau, Alaska, working as a single thirty-year-old cook.[20]

The second former soldier was Harry Andrews, who was one of the three members of Company L arrested for the Skagway saloon riot in October 1900. Sentenced to three months at Sitka, the army discharged him without honor in December 1900. After release from prison, he landed in Juneau and joined the Black community there. In

1910 Andrews was still single, thirty-nine years old, and working as a janitor.[21]

The third and last former Buffalo Soldier to make Juneau his temporary home was John W. Oby, who ended his service honorably in March 1902 with a character rating of excellent. He played baseball on the soldier teams in 1900 and 1901. Oby, who was a barber before he enlisted in the army, found employment cutting hair in Juneau in 1910, still single and thirty-three years old. He was the only one of the three in Juneau who remained after separation from the army by choice.[22]

These three ex-soldiers apparently learned that their military experience had no impact on post-army civilian employment. The jobs they found in Juneau reflected the positions open to Blacks in this era: cooks, janitors, and barbers. The one common thread that bound Oby, Andrews, and Perkins was their hometown of Philadelphia. All three enlisted within a month of each other in the City of Brotherly Love, so this may have been the reason they remained together in Juneau.

Living with them in the Black community of Juneau were four others with varied backgrounds. The first, Peter Brown, was a fifty-five-year-old Jamaican-born man who had been living in Skagway in 1900 working as a cook. Perhaps he, like the soldiers, moved on to Juneau after he was no longer welcome in Skagway. The second man, from California, was thirty-four-year-old James Hall, who worked as a cook and shared a house with Oby. The third was a thirty-two-year-old widow named Laura Williams, also working as a cook. Conceivably, she was the Mrs. Williams who had been listed as part of the Skagway Black community in 1901.[23]

The last of the seven members of the Black community in Juneau, and the fourth of the non-military members, William N. C. Waddleton, possessed a rare vocation for a Black man at the time. William Nathaniel Colcock Waddleton, born in South Carolina, was a fifty-two-year-old lawyer who had moved to Alaska in 1893, a pioneer seeking his fortune in the gold rush. He had trekked his way up the Pacific coast to Juneau, working as a cook in Fresno, California, in 1888, and a newspaper reporter in Seattle in 1892. By 1910 he had established a successful law practice in Juneau.[24]

Sometime before 1920, all the former Buffalo Soldiers had abandoned the Black community in Juneau. The city still had six Black residents, but only Waddleton remained of the seven from 1910. Oby had moved to Seattle, where he continued to work as a barber for many years. Andrews and Perkins left Juneau and disappeared from the records.

Three other soldiers, all former corporals from Company L who ended their service honorably, enjoyed more successful lives in other parts of Alaska. They may have initially lingered in Skagway; one of the trio married a woman from the Black community there. Yet instead of relocating south to Juneau, they traveled north to the gold fields of Alaska.

The first, Corporal George L. Wilson, settled in Alaska and Canada after his release from active duty. George Levi Wilson, born in 1866 in Boston, Massachusetts, served with Company L, Sixth Massachusetts Volunteers, during the Spanish-American War. His father was born in Scotland and his mother in New Brunswick, Canada. He was rated by Captain Hovey as excellent when discharged from the army in January 1902. He, like the others, might have initially stayed in Skagway before striking out for Canada.[25]

In 1908 Wilson registered as a U.S. citizen with the American Consulate in Dawson, Yukon Territory, Canada. He had been in Dawson since the previous year and worked in the mining business. He registered again in 1909 at the consulate, still occupied as a miner. By 1920, however, he had moved to Hot Springs, Alaska, where he was engaged as a prospector. Sometime before 1929 Wilson moved to Fairbanks, where he worked as a messenger.[26]

George Wilson died on January 8, 1940, in Fairbanks, Alaska, at the age of seventy-four years. He had been ill since October and succumbed to pneumonia and heart disease at his house. The newspaper noted that he was a widower and long-time resident of Fairbanks. He was provided a veteran's funeral service by the Dorman H. Baker Post of the American Legion as well as a Legion plot in the Fairbanks cemetery. The Legion post adjutant requested all members attend the funeral, so it appears he was well known in the organization.[27]

The second soldier was Corporal Benjamin Green, who had been the captain of the soldier baseball team until he ended his service in the army in March 1902. He was also a talented singer and leader of the Magnolia Four that performed in Skagway. Though a junior non-commissioned officer when he ended his enlistment, he had joined as a new private three years earlier in Dayton, Ohio. From his service record at Fort Wrangel and Skagway, he possessed excellent leadership skills and would have had a fine future in the army. Yet, he chose to resume life as a civilian in Alaska.[28]

Green might have remained in Skagway and joined the Black community there after his term of enlistment ended. He had leadership skills refined during his service with the company along with his previous competence as a teamster handling horses and mules. Green later lived at Fort Gibbon, near Tanana, Alaska, on the Yukon River, employed as a teamster or muleskinner. In 1930 he worked as a teamster in the freighting industry in Fairbanks, Alaska.[29]

Green made a living in Fairbanks running a shoeshine stand for many of his later years and was well liked by the community. Ben Green, as he was known to residents of Fairbanks, never married. A front-page newspaper article in 1939 recounted how he loved to tell children stories based on his army experiences. He was a big man, standing six feet tall and weighing about 260 pounds before a heart ailment caused him to lose considerable weight. Green "dropped dead of heart trouble" on March 17, 1940, in Fairbanks, at the age of sixty-four.[30]

The newspaper noted funeral services were held for veteran Ben Green under the auspices of the Fairbanks Dorman H. Baker Post of the American Legion, with the Legion commander for the Department of Alaska, the Fairbanks post commander, and several past commanders acting as pallbearers. He was buried in the American Legion plot of the Fairbanks cemetery. The service, burial, and pallbearers indicate he was active and respected in the American Legion.[31]

The third known soldier to stay in Alaska was Corporal Eugene Swanson. Swanson, born in Rockford, Alabama, in 1868, remained in Alaska after his discharge in Skagway in April 1902. With a character rating of excellent, he, like Corporal Green, had shown superb leadership skills and might have done well in the army. Yet he chose to try his hand at prospecting for gold in Alaska.[32]

According to Swanson's own account, his time in Skagway was not his first experience living in the north. He claimed he had come to seek his fortune in gold in the Atlin District of British Columbia in 1896 but gave up after a year. He said he traveled to Seattle, where he enlisted in the army and was assigned to the Ninth Cavalry. Swanson boasted he charged up San Juan Hill during the Spanish-American War.[33]

Swanson recounted that after his discharge in Skagway, he spent time mining in Dawson, Yukon, and Nome, Alaska. He finally settled in Rampart, Alaska, in 1904, where he is said to have "done comfortably well in mining." Rampart is on the Yukon River and about fifty river miles from where Benjamin Green lived in Tanana.[34]

Swanson was working as a teamster in Rampart, Alaska, in January 1920, likely in the mining business. He was listed as sixty years old and living with his wife, Amelia Beckwith, who he met during his army days in Skagway. He and Amelia had a ten-year-old daughter, Gracie, born in Rampart in 1910.[35]

In 1929 Eugene Swanson still lived in Rampart, widowed and working as a miner for placer gold. A Fairbanks newspaper reported Swanson ran the largest mining operation in the Rampart District, employing a six-man crew and a woman cook at Hunter Creek. He made a name for himself using the pioneer methods of drift mining instead of heavy equipment.[36]

In 1935 Eugene married Alice Graves from Fairbanks, Alaska. By December 1939, the seventy-five-year-old Swanson was operating a gold mine on Hess Creek in Tolovana, Alaska. He was still married but living with a divorced forty-eight-year-old Black "servant" named Estella M. Harris. In 1941 Swanson's Hunter Creek holdings were sold at a marshal's sale, and his career in the gold-mining industry ended. He appointed attorney Earnest B. Collins as executor of his estate.[37]

After his mining ventures ended, Swanson moved to Fairbanks, where he applied for and was granted a divorce from his wife, Alice. A reporter from the *Fairbanks Daily News-Miner* did a lengthy interview with Swanson in March 1942 titled "OLD WAR HORSE PRANCES." It was in this newspaper story Swanson said he served with the Ninth Cavalry when it "scaled the hill of San Juan to spike the guns of the Spanish batteries that raked us with terrible accuracy as we made the ascending charge." He joked with the reporter about joining the army again, which was then fighting in World War II. This time around, he noted: "I'd like to drive a tank."[38]

Swanson died in Fairbanks, Alaska, on December 30, 1942, having lived in Alaska for nearly forty-four years. He was seventy-eight years old and had been admitted to Saint Joseph's Hospital in Fairbanks in October, suffering from cancer. The Veterans of Foreign Wars in Fairbanks conducted his funeral service, and "Six Negro soldiers were pallbearers and gave a military flavor to the services." It is possible former members of Company L from Skagway were among the pallbearers.[39]

When laid to rest in the Fairbanks Clay Street Cemetery, Eugene Swanson joined his former barracks-mates George Wilson and Ben Green. Three former corporals from the Buffalo Soldiers who served in Skagway found their well-deserved final rest in Alaskan soil.

In newspaper obituaries, the white members of the Fairbanks American Legion and Veterans of Foreign Wars honored Wilson, Green, and Swanson for their service during the Spanish-American War and in Skagway. During Memorial Day 1943, the Buffalo Soldiers were honored alongside white veterans buried at Clay Street Cemetery, just as the soldiers of Company L honored Civil War veterans buried at the Skagway Cemetery forty-three years earlier.

The experiences of the white officers and Black soldiers of Company L at Fort Wrangel and in Skagway marked them in largely positive ways. Many, though not all, enjoyed professional success in the military after leaving Alaska, drawing on the positive experiences garnered in three years of service there. As with Jack London, their time in the north built character and provided the grist for many memorable tales.

Those Buffalo Soldiers who chose to remain in Alaska did leave a trace. When they did not find acceptance in Skagway, a few moved on to Juneau to join the small Black community there. Others journeyed to the gold fields of Nome and Rampart to seek their fortunes. And at least three did succeed in finding some measure of success and acceptance in Alaska, first in the gold fields, and later in Fairbanks.

Semper paratus.[40]

APPENDIX A

Biographies of Officers and Soldiers of Company L

Altmann, Webster: born March 1878, New York City, New York; enlisted February 11, 1899, New York City, New York, laborer, assigned Company L, Twenty-Fourth Infantry; discharged April 25, 1901, Washington DC, disability, private, "good"; died May 27, 1943, New York City, New York; buried Long Island National Cemetery, Farmingdale, New York

Andrews, Harry: born January 1870, Philadelphia, Pennsylvania; enlisted February 11, 1899, Philadelphia, Pennsylvania, laborer, assigned Company L, Twenty-Fourth Infantry; discharged December 8, 1900, Skagway, Alaska, private, "without honor"; living in Juneau, January 1910, working as a janitor

Ashton, George L.: born February 1880, Washington DC; enlisted September 26, 1898, Washington Barracks, DC, laborer, assigned Company L, Twenty-Fourth Infantry; discharged January 27, 1899, Camp Douglas, Utah, private, "very good"; enlisted February 9, 1899, Washington Barracks, DC, soldier, assigned Company L, Twenty-Fourth Infantry; discharged Camp Skagway, Alaska, February 8, 1902, private, "excellent"; enlisted March 12, 1902, Washington DC, soldier, assigned Hospital Corps; discharged March 11, 1908, Camp Overton, Mindanao, Philippines, private first class, "excellent"; enlisted March 12, 1908, Leyte, Philippines, soldier, Hospital Corps; discharged March 11, 1911, Fort Lawton, Washington, private first class, "excellent"; enlisted March 12, 1911, Fort Lawton, Washington, Hospital Corps; discharged March 11, 1914, Schofield Barracks, Hawaii Territory, hospital technician first class, "excellent"

Bailey, Lafayette: born March 1877, Manson, North Carolina; discharged April 3, 1899, from Company K, Eighth Illinois Volunteer Infantry; enlisted September 28, 1900, Chicago, Illinois, soldier, assigned Company L, Twenty-Fourth Infantry; arrived November 3, 1900, Camp Skagway, Alaska; discharged July 24, 1902 at Fort Missoula, Montana, private, "excellent"

Ballard, James H.: born September 13, 1868, Alexandria, Virginia; enlisted July 15, 1891, Washington DC, laborer, assigned Company D, Twenty-Fifth Infantry; discharged July 14, 1896, Fort Custer, Montana, private, "very good"; enlisted September 5, 1896, Washington Barracks, DC, assigned Company C, Twenty-Fifth Infantry; transferred to Company I, Twenty-Fifth Infantry; discharged September 4, 1899, Caloocan, Luzon, Philippines, sergeant, "excellent"; enlisted October 16, 1900, Baltimore, Maryland, soldier, assigned Company L, Twenty-Fourth Infantry; arrived November 3, 1900, Camp Skagway, Alaska; discharged October 15, 1903, Fort Missoula, Montana, private, "very good"; enlisted November 13, 1903, Washington DC, assigned Company D, Twenty-Fifth Infantry; discharged November 12, 1906, Fort Reno, Oklahoma Territory, corporal, "excellent"; died February 17, 1955; buried February 23, 1955, Arlington National Cemetery, Virginia

Banks, James M.: born October 1878, Monroe County, Illinois; discharged January 20, 1899, Company A, First Indiana Volunteer Infantry; enlisted March 22, 1899, Knoxville, Tennessee, soldier, assigned Company L, Twenty-Fourth Infantry; discharged March 21, 1902, Camp Skagway, Alaska, private, "excellent"

Barnett, Peter W.: born February 1871, Carrsville, Kentucky; discharged January 20, 1899, Company A, First Indiana Volunteer Infantry; enlisted March 13, 1899, Indianapolis, Indiana, soldier, assigned Company L, Twenty-Fourth Infantry; discharged March 12, 1900, Fort Wrangel, Alaska, private, "excellent"; died December 31, 1900, Honolulu, Hawaii, tuberculosis

Bayard, Levi H.: born March 1871, Cecil County, Maryland; enlisted March 10, 1899, Philadelphia, Pennsylvania, laborer, assigned Company L, Twenty-Fourth Infantry; discharged August 24, 1899, disability, private, "very good"

Belcher, Thomas A.: born March 1878, Franklin County, Virginia; enlisted March 14, 1899, Columbus Barracks, Ohio, farmer, assigned Company L, Twenty-Fourth Infantry; discharged March 13, 1902, Camp Skagway, Alaska, private, "excellent"; admitted July 28, 1911, National Home for Disabled Volunteers, Fall River, South Dakota; died September 21, 1911, pulmonary tuberculosis; buried National Home for Disabled Volunteers Cemetery, Fall River, South Dakota

Belcher, Walter: born December 1874, Franklin County, Virginia; discharged January 28, 1899, Company B, Ninth Battalion, Ohio Volunteer Infantry; enlisted March 14, 1899, Columbus Barracks, Ohio, teamster, assigned Company L, Twenty-Fourth Infantry; discharged March 13, 1902, Camp Skagway, Alaska, private, "excellent"; enlisted April 16, Washington Barracks, DC, soldier, assigned C Troop, Ninth Cavalry; discharged March 4, 1905, Fort Riley, Kansas, private, disability

Bordinghammer, Edward: born March 1852, Giles County, Tennessee; enlisted September 5, 1870, Pulaski, Tennessee, laborer, assigned Company K, Twenty-Fourth Infantry; discharged September 5, 1875, Fort Ringgold, Texas, private, "good"; enlisted September 5, 1875, Ringgold Barracks, Texas, soldier, Company K, assigned Twenty-Fourth Infantry; discharged September 4, 1880, Grierson's Springs, Texas, sergeant, "good"; enlisted September 7, 1880, Concho, Texas, assigned Company K, Twenty-Fourth Infantry; discharged September 6, 1885, Fort Reno, Indian Territory, sergeant, "very good"; enlisted September 7, 1885, Fort Reno, Indian Territory, assigned Company K, Twenty-Fourth Infantry; discharged September 6, 1890, Fort Grant, Arizona Territory, sergeant, "excellent"; enlisted September 7, 1890, Fort Grant, Arizona Territory, assigned Company K, Twenty-Fourth Infantry; discharged September 6, 1895, Fort Bayard, New Mexico, musician, "good"; enlisted September 7, 1895, Fort Bayard, New Mexico, assigned Company E, Twenty-Fourth Infantry; discharged September 6, 1898, Camp Wikoff, New York, musician, "good"; enlisted September 7, 1898, Montauk, New York, assigned Company E, Twenty-

Fourth Infantry; transferred to Company L, Twenty-Fourth Infantry; retired August 2, 1900, Camp Skagway, Alaska, musician; employed, 1903, Washington Naval Yard, Washington DC; died November 26, 1919, Washington DC; buried Arlington National Cemetery, Arlington, Virginia

Bracy, George: born April 1878, Congaree, South Carolina; enlisted February 9, 1899, Columbia, South Carolina, expressman, assigned Company L, Twenty-Fourth Infantry; discharged February 8, 1902, Camp Skagway, Alaska, private, "excellent"; enlisted February 27, 1905, Columbia, South Carolina, fireman, assigned Company L, Twenty-Fifth Infantry; discharged April 3, 1905, Fort Niobrara, Nebraska, disability, private, "very good"

Brown, Frank B.: born June 1862, Westchester, Pennsylvania; enlisted January 1, 1901, Boston, Massachusetts, assigned Company L, Twenty-Fourth Infantry; joined Company L, Twenty-Fourth Infantry, July 20, 1901; discharged January 3, 1904, Fort Missoula, Montana, private, "excellent"

Bullitte, Marion P.: born April 1877, Simpsonville, Kentucky; enlisted July 20, 1898, Louisville, Kentucky, cook, assigned Company A, Twenty-Fourth Infantry; discharged February 1, 1899, Fort Douglas, Utah, private, "good"; enlisted September 24, 1900, Louisville, Kentucky, musician, assigned Company L, Twenty-Fourth Infantry; arrived November 3, 1900, Camp Skagway, Alaska; discharged October 28, 1901, Camp Skagway, Alaska, private, "without honor"; inmate, Montana State Prison, May 9, 1910; living in Rock Island, Illinois, September 12, 1918; died February 22, 1926, Kansas City, Missouri

Callaway, Andy: born January 1870, Meriwether, Georgia; enlisted July 7, 1898, Nashville, Tennessee, plasterer, assigned Company K, Twenty-Fourth Infantry; discharged February 4, 1899, Camp Pilot, Butte, Wyoming, private, "good"; enlisted March 11, 1899, Nashville, Tennessee, plasterer, assigned Company B, Twenty-Fourth Infantry; reassigned Company L, Twenty-Fourth Infantry; discharged March 10, 1902, Camp Skagway, Alaska, private, "excellent"; filed February 15, 1907, as invalid, Tennessee; living 1910, Spring City, Tennessee

Casselle, Nelson A. (birth name Nathan A. Collins): born March 1877, Saint Louis, Missouri; discharged February 17, 1899, Company D, Seventh U.S. Volunteer Infantry; enlisted October 11, 1900, Lexington, Kentucky, painter, assigned Company L, Twenty-Fourth Infantry; arrived November 3, 1900, Camp Skagway, Alaska; deserted June 21, 1902, surrendered, July 27, 1902, Jefferson Barracks, Missouri, found guilty of AWOL; discharged December 11, 1902, Fort Leavenworth, Kansas, private, "good"; died May 29, 1977, Danville, Virginia; buried Oak Hill Cemetery, Danville, Virginia

Caughman, David: born April 1879, Columbia, South Carolina; enlisted January 8, 1899, Columbia, South Carolina, bell porter, assigned Company L, Twenty-Fourth Infantry; discharged February 7, 1902, Camp Skagway, Alaska, private, "excellent"; enlisted April 2, 1902, Charlotte, North Carolina, soldier, assigned to Tenth Cavalry; transferred to Company L, Twenty-Fourth Infantry; discharged November 26, 1902, Fort Missoula, Montana, private, "without honor"

Coats, Lafayette: born February 1872, Hart County, Kentucky; enlisted November 1, 1894, Louisville, Kentucky, farmer, assigned Company G, Twenty-Fourth Infantry; discharged October 31, 1897, Fort Douglas, Utah, private, "good"; enlisted May 17, 1898, Indianapolis, Indiana, soldier, assigned M Troop, Ninth Cavalry; discharged January 27, 1899, Fort Grant, Arizona Territory, private, "good"; enlisted January 31, 1899, Fort Grant, Arizona Territory, soldier, assigned Company L, Twenty-Fourth Infantry; discharged January 30, 1902, Camp Skagway, Alaska, private, "excellent"; enlisted March 21, 1902, Louisville, Kentucky, soldier, assigned Company L, Twenty-Fourth Infantry; discharged March 20, 1905, Fort Bayard, New Mexico, private, "very good"

Collier, Emery: born March 1877, Dayton, Ohio; enlisted March 15, 1899, Anniston, Alabama, cook, assigned Company L, Twenty-Fourth Infantry; discharged May 22, 1900, Camp Skagway, Alaska, private, "without honor"

Collier, Frank: born January 1873, Portsmouth, New Hampshire; enlisted February 15, 1899, Boston, Massachusetts, machinist, assigned Company L, Twenty-Fourth Infantry; discharged February 14, 1902, Camp Skagway, Alaska, private, "very good"

Collins, Edward J.: born July 1875, Piqua, Ohio; enlisted February 15, 1899, Piqua, Ohio, laborer, assigned Company L, Twenty-Fourth Infantry; discharged February 14, 1902, private, "excellent"; April 16, 1910, laborer, Piqua, Ohio; died September 7, 1958, Dayton, Ohio; buried Dayton National Cemetery, Dayton, Ohio

Cotton, Robert: born May 6, 1863, Boyle County, Kentucky; enlisted December 13, 1885, Fort Sill, Indian Territory, farmer, assigned Company I, Twenty-Fourth Infantry; discharged December 12, 1890, Fort Thomas, Arizona Territory, private, "excellent"; enlisted December 15, 1890, Fort Thomas, Arizona Territory, soldier, assigned Company E, Twenty-Fourth Infantry; discharged December 12, 1895, Fort Bayard, New Mexico, private, "very good"; enlisted December 13, 1895, Fort Bayard, New Mexico, soldier, assigned Company E, Twenty-Fourth Infantry; transferred to Hospital Corps, June 30, 1895, Fort Duchesne, Utah; discharged December 12, 1898, Fort Duchesne, Utah, private, "excellent"; enlisted December 17, 1898, Fort Douglas, Utah, soldier, assigned Company L, Twenty-Fourth Infantry; discharged December 16, 1901, Camp Skagway, Alaska, private, "excellent"; enlisted December 17, 1901, Camp Skagway, Alaska, soldier, assigned Company L, Twenty-Fourth Infantry; discharged August 8, 1902, Fort Missoula, Montana, private, "excellent"; enlisted July 3, 1903, Lexington, Kentucky, farmer, assigned Company L, Twenty-Fourth Infantry; discharged November 22, 1905, Fort Missoula, Montana, private, "excellent"; enlisted November 23, 1905, Fort Missoula, Montana, soldier, assigned Company L, Twenty-Fourth Infantry; discharged November 22, 1908, Madison Barracks, New York, corporal, "excellent"; enlisted November 23, 1908, Madison Barracks, New York, soldier, assigned Company L, Twenty-Fourth Infantry; discharged November 22, 1911, Madison Barracks, corporal, "excellent"; enlisted November 23, 1911, Madison Barracks, New York, farmer, assigned Company L, Twenty-Fourth Infantry; retired April 7, 1912, Fort McDowell, California, first sergeant; died February 9, 1956; buried Locust Grove Cemetery, Nicholasville, Kentucky

Cropper, Samuel: born March 1861, Texana, Texas; enlisted March 10, 1882, Baltimore, Maryland, laborer, assigned K Troop, Tenth Cavalry; discharged March 9, 1887, Fort Grant, Arizona Territory, private, "good"; enlisted March 26, 1887, Baltimore, Maryland, soldier, assigned Company G, Twenty-Fourth Infantry; discharged March 25, 1892, Fort Bayard, New Mexico, private, "very good"; enlisted April 8, 1892, Baltimore, Maryland, soldier, assigned Company F, Twenty-Fifth Infantry; discharged April 7, 1897, Fort Missoula, Montana, private, "good"; enlisted April 16, 1897, Baltimore, Maryland, soldier, assigned Company D, Twenty-Fourth Infantry, transferred to Company L, Twenty-Fourth Infantry; discharged April 15, 1900, Camp Skagway, Alaska, private, "very good"; enlisted October 13, 1903, Baltimore, Maryland, soldier, assigned Company D, Twenty-Fourth Infantry; discharged November 18, 1903, Fort Harrison, Montana, private, "very good"; discharged November 18, 1905, Fort Harrison, Montana; enlisted November 19, 1905, Fort Harrison, Montana, soldier, assigned Company D, Twenty-Fourth Infantry; discharged November 18, 1908, Madison Barracks, New York, private, "very good"; enlisted November 24, 1908, Ontario, New York, soldier, assigned Company F, Twenty-Fourth Infantry; discharged Fort Ontario, New York, private, "good"; enlisted November 29, 1911, Ontario, New York, soldier, assigned Company H, Twenty-Fourth Infantry; retired August 12, 1912, Fort McDowell, California, cook

Daily, William: born July 1867, Stateburg, South Carolina; enlisted February 14, 1899, Columbia, South Carolina, porter, assigned Company L, Twenty-Fourth Infantry; discharged, February 8, 1902, Camp Skagway, Alaska, private, "excellent"; enlisted April 4, 1902, Charlotte, North Carolina, soldier, assigned Company D, Twenty-Fourth Infantry; discharged April 13, 1905, Fort Harrison, Montana, private, "good"; enlisted April 24, 1905, Fort Harrison, Montana, soldier, assigned Company D, Twenty-Fourth Infantry; discharged April 23, 1908, Madison Barracks, New York, private, "good"; enlisted April 25, 1911, Madison Barracks, New York, soldier, assigned Company D, Twenty-Fourth Infantry; discharged April 24, 1914, Manila, Philippines, private, "very good"

Dalton, Kitt: born June 1873, Hartsville, Tennessee; enlisted January 13, 1899, Indianapolis, Indiana, farmer, assigned Company L, Twenty-Fourth Infantry; discharged January 12, 1902, Camp Skagway, Alaska, corporal, "excellent"; enlisted May 25, 1911, Vancouver Barracks, Washington, laborer, assigned Company M, Twenty-Fifth Infantry; discharged May 25, 1914, Schofield Barracks, Hawaii Territory, artificer, "excellent"

Davis, John E.: born July 1877, Mecklenburg, Virginia; enlisted March 2, 1899 Philadelphia, Pennsylvania, laborer, assigned Company L, Twenty-Fourth Infantry; discharged March 1, 1902, Camp Skagway, Alaska, artificer, "excellent"; enlisted March 2, 1902, Camp Skagway, Alaska, soldier, assigned Company L, Twenty-Fourth Infantry; discharged March 1, 1905, Fort Missoula, Montana, artificer, "excellent"; enlisted May 23, 1905, Norfolk, Virginia, soldier, assigned Company L, Twenty-Fourth Infantry; discharged May 22, 1908, Madison Barracks, New York, corporal, "excellent"; enlisted May 23, 1908, Madison Barracks, New York, soldier, assigned Company L, Twenty-Fourth Infantry; discharged May 22, 1911, Madison Barracks, New York, cook, "excellent"; enlisted May 23, 1911, Madison Barracks, New York, soldier, assigned Company L, Twenty-Fourth Infantry; discharged July 1, 1913, Fort Bayard, New Mexico, disability, private, "good"

Davis, Reid W.: born February 1878, Saint Augustine, Florida; enlisted March 10, 1899, Camp George H. Thomas, Georgia, laborer, assigned Company L, Twenty-Fourth Infantry; discharged March 9, 1902, Camp Skagway, Alaska, private, "excellent"; living April 28, 1910, Springfield City, Massachusetts; died February 3, 1926, New York City; buried City Cemetery

Dawson, Junius: born June 1876, Fredericksburg, Virginia; enlisted March 14, 1899, Philadelphia, Pennsylvania, laborer, assigned Company L, Twenty-Fourth Infantry; discharged March 13, 1902, Camp Skagway, Alaska, private, "excellent"; enlisted May 26, 1902, Philadelphia, soldier, assigned Company L, Twenty-Fourth Infantry; discharged May 25, 1905, Fort Missoula, Montana, corporal, "excellent"; enlisted May 26, 1905, Fort Missoula, Montana, soldier, assigned Company L,

Twenty-Fourth Infantry; discharged May 25, 1908; Madison Barracks, New York, first sergeant, "excellent"; enlisted May 26, 1908, Madison Barracks, New York, soldier, assigned Company L, Twenty-Fourth Infantry; discharged May 25, 1911, sergeant, "excellent"; enlisted May 26, 1911, Madison Barracks, New York, soldier, assigned Company L, Twenty-Fourth Infantry; discharged May 25, 1914, Fort William McKinley, Philippines, sergeant, "excellent"

Dewey, Edward G.: born April 24, 1878, New Bern, North Carolina; discharged Company L, Sixth Massachusetts Volunteer Infantry, January 21, 1899; enlisted January 23, 1899, Boston, Massachusetts, metal polisher, assigned Company H, Twenty-Fourth Infantry; reassigned Company L, Twenty-Fourth Infantry; discharged January 22, 1902, Hot Springs, Alaska, corporal, "good"; enlisted January 23, 1902, Hot Springs, Alaska, soldier, assigned Company L, Twenty-Fourth Infantry; discharged on disability, March 9, 1902, Hot Springs, Alaska, private, "excellent"

Doolin, Joseph H.: born September 1880, Jessamine County, Kentucky; enlisted October 15, 1898, Lexington, Kentucky, laborer, assigned Company K, Twenty-Fifth Infantry; discharged March 1, 1899, Fort Logan, Colorado, private, "good"; enlisted October 9, 1900, Lexington, Kentucky, farmer, assigned Company L, Twenty-Fourth Infantry; arrived November 3, 1900, Camp Skagway, Alaska; discharged November 26, 1902, Fort Missoula, Montana, private, "excellent"

Ellis, Thomas: born Shoenis City, Alabama, January 1878; enlisted September 28, 1900, Birmingham, Alabama, laborer, assigned Company L, Twenty-Fourth Infantry; arrived November 3, 1900, Camp Skagway, Alaska; discharged September 26, 1903, Fort Missoula, Montana, private, "excellent"

Fletcher, Charles: born March 1864, Laurinburg, North Carolina; enlisted February 8, 1899, Columbia, South Carolina, painter, assigned Company L, Twenty-Fourth Infantry; discharged February 7, 1902, Camp Skagway, Alaska, private, "very good"; enlisted March 21, 1902, Charlotte, North Carolina, soldier, assigned K Troop, Tenth Cavalry; discharged November 29, 1902, Fort Robinson, Nebraska, private, "fair"

Fox, William: born April 1865, Richmond, Virginia; enlisted March 3, 1884, Louisville, Kentucky, laborer, assigned Company D, Twenty-Fourth Infantry; discharged March 2, 1889, Fort Bayard, New Mexico, private, "good"; enlisted April 3, 1889, Fort Bayard, New Mexico, assigned Company D, Twenty-Fourth Infantry; discharged April 2, 1894, Fort Bayard, New Mexico, Wagoner, "good"; enlisted April 3, 1894, Fort Bayard, New Mexico, assigned Company D, Twenty-Fourth Infantry; discharged July 2, 1897, Fort Douglas, Utah, private, "good"; enlisted August 2, 1897, Fort Douglas, Utah, assigned Company D, Twenty-Fourth Infantry; discharged September 1, 1900, Fort Harrison, Montana, private; enlisted April 17, 1901, Fort Harrison, Montana, assigned Company L, Twenty-Fourth Infantry; arrived Camp Skagway, Alaska, April 27, 1901; discharged April 16, 1904, Fort Missoula, Montana, corporal, "excellent"; enlisted April 17, 1904, Fort Missoula, Montana, assigned Company L, Twenty-Fourth Infantry; discharged November 22, 1904, Fort Missoula, Montana, quartermaster sergeant, "excellent"; enlisted November 23, 1905, Fort Missoula, Montana, assigned L Troop, Ninth Cavalry; discharged November 22, 1908, Madison Barracks, New York, corporal, "excellent"; enlisted November 23, 1908, Madison Barracks, New York, assigned Company L, Twenty-Fourth Infantry; discharged November 22, 1911, Madison Barracks, New York, corporal, "excellent"; enlisted November 23, 1911, Madison Barracks, New York, assigned Company L, Twenty-Fourth Infantry; retired February 10, 1913, Fort McDowell, California, first sergeant; died October 10, 1917, Watertown, New York; buried Sackets Harbor Military Cemetery

Franklin, John: born February 1873, Nashville, Tennessee; enlisted January 8, 1992, Evansville, Indiana, laborer, assigned Company H, Twenty-Fourth Infantry; discharged January 7, 1897, Fort Douglas, Utah, private, "excellent"; enlisted January 11, 1897, Fort Douglas, Utah, soldier, assigned Company H, Twenty-Fourth Infantry; reassigned Company L, Twenty-Fourth Infantry; discharged January 10, 1900, Fort Wrangel, Alaska, corporal, "very good"; enlisted April 9, 1900, Portland, Oregon, assigned L Troop, Ninth Cavalry; discharged April

8, 1903, San Francisco, California, corporal, "excellent"; discharged November 17, 1908; enlisted November 18, 1908, Camp McGrath, Philippines, assigned H Troop, Ninth Cavalry, assigned Army War College, Washington DC; discharged November 17, 1911, Fort Meyer, Virginia, private, "excellent"; enlisted November 18, 1911, Fort Meyer, Virginia, assigned Army War College, Fort Meyer, Virginia; honorably discharged November 17, 1914

Freeman, William: born December 1877, Madison, Georgia; enlisted September 20, 1900, Macon, Georgia, laborer, assigned Company L, Twenty-Fourth Infantry; arrived November 3, 1900, Camp Skagway, Alaska; discharged November 26, 1902, Fort Missoula, Montana, corporal, "excellent"; enlisted December 30, 1902, Macon, Georgia, assigned Company C, Twenty-Fifth Infantry; discharged December 29, 1905, Fort Niobrara, Nebraska, corporal, "excellent"

Gant, Frank: born December 1867, Washington DC; enlisted March 9, 1899, Philadelphia, Pennsylvania, assigned Company L, Twenty-Fourth Infantry; discharged January 24, 1901, Camp Skagway, Alaska, private, "without honor"; living 1901, Washington DC

Grant, Robert: born November 1876, Philadelphia, Pennsylvania; enlisted in U.S. Navy June 28, 1898, served on USS *Vermont*, USS *Siren*, USS *Franklin*; discharged honorably October 8, 1898, ordinary seaman; enlisted October 10, 1898, U.S. Navy; deserted December 24, 1898, New York City, New York; enlisted December 27, 1898, New York City, New York, sailor, assigned Company L, Twenty-Fourth Infantry; transferred Hospital Corps, January 6, 1900; serving civilian jail term, April–June 1901, Sitka, Alaska; deserted September 7, 1901; dropped as deserter, September 17, 1901

Graves, John: born May 1874, Staunton, Virginia; enlisted February 13, 1899, Pittsburgh, Pennsylvania, laborer, assigned Company L, Twenty-Fourth Infantry; discharged January 11, 1900, Camp Skagway, Alaska, private, "without honor"

Green, Benjamin: born August 1875, Piqua, Ohio; enlisted March 22, 1899, Dayton, Ohio, teamster, assigned Company L, Twenty-Fourth Infantry; discharged March 21, 1902, Camp Skagway, Alaska, corporal, "excellent"; lived December 4, 1910, in Tanana Town, Fort Gibbon, Alaska, working as a teamster; lived October 23, 1929 in Fairbanks, Alaska, working as a teamster; died March 17, 1940, Fairbanks, Alaska; buried Clay Street Cemetery, Fairbanks, Alaska

Hanson, William: born August 27, 1852, Simpsonville, Kentucky; enlisted August 20, 1872, Louisville, Kentucky, farmer, assigned E Troop, Tenth Cavalry; discharged June 1, 1877, San Felipe, Texas, private, "good"; enlisted April 23, 1878, Cincinnati, Ohio, laborer, assigned Company G, Twenty-Fifth Infantry; discharged April 22, 1883, Fort Hale, Dakota Territory, private, "good"; enlisted May 1, 1883, Fort Snelling, Minnesota, assigned Company B, Twenty-Fifth Infantry; discharged April 30, 1888, Fort Snelling, Minnesota, corporal, "very good"; enlisted May 1, 1888, Fort Snelling, Minnesota, assigned Company B, Twenty-Fifth Infantry; discharged May 27, 1891, Fort Shaw, Montana, corporal, "good"; enlisted December 7, 1899, Saint Paul, Minnesota, assigned Company D, Twenty-Fifth Infantry; discharged December 6, 1898, Fort Douglas, Utah, corporal, "excellent"; enlisted December 7, 1898, assigned Company L, Twenty-Fourth Infantry; discharged December 6, 1901, Camp Skagway, Alaska, sergeant, "excellent"; enlisted December 7, 1901, Camp Skagway, Alaska, assigned Company L, Twenty-Fourth Infantry; discharged December 6, 1904, Fort Missoula, Montana, quartermaster sergeant, "excellent"; enlisted December 7, 1904, Fort Missoula, Montana, assigned to color guard, Twenty-Fourth Infantry; retired June 25, 1905, Fort Missoula, Montana, color sergeant

Harrill, Doc L.: born August 1873, Rutherfordton, North Carolina; enlisted January 18, 1899, Chattanooga, Tennessee, railroad man, assigned Company L, Twenty-Fourth Infantry; discharged January 17, 1902, Camp Skagway, Alaska, private, "excellent"; enlisted February 12, 1902, Chattanooga, Tennessee, assigned Company K, Twenty-Fifth Infantry; discharged February 11, 1905, Fort Niobrara, Nebraska, corporal, "excellent"; enlisted February 12, 1905, Fort Niobrara, Nebraska, assigned Company K, Twenty-Fifth Infantry; discharged February 5, 1907, Fort McIntosh, Texas, sergeant, "excellent"; enlisted February 6, 1910, Fort George Wright, Washington, assigned Company K, Twenty-Fifth Infantry; discharged December 23, 1912, sergeant, "very good"; lived in Spokane, Washington 1915–31; worked as a railway porter, 1920

Harris, Ovid C.: born January 1979, Dallas, North Carolina; enlisted October 8, 1900, Birmingham, Alabama, student, assigned Company L, Twenty-Fourth Infantry; arrived November 3, 1900, Camp Skagway, Alaska; discharged November 26, 1902, Fort Missoula, Montana, private, "excellent"

Harris, Robert: born August 1866, Martinsville, Virginia; enlisted June 19, 1893, Cincinnati, Ohio, laborer, assigned Company C, Twenty-Fourth Infantry; discharged September 18, 1896, Fort Huachuca, Arizona Territory, private, "good"; enlisted December 12, 1896, Cincinnati, Ohio, soldier, assigned Company D, Twenty-Fourth Infantry; reassigned Company L, Twenty-Fourth Infantry; discharged December 11, 1899, Fort Wrangel, Alaska, private, "without honor"

Hayes, Allen: born October 1862, Cherokee County, North Carolina; enlisted September 9, 1881, Saint Louis, Missouri, laborer, assigned Company I, Twenty-Fourth Infantry; discharged September 8, 1886, Fort Sill, Indian Territory, private, "good"; enlisted September 13, 1886, Fort Sill, Indian Territory, assigned Company G, Twenty-Fourth Infantry; discharged September 12, 1891, San Carlos, Arizona Territory, private, "very good"; enlisted September 14, 1891, San Carlos, Arizona Territory, assigned Company G, Twenty-Fourth Infantry; discharged September 13, 1896, Fort Bayard, New Mexico, private, "good"; enlisted September 17, 1896, Fort Bayard, New Mexico, assigned Company E, Twenty-Fourth Infantry; reassigned Company L, Twenty-Fourth Infantry; discharged September 16, 1899 Fort Wrangel, Alaska, sergeant, "very good"; enlisted September 17, 1899, Fort Wrangel, Alaska, assigned Company L, Twenty-Fourth Infantry; discharged September 16, 1902, Fort Missoula, Montana, private, "very good"; enlisted September 17, 1902, Fort Missoula, Montana, assigned Company L, Twenty-Fourth Infantry; discharged September 16, 1905, Fort Missoula, Montana, corporal, "excellent"; enlisted September 17, 1905,

Fort Missoula, Montana, assigned Company L, Twenty-Fourth Infantry, assigned to color guard, retired April 6, 1908, Madison Barracks, New York, color sergeant

Hayman, Charles A.: born August 1872, Hamilton, Virginia; enlisted September 27. 1898, Washington DC, driver, assigned Company L, Twenty-Fourth Infantry; discharged January 28, 1899, Fort Douglas, Utah, private, "good"; enlisted February 7, 1899, Washington DC, assigned Company L, Twenty-Fourth Infantry; discharged November 28, 1899, Fort Wrangel, Alaska, disability, private, "good"

Henry, Oscar D.: born December 1870, Atlanta, Georgia; enlisted March 22, 1899, Chattanooga, Tennessee, laborer, assigned Company L, Twenty-Fourth Infantry; died May 4, 1901, Fort Bayard, New Mexico, private, pulmonary tuberculosis

Holland, James H.: born May 1873, Norfolk, Virginia; enlisted March 2, 1899, Boston, Massachusetts, sailor, assigned Company L, Twenty-Fourth Infantry; discharged March 1, 1902, Camp Skagway, Alaska, private, "excellent"; enlisted October 28, 1911, cook, assigned Company H, Twenty-Fourth Infantry; honorably discharged October 21, 1914; living in San Francisco, California, April 5, 1930

Holloway, Ike: born March 1875, Columbus, Alabama; enlisted March 30, 1899, Anniston, Alabama, painter/carpenter, assigned Company L, Twenty-Fourth Infantry; discharged April 16, 1900, Fort Wrangel, Alaska, private, "without honor"

Hovey, Henry W.: born September 1, 1852, Vassalboro, Maine; married February 13, 1878, to Carrie French Tower, Saint Ann's Church, New York City, New York; commissioned second lieutenant, 1869, Company B, Seventh Infantry Regiment, New York National Guard, New York City, New York; 1880, commissioned second lieutenant, Twenty-Fourth Infantry; daughter Clara Drummond Hovey born December 20, 1882, Fort Sill, Oklahoma Territory; son Bradford Pierce Hovey born April 3, 1886, Fort Sill, Oklahoma Territory; promoted May 1888 to first lieutenant; assigned September 1895 as professor of military science and tactics, Norwich University, Northfield, Vermont; promoted April 26, 1898 to captain; rejoined March 1899 commanding Company L, Twenty-Fourth Infantry, Fort Douglas, Utah; promoted August 14, 1903 to major; deployed July 1906 to Philippine Islands; retired November 7, 1907 for disability; died November 15, 1908, Northfield, Vermont; buried Center Cemetery, Northfield, Vermont

Howard, William: born May 1873, Philadelphia, Pennsylvania; enlisted March 10, 1899, Philadelphia, Pennsylvania, laborer, assigned Company L, Twenty-Fourth Infantry; discharged March 9, 1902, Camp Skagway, Alaska, private, "good"; enlisted May 17, 1902, Philadelphia, Pennsylvania, soldier, assigned Company M, Twenty-Fourth Infantry; discharged May 16, 1905, Fort Missoula, Montana, private, "good"; enlisted May 19, 1905 Fort Missoula, Montana, soldier, assigned B Troop, Tenth Cavalry; discharged May 18, 1908, Camp Wallace, Philippines, private, "good"; enlisted June 8, 1908, Fort William McKinley, Philippines, laborer, assigned L Troop, Tenth Cavalry; discharged June 7, 1911, Fort Ethan Allen, Vermont, private, "good"; enlisted June 16, 1911, Jefferson Barracks, Missouri, soldier, assigned M Troop, Ninth Cavalry; discharged June 15, 1911, Douglas, Arizona Territory, private, "good"

Hutson, Julius: born February 1879, Gallatin, Tennessee; enlisted September 14, 1898, Russellville, Kentucky, farmer, assigned Company L, Twenty-Fourth Infantry; discharged January 29, 1899, Fort Douglas, Utah, private, "good"; enlisted February 11, 1899, Indianapolis, Indiana, assigned Company L, Twenty-Fourth Infantry; discharged February 10, 1902, Camp Skagway, Alaska, private, "excellent"; enlisted March 31, 1902, Indianapolis, Indiana, assigned I Troop, Ninth Cavalry; discharged March 30, 1905, Jefferson Barracks, Missouri, private, "good"; enlisted August 24, 1905, Saint Louis, Missouri, assigned Company E, Twenty-Fourth Infantry; discharged August 23, 1908, Stony Point Rifle Range, Henderson, New York, private, "very good"; enlisted October 1, 1908, Fort McDowell, California, assigned I Troop, Ninth Cavalry; discharged October 1, 1911, Fort D. A. Russell, Wyoming, private, "good"

Jackson, Landon: born February 21, 1879, Rising Fawn, Georgia; enlisted January 18, 1899, Chattanooga, Tennessee, waiter, assigned Company L, Twenty-Fourth Infantry; discharged January 17, 1902, Camp Skagway, Alaska, private, "excellent"; enlisted February 12, 1902, Chattanooga, Tennessee, assigned Company K, Twenty-Fifth Infantry; discharged February 11, 1905, Fort Niobrara, Nebraska, private, "excellent"; enlisted February 6, 1907, Fort McIntosh, Texas, soldier, assigned Company K, Twenty-Fifth Infantry; discharged February 5, 1910, Fort George Wright, Washington, private, "excellent"; enlisted February 6, 1910, Fort George Wright, Washington, assigned Company K, Twenty-Fifth Infantry; discharged February 5, 1913, Schofield Barracks, Hawaii Territory, corporal, "excellent"; arrived June 1917, San Francisco, California, Sergeant, Company K, Twenty-Fifth Infantry; commissioned first lieutenant, October 15, 1917, Camp Des Moines, Iowa, assigned to Camp Grant, Illinois; retired July 21, 1924, first lieutenant; lived in Leavenworth, Kansas, May 1, 1930; promoted to first lieutenant, Regular Army, May 7, 1932; died March 9, 1958; buried Fort Leavenworth National Cemetery, Kansas

Jenks, Isaac C.: born February 3, 1867, Dedham, Massachusetts; appointed June 16, 1887, cadet, United States Military Academy, West Point, New York; commissioned June 12, 1891, second lieutenant, Twenty-Fourth Infantry; married June 16, 1897, to Alice A. Stevenson, Salt Lake City, Utah; promoted April 26, 1898, first lieutenant; daughter Dorthy Alice Jenks born October 24, 1898, Salt Lake City, Utah; promoted February 2, 1901, captain; promoted February 1, 1913, major; promoted May 15, 1917, lieutenant colonel; promoted August 5, 1917, colonel; died January 3, 1931, Pittsburgh, Pennsylvania; buried Arlington National Cemetery, Arlington, Virginia

Jennings, William: born 1868, Somerset County, New Jersey; enlisted February 11, 1899, Philadelphia, Pennsylvania, laborer, assigned Company L, Twenty-Fourth Infantry; discharged February 10, 1902, private, "excellent"

Johnson, Albert L.: born May 1875, Forreston, Illinois; enlisted May 24, 1898, Chicago, Illinois, assigned Company C, Twenty-Fourth Infantry; discharged May 23, 1901, Carraglan, Philippines, private, "very good"; enlisted July 21, 1901, Portland, Oregon; joined Company L,

Twenty-Fourth Infantry, September 3, 1901; discharged December 30, 1902, Fort Bayard, New Mexico, disability, private, "good"

Johnson, Charles S.: born May 1872, Columbus, Ohio; enlisted January 28, 1899, Columbus Barracks, Ohio, hostler, assigned Company M, Twenty-Fourth Infantry; reassigned Company L, Twenty-Fourth Infantry; dishonorable discharge November 25, 1899, Vancouver Barracks, Washington, private

Johnson, Ernest L.: born April 1872, Baltimore, Maryland; enlisted March 9, 1899, Philadelphia, Pennsylvania, butcher, assigned Company L, Twenty-Fourth Infantry; discharged March 8, 1902, Camp Skagway, Alaska, private, "excellent"

Johnson, John J.: born April 1868, Knox County, Tennessee; enlisted December 10, 1892, Lexington, Kentucky, assigned D Troop, Ninth Cavalry; discharged March 9, 1996, Fort Duchesne, Utah, private, "good"; enlisted December 17, 1896, Fort Douglas, Utah, assigned Company H, Twenty-Fourth Infantry; reassigned Company L, Twenty-Fourth Infantry; discharged December 16, 1899, Camp Skagway, Alaska, corporal, "excellent"; enlisted December 17, 1899, Camp Skagway, Alaska, assigned Company L, Twenty-Fourth Infantry; discharged December 16, 1902, Fort Missoula, Montana, private; discharged November 22, 1905; enlisted November 23, 1905, Fort Missoula, Montana; died April 25, 1908, General Hospital, San Francisco, California, uremia, private

Johnson, Samuel: born January 1879, Woodford County, Kentucky; enlisted September 11, 1900, Lexington, Kentucky, farmer, assigned Company L, Twenty-Fourth Infantry; arrived November 3, 1900, Camp Skagway, Alaska; discharged November 26, 1902, Fort Missoula, Montana, private, "excellent"

Johnston, Henry: born March 1877, Thompson, Georgia; enlisted September 29, 1900, laborer, assigned Company L, Twenty-Fourth Infantry; arrived November 3, 1900, Camp Skagway, Alaska; discharged June 9, 1902, Fort Missoula, Montana, private, "without honor"

Joiner, Fred: born April 1876, South Charleston, Ohio; discharged January 28, 1899, Company B, Ninth Battalion, Ohio Volunteer Infantry;

enlisted February 9, 1899, Columbus Barracks, Ohio, laborer, assigned Company L, Twenty-Fourth Infantry; discharged December 27, 1899 Fort Wrangel, Alaska, private, "without honor"

Jones, Thomas J.: born October 1879, Pulaski, Tennessee; enlisted March 15, 1899, Anniston, Alabama, laborer, assigned Company L, Twenty-Fourth Infantry; discharged March 14, 1902, Camp Skagway, Alaska, private, "good"; enlisted February 23, 1907, Columbus Barracks, Ohio, laborer, assigned Company E, Twenty-Fifth Infantry; discharged February 22, 1910, Fort George Wright, Washington, private, "good"; enlisted February 23, 1910, Fort George Wright, Washington, assigned Company E, Twenty-Fifth Infantry; discharged December 23, 1912, Fort George Wright, Washington, private, "excellent"

Jordan, Harry V.: born January 1868, Greencastle, Pennsylvania; enlisted March 1, 1899, Boston, Massachusetts, cook, assigned Company L, Twenty-Fourth Infantry; discharged December 8, 1900, Camp Skagway, Alaska, private, "without honor"

Jordan, Robert W.: born December 1872, Nashville, Tennessee; enlisted March 22, 1899, Dayton, Ohio, laborer, assigned Company L, Twenty-Fourth Infantry; discharged December 1, 1899, Fort Wrangel, Alaska, private, "without honor"

Kennedy, Thomas: born April 1876, Lincoln County, Kentucky; discharged June 30, 1901, Company D, Forty-Ninth U.S. Volunteer Infantry; enlisted July 27, 1901, Indianapolis, Indiana, soldier, assigned Company L, Twenty-Fourth Infantry; joined August 13, 1901; killed October 18, 1903, Fort Missoula, Montana, private

Kimball, John: born April 1876, Atlanta, Georgia; enlisted June 7, 1898, Atlanta, Georgia, confectioner, assigned Company A, Twenty-Fifth Infantry; discharged February 28, 1899, Fort Huachuca, Arizona Territory, private, "good"; enlisted March 13, 1899, Fort McPherson, Georgia, assigned Company L, Twenty-Fourth Infantry; sick February 10–April 2, 1900, Vancouver Barracks, Washington; discharged March 12, 1902, Camp Skagway, Alaska, private, "good"

Kincaid, Orestus J.: born July 1877, Stanford, Kentucky; discharged January 20, 1899, Company A, First Indiana Volunteer Infantry; enlisted

March 7, 1899, Indianapolis, Maryland, assigned Company L, Twenty-Fourth Infantry; discharged March 6, 1902, Camp Skagway, Alaska, sergeant, "excellent"; enlisted August 14, 1905, Indianapolis, Indiana, porter, assigned Company L, Twenty-Fourth Infantry; discharged February 5, 1907, Fort Reno, Oklahoma Territory, Quartermaster sergeant, "excellent"; enlisted February 6, 1907, Fort Reno, Oklahoma Territory, assigned Company A, Twenty-Fifth Infantry; discharged February 5, 1910, Fort Lawton, Washington; enlisted February 6, 1910, Fort Lawton, Washington, assigned Company A, Twenty-Fifth Infantry; discharged February 5, 1913, Schofield Barracks, Hawaii Territory, quartermaster sergeant, "excellent"

King, Robert: born October 1871, King George County, Virginia; enlisted September 27, 1898, Philadelphia, Pennsylvania, groom, assigned Company I, Twenty-Fifth Infantry; discharged February 28, 1899, Fort Logan, Colorado, private, "good"; enlisted March 9, 1899, Philadelphia, Pennsylvania, assigned Company L, Twenty-Fourth Infantry; discharged march 8, 1902, Camp Skagway, Alaska, private, "excellent"

Knox, Elijah H.: born June 1871, New Bedford, Massachusetts; discharged January 21, 1899, Company L, Sixth Massachusetts Volunteer Infantry; enlisted February 3, 1899, Boston, Massachusetts, porter, assigned Company L, Twenty-Fourth Infantry; discharged October 31, 1900, Camp Skagway, Alaska, disability, private, "good"

Lee, Elijah: born March 1877, Paducah, Kentucky; discharged March 6, 1899, Company H, Eighth U.S. Volunteer Infantry; enlisted March 10, 1899, Camp George H. Thomas Georgia, cook, assigned Company L, Twenty-Fourth Infantry; discharged March 9, 1902, Camp Skagway, Alaska, cook, "excellent"; enlisted March 10, 1902, Camp Skagway, Alaska, assigned Company L, Twenty-Fourth Infantry; discharged March 9, 1905, Fort Missoula, Montana, private, "very good"; enlisted March 11, 1905, Fort Missoula, Montana, assigned Company L, Twenty-Fourth Infantry; discharged January 24, 1908, General Hospital, San Francisco, California, disability, private, "excellent"

Mack, Thomas: born February 1873, Dickenson, Virginia; discharged January 28, 1899, Company D, Ninth Battalion, Ohio Volunteer Infantry; enlisted February 11, 1899, Columbus Barracks, Ohio, soldier, assigned Company L, Twenty-Fourth Infantry; discharged February 10, 1902, Camp Skagway, Alaska, private, "excellent"

Mack, William: born December 1877, Spartanburg, South Carolina; discharged March 8, 1899, Company H, Tenth U.S. Volunteer Infantry; enlisted March 20, 1899, Greenville, South Carolina, soldier, assigned Company L, Twenty-Fourth Infantry; died November 5, 1901, Fort Bayard, New Mexico, private, pulmonary tuberculosis

Martin, Henry C.: born August 12, 1879, Faunsdale, Alabama; enlisted March 13, 1899, Mobile, Alabama, schoolteacher, assigned Company L, Twenty-Fourth Infantry; discharged October 31, 1900, Camp Skagway, Alaska, disability, private, "good"; living, 1918, Washington DC; living 1942, Columbus, Ohio

Martin, Thomas: born May 1875, Martinsville, Virginia; discharged January 28, 1899, Company D, Ninth Battalion, Ohio Volunteer Infantry; enlisted February 9, 1899, Columbus Barracks, Ohio, soldier, assigned Company L, Twenty-Fourth Infantry; discharged February 8, 1902, Camp Skagway, Alaska, corporal, "excellent"; enlisted March 14, 1902, Portland, Oregon, assigned Company E, Twenty-Fifth Infantry; discharged March 13, 1905, Fort Reno, Oklahoma Territory, private, "excellent"; enlisted April 6, Washington Barracks, DC, assigned Company L, Twenty-Fourth Infantry; transferred Hospital Corps; discharged April 5, 1908 Division Hospital, Manila, Philippines, private first class, "excellent"; enlisted April 12, 1908, Cebu, Philippines, assigned Hospital Corps; discharged April 11, 1911, Camp Jossman, Philippines, private first class, "excellent"; enlisted April 12, 1911, Camp Jossman, Philippines, assigned Hospital Corps; discharged April 11, 1914, Camp Avery, Philippines, private first class, "excellent"

Matthews, James C.: born December 1877, Charleston, South Carolina; enlisted February 8, 1899, Philadelphia, Pennsylvania, laborer, assigned Company L, Twenty-Fourth Infantry; discharged February 7, 1902, Camp Skagway, Alaska, private, "very good"

McClellan, George A.: born March 1880, Talladega, Alabama; enlisted March 22, 1899, Chattanooga, Tennessee, laborer, assigned Company

L, Twenty-Fourth Infantry; discharged March 21, 1902, Camp Skagway, Alaska, private, "excellent"; enlisted May 15, 1902, Saint Paul, Minnesota, assigned Company A, Twenty-Fourth Infantry; transferred to Hospital Corps; discharged April 24, 1905, Fort McDowell, California, private, "very good"; enlisted December 7, 1905, Fort Des Moines, Iowa, assigned Hospital Corps; discharged December 6, 1908, Camp Ward Cheney, Philippines, private first class, "very good" enlisted December 7, 1908, Camp Ward Cheney, Philippines, assigned Hospital Corps; discharged December 6, 1911, Fort Ethan Allen, Vermont, private first class, "very good"; enlisted January 20, 1912, Fort Des Moines, Iowa, assigned Hospital Corps; honorably discharged January 16, 1915

McClinton, Willis: born June 14, 1872, Russell County, Alabama; enlisted March 7, 1898, Fort Logan H. Roots, Arkansas, laborer, assigned Company D, Twenty-Fourth Infantry; reassigned Company L, Twenty-Fourth Infantry; discharged March 6, 1901, Camp Skagway, Alaska, corporal, "excellent"; lived 1917–58, Seattle, Washington; died October 28, 1958, Seattle, Washington

McGee, Allen: born November 1861, Kingston, North Carolina; enlisted January 23, 1886, Baltimore, Maryland, hostler, assigned M Troop, Tenth Cavalry; discharged January 22, 1891, Fort Grant, Arizona Territory, private, "good"; enlisted February 17, 1891, Cincinnati, Ohio, assigned D Troop, Tenth Cavalry; discharged February 16, 1896, Fort Assiniboine, Montana, private, "good"; enlisted March 16, 1898, San Francisco, California, assigned Company C, Twenty-Fourth Infantry; reassigned Company L, Twenty-Fourth Infantry; discharged March 15, 1899, Fort Douglas, Utah, corporal, "excellent"; enlisted March 16, 1899, Fort Douglas, Utah, assigned Company L, Twenty-Fourth Infantry; discharged March 15, 1902, Camp Skagway, Alaska, sergeant, "excellent"; enlisted March 16, 1902, Camp Skagway, Alaska, assigned Company L, Twenty-Fourth Infantry; discharged March 15, 1905, Fort Missoula, Montana, sergeant, "excellent"; enlisted March 22, 1905, Saint Paul, Minnesota, assigned Company L, Twenty-Fifth Infantry; discharged February 5, 1907, Fort McIntosh, Texas, corporal, "excellent"; enlisted February 6, 1907, Fort McIntosh, Texas, assigned Company L, Twenty-Fifth Infantry; discharged February 5, 1910, Fort George Wright, Washington, corporal, "good"; enlisted February 11, 1910, Jefferson Barracks, Missouri, assigned Company D, Twenty-Fourth Infantry; retired March 5, 1911, Madison Barracks, New York, sergeant

McIntyre, David: born January 1879, Cambridge, Massachusetts; enlisted February 14, 1899, Boston, Massachusetts, barber, assigned Company L, Twenty-Fourth Infantry; sentenced April 6, 1900, to five months' jail time in Sitka, Alaska; discharged May 7, 1900, Fort Wrangel, Alaska, private, "without honor"

McMurry, Walter: born April 1881, Owensboro, Kentucky; discharged January 20, 1899, Company A, First Indiana Volunteer Infantry; enlisted February 8, 1899, Evansville, Indiana, volunteer soldier, assigned Company L, Twenty-Fourth Infantry; deserted October 1, 1899, Camp Skagway, Alaska

Merritt, Edgar: born January 1879, Hopkinsville, Kentucky; discharged January 20, 1899, Company A, First Indiana Volunteer Infantry; enlisted February 8, 1899, Evansville, Indiana, volunteer soldier, assigned Company L, Twenty-Fourth Infantry; discharged February 7, 1902, Camp Skagway, Alaska, private, "good"; enlisted March 12, 1902, Chicago, Illinois, assigned Company L, Twenty-Fourth Infantry; discharged March 11, 1905, Fort Missoula, Montana, private, "good"; enlisted April 18, 1905, Chicago, Illinois, assigned Company K, Twenty-Fifth Infantry; discharged May 23, 1905, Fort Niobrara, Nebraska, disability, private, "good"

Miller, Robert: born October 1866, Rutherford County, Tennessee; discharged January 26, 1899, Company K, Twenty-Fourth Infantry; enlisted October 12, 1900, Nashville, Tennessee, laborer, assigned Company L, Twenty-Fourth Infantry; arrived November 3, 1900, Camp Skagway, Alaska; discharged October 11, 1903, Fort Missoula, Montana, private, "excellent"; enlisted October 21, 1903, Nashville, Tennessee, assigned Company L, Twenty-Fourth Infantry; discharged November 22, 1905, Fort Missoula, Montana, private, "excellent"; enlisted November 23, 1905, Fort Missoula, Montana, assigned Company L, Twenty-Fourth Infantry; discharged May 10, 1907, Presidio, San Francisco, California, disability, private, "excellent"

Moore, Loney: born November 1872, Penola, Virginia; enlisted June 7, 1890, Saint Paul, Minnesota, cook, assigned Company A, Twenty-Fifth Infantry; discharged June 6, 1895, Fort Custer, Montana; enlisted June 15, 1895, Saint Paul, Minnesota, assigned Company B, Twenty-Fourth Infantry; discharged June 14, 1898, on board *City of Washington*, private, "good"; enlisted June 16, 1898, on board *City of Washington*, off Matanzas, Cuba, soldier, assigned to Company A, Twenty-Fourth Infantry; wounded July, 1, 1898, Battle of San Juan Hill; discharged January 27, 1899, Fort Douglas, Utah, corporal, "excellent"; enlisted January 28, 1899, Fort Douglas, Utah, assigned Company L, Twenty-Fourth Infantry; discharged May 15, 1900, Camp Skagway, Alaska, private, "without honor"; applied for pension as invalid, December 1, 1928, California

Morris, Ernest C.: born January 1874, Cairo, Illinois; discharged March 6, 1899, Company D, Eighth U.S. Volunteer Infantry; enlisted March 10, 1899, Camp George H. Thomas, Georgia, hostler, assigned Company L, Twenty-Fourth Infantry; discharged March 9, 1902, Camp Skagway, Alaska, private, "excellent"; arrested July 1902, Skagway, Alaska, for theft; acquitted October 14, 1902, Skagway, Alaska, by grand jury

Morton, Thomas: born May 1869, Bourbon County, Kentucky; enlisted February 7, 1899, Lexington, Kentucky, laborer, assigned Company L, Twenty-Fourth Infantry; discharged January 2, 1902, Fort Bayard, New Mexico, disability, private, "excellent"

Moulton, Prince A.: born April 1863, Warrensburg, Missouri; discharged April 1, 1895, Fort Bayard, New Mexico; enlisted April 2, 1895, Fort Bayard, New Mexico, assigned Company D, Twenty-Fourth Infantry; discharged April 1, 1898, Fort Douglas, Utah, musician, "good"; enlisted April 6, 1898, Fort Douglas, Utah, assigned Company D, Twenty-Fourth Infantry; discharged April 5, 1901, Fort Harrison, Montana, private, "good"; enlisted April 17, 1901, Fort Harrison, Montana, assigned Company L, Twenty-Fourth Infantry; arrived Camp Skagway, Alaska, April 27, 1901; discharged April 16, 1904, Fort Missoula, Montana, private, "excellent"

Mozeak, Thomas: born May 1879, Morgantown, North Carolina; discharged January 31, 1899, Company G, Third North Carolina Volunteer Infantry; enlisted March 10, 1899, Greenville, South Carolina, waiter, assigned Company L, Twenty-Fourth Infantry; discharged March 9, 1902, Camp Skagway, Alaska, private, "excellent"

Nash, Joseph A.: born February 1871, London, Ohio; discharged March 8, 1899, Company B, Tenth U.S. Volunteer Infantry; enlisted March 25, 1899, Richmond, Virginia, soldier, assigned Company L, Twenty-Fourth Infantry; discharged March 22, 1902, Camp Skagway, Alaska, musician, "excellent"

Oby, John W.: born April 9, 1876, Woodstock, Virginia; enlisted March 21, 1899, Pittsburgh, Pennsylvania, barber, assigned Company L, Twenty-Fourth Infantry; discharged March 20, 1902, Camp Skagway, Alaska, musician, "excellent"; living January 22, 1910, Juneau, Alaska, working as a barber; registered for World War I draft, September 9, 1918, Seattle, Washington, working as cook for Alaska Steamship Company; living April 7, 1930, Seattle, Washington, working as barber; applied December 1941, for Social Security; living 1942, Seattle, Washington

O'Connor, Robert: born June 1872, Gaston County, North Carolina; enlisted June 14, 1892, Albany, New York, laborer, assigned F Troop, Tenth Cavalry; discharged September 13, 1895, Fort Assiniboine, Montana, private, "good"; enlisted November 18, 1895, Saint Louis, Missouri, assigned Company C, Twenty-Fourth Infantry; discharged November 12, 1898, Fort Douglas, Utah, sergeant, "excellent"; enlisted November 13, 1898, Fort Douglas, Utah, assigned Company L, Twenty-Fourth Infantry; married April 3, 1899, to Louisa Withers, Salt Lake City, Utah; discharged, November 12, 1901, Camp Skagway, Alaska, sergeant, "good"; enlisted November 13, 1901, Camp Skagway Alaska, assigned Company L, Twenty-Fourth Infantry; discharged November 12, 1904, Fort Missoula, Montana, private, "very good"; enlisted December 3, 1904, Saint Louis, Missouri, assigned to Company F, Twenty-Fourth Infantry; discharged November 15, 1905, Fort Assiniboine, Montana, corporal, "very good"; enlisted November 16, 1905, Fort Assiniboine, Montana, assigned to Company F, Twenty-Fourth Infantry; dishonorable discharge, June 10, 1907, Camp Bumpus, Philippines, private; committed November 10, 1910, Stockton, California State Hospital, diagnosis of insanity, revised to alcoholism; discharged February 9, 1911, recovered

Pate, William: born May 1879, New Bern, North Carolina; discharged January 21, 1899, Boston, Massachusetts, Company L, Sixth Massachusetts Volunteer Infantry; enlisted January 23, 1899, Boston, Massachusetts, coachman, assigned Company L, Twenty-Fourth Infantry; discharged January 22, 1902, Camp Skagway, Alaska, private, "excellent"; enlisted January 3, 1903, Worchester, Massachusetts, coachman, Company M, Twenty-Fifth Infantry; dishonorable discharge November 3, 1905, Fort Niobrara, Nebraska

Payne, George M.: born October 1872, Washington DC; enlisted January 26, 1899, Indianapolis, Indiana, butler, assigned Company L, Twenty-Fourth Infantry; discharged December 8, 1900, Camp Skagway, Alaska, private, "without honor"

Perkins, John A.: born February 1879, Buckingham, Virginia; enlisted March 16, 1899, Philadelphia, Pennsylvania, laborer, assigned Company L, Twenty-Fourth Infantry; discharged March 15, 1902, Camp Skagway, Alaska, private, "not good"; resided in Skagway, Alaska, after discharge; sentenced May 10, 1902, to six months in jail in Sitka, Alaska; living January 10, 1910, Juneau, Alaska, working as a cook

Perry, Joseph: born October 1875, Summerville, South Carolina; enlisted September 28, 1900, Savannah, Georgia, laborer, assigned Company L, Twenty-Fourth Infantry; arrived November 3, 1900, Camp Skagway, Alaska; discharged November 26, 1902, Fort Missoula, Montana, private, "excellent"

Pon, Jacob A.: born August 1873, Orangeburg, South Carolina; discharged February 6, 1899, Company K, Third North Carolina Volunteer Infantry; enlisted March 3, 1899, Greenville, Alabama, fireman, assigned Company L, Twenty-Fourth Infantry; discharged March 2, 1902, Camp Skagway, Alaska, cook, "excellent"; enlisted March 3, 1902, Camp Skagway, Alaska, assigned Company L, Twenty-Fourth Infantry; discharged March 2, 1905, Fort Missoula, Montana, cook, "excellent";

enlisted March 3, 1905, cook, Fort Missoula, Montana; discharged November 20, 1905, Fort Missoula, Montana; enlisted November 23, 1905, Fort Missoula, Montana, assigned Company L, Twenty-Fourth Infantry; discharged November 22, 1908, Madison Barracks, New York, cook, "excellent"; enlisted November 23, 1908, Madison Barracks, New York, assigned Company L, Twenty-Fourth Infantry; reassigned Mounted Service School, Fort Riley, Kansas; discharged November 22, 1911, Fort Riley, Kansas, cook, "excellent"

Rains, Edward L.: born June 30, 1877, Nashville, Tennessee; enlisted April 14, 1898, Nashville, Tennessee, druggist, assigned Battery K, Sixth Artillery; transferred to Hospital Corps; discharged May 8, 1900, Fort Baker, California, to accept commission, "excellent"; commissioned July 25, 1900, second lieutenant, Twenty-Fourth Infantry; arrived August 27, 1900, Camp Skagway, Alaska; married January 26, 1901, to Ella Burns Hays, Tacoma, Washington; deserted 1908; dropped from the rolls March 6, 1909; married Madge P. Rains prior to 1920; married February 27, 1923, to Helen Cornelia MacVichie, Oakland, California; died September 1, 1924, Salt Lake City, Utah

Randall, Ernest C.: born December 1876, Worcester, Massachusetts; discharged November 18, 1898, Heavy Battery B, Connecticut Volunteer Artillery; enlisted December 27, 1898, New York City, New York, soldier, assigned Company L, Twenty-Fourth Infantry; discharged December 26, 1901, Camp Skagway, Alaska, private, "excellent"

Rare, James: born March 1871, Mount Sterling, Kentucky; enlisted February 14, 1899, Lexington, Kentucky, assigned Company L, Twenty-Fourth Infantry; discharged October 1, 1899, private, "without honor"

Ray, Charles F.: born April 1876, Bristol, Tennessee; enlisted March 22, 1899, Wilmington, Delaware, laborer, assigned Company L, Twenty-Fourth Infantry; discharged March 21, 1902, Camp Skagway, Alaska, private, "excellent"

Reed, Charles: born December 1866, Clark County, Virginia; enlisted September 20, 1898, Pittsburgh, Pennsylvania, hostler, assigned Company L, Twenty-Fourth Infantry; discharged January 27, 1899, Fort Douglas, Utah, wagoner, "very good"; enlisted February 10, 1899, Pittsburgh, Pennsylvania, assigned Company L, Twenty-Fourth Infantry; discharged February 9, 1902, Camp Skagway, Alaska, quartermaster sergeant, "excellent"; enlisted April 21, 1902, Pittsburgh, Virginia, assigned Company L, Twenty-Fourth Infantry; discharged April 20, 1905, Fort Missoula, Montana, private, "excellent"; enlisted April 21, 1905, Fort Missoula, Montana, assigned Company L, Twenty-Fourth Infantry; discharged April 20, 1908, Madison Barracks, New York, quartermaster sergeant, "excellent"; enlisted April 21, 1908, Madison Barracks, New York, assigned Company L, Twenty-Fourth Infantry; discharged March 20, 1911, Madison Barracks, New York, quartermaster sergeant, "excellent"; enlisted March 21, 1911, Madison Barracks, New York, assigned Company L, Twenty-Fourth Infantry; discharged March 20, 1914, Camp McGrath, Philippines, first sergeant, "excellent"

Reed, James E. B.: born October 1869, Charleston, Ohio; enlisted December 13, 1898, Buffalo, New York, printer, assigned Company L, Twenty-Fourth Infantry; discharged December 14, 1901, Camp Skagway, Alaska, private, "excellent"; married Julia Ann Gay, April 4, 1904, Seattle, Washington; worked, January 1904, as editor of the *Georgetown South Seattle News*; worked as printer, 1920, Butte, Montana; worked as printer, 1933, Toledo, Ohio; died April 29, 1942, Toledo, Ohio

Richards, Charles D.: November 1879, Paschalville, Pennsylvania; enlisted February 4, 1899, Philadelphia, Pennsylvania, laborer, assigned Company L, Twenty-Fourth Infantry; discharged February 3, 1902, Camp Skagway, Alaska, private, "excellent"

Roberts, Wilkins G.: born September 1878, Burke County, Georgia; enlisted October 12, 1900, Savannah, Georgia, laborer, assigned Company L, Twenty-Fourth Infantry; arrived November 3, 1900, Camp Skagway, Alaska; discharged November 26, 1902, Fort Missoula, Montana, private, "very good"

Robinson, Henry C.: born October 1864, Albemarle County, Virginia; enlisted September 27, 1886, Washington DC, waiter, assigned Company K, Twenty-Fifth Infantry; discharged September 26, 1891, Fort Buford, North Dakota, private, "good"; enlisted November 29, 1892, Washington DC, assigned Company F, Twenty-Fourth Infantry; discharged November 28, 1897, Fort Douglas, Utah, corporal, "excellent"; enlisted November 29, 1897, Fort Douglas, Utah, assigned Company F, Twenty-Fourth Infantry; transferred to Company L, Twenty-Fourth Infantry; married September 30, 1898, to Sarah Clemmens; discharged November 28, 1900, Camp Skagway Alaska, sergeant, "excellent"; enlisted December 18, 1900, Camp Skagway, Alaska, assigned Company L, Twenty-Fourth Infantry; discharged December 17, 1903, Fort Missoula, Montana, first sergeant, "excellent"; enlisted December 18, 1903, Fort Missoula, Montana, assigned Company L, Twenty-Fourth Infantry; discharged November 22, 1905, Fort Missoula, Montana, sergeant, "excellent"; enlisted November 23, 1905, Fort Missoula, Montana, assigned Company L, Twenty-Fourth Infantry; discharged November 22, 1908, Madison Barracks, New York, first sergeant, "excellent"; enlisted November 23, 1908, Madison Barracks, New York, assigned Company L, Twenty-Fourth Infantry; discharged November 22, 1911, Madison Barracks, first sergeant, "excellent"; enlisted November 23, 1911, Madison Barracks, New York, assigned Company L, Twenty-Fourth Infantry; retired July 11, 1912, Fort McDowell, California, first sergeant

Rollins, William: born March 1870, Christian County, Kentucky; enlisted April 23, 1901, Portland, Oregon, porter, assigned Company L, Twenty-Fourth Infantry; arrived May 2, 1901, Camp Skagway, Alaska; discharged April 22, 1904, Fort Missoula, Montana, sergeant, "excellent"

Rucker, Edward: born April 1877, Shelbyville, Kentucky; enlisted September 29, 1900, Louisville, Kentucky, teamster, assigned Company L, Twenty-Fourth Infantry; arrived November 3, 1900, Camp Skagway, Alaska; deserted April 28, 1901, Camp Skagway, Alaska

Rucker, John: born September 1876, Simpsonville, Kentucky; enlisted September 29, 1900, Louisville, Kentucky, laborer, assigned Company L, Twenty-Fourth Infantry; arrived November 3, 1900, Camp Skagway, Alaska; discharged June 1, 1902, Fort Missoula, Montana, private, "without honor"

Rudisell, William: born October 1879, Williamstown, Texas; discharged Camp Thomas, Georgia, March 6, 1899, Company D, Eighth U.S. Volunteer Infantry; enlisted March 13, 1899, Mobile, Alabama, soldier, assigned Company L, Twenty-Fourth Infantry; discharged March 12, 1902, Camp Skagway, Alaska, private, "excellent"

Sanders, Chester: February 22, 1879, Carrollton, Kentucky; inducted into federal service, July 25, 1898, assigned Company D, Eighth U.S. Volunteer Infantry; discharged March 6, 1899, Camp Thomas, Georgia; enlisted March 9, 1899, Camp Thomas, Georgia, porter, assigned Company L, Twenty-Fourth Infantry; discharged March 8, 1902, Camp Skagway, Alaska, private, "excellent"; enlisted March 9, 1902, Camp Skagway, Alaska, assigned Company L, Twenty-Fourth Infantry; discharged March 8, 1905, Fort Missoula, Montana, sergeant, "excellent"; enlisted March 9, 1905, Fort Missoula, Montana, assigned Company L, Twenty-Fourth Infantry; discharged November 22, 1905, sergeant, "excellent"; enlisted November 23, 1908, Fort Ontario, New York, assigned noncommissioned staff, Twenty-Fourth Infantry; discharged November 22, 1911, Madison Barracks, New York, battalion sergeant major, "excellent"; enlisted November 23, 1911, Fort Ontario, New York, assigned noncommissioned staff, Twenty-Fourth Infantry; honorable discharge, November 22, 1914; commissioned captain, October 15, 1917, Camp Des Moines, Iowa, assigned to 270th Infantry, Camp Grant, Illinois; discharged November 8, 1920, 370th Infantry, Camp Meade, Maryland, captain; died February 10, 1962; buried Los Angeles, California

Shannon, Huston: born March 1875, Bowling Green, Kentucky; enlisted March 22, 1899, Boston, Massachusetts, waiter, assigned Company L, Twenty-Fourth Infantry; discharged February 10, 1900, Camp Skagway, Alaska, private, "without honor"

Simmons, Esaw: born April 1878, Dugan County, North Carolina; discharged March 6, 1899, Company D, Eighth U.S. Volunteer Infantry; enlisted March 10, 1899, Camp Thomas, Georgia, assigned Company L, Twenty-Fourth Infantry; died March 6, 1901, Camp Skagway, Alaska, private, acute influenza

Sims, William: September 1877, Carlisle, South Carolina; discharged March 8, 1899, Company H, Tenth U.S. Volunteer Infantry; enlisted March 20, 1899, Greenville, South Carolina, butler, assigned Company

L, Twenty-Fourth Infantry; discharged March 19, 1902, Camp Skagway, Alaska, private, "excellent"; enlisted May 22, Macon, Georgia, assigned Company L, Twenty-Fourth Infantry; discharged November 27, 1902, Fort Missoula, Montana, disability, private, "excellent"

Slone, Leroy H.: born April 1874, Portsmouth, Ohio; enlisted January 29, 1899, Columbus, Barracks, Ohio, laborer, assigned Company L, Twenty-Fourth Infantry; discharged January 28, 1902, Camp Skagway, Alaska, private, "excellent"; enlisted March 4, 1902, Columbus Barracks, Ohio, assigned Company K, Twenty-Fourth Infantry; discharged March 3, 1905, Fort Missoula, Montana, private, "excellent"

Smith, David: born January 1881, Lexington, Kentucky; enlisted October 9, 1900, Lexington, Kentucky, laborer, assigned Company L, Twenty-Fourth Infantry; arrived November 3, 1900, Camp Skagway, Alaska; discharged November 26, 1902, Fort Missoula, Montana, private, "excellent"; enlisted October 27, 1903, Lexington, Kentucky, laborer, assigned Company D, Twenty-Fourth Infantry; discharged November 17, 1905, Fort Harrison, Montana, private, "good"; enlisted November 18, 1905, Fort Harrison, Montana, assigned Company D, Twenty-Fourth Infantry; discharged November 17, 1908, Madison Barracks, New York, private, "good"; enlisted November 21, 1908, Columbus Barracks, Ohio, assigned Company D, Twenty-Fourth Infantry; discharged November 22, 1911, Madison Barracks, New York, private, "good"; enlisted December 3, 1911, Fort Slocum, New York, assigned H Troop, Tenth Cavalry; discharged December 13, 1914, "without honor"

Smith, James: born January 1877, Jefferson County, Alabama; enlisted October 13, 1900, Cincinnati, Ohio, laborer, assigned Company L, Twenty-Fourth Infantry; arrived November 3, 1900, Camp Skagway, Alaska; discharged November 26, 1902, Fort Missoula, Montana, private, "excellent"

Snoten, Augustus: born April 1849, Sumner County, Tennessee; enlisted April 26, 1876, Nashville, Tennessee, laborer, assigned Company C, Twenty-Fourth Infantry; discharged April 25, 1881, Fort Sill, Indian Territory, private, "good"; enlisted April 26, 1881, Fort Sill, Indian Territory, assigned Company C, Twenty-Fourth Infantry; discharged April

25, 1886, Fort Sill, Indian Territory, private, "good"; enlisted April 26, 1886, Fort Sill, Indian Territory, assigned Company C, Twenty-Fourth Infantry; discharged April 25, 1891, Fort Grant, Arizona Territory, private, "good"; enlisted April 26, 1891, Fort Grant, Arizona Territory, assigned Company C, Twenty-Fourth Infantry; discharged April 25, 1896, Fort Huachuca, Arizona Territory, private, "very good"; enlisted April 26, 1896, Fort Huachuca, Arizona Territory, assigned Company C, Twenty-Fourth Infantry; wounded July 1, 1898, Battle of San Juan Hill; reassigned Company L, Twenty-Fourth Infantry; discharged April 25, 1899, Presidio of San Francisco, California, private, "excellent"; enlisted April 26, 1899, Presidio of San Francisco, California, assigned Company L, Twenty-Fourth Infantry; discharged April 25, 1902, Camp Skagway, Alaska, corporal, "very good"; enlisted April 26, 1902, Camp Skagway, Alaska, assigned Company L, Twenty-Fourth Infantry; retired September 21, 1904, Fort Missoula, Montana, color sergeant

Sterling, Develor: born August 1882, Tazewell, Tennessee; enlisted October 13, 1900, Knoxville, Tennessee, laborer, assigned Company L, Twenty-Fourth Infantry; arrived November 3, 1900, Camp Skagway, Alaska; discharged November 26, 1902, Fort Missoula, Montana, private, "excellent"; enlisted July 22, 1903, Knoxville, Tennessee, laborer, assigned C Troop, Ninth Cavalry; discharged July 27, 1906, Abilene, Kansas, private, "without honor"

Stewart, Harry: born December 1876, Xenia, Ohio; discharged March 6, 1899, Company C, Eighth U.S. Volunteer Infantry; enlisted March 13, 1899, Indianapolis, Indiana, soldier, assigned Company L, Twenty-Fourth Infantry; discharged March 12, 1902, Camp Skagway, Alaska, private, "very good"; enlisted March 13, 1902, Camp Skagway, Alaska, assigned Company L, Twenty-Fourth Infantry; discharged May 31, 1903, Fort Missoula, Montana, private, "without honor"

Stokes, Edward: born February 1878, Wilmington, North Carolina; enlisted March 10, 1899, Philadelphia, Pennsylvania, laborer, assigned Company L, Twenty-Fourth Infantry; discharged March 9, 1902, Camp Skagway, Alaska, private, "excellent"; enlisted May 17, 1902, Philadelphia, Pennsylvania, assigned Company M, Twenty-Fifth Infantry;

discharged May 16, 1905, Fort Niobrara, Nebraska, private, "good"; assigned Company B, Twenty-Fourth Infantry; discharged October 24, 1909; enlisted January 28, 1910, Jefferson Barracks, Missouri, assigned Company K, Twenty-Fifth Infantry; discharged December 23, 1912, Fort George Wright, Washington, private, "very good"

Swanson, Eugene: born December 1868, Rockford, Alabama; enlisted April 10, 1899, Chattanooga, Tennessee, painter, assigned Company L, Twenty-Fourth Infantry; discharged April 9, 1902, Camp Skagway, Alaska, corporal, "excellent"; married Amelia Beckwith, Skagway, Alaska; worked as teamster, January 6, 1920, Rampart, Alaska; applied for pension, July 17, 1926, Alaska; worked as miner, December 19, 1929, Rampart, Alaska; married Alice Graves, January 17, 1935, Fairbanks, Alaska; worked as miner, December 13, 1939, Hess Creek, Tolovana, Alaska; died December 30, 1942, Fairbanks, Alaska; buried Clay Street Cemetery, Fairbanks, Alaska

Taylor, John: born January 1879, Jeffersonville, Georgia; enlisted March 8, 1899, Macon, Georgia, assigned Company L, Twenty-Fourth Infantry; discharged March 7, 1902, Camp Skagway, Alaska, private, "excellent"; enlisted May 22, 1902, Macon, Georgia, assigned Company L, Twenty-Fourth Infantry; discharged May 21, 1905, Fort Harrison, Montana, private, "good"

Terrell, Robert: born February 1874, Crawford, Alabama; enlisted October 6, 1900, Macon, Georgia, laborer, assigned Company L, Twenty-Fourth Infantry; arrived November 3, 1900, Camp Skagway, Alaska; discharged November 26, 1902, Fort Missoula, Montana, corporal, "excellent"

Thornell, George: born August 1876, Salisbury, Virginia; enlisted February 13, 1899, Pittsburgh, Pennsylvania, laborer, assigned Company L, Twenty-Fourth Infantry; discharged February 12, 1902, Camp Skagway, Alaska, private, "good"; arrested July 12, 1902, Skagway, Alaska, for vagrancy

Trice, Benton: born January 1878, Almagro, Virginia; discharged January 28, 1899, Company B, Ninth Battalion, Ohio Volunteer Infantry; enlisted March 9, 1899, Philadelphia, Pennsylvania, soldier, assigned

Company L, Twenty-Fourth Infantry; discharged March 8, 1902, Camp Skagway, Alaska, private, "excellent"; enlisted October 5, 1905, Seattle, Washington, carpenter, assigned A Troop, Ninth Cavalry; discharged October 4, 1908, Camp McGrath, Philippines, corporal, "excellent"; living April 11, 1940, San Francisco, California; died January 21, 1941, San Francisco, California; buried January 24, 1941, San Francisco, California

Turner, Ellis: born January 1877, Wytheville, Virginia; enlisted August 26, 1898, Cincinnati, Ohio, laborer, assigned Company L, Twenty-Fourth Infantry; discharged January 28, 1899, Fort Douglas, Utah, private, "good"; enlisted February 15, 1899, Cincinnati, Ohio, soldier, assigned Company L, Twenty-Fourth Infantry; died October 9, 1900, Vancouver Barracks, Washington, private, pulmonary tuberculosis

Washington, James: born May 1862, Gainesville, Alabama; enlisted August 28, 1886, Washington DC, laborer, assigned Company G, Twenty-Fifth Infantry; discharged August 27, 1891, Fort Missoula, Montana, private, "good"; enlisted August 28, 1891, Fort Missoula, Montana, assigned Company G, Twenty-Fifth Infantry; discharged August 27, 1896, Fort Missoula, Montana; enlisted September 2, 1896, Fort Sherman, Idaho, assigned Company G, Twenty-Fourth Infantry; transferred to Company L, Twenty-Fourth Infantry; discharged September 1, 1899, Fort Wrangel, Alaska, sergeant, "excellent"; enlisted September 2, 1899, Fort Wrangel, Alaska, assigned Company L, Twenty-Fourth Infantry; married September 11, 1899, to Alice Cooper, Seattle, Washington; discharged September 1, 1902, Fort Missoula, Montana, sergeant, "excellent"; enlisted September 2, 1902, Fort Missoula, Montana, assigned Company L, Twenty-Fourth Infantry; transferred to assigned Company C, Twenty-Fourth Infantry; discharged September 1, 1905, Fort Harrison, Montana, corporal, "excellent"; enlisted September 2, 1905, Fort Harrison, Montana, assigned Company C, Twenty-Fourth Infantry; discharged September 1, 1908, Madison Barracks, New York, sergeant, "excellent"; enlisted September 2, 1908, Madison Barracks, New York, assigned Company C, Twenty-Fourth Infantry; discharged September 1, 1911, Madison

Barracks, New York, first sergeant, "excellent"; enlisted September 2, 1911, Madison Barracks, New York, assigned Company C, Twenty-Fourth Infantry; retired September 18, 1911, Madison Barracks, New York, first sergeant

Waters, James A.: born June 1877, Pocomoke City, Maryland; enlisted February 27, 1899, Philadelphia, Pennsylvania, teacher, assigned Company L, Twenty-Fourth Infantry; discharged February 26, 1902, Camp Skagway, Alaska, private, "excellent"

Watkins, Leonard: born February 5, 1875, Baldwin, Georgia; enlisted March 13, 1899, Lexington, Kentucky, laborer, assigned Company L, Twenty-Fourth Infantry; discharged February 12, 1902, Camp Skagway, Alaska, private, "excellent"; enlisted May 7, 1902, Macon, Georgia, assigned Company M, Twenty-Fourth Infantry; discharged May 6, 1905, Fort Missoula, Montana, private, "very good"

Watson, Frank W.: born February 1877, Amanda, Tennessee; enlisted March 22, 1899, Chattanooga, Tennessee, farmer, assigned Company L, Twenty-Fourth Infantry; discharged March 21, Camp Skagway, Alaska, private, "good"; enlisted May 21, 1902, Chattanooga, Tennessee, assigned Company L, Twenty-Fourth Infantry; discharged November 27, 1902, Fort Missoula, Montana, disability, private, "fair"

Wesley, Maris P.: born July 1875, Lancaster County, Pennsylvania; enlisted February 4, 1899, Philadelphia, Pennsylvania, laborer, assigned Company L, Twenty-Fourth Infantry; discharged February 4, 1902, Camp Skagway, Alaska, private, "excellent"

Wheeler, Arthur: born August 1882, Cane Ridge, Kentucky; enlisted October 9, 1900, Lexington, Kentucky, farmer, assigned Company L, Twenty-Fourth Infantry; arrived November 3, 1900, Camp Skagway, Alaska; died December 6, 1901, Camp Skagway, Alaska, private, typhoid fever

White, Charlie J.: born January 1877, Cape May, New Jersey; enlisted March 6, 1899, Philadelphia, Pennsylvania, laborer, assigned Company L, Twenty-Fourth Infantry; discharged March 5, 1902, Camp Skagway, Alaska, corporal, "excellent"

White, William H.: born April 1874, Martins Ferry, Ohio; enlisted February 7, 1899, Pittsburgh, Pennsylvania, coachman, assigned Company L, Twenty-Fourth Infantry; deserted October 16, 1900, Camp Skagway, Alaska

Williams, Edward: born February 1857, Hickman County, Tennessee; enlisted February 11, 1901, Fort Douglas, Utah, soldier, assigned Company L, Twenty-Fourth Infantry; arrived Camp Skagway, Alaska, April 11, 1901; discharged February 10, 1904, Fort Missoula, Montana, sergeant, "excellent"

Williams, Edward: born March 1875, Lincoln County, Kentucky; enlisted September 22, 1898, Louisville, Kentucky, laborer, assigned Company L, Twenty-Fourth Infantry; discharged January 28, 1899, Fort Douglas, Utah, private, "good"

Williams, Herbert: born July 1876, Columbus, Ohio; enlisted February 15, 1899, Columbus Barracks, Ohio, laborer, assigned Company L, Twenty-Fourth Infantry; discharged February 14, 1902, Camp Skagway, Alaska, corporal, "excellent"; enlisted February 15, 1902, Camp Skagway, Alaska, assigned Company L, Twenty-Fourth Infantry; discharged February 14, 1904, Fort Missoula, Montana, sergeant, "excellent"; enlisted February 15, 1905, Fort Missoula, Montana, assigned Company L, Twenty-Fourth Infantry; discharged November 22, 1905, Fort Missoula, Montana, sergeant, "excellent"; enlisted November 23, 1905, Fort Missoula, Montana, assigned Company L, Twenty-Fourth Infantry; reassigned Hospital Corps; discharged November 22, 1908, Malabang, Philippines, private, "excellent"; enlisted November 23, Malabang, Philippines, assigned Company K, Twenty-Fifth Infantry, Hospital Corps; transferred to Army Staff School, Fort Leavenworth, Kansas; discharged November 22, Fort Leavenworth, Kansas, private, "excellent"; enlisted November 24, 1911, Fort Leavenworth, Kansas, assigned Army Staff School; honorably discharged November 24, 1914

Williams, Thomas: born November 1876, Barbados, British West Indies; enlisted February 1, 1899, Columbus Barracks, Ohio, bricklayer, assigned Company L, Twenty-Fourth Infantry; discharged July 13, 1901, Camp Skagway, Alaska, private, "without honor"

Wilson, George Levi: born July 10, 1866, Boston, Massachusetts; discharged January 1, 1899, Company L, Sixth Massachusetts Volunteer Infantry; enlisted January 27, 1899, Boston, Massachusetts, laborer, assigned Company L, Twenty-Fourth Infantry; discharged January 26, 1902, Camp Skagway, Alaska, private, "excellent"; lived July 1907, Dawson, Yukon, Canada; registered as a U.S. citizen November 21, 1908, at the U.S. Consulate in Dawson, Yukon, Canada, working in the mining business; registered as a U.S. citizen November 20, 1909, at the U.S. Consulate in Dawson, Yukon, Canada, working in the mining business; lived 1920, Hot Springs, Alaska, working as a prospector; lived November 28, 1929, Fairbanks, Alaska, working as a messenger; died January 9, 1940, Fairbanks, Alaska; buried Clay Street Cemetery, Fairbanks, Alaska

APPENDIX B

Buffalo Soldier Regiments

To appreciate the service and experiences of the African American soldiers who served in Skagway from 1899 to 1902, it is important to know who they were and where they came from. The citizens of Skagway then would have been as unfamiliar as today's readers with the origins of the Black regulars. The Buffalo Soldier regiments were founded thirty years before Skagway became a gold rush boomtown. This short history provides a basis to evaluate their mission and performance in Skagway three decades later.

Origins

Black Americans have served and sacrificed in U.S. conflicts from the Revolutionary War onward, yet it was during the Civil War that they first fought in large numbers and in organized Black regiments. The service of 178,975 Black volunteers during the Civil War, composing about 10 percent of the total Union manpower by the end of the bitter struggle, granted Blacks the right to serve in the Regular Army in the postwar era. Black regiments fought in all the major theaters of combat and suffered 36,847 dead. As the Union Army demobilized the last of the Black volunteer regiments after the end of the war, Congress passed legislation in 1866 establishing Black Regular Army cavalry and infantry regiments. This marked the first time the United States permitted Blacks to enlist as regulars and as soldiers in the nation's standing army. These Black regulars came to be known as the Buffalo Soldiers.[1]

Today we use the term "Buffalo Soldier," but in the post–Civil War era the Black soldiers would have been known as "colored troops" who served in "Negro regiments." The sobriquet Buffalo Soldier came into popular use in the twentieth century, though it had roots in nineteenth-century Native coinage. The Cheyennes and Comanches used the expression first in the late 1860s and early 1870s for the members of the Black Regular regiments.[2]

The press used the term "Buffalo Soldier" occasionally, and it appeared in a private letter in 1877, yet the soldiers of the period did not use the term. Most agree the name referred to the soldiers' dark skin and black curly hair, similar in the view of some Cheyennes or Comanches to that of the buffalo. There is a great deal of disagreement in any meaning beyond this visual similarity. Certainly, there was no empathetic connection between Native Americans and Black regulars: Native Americans viewed the African American soldier, like the rest of the U.S. military, as a blue-clad enemy bent on destroying their way of life.[3]

Establishment

The Buffalo Soldiers originated in post–Civil War legislation to set the size of the peacetime army and establish Black Regular Army regiments. Congress approved an act on July 28, 1866, adding four cavalry regiments and twenty-six new infantry regiments to the army, that legislation earmarking two cavalry and four infantry regiments of Black soldiers. This was a major triumph for African Americans who, so recently freed from their slave shackles in the South, had sacrificed so much during the Civil War. By August 1866 military departments began recruiting Black soldiers and white officers from former Civil War volunteer regiments to fill the ranks of the Ninth and Tenth U.S. Cavalry and the Thirty-Eighth, Thirty-Ninth, Fortieth, and Forty-First U.S. Infantry Regiments.[4]

In 1869 and subsequent years, Congress moved to reduce the size of the peacetime Regular Army by limiting its enlisted strength to fewer than thirty thousand, the strength the army maintained throughout the Indian Wars. This mandate forced the army to reduce the number of infantry regiments to twenty-five but left the number of cavalry regiments at ten. The Ninth and Tenth Cavalry Regiments survived intact, but the Thirty-Ninth and Fortieth Regiments combined to form the new Twenty-Fifth Infantry Regiment, and the Thirty-Eighth and Forty-First Regiments formed the new Twenty-Fourth. These four Buffalo Soldier regiments composed only 10 percent of the post–Civil War Regular Army strength yet played a key role in the Indian Wars on the western frontier between 1866 and 1890.[5]

Enlisted Men

Shortly after legislation created Buffalo Soldier regiments in 1866, the army dispatched recruiting officers to enlist members of the former U.S. Colored Troops into the new units. Nearly half of the Black soldiers recruited were Civil War veterans, and most were formerly enslaved and illiterate, with few skills beyond those of field hands or farm laborers. Black soldiers earned the same wage as their white counterparts in the Regular Army, a situation unparalleled in the civilian world at the time. It did not take long to fill the ranks, and the regiments were soon deployed to the frontier to begin the nation-building tasks of fighting Native Americans, protecting settlers, guarding strategic points, building roads, stringing telegraph lines, maintaining military posts, securing reservations, and endless tours of escort and guard duty.[6]

With congressional limits placed on its size after the Civil War, the Regular Army struggled to keep the peace with 430 companies garrisoning roughly 200 scattered posts across the vast western frontier of the United States. Forty-four of these companies were Buffalo Soldiers, and Black and white units commonly served together at the same isolated frontier forts.

The official record shows a far from equitable picture of race relations on frontier posts. At Fort Robinson, Nebraska, the post commander noted with alarm in 1887 that Black soldiers received court-martials at more than twice the rate of whites. Fort Robinson's mix of large numbers of Black cavalry troopers and white infantry soldiers proved a fertile breeding ground for racism. Whites in the military might have grudgingly accepted that Blacks could be molded into capable soldiers but continued to believe that they were dependent on their white officers for leadership. Buffalo Soldiers could not escape the ubiquitous racism and stereotypes of the time, no matter how well or consistently they performed their duties.[7]

On the other hand, the bureaucratic machinery of the army housed, uniformed, equipped, and mounted Black and white Regular Army troops the same. If a quartermaster issued a Black Regular unit threadbare uniforms, foul rations, or swayback horses, it was due to an overburdened procurement system and insufficient congressional appropriations rather than racism. Similar treatment might befall a white regiment. The army simply could not afford to cripple one-tenth of its combat power by deliberately issuing substandard items to the Black regiments. Army bureaucracy was by regulation colorblind when it came to all things official, such as recruiting, medical services, pay, pensions, and admission to the government-sponsored Soldiers' Home in Washington DC.[8]

Individual Buffalo Soldiers compiled an impressive record during twenty-five years of campaigning and received a number of Medals of Honor, continuing their record begun during the Civil War and further dispelling the myth that Blacks lacked military virtue. Congress awarded eighteen Black soldiers the Medal of Honor between 1870 and 1890. These Black regulars personified the best qualities of the American soldier, willing to risk their lives for their brothers in arms. Six white officers who served with the Buffalo Soldiers also received the coveted award, showing their willingness to risk their lives for the Black soldiers they led and respected.[9]

By the 1890s the Buffalo Soldiers boasted a core of long-service, experienced frontier veterans. In an era when desertion was a chronic problem for the Regular Army, Black soldiers rarely deserted. Black regulars also had a consistently higher reenlistment rate than white units. These and other factors helped the Buffalo Soldier regiments develop a high esprit de corps, which in turn won the grudging respect of most of their white officers.[10]

White Officers

Congress required all lieutenant positions and two-thirds of the captain and field-grade positions in the new infantry and cavalry regiments created in 1866 be set aside for volunteers who served at least two years of field service in the Civil War. The remaining third comprised Regular Army officers, and most of these were graduates of West Point. Though at least one hundred Black officers served in the United States Colored Troops during the Civil War, none received commissions in the Buffalo Soldier regiments, most not having the minimum two years of field service. All the volunteer officers competing for commissions in the new Black and white regiments had to pass an examination before a board of officers. Ultimately, the quality of the officers in the Black regiments ran the gamut from indifferent and incompetent to highly capable and was probably no different than that in the other regiments in the Regular Army.[11]

A frank letter quoted in the *Army and Navy Journal* in 1887 by an unidentified white officer serving in a Black regiment illustrates his respect for Black soldiers as well as his conflicting emotions. The officer emphasized that he was "no admirer of the African, believing he will *ultimately destroy the white race,*" but he confessed that he would have been as prejudiced or perhaps worse than his peers had he not served with Black soldiers. He referred to himself as a "colored officer," or an officer serving in a colored regiment, and admitted that he took the attendant "prejudices, remarks, slurs, etc., good humoredly." His service in the Buffalo Soldiers caused him to "think the world of the men" in his company. When he looked at them he did "not see their black faces" but "something beyond." He considered them "far ahead of white troops" and "more like a lot of devoted servants and retainers, *faithful and trustworthy in every respect,* and *brave* and *gallant.*"[12]

Another white officer, Louis H. Rucker, was among the white officers awarded Regular Army commissions in the Ninth Cavalry when it formed in 1866, and he served with the unit until 1897. Rucker began his career as an enlisted volunteer in the Civil War in 1861 and was a first lieutenant by the end of the war. In the Ninth he proved an able second lieutenant, an efficient first lieutenant regimental quartermaster, and a superb troop commander after promotion to captain in 1879. Rucker served as one of the exemplary company commanders in the Ninth Cavalry during this period, a low-key officer who treated his enlisted and noncommissioned officers with respect and whose smaller-than-average troop desertion and dishonorable discharge rates reflected his effectiveness. Rucker served as a key mentor to Black officers John Alexander and Charles Young during their formative years as second lieutenants with the Ninth.[13]

Frank B. Taylor was the opposite of Rucker. With no Civil War experience, Taylor used political connections to obtain a commission in the Twenty-Fifth Infantry in 1867. He transferred to the white Eighteenth Infantry in 1869, where his regimental commander tried to discharge him, and later moved to the Ninth Cavalry, where in 1881 he was court-martialed for verbally abusing, pistol-whipping, and beating a Black trooper with the butt of a carbine. The board recommended he be dismissed, but President Chester Arthur reduced his sentence, and he continued to serve. In addition to his contempt for Black enlisted men, Taylor avoided service in the same troop with the two Black officers then on active service. Within a week of Lieutenant Charles Young joining his troop at Fort Robinson, Nebraska, in 1889, Captain Taylor fell "ill" and remained on the sick list for nine months. Two years earlier, after Lieutenant John Alexander was assigned to his troop, Taylor had found convenient ways to be out on detached service for five months and was then reassigned. For the leadership of the regiment to condone such behavior indicates an unhealthy racial climate that could not have been lost on Young or Alexander.[14]

Black Officers

Only three Black Regular Army line officers served in the U.S. Army during the period 1866 to 1890, and all were graduates of West Point. Of the thirteen Blacks who attended the United States Military Academy in this postwar period, only three graduated: Henry O. Flipper in 1877, John H. Alexander in 1887, and Charles Young in 1889. The War Department assigned these Black officers solely to the Buffalo Soldier regiments after graduation from West Point, and the three had diverse careers and mixed successes.[15]

Henry Flipper, the first Black alumnus of the academy, chose the Tenth U.S. Cavalry after he graduated in 1877. Initially stationed at Fort Sill, Oklahoma Territory, Flipper performed his duties admirably. Flipper's otherwise bright career came to a disastrous end with a court-martial in 1881. As a commissary officer at a new station at Fort Davis, Texas, his commanding officer charged him with embezzling funds. He was cleared of the embezzlement charge but convicted of "conduct unbecoming of an officer" for submitting inaccurate statements concerning the funds to his commanding officer. A court-martial board dismissed Flipper from the service, and the decision was approved by President Chester Arthur. (The U.S. Army issued Flipper a posthumous honorable discharge in 1976.)[16]

John Alexander, the second Black graduate of West Point, joined the Ninth U.S. Cavalry upon graduation in 1887. Initially posted to Fort Robinson, Nebraska, Alexander later served at Fort Duchesne, Utah, both posts occupied by the Ninth Cavalry. He won high praise from his commanders and quickly mastered the challenging duties of a second lieutenant on the frontier. Alexander's promising career in the army ended when he died unexpectedly of a heart attack in 1894. This left only Young on the active list to carry the torch for his race in the U.S. Army thereafter.[17]

Charles Young graduated from West Point in 1889, and like Alexander selected the Ninth Cavalry. He joined his unit at Fort Robinson, Nebraska, after graduation, and in 1890 rotated to Fort Duchesne,

Utah, just before the Ninth participated in the Pine Ridge Campaign, the end of the wars with the Plains Indians. Young matured and honed his skills as a leader at Fort Duchesne while maintaining the peace with the Ute Indians, serving there until 1894. Unlike the two Black academy graduates preceding him, Young went on to a long and distinguished career and eventually attained the rank of colonel.[18]

End of the Indian Wars

By 1890 the serious troubles with the Plains Indians were over, so the soldiers of the Black Regular regiments, like white frontier troops, spent much of their time performing routine garrison duties such as drill, training, target practice, and exercise marches. Once the Indians were removed to reservations, the operational role of the army in the West changed, which facilitated improvements in the lives of the soldiers, Black and white. General John M. Schofield, the serving commander in chief of the army, declared in 1884: "The period of 'temporary huts' for the troops has passed." In this new role, the army concentrated troops near the reservations where they might be needed, and those posts selected for retention were provided appropriations for permanent, comfortable buildings. The spread of the railroad and telegraph meant these forts were no longer inaccessible; instead, they were regularly supplied with food and other goods. White settlements sprang up around posts ending the soldiers' isolation.[19]

Perhaps more important to the everyday lives of the Buffalo Soldiers were the creature comforts afforded by the new permanent posts. Congress approved appropriations in 1886 to complete improvements in the barracks and other buildings at various posts, among them Fort Robinson, Nebraska. After the Ninth Cavalry moved its headquarters to Fort Robinson in 1887, the members of the Ninth moved into new barracks with all the amenities they could ask for. At times in the previous two decades, the Ninth Cavalry had spent tours in tents and temporary shelters at various postings in the Southwest, so their new living quarters were a welcome change. And it was certainly not lost on the Black troopers of the Ninth that they lived in buildings that were identical to those of their counterparts in the all-white Eighth Infantry. The army achieved this equality of housing not by design but by practical circumstance; they had no idea whether a white or Black regiment would occupy the barracks they constructed.

Twenty-Fourth in Cuba

At the end of the Indian Wars, the Twenty-Fourth Infantry Regiment consolidated at one of the large permanent posts in Fort Huachuca, Arizona Territory, in 1892. Then, in 1896, the regiment pulled up stakes and moved to another big base at Fort Douglas, Utah. At the start of the Spanish-American War in 1898, the Twenty-Fourth was serving in the Department of the Colorado with its companies split between Fort Douglas, Utah, and Fort D. A. Russell, Wyoming.[20]

With the outbreak of war with Spain in April 1898, the U.S. Army deployed the Twenty-Fourth Infantry to the Caribbean, where it earned combat fame in Cuba. It participated in the assault on the blockhouse and trenches atop San Juan Hill the first three days of July 1898. The regiment suffered seventeen killed and eighty-two wounded in this action, with sixteen members cited for extraordinary valor. The war was short, less than four months, and the officers and men soon redeployed to their home stations at Fort Douglas, Utah, and Fort D. A. Russell, Wyoming, in late 1898. Some were recovering from wounds suffered in battle, and many more were suffering from yellow fever and malaria.

After the United States declared war on Spain on April 25, 1898, Congress added two companies to each of the infantry regiments to bring them up to a wartime strength of twelve companies. Yet the war ended so quickly with an American victory that the regiments did not add the extra companies until after the war. These extra companies were needed to respond to contingencies that arose with the newly acquired American overseas empire.

Summary

Black volunteer soldiers who served during the Civil War paved the way for Blacks to enlist as regulars in the postwar standing army. Soon after they arrived on the western plains, the Native American tribes gave the members of the Black regiments the nickname "Buffalo Soldiers," likely because of their dark skin and black curly hair. Dispersed among several hundred isolated posts across the country, they served and fought side by side with white regiments, though not always in racial harmony. Except for three Black West Point graduates and two chaplains, white officers led these regiments. Many Black soldiers and white officers developed mutual trust and respect.

The four regiments of Buffalo Soldiers played a critical role in the settling of the Western frontier from 1866 to 1890. They proved capable soldiers and established a creditable record. They were the only Black Americans at the time afforded equal recruitment, pay, housing, and pensions. In all things official, Black soldiers were treated as equals, though racial bias persisted in all social or off-duty situations. These Black regulars served competently with white regulars despite the pervasive racial prejudice of the age.

After the Indians Wars, Buffalo Soldier regiments added battle streamers to their colors in action in Cuba. The army shipped all four of the Black Regular regiments to Cuba, and they played key roles in the swift victory against the Spanish. After the war, they returned to their garrisons in the West to recover and prepare for the missions in the United States' newly won overseas empire.

APPENDIX C

Minstrel Show Programs

Jubilee Concert, July 24, 1901

PART 1.

Chorus of the Trinity. (original)	Full Chorus (Including solos, duets, and quartets)
The Old Home	Chorus
The Singer and the Song	E.J. Collins
Rocked in the Cradle of the Deep	N.A. Casselle
Jubilee Song	Troubadour Four
She's My Sweetheart	B. Green
The Fortune Telling Man	Caughman
Play on Your Harp	Chorus
You Tell Me Your Dream and I'll Tell you Mine	Dora Clark
Mid the Green Fields of Virginia	Geo. H. Williams
Song (selected)	Troubadour Four
My Creole Sue	Full Chorus

PART II.

Sycamore River Camp Meeting	Pate and Williams (Original sketch)
When the Hawaii Days are Over	Fran Poole
When the Big Bell Rings the Day	Magnolia Four
Sing Me a Song of the South	Geo. H. Williams (Character song and sketch)
My Old Kentucky Home Duet	Freeman and Poole Full Chorus

PART FIRST.

Introducing night in the park.

Stars and Stripes.

Introduction:—

"Give me my money."

"Grace O'More."

"Carolina."

"Maggie McGuire."

"My aunt Aliza."

Hulu Hulu dance.

SONG:—"You'll get all that's coming to you," by Private Pate

SONG:—"When the Harvest days are Over," by Private Collins

SONG:—"She's Just Come to Town," by Corporal Banks

SONG:—"Sing Me a Song of the South," by Corporal Green

SONG:—"Goo goo Eyes," by Corporal White

SONG:—"I Won't Play Second Fiddle to Any Girl," by M[usician] Williams

SONG:—"Asleep in the Deep," by Private Casselle

SECOND PART.

1. Animated Song Sheet.

2. An old plantation scene

Old slave deserts his owner and comes back to find his children grown.

CAST:

Old Ephe (slave) Corporal Green

Sandy (his son) Pvt. Pate

Little Ephe (his son) Corp. Banks

Mr. Stevenson, a planter Pvt. Freeman

Cloey (Ephe's wife) Mrs. Thomas

Georgia (Stevenson's niece) Mrs. Hayes

Miss Stevenson Mrs. Beckwith

IRISH SONG:—"Mulligan's Mule," by Private Grant

Second Part of Plantation Scene.

Showing cotton pickers at work; planter catches Old Ephe making merry with the cotton pickers; orders him off the place; the old darky starts to go but falls dead just as he is leaving. One of the most pathetic scenes on record and is true to the condition that existed in the South in the days of slavery.

THIRD PART.

OVERTURE.

Comic Song—"Coon, Coon, Coon, Au Revoir," Corp White and M[usician] Williams

SONG:—"Blue and Gray," Pvt. Caughman

Cake Walk:—

Leader, Corporal Banks

Corporal Green and Mrs. Beckwith

Mr. and Mrs. Williams

Private Pate and Mrs. Hayes

Private Watson and Mrs. Thompson

Corporal White and Mrs. O'Conner

QUARTET:—

By the Magnolia Four Quartet

SONG:—"The girl I left in Sunny Tennessee, only me."

DIANA LEE'S WEDDING.

SONG:—

"Coons have Grace and Love their Hounds."

"All I want is my Black Baby Back."

Dance:—"Comin' thru the Rye."

Song:—"Chicken"

Clog and Buck Dancing.

APPENDIX D

Tribute to Captain Hovey

A FITTING TRIBUTE TO CAPT. HOVEY

*Complete Report of the Speech Delivered
by R.W. Jennings Saturday*

Capt. Hovey, whom all the people of Skagway have learned to count as one of themselves, will depart from the city today for the scene of his new duties. The *Daily Alaskan* has been enabled to get an accurate report of the speech delivered to Capt. Hovey by R.W. Jennings at the banquet Saturday night, and it so fittingly represents the feelings of the people of this city that it is published today in full as a last tribute to him whom all have learned to love.

Mr. Jennings said:

The time has almost arrived, as we are informed, when you and the officers and men in your command are to leave the city of Skagway to take up your station at some other post. The good citizens of Skagway, everyone of whom is your personal admirer and many of whom are your warm friends, were unwilling that you should depart without bearing with you the memory of some public expression of the regard in which you personally and your command as a whole is held by them, and to that end was born the idea of this dinner.

You came among us three years ago almost to the day. Of those who were citizens of Skagway at that time many are present here this evening, and to those present here now who were not citizens of Skagway at that time the rumor of your good deeds has been so often repeated that they feel almost as if they too had been with you from the beginning. At the time of your arrival here it must be confessed the surroundings were far from cheerful. The conveniences of life were few and far between. The facilities of government were meager indeed. There was no lawfully authorized city government: no adequate police or fire protection. But a single court, sitting then at Sitka, administered the laws throughout the entire district of Alaska. From Juneau north there was but a single deputy U.S. marshal to serve process or preserve the peace. There were many lawless characters in and about the town, and no one knew when the civil authority might be powerless to enforce process of the courts; no one knew when there might be some kind of trouble with the Indians under their law of a life for life, and all lived in dread lest the morning might find the entire town reduced to a heap of ashes and all its citizens without shelter and without food and at the mercy of the cold and cutting winds that rush from the passes of the mountains. From the very moment of your arrival you put yourself to work to thoroughly understand the situation and to meet its wants. You did thoroughly master the conditions and have ever held yourself and your men in readiness to prevent disaster or to ameliorate it if, in spite of your efforts, it should in any form overtake us. The very presence at this point of the military has exercised a wholesome restraining influence upon some who might otherwise be dispensed to do evil. The knowledge that you were here with your men has, we have no doubt, prevented any concerted action on the part of the natives, who, excited by whisky or the passion of revenge, might have wrought sad havoc. The fact of your presence and that of your men has been a guarantee that the process of the courts should be duly enforced. The knowledge that you had established a fire patrol and that on the darkest and coldest and wildest nights your faithful guards were at their posts or on their beats about the town, and that on alarm of fire they would all turn out and, directed by your cool judgment and incisive commands, would do everything possible to save property and life has been to all our citizens a consoling assurance. We have all felt that our own fire department, prompt, efficient and worthy as it is and able to cope with all ordinary fires, would in the event of a general conflagration have the hearty and cheerful support and assistance of a well-organized and thoroughly disciplined body of men led by one who knew the right thing to do and when to do it.

Your efforts to secure the location in this city of a permanent army post, efforts which we hope are soon to be crowned by complete success, are known to and appreciated by all. While discharging your duty to the government you have not been unmindful of the interests of Skagway. We are not aware of any movement working to the general welfare in which you have not manifested a lively concern and done more than your share. You have entered actively into the personal, social and business life of the city. In fact, you have become and are now a citizen of Skagway in spite of that prominence of the law which declares that no person shall either acquire or lose citizenship by reason of his service in the military or naval forces of the United States. You did not wrap yourself in a mantle of exclusiveness and from the height of power which was yours look down with condescension upon poor civilians, thanking God that you were not as other men were. You did not draw around your form some awful circle within whose confines no ordinary mortal dared venture; you did not pass with an air of conscious superiority as if to say, "I am Sir Oracle and when I open my lips let no dog bark." On the contrary, you became one of us; you mingled with our citizens: you entered into our sports, our joys, our cares; you joined our lodges; you even passed the hat around in church. And yet you lost none of the dignity that attached to your position nor forfeited one whit of the respect that was due to you. Though kind, you were not soft; though friendly, you were not familiar: though powerful, you were not officious.

Stationed as you were far from the seat of government, with no speedy communication with the powers that be, it was yours, had you so chosen, to excel the military above the civil power, to so conduct yourself and to so direct those under your command as to make that portion of the army an engine of oppression; but instead of so doing you have uniformly and consistently refused to use your company except as an aid to the civil authorities when requested by them. We soon came to feel that you believe that it was glorious to have the strength of a giant but that it was tyrannous to use it as a giant. We soon came to believe that you felt that "the voice of the law was the harmony of the world; that all things in heaven and earth did her homage—the very least as feeling her care and the greatest as not exempt from her power." We saw by your every action that before the president's commission had made you a captain great nature had made you a man and a citizen. Though it is a maxim of the law that among arms the laws are silent, you have acted on the principle that among the laws arms are silent. Not one officious act have you performed; not one false step have you taken, and your men, inspired by your example, have followed in your footsteps. There has been no complaint that by virtue of your position or their arms a republic's true dividing line between the civil and the military has at any time been over-stepped or even infringed upon. Did one of your men violate the city ordinances or the general laws of Alaska he was promptly and without cavil handed over to the civil authorities, to be dealt with as the statute requires.

Captain, you are quite a decent man. We have no doubt that in all your effort you have been ably seconded by Capt. Jenks, Lieut. Rains and Dr. Bailey, and we have no anxiety but the policy which you have adopted will not be continued under the gallant officers who will succeed you.

We know not in what quarter of the country or of the world the exigencies of the service may call you. It may be your lot to be stationed on the wind swept plains of Kansas or Nebraska, or the torrid mesas of Arizona or New Mexico, or near some great city where social diversions will vary the monotony of a soldier's life in time of peace. You may go down among the Mormons and from the height of Fort Douglas muse upon that wonderful temple. Or you may be called upon to fight the lusty natives in the jungles of the Philippines, or the heathen Chinese under the walls of Pekin; or among the palms and pines, the oranges and bananas, the cocoanuts and citron groves and white magnolias of

Porto Rico, lulled by the mocking bird's heavenly strain and fanned by the zephyrs of eternal summer to fall asleep dreaming that life is beauty.

Wherever it be, wherever you go you will carry with you the best wishes of the citizens of Skagway. None, more than they, will rejoice in the advancement of rank which is soon and sure to come. We feel certain that the blade which has been stainless here will be unstained forever. Accept, then, this our tribute. Our hoard is but little, but our hearts are great.

Daily Alaskan, May 15, 1902

NOTES

Prologue

1. Bearss, "Proposed Klondike Gold Rush National Historical Park," 114. Superintendent Samuel Steele of the Northwest Mounted Police called Skagway "little better than a hell on earth."
2. *Daily Alaskan*, July 6, 1901, 4.
3. *Daily Alaskan*, July 6, 1901, 4.
4. *Daily Alaskan*, July 6, 1901, 4.
5. *Daily Alaskan*, July 4, 1901, 4, and July 6, 1901, 4.
6. *Daily Alaskan*, July 6, 1901, 4. The army had a long history of organized contests between baseball teams reaching back to the Civil War.
7. *Daily Alaskan*, July 6, 1901, 4.

1. North to Alaska

1. Twenty-Fourth Infantry Regimental Return, April–May 1899, Returns from Regular Army Infantry Regiments, June 1821–December 1916, Microfilm M665, RG 94, National Archives and Records Administration, Washington DC (NARA), hereafter Twenty-Fourth Infantry Regimental Return.
2. The Second Battalion comprised Companies B, D, L, and M, which were stationed at Fort Wright, Washington; Fort Harrison, Montana; Dyea, Alaska; and Fort Wright, Washington, respectively.
3. Muller, *Twenty-Fourth Infantry*, 18–32. The Twenty-Fourth Infantry headquarters and the first battalion of four companies arrived in Manila in July; the second battalion of four companies arrived in August 1899.
4. Heitman, *Historical Register of the U.S. Army*, 1:619; Fort Douglas Post Return, October 1898–March 1899, Returns from U.S. Military Posts, 1800–1916, Microfilm M617, RG 94, NARA.
5. Muller, *Twenty-Fourth Infantry*, 18–32.

6. Company L, Twenty-Fourth Infantry Regimental Return, June 1899. (When companies operated independently from the regiment, they submitted separate company returns that were appended to the monthly regimental return.) Privates James Banks, Landon Jackson, Harry Stewart, James A. Waters, and William H. White were hospitalized on May 2, 1899. Privates John A. Perkins and James Rare were left in confinement on May 2, 1899.

7. Twenty-Fourth Infantry Regimental Return, May 1899; Company L, Twenty-Fourth Infantry Regimental Return, June 1899. Privates Lafayette Coats and Benton Trice were hospitalized on May 14, 1899.

8. Twenty-Fourth Infantry Regimental Return, May 1899; *Daily Alaskan*, January 1, 1900.

9. Heitman, *Historical Register of the U.S. Army*, 1:545; Dodge, *Norwich University, 1819-1911*, 81.

10. Twenty-Fourth Infantry Regimental Return, March 1881. Columbus Barracks, Ohio, and Davids Island, New York, trained infantry soldiers, while Jefferson Barracks, Missouri, trained cavalry troopers. Black and white soldiers were trained at all three of these depots.

11. Twenty-Fourth Infantry Regimental Return, June 1882; Dodge, *Norwich University, 1819-1911*, 81.

12. Twenty-Fourth Infantry Regimental Return, May 1888; Dodge, *Norwich University, 1819-1911*, 81.

13. Twenty-Fourth Infantry Regimental Return, 1881-1885.

14. Twenty-Fourth Infantry Regimental Return, 1888-1885.

15. Twenty-Fourth Infantry Regimental Return, 1885.

16. Heitman, *Historical Register of the U.S. Army*, 1:545; Dodge, *Norwich University, 1819-1911*, 81.

17. Heitman, *Historical Register of the U.S. Army*, 1:545; Dodge, *Norwich University, 1819-1911*, 81.

18. Twenty-Fourth Infantry Regimental Return, October 1898-March 1899; *Sixty-Second Annual Report*, 282-95. For his first two years at West Point, Jenks observed Charles Young's struggle to become the third Black graduate of West Point in 1889. Upon graduation, Young was assigned to the Ninth Cavalry, one of two Black cavalry regiments in the Regular Army. Young and the other two Black graduates who preceded him, Henry O. Flipper in 1877 and John H. Alexander, 1887, were forced to accept commissions in one of the four Black regiments. U.S. Army policy restricted Black officers to assignments in Black units, where they would command only Black soldiers. Shellum, *Black Cadet in a White Bastion*, 43-47, 94-130. Though authorized

a captain, a first lieutenant, and a second lieutenant, infantry companies rarely had their full complement of three commissioned officers.

19. *Sixty-Second Annual Report*, 282–95; Association of Graduates, *Register of Graduates of the United States Military Academy*, 4–68.

20. Cullum, *Biographical Register*, 528; *Sixty-Second Annual Report*, 282–95; Association of Graduates, *Register of Graduates of the United States Military Academy*, 4–68.

21. Cullum, *Biographical Register*, 528; *Sixty-Second Annual Report*, 282–95.

22. Twenty-Fourth Infantry Regimental Return, March 1881; Muller, *Twenty-Fourth Infantry*, 17. Jenks led detachments of troops to supervise the closing of nearby Fort Selden and disinter the remains of soldiers buried there.

23. Twenty-Fourth Infantry Regimental Return, March 1881; Muller, *Twenty-Fourth Infantry*, 17.

24. Twenty-Fourth Infantry Regimental Return, November 1893; *Sixty-Second Annual Report*, 282–95.

25. Twenty-Fourth Infantry Regimental Return, March 1881.

26. Twenty-Fourth Infantry Regimental Return, March 1881; Utley, *Frontier Regulars*, 399–400.

27. *Utah, County Marriages, 1887–1937*, Ancestry.com. Alice was married previously and brought a daughter named Marion into the new family. Her previous marriage had been a short affair with a man who was an alcoholic. She was born Alice A. Girard, used Alice A. Stevenson after her first marriage, and used Alice G. Jenks after her marriage to Isaac C. Jenks.

28. Twenty-Fourth Infantry Regimental Return, March 1881.

29. Letter from Jenks to his father, Henry Jenks, on July 18, 1898, Isaac C. Jenks Papers, Isaac C. Jenks Collection, private collection, Hanover NH, hereafter Jenks Papers.

30. Letter from Jenks to his father, Henry Jenks, on July 18, 1898, Jenks Papers; Twenty-Fourth Infantry Regimental Return, March 1881; *Sixty-Second Annual Report*, 282–95; Muller, *Twenty-Fourth Infantry*, 18–32.

31. Twenty-Fourth Infantry Regimental Return, March 1881; Muller, *Twenty-Fourth Infantry*, 18–32.

32. *Utah, County Marriages, 1887–1937*.

33. U.S. Census, 1900, Skagway, Alaska, Bureau of the Census, Twelfth Census of the United States, T623, NARA, hereafter Census, Skagway, 1900.

34. Enlistment of Robert O'Connor, June 14, 1892, Register of Enlistments in the U.S. Army, 1798–1914, Microfilm M233, RG 94, NARA, hereafter Register of Enlistments; Glass, *History of the Tenth Cavalry*, 28–29. For example, Tenth

Cavalry Medal of Honor winner Lieutenant Powhatan H. Clarke drowned in the Little Big Horn River in 1893, and First Sergeant James Brown froze to death in a blizzard in 1895.

35. Enlistment of Robert O'Connor, November 13, 1895, Register of Enlistments; Twenty-Fourth Infantry Regimental Return, 1895–1896.

36. Twenty-Fourth Infantry Regimental Return, April–October 1898.

37. Twenty-Fourth Infantry Regimental Return, October 1898; Enlistment of Robert O'Connor, November 13, 1898, Register of Enlistments.

38. Census, Skagway, 1900.

39. Census, Skagway, 1900; Enlistment of James Washington, August 28, 1886, Register of Enlistments.

40. Twenty-Fifth Infantry Regimental Return, 1886–1896, Returns from Regular Army Infantry Regiments, June 1821–December 1916, Microfilm M665, RG 94, NARA, hereafter Twenty-Fifth Infantry Regimental Return.

41. Twenty-Fifth Infantry Regimental Return, 1888–1891; Enlistment of James Washington, August 28, 1891, Register of Enlistments.

42. Twenty-Fifth Infantry Regimental Return, 1896; Enlistment of James Washington, September 2, 1896, Register of Enlistments.

43. Twenty-Fourth Infantry Regimental Return, 1896–1898.

44. Twenty-Fourth Infantry Regimental Return, October 1896–April 1898.

45. Twenty-Fourth Infantry Regimental Return, July–October 1898; Muller, *Twenty-Fourth Infantry*, 18–32.

46. Twenty-Fourth Infantry Regimental Return, August–October 1898; Muller, *Twenty-Fourth Infantry*, 18–32.

47. Census, Skagway, 1900.

48. Enlistment of Peter Snoten, April 8, 1876; and Augustus Snoten, April 26, 1876, Register of Enlistments. Augustus Snoten served his entire career in the Twenty-Fourth Infantry, while Peter served in both the Twenty-Fourth Infantry and the Ninth Cavalry.

49. Enlistment of Augustus Snoten, April 26, 1881, 1886, 1891, 1896, and 1899, Register of Enlistments.

50. Enlistment of Augustus Snoten, April 26, 1881, Register of Enlistments; Muller, *Twenty-Fourth Infantry*, 18–24.

51. Twenty-Fourth Infantry Regimental Return, April–October 1898; Muller, *Twenty-Fourth Infantry*, 18–24.

52. Enlistment of Edward Bodenhammer, September 5, 1870, Register of Enlistments. He enlisted in 1870 with the name Bodenhammer but used Bordinghammer in all subsequent enlistments. He probably lied about his age

to avoid needing to obtain his parents' consent and was not yet eighteen when he enlisted.

53. Muller, *Twenty-Fourth Infantry*, 7–9.

54. Enlistment of Edward Bordinghammer, September 5, 1875, September 7, 1880, September 7, 1885, September 7, 1890, September 7, 1895, and September 7, 1898, Register of Enlistments.

55. Enlistment of Edward Bordinghammer, September 5, 1875, September 7, 1880, September 7, 1885, September 7, 1890, September 7, 1895, and September 7, 1898, Register of Enlistments; Muller, *Twenty-Fourth Infantry*, 18–24.

56. Twenty-Fourth Infantry Regimental Return, April–October 1898; Muller, *Twenty-Fourth Infantry*, 18–24.

57. Enlistment of Benjamin Green, March 22, 1899, Register of Enlistments.

58. Census, Skagway, 1900; Sawyer, *A Biography of John Randolph*, 107–8.

59. *Toledo Evening Bee*, July 16, 1884, 4; *Fairbanks Daily News-Miner*, March 18, 1940, 7; Zang, *Fleet Walker's Divided Heart*, 40–47.

60. Twenty-Fourth Infantry Regimental Return, March–April 1899.

61. Enlistment of Eugene Swanson, April 10, 1899, Register of Enlistments; Twenty-Fourth Regimental Return, April 1899.

62. "Old War Horse Prances," *Fairbanks Daily News-Miner*, March 7, 1942, 1.

63. Enlistment of George L. Wilson, January 27, 1899, Register of Enlistments.

64. Johnson, "In Search of Freedom," 32–39.

65. General Index to Compiled Service Records of Volunteer Soldiers Who Served during the War with Spain, Records of the Adjutant General's Office, 1780–1917, Microfilm M871, RG 94, NARA; Johnson, "In Search of Freedom," 32–39.

66. *Annual Report of the War Department, 1900*, 68–101; Johnson, *African American Soldiers*, 63; Steward, *Colored Regulars*, 282–87; Cunningham, "'We Are an Orderly Body of Men,'" 1–14. Nelson Ballard, who served as Young's battalion adjutant in the Ninth Ohio, wrote an "Outline History of the Ninth (Separate) Battalion Ohio Volunteer Infantry," which is printed at the end of Steward, *Colored Regulars*.

67. *Annual Report of the War Department, 1900*, 68–101; Cirillo, *Bullets and Bacilli*, 97, 161; Scott, *The Unwept*, 60; Johnson, *African American Soldiers*, 60–61; Steward, *Colored Regulars*, 282; Cunningham, "'We Are an Orderly Body of Men,'" 1–14.

68. Enlistment of William Pate, January 23, 1899; Edward G. Dewey, January 23, 1899; Elijah H. Knox, February 3, 1899, Register of Enlistments. The Sixth

Massachusetts entered federal service on May 13, 1898, and mustered out on January 21, 1899, in Boston.

69. Shellum, *Black Officer in a Buffalo Soldier Regiment*, 70–92. The Ninth Ohio was mustered into the U.S. federal service on May 14, 1898, and mustered out January 28, 1899.

70. Enlistment of Walter Belcher, March 14, 1899; Fred Joiner, February 9, 1899; Benton Trice, March 3, 1899; Thomas Mack, February 11, 1899; and Thomas Martin, March 14, 1899, Register of Enlistments.

71. Enlistment of James M. Banks, March 22, 1899; Peter Barnett, March 13, 1899; Orestus Kincaid, March 7, 1899; and Edgar Merritt, February 8, 1899, Register of Enlistments.

72. Enlistment of Ernest C. Randall, December 27, 1898, Register of Enlistments; Cole, *Connecticut Men in the Spanish-American War*, 173.

73. The Eighth Immunes mustered in the summer of 1898 in New Jersey, Tennessee, the District of Columbia, Kentucky, and West Virginia. The Tenth Immunes mustered in the summer of 1898 in the District of Columbia, Virginia, Georgia, South Carolina, and Florida. Both regiments mustered out in March 1899.

74. Twenty-Fourth Regimental Return, May–October 1898.

75. Twenty-Fourth Regimental Return, May–September 1898.

76. Twenty-Fourth Regimental Return, September–October 1898.

77. Heitman, *Historical Register of the U.S. Army*, 1:620–21. This authorized strength increased slightly in a subsequent reorganization in 1901.

78. "Army Food Service," 8, undated PDF, www.quartermaster.army.mil; *Manual for Army Cooks*.

79. Twenty-Fourth Regimental Return, October 1898. An artificer took care of equipment and made minor repairs on the unit's weapons and other gear.

80. Twenty-Fourth Regimental Return, August–November 1898.

81. Moss, *Officers' Manual*, 178–79.

82. Twenty-Fourth Regimental Return, January–March 1899.

2. Dyea Barracks

1. Company L, Twenty-Fourth Infantry Return, May–August 1899. Hovey completed two returns at the end of each month: a Company L Return forwarded to his battalion headquarters and a Post Return forwarded to the Department of the Columbia.

2. Brunet-Jailly, *Border Disputes*, 534.

3. Brady, *Skagway*, 6, 29, 152.

4. The North West Mounted Police were renamed the Royal North West Mounted Police in 1904 and Royal Canadian Mounted Police in 1920, so I use the term North West Mounted Police and the acronym NWMP in this book. Brady, *Skagway*, 52–57; Mike Coppock, "Jack London's Alaska," *True West*, February 11, 2014, https://truewestmagazine.com/jack-londons -alaska/.

5. Brady, *Skagway*; Coppock, "Jack London's Alaska."

6. National Park Service, *Chilkoot Trail*, 39; *Daily Alaskan*, July 7, 1899, 1.

7. James, "Canada, Sovereignty and the Alaska Boundary Dispute."

8. Brady, *Skagway*, 152; Neufeld, *Chilkoot Trail*, 134.

9. Coleman, *Pig War*. It was called the Pig War because it was triggered by an American farmer's shooting a pig owned by an Irish employee of the Hudson Bay Company.

10. Convention between Great Britain and the United States of America for the Adjustment of the Boundary between the Dominion of Canada and the Territory of Alaska, Signed at Washington, January 24, 1903; Munro, "English-Canadianism," 189–203.

11. Brady, *Skagway*, 377. The army unit in Dyea was called on five times during the year before Hovey's arrival to assist civilian authorities.

12. "Dyea," National Park Service, https://www.nps.gov/klgo/learn/historyculture /dyea.htm.

13. Haycox, *Alaska*, 196–97.

14. *Annual Report of the War Department, 1898*, Vol. 1, Pt. 2, 179–81; Gurcke, "Company L," 1.

15. *Annual Report of the War Department, 1898*, Vol. 1, Pt. 2, 179–81; Gurcke, "Company L," 1.

16. *Annual Report of the War Department, 1898*, Vol. 1, Pt. 2, 179–81; Gurcke, "Company L," 1. Louis H. Rucker served as a volunteer enlisted man and officer during the Civil War, was commissioned a lieutenant in the Ninth Cavalry when it formed in 1866, and served with the Ninth until he transferred to the Fourth Cavalry to facilitate his promotion to major in January 1897. See comments about his service in the Ninth Cavalry in appendix B.

17. *Annual Report of the War Department, 1898*, Vol. 1, Pt. 2, 179–81; "Alaska Relief Expedition," *U.S. Army and Navy Journal*, February 5, 1897; Ninth Cavalry Regimental Return, December 1897–April 1898, Returns from Regular Army Cavalry Regiments, 1833–1916, Microfilm M744, RG 391, NARA, hereafter Ninth Cavalry Regimental Return.

18. *Annual Report of the War Department, 1898*, Vol. 1, Pt. 2, 179–81; Gurcke, "Company L," 2. Most of the reindeer starved until their handlers found a local Alaskan moss they could substitute for their natural forage.

19. Company L, Twenty-Fourth Infantry Return, July–August 1899. Bailey's duties as well as the organization of the army hospital will be discussed in detail in chapter 4.

20. Camp Skagway Post Return, July–August 1899, Returns from U.S. Military Posts, 1800–1916, Microfilm M617, RG 94, NARA, hereafter Camp Skagway Post Return.

21. Moss, *Officers' Manual*, 306–8. The soldiers in the company would have referred to these men who worked for Hovey derisively as "dog-robbers."

22. Camp Skagway Letters Sent, 1899–1904, Records of U.S. Army Commands, 1821–1920, Entry 435-5, Vol. 1, RG 393, NARA, hereafter Camp Skagway Letters Sent.

23. Company L, Twenty-Fourth Infantry Return, July–August 1899.

24. Company L, Twenty-Fourth Infantry Return, July–August 1899.

25. Company L, Twenty-Fourth Infantry Return, October 1898; Plat of U.S. Survey No. 146, Office of the Surveyor General, Sitka, Alaska, February 1, 1899, copy obtained from the Klondike Gold Rush National Monument (KLGO).

26. Gurcke, "Company L."

27. General Order No. 6, January 14, 1899, General Orders and Circulars, 1797–1910, Records of the Adjutant General's Office, 1780–1917, RG 94, NARA.

28. "Testimony Secured in the 1899 among the Chilkat Indians," July 24, 1899, *Elihu Root Collection of United States Documents*, 543–44. Through the generosity of Bourn's descendants, the Alaska State Library has just about the only photographs of the DKT wharf site (ASL, Frank B. Bourn Collection, PCA 099). Tweedale owned a remarkable military pedigree. During the Civil War he enlisted as a private in Company B, Fifteenth Pennsylvania Cavalry and was awarded the Medal of Honor for gallantry in action at Stones River, Tennessee. After the war Tweedale completed his law degree at Columbian University (now George Washington University) in Washington DC and pursued a career in the Regular Army. Heitman, *Historical Register of the U.S. Army*, 1:976.

29. "Testimony Secured," 543–44; *Proceedings of the Alaskan Boundary Tribunal*.

30. "Testimony Secured," 543–44. The chiefs voiced a dislike for Canadian officials who made them pay duties on goods when they crossed the border into territory that had traditionally belonged to the Chilkat.

31. "Testimony Secured," 543–44. The names of the Chilkat chiefs who gave testimony included Koo-too-at, George Sha-trage, Jack Kitchk, Da-na-wak, Skin-ya, George Kah-oosh-tey, Yel-hak, Koow-tey-na-ah, David Ye-ka-sha, and Yen-sheesh Johnson.

32. Gurcke, "Company L."

33. Gurcke, "Company L," 14–23. First Sergeant O'Connor supervised the daily flow of activities at the wharf barracks. He maintained a guard roster with a sergeant of the guard, who supervised a corporal, and sentries walking the perimeter who were responsible for keeping unwelcome guests outside and straying soldiers inside the camp.

34. PCA 099-085, KLGO DKT-4-9513, and PCA 099-164, KLGO DKT-7-9538, Frank B. Bourn Collection, Alaska State Library; Gurcke, "Company L," 16–17.

35. PCA 099-160, KLGO DKT-5-953, Frank B. Bourn Collection, Alaska State Library; Gurcke, "Company L," 18.

36. Gurcke, "Company L," 14; Cole, "Survey of U.S. Army Uniforms," 29–37.

37. Gurcke, "Company L," 14; Cole, "Survey of U.S. Army Uniforms," 48–53. A .30-caliber or 7.62-millimeter-diameter bullet propelled by 40 grains or 3 grams of smokeless powder.

38. Gurcke, "Company L," 14; Cole, "Survey of U.S. Army Uniforms," 38–47.

39. Gurcke, "Company L," 14; Cole, "Survey of U.S. Army Uniforms," 29–53.

40. There was no direct land route between Dyea and Skagway, other than a hard march via heavily wooded mountain trails. The main conveyance between the towns was by boat or steamer.

41. Gurcke, "Company L." It was customary at the time for professionals to mark their exclusive photographs with their name in the bottom right corner, and none of the images bear a notation.

42. Gurcke, "Company L," 20–23. The photos of Company L on the DKT wharf were likely taken by Tweedale prior to the trip to Skagway on July 3. The series of photos of Company L marching in Skagway were taken on July 4, as was the posed and higher-quality image of the company on Fifth Avenue taken by Barley.

43. Gurcke, "Company L," 20–23.

44. Company L, Twenty-Fourth Infantry Return, July 1899.

45. Hovey to Deputy Marshal Tanner, July 6, 1899, Camp Skagway, Camp Skagway Letters Sent.

46. *Daily Alaskan*, July 7, 1900, as it appears in Brady, *Skagway*, 177–78.

47. Hovey to Adjutant General, Department of the Columbia, July 14, 1899, Camp Skagway Letters Sent.

48. Company L, Twenty-Fourth Infantry Return, July–August 1899.
49. Special Field Return, Company L, Twenty-Fourth Infantry Return, July 29, 1900.
50. Hovey to Adjutant General, U.S. Army, Washington DC, August 14, 1899, Camp Skagway Letters Sent.
51. Special Field Return, Company L, Twenty-Fourth Infantry Return, July 29, 1900; Hovey to Adjutant General, Department of Columbia, July 26, 1899, Camp Skagway Letters Sent; *Daily Alaskan*, January 1, 1900.
52. "Dyea," National Park Service.

3. Fort Wrangel

1. Lieutenant Jenks referred to the post as Fort Wrangel in his monthly reporting. The *Stikeen River Journal*, published weekly in the town, listed its home as Fort Wrangel, Alaska. The 1900 U.S. Census listed the town as Fort Wrangel. Fort Wrangel will be used throughout the chapter to describe both the fort and city. The name of the town was changed from Fort Wrangel to Wrangell in 1903 when it incorporated.
2. Orth, *Dictionary of Alaska Place Names*, 1060–61; Demerjian, *Wrangell*, 7–8.
3. Hunt, *Alaska*, 30–42.
4. Harring, "Incorporation of Alaska Natives under American Law," 295–96. The father was acting for his clan, trying to impress on the Americans the importance of respecting Tlingit law. Tlingit extensively used "peace ceremonies" to settle disputes that might lead to violence, yet U.S. authorities insisted on imposing common law and refused to recognize Tlingit indigenous law.
5. Harring, "Incorporation of Alaska Natives under American Law," 295–96. This was the first American application of the death penalty in Alaska.
6. Demerjian, *Wrangell*, 7–8; Scidmore, "Stikine River," 1–15. It initially competed favorably with Dyea and Skagway, and Canada considered building a railroad line along the Stikine River.
7. "History of Wrangell," Wrangell, http://www.wrangell.com/visitorservices /history-wrangell. Fort Wrangel had 2 sawmills, 1 cigar factory, 2 jewelers, 1 fish cannery, 3 tin shops, 2 blacksmiths, several carpenter shops, 1 shipyard, 10 laundries, 1 plumber, 1 copper shop, 2 breweries, 2 newspapers, numerous lodging houses, several restaurants, and too many bars.
8. Demerjian, *Wrangell*, 7–8; Scidmore, "Stikine River," 1–15.
9. Muir, *Travels in Alaska*.

10. Fort Wrangel Post Return, May–June 1899, Returns from U.S. Military Posts, 1800–1916, Microfilm M617, RG 94, NARA, hereafter Fort Wrangel Post Return.

11. *Stikeen River Journal,* May 20, 1899, 1. The *Stikeen River Journal* was a weekly newspaper published in Fort Wrangel from 1898 to 1899, and all issues were accessed via the Wrangell Public Library.

12. *Stikeen River Journal,* May 20, 1899, 1. Jenks arrived with forty-six enlisted men, not forty-nine. The newspaper may have been counting the three enlisted members of the hospital detachment.

13. Fort Wrangel Post Return, May–June 1899.

14. Fort Wrangel Post Return, May–June 1899. A "striker" or personal orderly had a long tradition in the army. Though the army had officially forbidden officers to employ strikers, they continued to do so informally.

15. Demerjian, *Wrangell,* 10–14. This book has good period photos of the military buildings at Fort Wrangel.

16. Moss, *Officers' Manual,* 305. By army regulation, an infantry company was supplied with two G trumpets with F slides.

17. Enlistment of Joseph A. Nash, March 25, 1899, Register of Enlistments, 1798–1914; U.S. Census, 1880, Circleville, Ohio, Bureau of the Census, Tenth Census of the United States, T9, NARA. Nash, born in London, Ohio, was the twenty-eight-year-old son of a clergyman, who likely fostered his talent with music.

18. Enlistment of James Washington, September 2, 1896; and Allen Hayes, September 13, 1886, Register of Enlistments. Every soldier when discharged had to be provided a discharge certificate. As a post commander, Jenks had a stack of blank forms for this purpose. Jenks issued discharges marked "honorably" to those who ended their terms as such, like Washington and Hayes. He issued discharges marked "without honor" to those soldiers who were in prison under sentence of a civil court, upon approval of the adjutant general of the U.S. Army. A "dishonorable discharge" could only be given to a soldier expressly imposed by sentence, normally by general court-martial.

19. Enlistment of Charles A. Hayman, February 7, 1899, Register of Enlistments.

20. Jenks to the Adjutant General, U.S. Army, November 16, 1899, *United States Congressional Serial Set,* 3–4.

21. U.S. Census, 1900, Fort Wrangel, Alaska, Bureau of the Census, Twelfth Census of the United States, T623, NARA, hereafter Census, Fort Wrangel, 1900.

22. *Stikeen River Journal*, August 6, 1898, 1, and August 27, 1898, 1; *Fort Wrangel News*, August 10, 1898, 1, as quoted in Levi, *Boom and Bust*, 121.

23. Demerjian, *Wrangell*, 15-17; Scidmore, "Stikine River," 2.

24. *Stikeen River Journal*, May 27, 1899, 1.

25. *Stikeen River Journal*, May 27, 1899, 1.

26. Enlistment of Harry V. Jordan, March 1, 1899; William Pate, January 23, 1899; Edward J. Collins, February 15, 1899; George M. Payne, January 26, 1899; and William Howard, March 10, 1899, Register of Enlistments.

27. *Stikeen River Journal*, June 10, 1899, 2.

28. *Stikeen River Journal*, June 10, 1899, 2.

29. *Stikeen River Journal*, June 10, 1899, 2.

30. *Stikeen River Journal*, June 10, 1899, 2.

31. *Stikeen River Journal*, July 8, 1899, 2.

32. *Stikeen River Journal*, July 8, 1899, 1.

33. *Stikeen River Journal*, July 1, 1899, 1.

34. *Stikeen River Journal*, July 1, 1899, 1, July 8, 1899, 1.

35. *Regulations for the Army of the United States, 1895*, 217-31; Winthrop, *Military Law and Precedents*, 81-109, 493-97.

36. Fort Wrangel Post Return, August–September 1899.

37. Fort Wrangel Post Return, September–October 1899; *Military Laws of the United States, 1901*, 518.

38. Fort Wrangel Post Return, September–October 1899.

39. *Manual for Courts-Martial*, 1898, 13; *Military Laws of the United States, 1901*, 518.

40. Fort Wrangel Post Return, October 1899; Enlistment of Robert W. Jordan, March 22, 1899, Register of Enlistments.

41. *Stikeen River Journal*, November 11, 1899, 1.

42. Fort Wrangel Post Return, November–December 1899. It is noteworthy Jenks referred to Harris as a musician in his monthly post return, since Jenks had only one assigned musician on his books: Joseph Nash. This indicates Jenks and Washington employed Harris as an extra trumpeter in addition to his normal duties. Harris was a thirty-three-year-old soldier from Martinsville, Virginia, on his second enlistment with the Twenty-Fourth Infantry. Joiner was one of the five soldiers who served in the Ninth Battalion, Ohio Volunteer Infantry, during the Spanish-American War before joining the Twenty-Fourth. Enlistments of Richard Harris, December 12, 1896, and Fred Joiner, February 9, 1899, Register of Enlistments.

43. Fort Wrangel Post Return, September 1899–February 1900; Enlistment of Huston Shannon, March 24, 1899, Register of Enlistments. The army issued orders directing Jenks to grant Shannon, a twenty-two-year-old from Bowling Green, Kentucky, a two-month furlough at the request of his mother in August. In October Jenks had received a letter from Stella B. Shannon requesting Private Shannon's discharge.

44. Fort Wrangel Post Return, February 1900; Enlistment of Ike Holloway, March 30, 1899, Register of Enlistments.

45. Fort Wrangel Post Return, April 1900; Enlistment of David McIntyre, February 14, 1899, Register of Enlistments.

46. Fort Wrangel Post Return, April 1900; Enlistment of Emery Collier, March 15, 1899, Register of Enlistments.

47. Fort Wrangel Post Return, May 1899–April 1900.

48. Ashburn, *History of the Medical Department*.

49. Emerson, *Encyclopedia of United States Army Insignia*, 183.

50. Fort Wrangel Post Return, December 1899–January 1900.

51. Fort Wrangel Post Return, December 1899–January 1900.

52. The term also may refer to the distaff, a decorated wooden household item used by women to spin flax into thread to weave clothing.

53. Last sentence suggested by Tom Phillips, email communication with author, January 23, 2020.

54. *Sixty-Second Annual Report*, 290.

55. Census, Fort Wrangel, 1900; photo of Jenks house, Jenks Papers.

56. *Army and Navy Journal*, October 8, 1899, 120.

57. Fort Wrangel Post Return, September 1899; Census, Fort Wrangel, 1900. The wives of a privileged few senior sergeants customarily traveled with the company when assigned to isolated frontier posts. These women often served as laundresses for the soldiers and performed other extra jobs to supplement their husbands' income. The enlisted soldiers had to ask the permission of their commanding officer to marry, and only a limited number could bring their wives on duty assignments. This was especially important for Company L, since they might be the only African American women present on the post.

58. Fort Wrangel Post Return, September 1899; Census, Fort Wrangel, 1900.

59. *Douglas Island News*, April 11, 1900, 3. Among others present were U.S. Commissioner Judge Fred Page Tustin, Mrs. Tustin, U.S. Customs Agent James H. Causton, Mrs. Causton, miner William Thomas, Mrs. Thomas, Associated Press reporter Henry Baron, Ketchikan businessman Henry C. Strong, Mrs.

Strong, J. F. Collins, Mrs. Collins, Special Treasury Agent John Shartzer, and Frank Tustin.

60. Fort Wrangel Post Return, May 1899–April 1900.

61. *Annual Report of the War Department, 1899*, Pt. 2, 411, 480, 956; *Annual Report of the War Department, 1899/1900*, Pt. 1, 4.

62. Heitman, *Historical Register of the U.S. Army*, 1:814. Randall enjoyed a storied career that began when he enlisted as a private in the Fourth Pennsylvania Volunteer Infantry in 1861. After receiving a Regular Army commission as a lieutenant in 1861, he rose rapidly in rank and earned six brevet promotions for gallantry in action during the Civil War and Indian Wars. Randall was awarded six brevets: captain (September 17, 1862) for Antietam; major (April 2, 1865) for Petersburg; lieutenant colonel and colonel of Volunteers (March 26, 1865) for the attack on Fort Stedman; lieutenant colonel (February 27, 1890) for actions against Indians at Turret Mountain, Arizona, on March 27, 1873, and Diamond Butte, Arizona, on April 22, 1873; and colonel (February 27, 1890) for action against Indians near Pinal, Arizona, March 8, 1874.

63. Fort Wrangel Post Return, April 1900.

64. Fort Wrangel Post Return, April 1900. Randall signed General Order No. 9, Headquarters Department of Alaska, on April 28, 1900, directing Jenks to abandon Fort Wrangel.

65. Fort Wrangel Post Return, April 1900; Demerjian, *Wrangell*, 9.

66. Fort Wrangel Post Return, April 1900. Private Victor Emmons, Company F, Seventh Infantry, was delivered to Jenks in April 1900 after serving a six-month prison sentence at Sitka.

4. Skagway Barracks

1. Brady, *Skagway*, 21–25.

2. Brady, *Skagway*, 25; Census, Skagway, 1900.

3. Spude, *"That Fiend in Hell,"* 6; Jarvis, *Great Gold Rush*, 30; Brady, *Skagway*, 134. Smith earned his nickname in Denver employing his "prize soap racket." Smith would open a display case on a street corner selling ordinary cakes of soap. As he spoke to crowds, he would wrap bills, ranging from one to one hundred dollars, depending on the size of the crowd, around a few of the cakes. He then wrapped each bar in plain paper, mixed the money-wrapped packages with others that contained no money, and finally sold each package for a dollar each. A shill planted in the crowd would buy a bar, open it, and proclaim he won money. This induced others to buy, until he auctioned

off all the remaining soap bars to the highest bidder. Through manipulation and sleight of hand, Smith removed the packages containing money or sold them to members of the gang planted in the crowd.

4. *Skagway News*, July 8, 1898; Smith, *Alias Soapy Smith*, 487–90; Brady, *Skagway*, 112–16.

5. *Daily Alaskan*, July 7, 1899; Brady, *Skagway*, 177–78.

6. *Daily Alaskan*, January 9, 1900, 9. According to the *Daily Alaskan*, Skagway also had 2 architects, 12 attorneys, 8 barber shops, 2 blacksmiths, 1 cigar manufacturer, 2 dentists, 5 druggists, 1 furniture manufacturer, 4 jewelers, 4 laundries, 3 photographers, 2 plumbers, 10 physicians, 5 tailors, 1 theater, and 1 undertaker.

7. Special Field Return, Company L, Twenty-Fourth Infantry Return, July 29, 1900; Gurcke, "Company L," 24–26.

8. Gurcke, "Company L," 24–26. Sibley tents were designed by U.S. Army officer Henry H. Sibley in 1856. Sibley was paid five dollars per tent manufactured due to his patent, but when he went south to the Confederacy during the Civil War, he forfeited his patent forever.

9. *Skagway News*, August 26, 1898, 1; *Daily Alaskan*, March 24, 1899, 1; Gurcke, "Company L," 27, 7.

10. Gurcke, "Company L," 7–8. "Scavenger" was a term for street cleaner, garbage collector, and night soil man, among other things.

11. Gurcke, "Company L," 8.

12. Gurcke, "Company L," 8–9.

13. *Daily Alaskan*, February 17, 1900, 4.

14. Gurcke, "Company L," 8–9.

15. Gurcke, "Company L," 8–9.

16. Gurcke, "Company L," 8–9.

17. Gurcke, "Company L," 8–9.

18. *Douglas Island News*, August 1, 1900, 1.

19. Email from Catherine Spude to the author, July 30, 2019, responding to my question on the *Douglas Island News* quote.

20. Spude, "Skagway's Bustling Saloon Era, 1897–1916," in Brady, *Skagway*, 225–28; Spude, *Saloons, Prostitutes, and Temperance*, 63.

21. Email from Catherine Spude to the author, July 30, 2019, responding to my question on the *Douglas Island News* quote.

22. *Military Laws of the United States, 1901*, 336–38. The monthly base pay of a private was thirteen dollars, plus or minus authorized deductions and clothing allowances.

23. *Daily Alaskan*, July 24, 1901.
24. Hovey's correspondence, August 1899–January 1900, Camp Skagway Letters Sent. Hovey kept a handwritten daily record of the official letters he sent in a large leather-bound ledger.
25. Hovey's correspondence, August 1899–January 1900, Camp Skagway Letters Sent.
26. In 1977, when the author was a second lieutenant deployed to Camp Irwin, California, with his tank battalion, he paid his men in cash in much the same fashion.
27. Hovey to Chief Paymaster, Department of the Columbia, August 19, 1899, and September 4, 1899, Camp Skagway Letters Sent.
28. Hovey to Chief Paymaster, Department of the Columbia, September 26 and October 25, 1899, Camp Skagway Letters Sent.
29. Hovey to Chief Paymaster, Department of the Columbia, December 24, 1899, January 19, 1900, and January 21, 1900, Camp Skagway Letters Sent.
30. Company L, Twenty-Fourth Infantry Return, June–August 1899.
31. Company L, Twenty-Fourth Infantry Return, August–October 1899.
32. Camp Skagway Post Return, August–September 1899.
33. Hovey, Certificate on Cause of Desertion, Camp Skagway Letters Sent.
34. Hovey to Adjutant General, Department of the Columbia, October 25, 1899, and Hovey to Adjutant General, U.S. Army, December 27, 1899, Camp Skagway Letters Sent.
35. Camp Skagway Post Return, October–December 1899, May–June 1900; Hovey to Adjutant General, Department of the Columbia, Vancouver Barracks WA, October 26, 1899, Camp Skagway Letters Sent. In May 1900 civilian authorities at Fort Wrangel turned over a deserter from the Seventh Infantry who Hovey tried, confined, and discharged.
36. Camp Skagway Post Return, November 1899; Norman E. Malcolm, U.S. Commissioner, Juneau, to Hovey, August 14, 1899, Camp Skagway Letters Sent.
37. *Daily Alaskan*, December 14, 1899.
38. Brady, *Skagway*, 223, 229.
39. *Daily Alaskan*, April 20, 1901.
40. *Daily Alaskan*, December 19, 1899, 1.
41. Camp Skagway Post Return, December 1899–January 1900.
42. *Daily Alaskan*, February 7, 1901.
43. *Daily Alaskan*, February 7, 1901; Enlistment of Loney Moore, June 15, 1895, and January 28, 1899, Register of Enlistments; Hovey to U.S. Marshal Shoup,

Juneau AK, May 16, 1900, Camp Skagway Letters Sent. Moore applied for an army pension on June 28, 1928, in California, which was denied because of his dishonorable discharge.

44. *Regulations for the Army of the United States, 1895*, 20–22; Moss, *Officers' Manual*, 306.

45. General Order 83, June 17, 1901, *Regulations for the United States Army, 1901*, Vol. 1861, 363–64.

46. General Order 83, June 17, 1901, *Regulations for the United States Army, 1901*, Vol. 1861, 363–64.

47. Camp Skagway Post Return, October 1899. Breckinridge joined the army during the Civil War and was captured, exchanged, and received two brevets for gallantry and meritorious service during the war. As a brigadier general he was appointed as the inspector general of the army in 1889, then served as a volunteer major general with the Fifth Corps in Cuba during the Spanish-American War. In the battles of El Caney and San Juan Hill in Cuba, he had his horse shot out from under him. After the war he resumed his duties as the inspector general of the army and served in that position until he retired in 1903. Heitman, *Historical Register of the U.S. Army*, 1:242.

48. Whitehorne, *Inspector Generals of the Army*, 494.

49. "Weather: Skagway," National Park Service, https://www.nps.gov/klgo /planyourvisit/weather.htm.

50. Hovey to Chief Quartermaster, Department of Alaska, Fort Saint Michael, August 13, 1900, Camp Skagway Letters Sent.

51. *Army and Navy Journal*, February 24, 1900, 601.

52. *Daily Alaskan*, December 20, 1899, 4.

53. *Daily Alaskan*, December 26, 1899, 1.

54. *Daily Alaskan*, December 27, 1899, 4.

55. Camp Skagway Post Return, June 1900; *Daily Alaskan*, October 29, 1901; "Buffalo Soldiers in Skagway," National Park Service, https://www.nps.gov /klgo/learn/historyculture/buffalo-soldiers.htm.

56. Census, Skagway, 1900.

57. Census, Skagway, 1900.

58. Dodge, *Norwich University, 1819–1911*, 81; U.S. Census, 1900, Northfield, Vermont, Bureau of the Census, Twelfth Census of the United States, T623, NARA.

59. Census, Skagway, 1900; Enlistment of Charles Clarkson, June 16, 1887, September 16, 1891, and September 16, 1896, Register of Enlistments.

60. Census, Skagway, 1900.

61. U.S. Census, 1870, Paris, Kentucky, Bureau of the Census, T132, NARA; U.S. Census, 1880, Emporia, Kansas, Bureau of the Census, Tenth Census of the United States, T9, NARA; *Utah, County Marriages, 1887-1937.*

62. Census, Skagway, 1900; *Official Register of the United States,* 457.

63. *Daily Alaskan,* January 9, 1900, 10. Hovey to E. C. Hawkins, General Manager for the White Pass & Yukon Route Railroad, Seattle, September 11, 1899, Camp Skagway Letters Sent.

64. *Official Register of the United States,* 460; Conner, "History of Weather Observations," 20. This paper gives a good description of the officers and enlisted men of the Hospital Corps, who in the frontier army had the mission of taking weather readings.

65. Census, Skagway, 1900; Enlistment of Gabriel Cushman, February 1, 1895, Register of Enlistments.

66. Conner, "History of Weather Observations," 21.

67. Census, Skagway, 1900. Sterly and Cushman both spoke German. Cushman also spoke Yiddish.

68. *Official Register of the United States,* 457.

69. Hovey to Commanding Officer, Vancouver Barracks, February 9, 1900, Camp Skagway Letters Sent; Enlistment of John Kimball, March 3, 1899, Register of Enlistments.

70. Hovey to Surgeon, December 28, 1899, Camp Skagway Letters Sent.

71. *Daily Alaskan,* January 9, 1900, 9.

72. *Daily Alaskan,* January 10, 1900, 4.

73. *Annual Report of the War Department, 1899,* Pt. 2, 411, 480, 956; *Annual Report of the War Department, 1899/1900,* Pt. 1, 4.

74. *Annual Report of the War Department, 1902,* 29; "Big War Works for Skagway," *Daily Alaskan,* January 9, 1900. This eventually led to the construction of Fort Seward at Haines, across the Chilkoot Inlet from Skagway, beginning in 1902.

75. *Daily Alaskan,* April 19, 1900, 9, April 25, 1900, 1, April 26, 1900, 1.

76. *Annual Report of the War Department, 1902,* 29.

77. Camp Skagway Post Return, May 1900. Randall signed General Order No. 9, Headquarters Department of Alaska, on April 28, 1900, directing Jenks to abandon Fort Wrangel and rejoin Company L. Not everyone was as pleased as the Skagwayans with the news of the creation of permanent military facilities in Alaska. The Alaska Miners Association, an organization of Nome miners, "were inclined to look with disfavor upon the decision." One member noted, "Nothing had ever transpired in Alaska to warrant the

presence of Federal troops." During a meeting, two other members told of their experience when soldiers dispersed a miners' assembly and tried to interfere in the miners claim-locating methods. Federal troops were not always welcome among independently minded miners who wanted to follow their own rules. Army troops were often used at the time by the civilian authorities to break up strikes by organized labor. *Daily Alaskan*, January 13, 1900, 4.

5. Company Reunited

1. Camp Skagway Post Return, May 1900.
2. Camp Skagway Post Return, May 1900.
3. Gurcke, "Lynch and Kennedy Dry Goods and Haberdashery (1900/1908)," 2–3. The barracks building was sawed in half and moved in 1908 to its current location on the corner of Broadway and Fourth Avenue, where it became the Trail Inn. It is now called the Lynch and Kennedy Building.
4. Gurcke, "Company L," 4, 7–11.
5. Camp Skagway Post Return, May 1900. Lieutenant Jenks no longer filled the first lieutenant position but had been carried on the books as the adjutant of the Second Battalion, Twenty-Fourth Infantry, since December 26, 1899. The first lieutenant position in the company did not stay vacant long. In November 1900 First Lieutenant Albert Laws was assigned to Company L from another company in the Twenty-Fourth Infantry. He did not join the company in Skagway, since he was serving in the Philippines at the time as a major with the Thirty-Fifth U.S. Volunteers (Laws was a major in the volunteers but remained a first lieutenant in the Regular Army). This assignment on paper facilitated his promotion to first lieutenant. An officer had to fill an authorized position appropriate to his new rank before he could wear his new bars. Laws was replaced by First Lieutenant Joseph L. Herring in June 1901. Again, the assignment was on paper, for promotion purposes only, and Herring remained with the regiment in the Philippines until it returned to the United States. Camp Skagway Post Return, November 1900.
6. *Regulations for the Army of the United States, 1895*, Article XXXII, paragraph 258, 37.
7. Hovey to Surgeon General, U.S. Army, April 9, 1900, and Hovey to Adjutant General, Department of Alaska, May 7, 1900, Camp Skagway Letters Sent.
8. Camp Skagway Post Return, May and June 1900.
9. *Daily Alaskan*, July 20, 1900.

10. Hovey to Adjutant General, Department of Alaska, April 30, 1900, Camp Skagway Letters Sent; Camp Skagway Post Return, May 1900.
11. *Daily Alaskan,* May 5, 1900.
12. Dobak and Phillips, *Black Regulars,* 148–49.
13. *Daily Alaskan,* May 5, 1900.
14. *Daily Alaskan,* May 2, 1900. This term comes from the Douglas MacArthur quote, "On the fields of friendly strife are sown the seeds that on other days, on other fields will bear the fruits of victory."
15. *Daily Alaskan,* May 19, 1900.
16. *Sixty-Second Annual Report,* 282.
17. *Daily Alaskan,* May 19, 1900.
18. Warrington, "Fight for Sunday Baseball."
19. *Daily Alaskan,* May 19, 1900. The article only gives the last names of the Skagway baseball players as Phelps, Randall, McGrath, Kenny, W. Cleveland, Durgin, Tharlson, and Van Zant. Some of the first names are known for individuals who played in later years. Others are the author's best guesses from the 1900 census and other city records. The newspaper was often inaccurate and inconsistent in spelling names. The full names of known players included John Phelps, Louis McGrath, William Cleveland, Edward Barry, Tom Cleveland, and Earl Dugin (not Durgin).
20. *Daily Alaskan,* May 19, 1900; Muller, *History of the Twenty-Fourth Infantry.*
21. *Daily Alaskan,* May 22, 1900.
22. *Daily Alaskan,* May 22, 1900.
23. *Daily Alaskan,* June 5, 1900.
24. *Daily Alaskan,* June 19, 1900.
25. *Daily Alaskan,* June 19, 1900. The Portland Webfeet, Seattle Hustlers, Spokane Bunchgrassers, and Tacoma Daisies played Minor League professional baseball in the Pacific Northwest League from 1890 to 1892.
26. *Douglas Island News,* June 27, 1900, 1.
27. *Daily Alaskan,* June 22, 1900.
28. Enlistment of Edward G. Dewey, January 23, 1899; Frank Gant, March 9, 1899; John W. Oby, March 21, 1899; Benjamin Green, March 22, 1899; William Jennings, February 11, 1899; Ernest L. Johnson, March 9, 1899; William Sims, March 20, 1899; James M. Banks, March 22, 1899; George Bracy, February 9, 1899; William Mack, March 20, 1899, Register of Enlistments.
29. The U.S. Census was a decennial counting of people mandated by Article 1, Section 2 of the U.S. Constitution. This section directed that a count of people be made every ten years to apportion representatives and taxes

among the states. Even though it was not a state, census coverage began in the District of Alaska in 1880.

30. Census, Skagway, 1900. Quoted statistics vary wildly, so I have used numbers and statistics quoted by Catherine Spude in *Saloons, Prostitutes, and Temperance*, 259–64. Spude did an extensive study on the 1900 population of Skagway for her PhD dissertation. The official enumeration for 1900 was 3,113, but this number included people on board ships in the harbor, men on the work gangs of the White Pass railroad, and a small settlement to the west called Smugglers Cove.

31. Census, Skagway, 1900. Though one soldier was born in the British West Indies, I have used the term "African American" as well as "Black" throughout this book to refer to the soldiers of Company L.

32. Spude, *Saloons, Prostitutes, and Temperance*, 262–63.

33. Census, Fort Wrangel and Skagway, 1900.

34. Census, Skagway, 1900. Company L: Alabama, 3; Arkansas, 1; District of Columbia, 3; Florida, 2; Georgia, 3; Illinois, 3; Indiana, 8; Kentucky, 5; Massachusetts, 9; Maryland, 2; North Carolina, 8; New Jersey, 1; New York, 3; Ohio, 6; Pennsylvania, 11; South Carolina, 5; Tennessee, 9; Virginia, 10; Virgin Islands, 1. Hospital staff: Arkansas, 1; Illinois, 1; Missouri, 1; New York, 1; Oregon, 1; Pennsylvania, 1; Virginia, 1; Washington, 1. Company F: Kentucky, 1.

35. Census, Skagway, 1900. The two cooks were twenty-three and twenty-six, the two musicians twenty-nine and forty-eight, and the artificer twenty-two years old. The average age of the Hospital Corps enlisted members was twenty-eight years.

36. Census, Skagway, 1900. The instructions to census takers directed they ask and enter "Yes" for all persons ten years of age and over who could read or write any language.

37. Census, Skagway, 1900.

38. Census, Skagway, 1900; email from Catherine Spude to the author, August 8, 2019, Subject: Charles Munson.

39. *Daily Alaskan*, March 15, 1900, 1.

40. Brady, *Skagway*, 157–59; Census, Skagway, 1900; Mielke, "Newlyweds Murdered in Chilkat Territory."

41. *Daily Alaskan*, June 27, 1900, 1; Brady, *Skagway*, 157–59.

42. *Douglas Island News*, June 27 and July 4, 1900, 1; Brady, *Skagway*, 157–59; Mielke, "Newlyweds Murdered in Chilkat Territory." The newspaper gives the names of those found guilty and sentenced as Jim Hanson, Jim Williams, Kitchikoo, Day Kauteen, Jack Lain, and Mark Clanet. The 1900 census lists

the following inmates in the Skagway jail: Paddie Anahooch, James Hanson, Day Kanteen, Dave A.W. Kanut, John Kanut, Jim Ketchitoo, James Konish, George White, James Williams, Jim Williams, and John Ketchitoo. All are listed as Chilkat Tlingit, except George White, who was Sitka Tlingit, and James Williams, who was Taku Tlingit. Jim Hanson converted hundreds of inmates to Salvationism at McNeil Island before dying of tuberculosis in 1905. All six died of tuberculosis by 1905 except Jack Lane, who was released in 1910 after his sentence was commuted to time served by President Howard Taft.

43. Hovey to Adjutant General, Department of Alaska, Fort Saint Michael, August 28, 1900, Camp Skagway Letters Sent.

44. *Daily Alaskan*, June 29, 1900. Juneau incorporated one day after Skagway.

45. Brady, *Skagway*, 211–12.

46. There were 360 votes cast (not all voters marked the incorporation ballot).

47. Census, Skagway, 1900. Hislop had also been elected mayor by the previous "illegitimate" city council.

48. Spude, *Saloons, Prostitutes, and Temperance*, 67; Brady, *Skagway*, 139, 307–12.

49. Spude, *Saloons, Prostitutes, and Temperance*, 67; Brady, *Skagway*, 139, 307–12.

50. *Daily Alaskan*, July 3 and 6, 1900.

51. *Daily Alaskan*, July 6, 1900. Skagway and Canadians teams played one another in 1898 and 1899 on July 4, which was close to the queen's birthday.

52. *Daily Alaskan*, July 3 and 6, 1900.

53. *Daily Alaskan*, July 3 and 6, 1900.

54. Hovey to the Adjutant General, Department of Alaska, May 10, 1900, Camp Skagway Letters Sent.

55. Hovey to the Adjutant General, U.S. Army, July 5, 1900, Camp Skagway Letters Sent.

56. *Daily Alaskan*, July 3, 1900.

57. *Daily Alaskan*, July 31, 1900.

58. *Daily Alaskan*, July 31, 1900; Brady, *Skagway*, 179–80; Graves, *On the "White Pass" Pay-Roll*.

59. *Daily Alaskan*, July 31, 1900; Brady, *Skagway*, 173–75, 181–82.

60. *Daily Alaskan*, July 31, 1900.

61. Camp Skagway Post Return, June 1900.

62. Hovey to Adjutant General, Department of Alaska, August 28, 1900, Camp Skagway Letters Sent; Camp Skagway Post Return, August 1900.

63. Hovey to Adjutant General, Department of Alaska, August 28, 1900, Camp Skagway Letters Sent; Camp Skagway Post Return, August 1900; Miller, *Canadian Career of the Fourth Earl of Minto*, 159.

64. *Daily Alaskan*, August 11, 1900. With him, aside from Lady Minto, were Arthur Guise, comptroller of the household, Captain Graham, aide de camp, T. F. Sladen, his private secretary, and Staff Sergeant T. Rogers, his enlisted aide.

65. Camp Skagway Post Return, August 1900.

66. Miller, *Canadian Career of the Fourth Earl of Minto*, 159.

67. Company L, Twenty-Fourth Infantry Return, August 1900.

68. *Genealogy of the Descendants of John White of Wenham and Lancaster, Massachusetts: 1638-1900*, accessed on Ancestry.com.

69. Heitman, *Historical Register of the U.S. Army*, 1:812; Camp Skagway Post Return, August 1900.

70. Heitman, *Historical Register of the U.S. Army*, 1:812; Camp Skagway Post Return, August 1900.

71. Coumbe, *History of the U.S. Army Officer Corps*, 3. Of the officers promoted from the ranks between 1900 and 1913, only two were African American. Benjamin O. Davis earned a commission as a second lieutenant in the Tenth Cavalry and John E. Green a commission as a second lieutenant in the Twenty-Fifth Infantry in February 1901. Green, who like Rains was born in Nashville, Tennessee, had served his enlisted time as a private and corporal in H Company, Twenty-Fourth Infantry, and was fighting with his unit in the Philippine Islands at the time of his commissioning. Green and Rains may well have crossed paths in the Philippines. Heitman, *Historical Register of the U.S. Army*, 1:357, 472.

72. Camp Skagway Post Return, September 1900.

73. Hovey to Adjutant General, Department of Alaska, September 24, 1900, Camp Skagway Letters Sent.

74. *Daily Alaskan*, September 25, 1900.

75. *Daily Alaskan*, September 25, 1900.

76. Hovey to Adjutant General, Department of Alaska, September 24, 1900, Camp Skagway Letters Sent.

77. *Regulations for the Army of the United States, 1895*, 64.

78. Hovey to Adjutant General, Department of Alaska, September 24, 1900, Camp Skagway Letters Sent; Lieber, *Use of the Army in Aid of the Civil Power*, 77-78; Laurie, *The Role of Federal Military Forces in Domestic Disorders, 1877-1945*, 19-20.

79. Hovey to Adjutant General, U.S. Army, October 9, 1900, Camp Skagway Letters Sent.

80. *Daily Alaskan*, September 25, 1900.

81. *Daily Alaskan*, September 25, 1900.

82. Company L, Twenty-Fourth Infantry Return, October 1900; *Douglas Island News*, October 17 and 24, 1900.
83. Enlistment of Harry Andrews, February 11, 1899; Harry V. Jordan, March 1, 1899; and George M. Payne, January 26, 1899, Register of Enlistments.
84. *Daily Alaskan*, October 9, 1900.
85. *Daily Alaskan*, October 9, 1900.
86. *Daily Alaskan*, October 11, 1900.
87. Company L, Twenty-Fourth Infantry Return, October 1900.
88. Hovey to Rains, October 9, 1900, Camp Skagway Letters Sent; Camp Skagway Post Return, October 1900.
89. Hovey to Rains, October 9, 1900, Camp Skagway Letters Sent; Camp Skagway Post Return, October 1900.
90. *Daily Alaskan*, October 10, 1900.
91. Hovey to Rains, October 29, 1900, Camp Skagway Letters Sent.
92. Hovey to Rains, October 29, 1900, Camp Skagway Letters Sent.
93. Hovey to Rains, October 29, 1900, Camp Skagway Letters Sent.
94. Hovey to Adjutant General, Department of Alaska, December 5, 1900, Camp Skagway Letters Sent.
95. Camp Skagway Post Return, November 1901.
96. Camp Skagway Post Return, May 1900 and January 1901.
97. *Military Laws of the United States, 1901*, 515.
98. Enlistment of Edward Bordinghammer, September 5, 1875, September 7, 1880, September 7, 1885, September 7, 1890, September 7, 1898, Register of Enlistments; Muller, *Twenty-Fourth Infantry*, 18–24.
99. Company L, Twenty-Fourth Infantry Return, October 1900.

6. Settling In

1. Hovey to Adjutant General, U.S. Army, February 26, 1901, Camp Skagway Letters Sent.
2. *Daily Alaskan*, September 21, 1900.
3. Hovey to Adjutant General, U.S. Army, February 26, 1901, Camp Skagway Letters Sent.
4. Hovey to Adjutant General, Department of Alaska, March 4, 1901, Camp Skagway Letters Sent.
5. Jenks to Adjutant General, U.S. Army, June 24, 1901, Camp Skagway Letters Sent; *Daily Alaskan*, June 23, 1901.
6. *Daily Alaskan*, June 23, 1901; "Customs Flag Incident," July 13, 1901, RG 2, Privy Council Office, Series A-1-a, Library and Archives Canada.

7. *Daily Alaskan*, June 23, 1901.
8. Jenks to Adjutant General, U.S. Army, June 24, 1901, Camp Skagway Letters Sent; "Customs Flag Incident."
9. Jenks to Adjutant General, U.S. Army, June 24, 1901, Camp Skagway Letters Sent; *Douglas Island News*, July 24, 1901.
10. Hovey to Adjutant General, U.S. Army, January 15, 1901, Camp Skagway Letters Sent.
11. Hovey to President, Alaska Chamber of Commerce, January 15, 1901, and Hovey to Adjutant General, Department of Alaska, March 4, 1901, Camp Skagway Letters Sent.
12. Jenks to Chief Quartermaster, Department of Columbia, May 15, 1901, Camp Skagway Letters Sent.
13. Jenks to Chief Quartermaster, Department of Columbia, May 15, 1901, Camp Skagway Letters Sent.
14. *Daily Alaskan*, January 9, 1900.
15. U.S. Ordnance Department, *Handbook of the Gatling Gun*, 21.
16. U.S. Ordnance Department, *Handbook of the Gatling Gun*, 21.
17. *Daily Alaskan*, September 6, 1900; Brunet-Jailly, *Border Disputes*, 534.
18. Keller, *Mr. Gatling's Terrible Marvel*, 168–70.
19. *Daily Alaskan*, December 13, 1900, 4, excerpt provided by KGLO.
20. Enlistment of Esaw Simmons, March 10, 1899, Register of Enlistments; Camp Skagway Post Return, March 1901.
21. *Seattle Star*, March 18, 1901, 3, courtesy of the Skagway Museum.
22. Hovey to Adjutant General, March 9, 1901, Camp Skagway Letters Sent.
23. Enlistment of Oscar D. Henry, March 22, 1899, Register of Enlistments; Camp Skagway Post Return, May 1901.
24. Camp Skagway Post Return, March–April 1901; Company L, Twenty-Fourth Infantry Return, March–April 1901.
25. Enlistment of Webster Altmann, March 11, 1899, Register of Enlistments; New York State Census, 1905, New York State Archives, Albany; 1925 New York State Census, 1925, New York State Archives, Albany, via Ancestry.com.
26. Enlistment of James Washington, August 28, 1886, Register of Enlistments; Camp Skagway Post Return, April–May 1901.
27. Coffman, *The Old Army*, 271–76; Brands, "'Unsatisfactory and Futile,'" 1067–94.
28. Coffman, *The Old Army*, 271–76; Hovey to Rains, February 13, 1901, Camp Skagway Letters Sent.
29. Hovey to Rains, February 13, 1901, Camp Skagway Letters Sent.

30. Jenks to Adjutant General, Department of Alaska, September 10, 1901, Camp Skagway Letters Sent.
31. Jenks to Adjutant General, Department of Alaska, September 10, 1901, Camp Skagway Letters Sent.
32. Camp Skagway Post Return, February 1900–April 1901.
33. Weigley, *History of the United States Army*, 290–91.
34. Camp Skagway Post Return, May–October 1901; *Sixty-Second Annual Report*, 286.
35. *Daily Alaskan*, May 23, 1901.
36. *Daily Alaskan*, May 23, 1901. The individuals named were L. A. Treen, T. Broemser, T. A. Shorthill, and Alexander Green.
37. *Daily Alaskan*, May 23, 1901.
38. *Daily Alaskan*, June 8, 1901.
39. *Daily Alaskan*, June 8, 1901.
40. *Daily Alaskan*, May 24, 1901.
41. *Douglas Island News*, June 5, 1901.
42. *Daily Alaskan*, May 24, 1901; *Douglas Island News*, May 29, 1901.
43. *Daily Alaskan*, May 24, 1901.
44. *Daily Alaskan*, June 2, 1901.
45. *Daily Alaskan*, July 4 and 6, 1901.
46. *Daily Alaskan*, July 4 and July 6, 1901.
47. *Daily Alaskan*, July 6, 1901.
48. *Daily Alaskan*, July 4 and 6, 1901.
49. *Daily Alaskan*, July 4 and 6, 1901.
50. *Daily Alaskan*, July 4 and 6, 1901.
51. Enlistment of Thomas Morton, February 7, 1899; William Pate, January 23, 1899; William Rollins, March 23, 1901; and William Freeman, September 20, 1900, Register of Enlistments.
52. Enlistment of James Banks, March 22, 1899; George Bracy, February 9, 1899; Edward Dewey, January 23, 1899; Frank Gant, March 9, 1899; William Mack, March 20, 1899, Register of Enlistments.
53. *Daily Alaskan*, July 4 and 6, 1901.
54. *Daily Alaskan*, July 4 and 6, 1901.

7. Command Change

1. Enlistment of Herbert Williams, February 15, 1899, Register of Enlistments; *Daily Alaskan*, February 20, 1901.
2. Marriage Certificate of William Snoten, June 18, 1924, and World War II Registration Card of William W. Snoten, undated, Ancestry.com.

3. Census, Skagway, 1900.

4. *Daily Alaskan*, July 17, 1901, 4.

5. *Daily Alaskan*, July 17, 1901, 4.

6. *Daily Alaskan*, December 11, 1900. We have pictures of Hovey, Jenks, and Bailey, and the man sitting in the barber chair is not one of them. The only other officer in Skagway in December 1900 was Lieutenant Rains.

7. *Daily Alaskan*, June 7, 1901.

8. *Daily Alaskan*, June 7, 1901.

9. *Daily Alaskan*, June 19, 1901, 1.

10. *Daily Alaskan*, June 19, 1901, 1, and June 22, 1901, 4.

11. *Daily Alaskan*, June 19, 1901, 1, and June 22, 1901, 4.

12. *Spude, Saloons, Prostitutes and Temperance*, 151.

13. Spude, *Saloons, Prostitutes and Temperance*, 92–101.

14. *Daily Alaskan*, November 16, 1901, 1, and November 19, 1901, 4.

15. Dodge, *Norwich University, 1819–1911*, 81; *Sixty-Second Annual Report*, 290; *Northfield Times*, November 17, 1908; Census, Skagway, 1900. The Military Order of the Loyal Legion of the United States was a patriotic order of military officers who served in the Civil War. It became hereditary society after the original members died out.

16. *Daily Alaskan*, November 14, 1900, 1; Bowman, *The Arctic Brotherhood*, 54.

17. *Sixty-Second Annual Report*, 288; *Daily Alaskan*, July 4, 1901, 1.

18. *Daily Alaskan*, September 29, 1901.

19. *Sixty-Second Annual Report*, 288; *Daily Alaskan*, July 4, 1901, 1.

20. *Daily Alaskan*, June 2 and October 10, 1901.

21. Bailey Consular Passport no. 911, issued in Swatow, China, February 16, 1894, Ancestry.com.

22. *Daily Alaskan*, December 4 and 10, 1901.

23. *Daily Alaskan*, May 4, 1901.

24. *Daily Alaskan*, May 4, and July 28, 1901. Bailey lost badly at Alaskan blackjack at a party hosted by Dr. and Mrs. Runnals in July 1901 and attended by Isaac and Alice Jenks as well as Florence Bailey. Ed Bailey won second prize playing High Five at a party at the Pullen House hosted by Mrs. Arnold L. Berdoe in September 1901.

25. *Washington County Marriages, 1855–2008*, Ancestry.com; *Daily Alaskan*, February 6, 1901.

26. *Daily Alaskan*, September 24, 1901. In September 1901 the *Daily Alaskan* reported Rains departed on a hunting trip with P. E. Kern, H. C. Barley, A. H. Brackett, M. R. Clemenger, and A. Brackett Jr. They departed on a Tuesday

from Dyea in boats and planned a trip to Sheep Camp in the mountains in search of bear until their planned return on Thursday.

27. Jenks to Adjutant General, U.S. Army, July 25, 1901, Camp Skagway Letters Sent.

28. Hovey to Adjutant General, Department of Alaska, March 4, 1901, Camp Skagway Letters Sent.

29. Hovey to Adjutant General, Department of Alaska, March 4, 1901, Camp Skagway Letters Sent; Camp Skagway Post Return, February 1901.

30. Camp Skagway Post Return, July and August 1901.

31. Woll, *Black Musical Theatre*, 1-2.

32. *Daily Alaskan*, August 14, 21, 1901. The Georgia Jubilee Singers was a popular name for many jubilee troupes and does not mean they came from Georgia.

33. *Daily Alaskan*, July 21, 1901.

34. *Daily Alaskan*, July 21, 1901.

35. *Daily Alaskan*, July 25, 1901.

36. *Daily Alaskan*, July 21, 25, 1901.

37. *Daily Alaskan*, August 20, 1901.

38. *Daily Alaskan*, August 20, 1901.

39. *Daily Alaskan*, August 20, 1901.

40. *Daily Alaskan*, August 20, 1901.

41. *Daily Alaskan*, August 20, 1901.

42. *Daily Alaskan*, August 20, 1901. Sergeant Allen Hayes was listed in the 1900 census as married, but his wife was not listed in Skagway. She could have joined him in Skagway after June 1900.

43. *Daily Alaskan*, August 21, 1901.

44. *Daily Alaskan*, September 11, 14, 1901; Woll, *Black Musical Theatre*, 1-2. It is likely Director George H. Williams was the same man who had performed with the Georgia Anniversary Jubilee Singers in July.

45. Woll, *Black Musical Theatre*, 6-13. Cole believed Blacks should compete with whites and prove their ability to act and sing on stage, while others such as Marion Cook thought African Americans should not imitate Black dialectic songs but rather create and elevate their own style.

46. *Daily Alaskan*, September 15, 1901.

47. *Daily Alaskan*, September 29, 1901.

48. *Daily Alaskan*, September 18, 19, 1901.

49. Morgan, *William McKinley and His America*, 15-248. Rutherford B. Hayes, another future president, also served in this Ohio unit.

50. Morgan, *William McKinley and His America*, 66–67, 193, 236, 479. The African American soldiers in Skagway did not have the opportunity to vote for President McKinley or his opponent in the election of 1900. U.S. military members serving overseas or on bases away from their home states were not granted the right to vote in elections for another eighty-six years. No Skagwayans voted either, since Alaska did not become a state for another fifty-nine years. U.S. Military and Uniformed Services, merchant marines, and other citizens overseas living on bases in the United States, abroad, or on board ship were granted the right to vote by the Uniformed and Overseas Citizens Absentee Voting Act of 1986. Alaskans achieved statehood in 1959 and voted in the first presidential election in 1960.

51. *Scribner's Magazine*, April 1899, 420–40.

52. *Annual Report of the Chief Signal Officer*, 9.

53. *Annual Report of the Chief Signal Officer*, 9.

54. *Annual Report of the Chief Signal Officer*, 10; Camp Skagway Post Return, August 1901.

55. Camp Skagway Post Return, August 1901; Skirbunt, "From Commissary Sergeant to U.S. President."

56. Enlistment of August Luttge, September 17, 1894, August 30, 1901, Register of Enlistments.

57. Camp Skagway Post Return, May to October 1901; *Sixty-Second Annual Report*, 286.

58. Camp Skagway Post Return, October 1901; *Daily Alaskan*, October 13, 1901, 1.

59. Hovey to Chief Quartermaster, Department of Columbia, May 15, 1901, Camp Skagway Letters Sent; "First Book of the Chronicles of Skagway," *Daily Alaskan*, January 1, 1900, 15.

60. Jenks to Adjutant General, Department of Alaska, May 15, 1901, Camp Skagway Letters Sent.

61. *Daily Alaskan*, June 16, 1901, 4, and June 17, 1901.

62. *Daily Alaskan*, October 6, 1901.

63. *Daily Alaskan*, October 12, 1901. Guests included C. M. Summers, C. E. Wynn-Johnson, A. B. Newell, C. V. Hall, J. P. Rogers, E. J. Shaw, A. L. Berdoe, C. G. K. Norse, and Dr. Bailey. Newell officiated as chairman, and Norse acted as the toastmaster.

64. DeArmond, *Klondike Newsman*, 33–35. The Pack Train never closed, and you could get a meal at any hour. It shared a building with the Pack Train Saloon, but Tony and Louie had no interest in the saloon, and a partition separated the two.

65. *Daily Alaskan*, October 13, 1901. The group played a "new and popular game of Progressive Coal Black Lady" during the early part of the evening on five tables. Black Lady was a combative variant of Whist, like Hearts for large groups, using two decks of cards. Later the group "indulged in old fashioned games that took those present back to their younger days."

66. Summary of military service, Jenks Papers.

8. Challenges

1. *Annual Report of the War Department, 1901,* 23; *Annual Report of the War Department, 1902,* 29.

2. "An Army Post Should Be Located in Skagway," *Daily Alaskan,* October 20, 1901; *Annual Report of the War Department, 1902,* 29. The six officers included his adjutant, Captain Wilds P. Richardson; chief surgeon, Major Rudolf G. Ebert; paymaster, Major William F. Tucker; quartermaster, Major Gonzales S. Bingham; and judge advocate, Captain Walter A. Bethel.

3. "An Army Post Should Be Located in Skagway."

4. *Annual Report of the War Department, 1902,* 29.

5. *Annual Report of the War Department, 1902,* 29.

6. *Annual Report of the War Department, 1902,* 35; Shellum, *Black Officer in a Buffalo Soldier Regiment,* 292. Randall noted that at Fort Saint Michael, Alaska, the local authorities issued licenses to persons "who established rum shops on the ice of the bay near the shoreline, and the post commander was powerless to prevent it."

7. Hovey to Adjutant General, Department of Columbia, February 10, 1902, Camp Skagway Letters Sent.

8. Spude, *Saloons, Prostitutes, and Temperance,* 27, 74.

9. "Soldier Threw Rocks," *Daily Alaskan,* October 11, 1901.

10. "Bullitte Sent to Sitka," *Daily Alaskan,* October 12, 1901.

11. "His Last Little Joke," *Daily Alaskan,* October 25, 1901.

12. "Costly Rock," *Daily Alaskan,* April 4, 1901.

13. "Costly Rock."

14. "Perforated Siwash," *Skaguay News,* January 6, 1899, 5; Spude, "Excerpts from Behind the Red Curtains" (draft manuscript).

15. Enlistment of Robert Grant, December 27, 1898, Register of Enlistments; Robert Grant, Abstracts of Spanish-American War Military and Naval Service Records, 1898–1902, Adjutant General's Office, New York State Archives.

16. Camp Skagway Post Return, April–November 1901; *Daily Alaskan,* April 4, 1901.

17. Spude, *Saloons, Prostitutes and Temperance*, 151; Camp Skagway Post Return, June 1901.

18. Hovey, Certificate on Cause of Desertion, Camp Skagway Letters Sent.

19. Spude, *Saloons, Prostitutes and Temperance*, 45, 74–75.

20. Glasrud and Searles, *Buffalo Soldiers in the West*, 76–80. During the Civil War, the army assigned Black chaplains to the Black volunteer regiments to provide religious services and educate the soldiers, many of whom were illiterate former slaves. This practice continued after the war in the Buffalo Soldier regiments. The Twenty-Fourth Infantry regimental chaplain, Captain Allen Allensworth, who was an outspoken advocate of education for Black soldiers, was with the regiment in the Philippines, so this task fell to others in Skagway.

21. *Daily Alaskan*, January 15, 1902.

22. Adjutant General's Office, Washington DC, October 19, 1899, Camp Skagway Letters and Telegrams and Endorsements Received, 1898–1904, Records of U.S. Army Commands, 1821–1920, Entry 435-4, Vol. 4, RG 393, NARA.

23. "Line Drawn," *Daily Alaskan*, August 16, 1900.

24. "Negro Progress," *Daily Alaskan*, February 16, 1900; "Full House Greets Mr. Reed," *Daily Alaskan*, February 17, 1900.

25. "Negro Progress."

26. "Line Drawn."

27. "Line Drawn."

28. "Line Drawn."

29. "Line Drawn"; *Daily Alaskan*, August 17, 1900.

30. *Daily Alaskan*, July 3 and 6, 1900.

31. Bielakowski, *U.S. Cavalryman*, 19–20; *Annual Report of the War Department, 1902*, 36.

32. Sawyer, *Our Rifles*, 198

33. *Daily Alaskan*, October 6, 1901.

34. *Daily Alaskan*, October 6, 1901. The Skagway Rifle Club members included J. W. Snook, C. E. Olsen, M. B. Clemenger, C. G. K. Nourse, F. B. McDonald, and E. A. Kindall.

35. *New York Times*, November 18, 1901; *San Francisco Call*, November 17, 1901.

36. *New York Times*, November 18, 1901; *San Francisco Call*, November 17, 1901.

37. Dumonceaux, "The Conspiracy," ii, 35, 38; Wood to Hovey, October 15, 1901, RG18, Vol. 3033, Microfilm C2145, Library and Archives Canada.

38. "Primrose in Disgrace," *Daily Alaskan,* October 22, 1901, 1; Dumonceaux, "The Conspiracy," 32–33; RG18, Royal Canadian Mounted Police Fonds, Vol. 229, File 149, Library and Archives Canada.

39. "Primrose in Disgrace," 1; Seeley to Wood, January 24, 1902, RG18, Vol. 3033, Microfilm C2145, Library and Archives Canada.

40. Letters Sent, September to October 1901, Camp Skagway Letters Sent.

41. *Daily Alaskan,* December 3, 1901, 1.

42. Hovey to Adjutant General, Department of Columbia, December 11, 1901, Camp Skagway Letters Sent.

43. *Regulations for the Army of the United States, 1895,* 14–15; *Military Laws of the United States, 1901,* 336–38, 509–13.

44. Camp Skagway Post Return, November 1902.

45. Camp Skagway Post Return, December 1901 and January 1902; *Military Laws of the United States, 1901,* 513–16; *Regulations for the Army of the United States, 1895,* 14–15. Privates James E. B. Reed and Earnest C. Randall did not reenlist.

46. *Daily Alaskan,* January 1, 1902, 4; Camp Skagway Post Return, February 1902.

47. *Daily Alaskan,* February 5, 1902, 2; Camp Skagway Post Return, February 1902.

48. Camp Skagway Post Return, January 1902 and March 1902. Corporals Kit Dalton and Edward G. Dewey departed, as well as privates Doc L. Harrill, Landon Jackson, William Pate, George L. Wilson, Leroy H. Slone, Thomas Morton, and Lafayette Coats. Dewey and Morton were given disability discharges. Coats, Harrill, Landon, and Slone later enlisted again.

49. Camp Skagway Post Return, February 1902; Company L, Twenty-Fourth Infantry Return, February 1902. Privates George L. Ashton, George Bracy, David Caughman, Frank Collier, Edward J. Collins, William Daily, Charles Fletcher, Julius Hutson, William Jennings, Thomas Mack, James C. Matthews, Charles D. Richards, George Thornell, James A. Waters, Leonard Watkins, and Maris J. Wesley left Alaska. Ashton, Caughman, Daily, Fletcher, Hutson, and Watkins later enlisted again.

50. *Daily Alaskan,* February 20, 1902; Company L, Twenty-Fourth Infantry Return, February and March 1902.

51. Company L, Twenty-Fourth Infantry Return, March 1902.

52. Camp Skagway Post Return, March 1902. Privates Thomas A. Belcher, Walter Belcher, Andy Callway, Reid W. Davis, Junius Dawson, James H. Holland, William Howard, Ernest L. Johnson, Thomas J. Jones, John Kimball, Rob-

ert King, George A. McClellan, Earnest Morris, Thomas Mozeak, John A. Perkins, Charles F. Ray, William Rudisell, Chester Sanders, William Sims, Harry Stewart, Edward Stokes, John Taylor, Benton Trice, and Frank W. Watson ended their enlistment. Only privates Sanders and Stewart enlisted and stayed in Skagway. Belcher, Dawson, Holland, Jones, McClellan, Sims, Stokes, Taylor, Trice, and Watson enlisted again after leaving Alaska.

53. Camp Skagway Post Return, April 1902.

54. Camp Skagway Post Return, November and December 1901; Army and Navy General Hospital, Hot Springs, Arkansas, Post Return, March 1902, Returns from U.S. Military Posts, 1800–1916, M617, RG 94, NARA.

55. Camp Skagway Post Return, May 1901–March 1902; *Daily Alaskan*, June 7, 1901. Thomas Williams was convicted before Judge Sehlbrede of larceny and was sentenced to three months at Sitka.

56. Camp Skagway Post Return, March 1902.

57. Hovey to Adjutant General, Department of Columbia, March 1, 1902, and 1st Indorsement, March 11, 1902, Camp Skagway Letters Sent.

9. Departure

1. Muller, *Twenty-Fourth Infantry*, 46–47.

2. Camp Skagway Post Return, April 1902. The artillerymen left Fort Lawton, Washington, on March 31, 1902, and arrived in Skagway five days later.

3. Smith, "Coast Artillery Organization," 419–20. Before 1901 the Artillery Corps had been divided into heavy and light artillery.

4. Camp Skagway Post Return, April 1902.

5. Camp Skagway Post Return, April 1902; Adjutant General, Department of Columbia, to Hovey, May 15, 1902, Camp Skagway Letters and Telegrams and Endorsements Received, 1898–1904.

6. *Daily Alaskan*, April 12, 1902.

7. *Daily Alaskan*, April 12, 1902.

8. *Daily Alaskan*, April 12, 1902.

9. *Daily Alaskan*, April 18, 19, 20, 1902. Newspapers in 1902 included the *Daily Alaskan*, *Daily Skaguay News*, *Alaska Traveler's Guide*, and *The Alaskan*. Boys' baseball teams also competed in Skagway. Under the headline "Play Ball," the *Daily Alaskan* noted a game planned between the newsboys and the schoolboys on the beach near the depot in April 1902. This game was played on a Sunday when both groups would be free to play. Newsboys were essential to newspaper distribution and sales, even in a small town like Skagway. In 1902 Skagway still had several newspapers, as well as sale outlets for major

dailies like the *Seattle Post-Intelligencer*, and it is noteworthy that there were enough newsboys in Skagway to field a baseball team. *Daily Alaskan*, April 13, 1902, 1.

10. *Daily Alaskan*, April 20, 1902, 1.

11. *Daily Alaskan*, April 19, 1902, 1.

12. *Daily Alaskan*, April 24, 1902.

13. *Daily Alaskan*, April 29, 1902.

14. *Daily Alaskan*, May 6, 1902.

15. *Daily Alaskan*, May 9, and May 10, 1902, 1. It is not clear when the slashing incident occurred. It was reported in the Friday, May 9, newspaper that Perkins was arrested on Wednesday night and sentenced on Friday. Yet Private Edward G. Davidson and another soldier from the Thirty-Second Company named Private Henry A. Hansen had summary court-martial charges preferred against them on May 5, 1902, so the incident may have occurred on Sunday, May 4, 1902.

16. 1st Endorsement by Captain Hovey, May 5, 1902, Camp Skagway Letters and Telegrams and Endorsements Received, 1898-1904; Enlistment of Edward G. Davidson, August 18, 1901; and Henry Hansen, August 20, 1901, Register of Enlistments.

17. Enlistment of John A. Perkins, March 16, 1899, Register of Enlistments.

18. Camp Skagway Post Return, July 1899.

19. *Daily Alaskan*, May 9, 10, 1902, 1.

20. *Daily Alaskan*, May 10, 1902.

21. *Daily Alaskan*, May 10, 11, 1902.

22. *Daily Alaskan*, May 13, 1902.

23. *Daily Alaskan*, May 13, 1902.

24. *Daily Alaskan*, May 13, 1902.

25. *Daily Alaskan*, May 13, 1902.

26. *Daily Alaskan*, May 13, 1902.

27. Enlistment of William Fox, April 4, 1884, April 3, 1889, April 3, 1894, September 2, 1897, Register of Enlistments.

28. Enlistment of Thomas Kennedy, July 7, 1901, Register of Enlistments. Kennedy was murdered by a fellow soldier named John Tully at Fort Missoula, Montana, on October 18, 1903. Though the murder took place on Fort Missoula, the local marshal arrested Tully and he was sentenced to hang. The U.S. Supreme Court later overturned the conviction because the local civilian court did not have jurisdiction for a crime committed on federal land.

29. *Daily Alaskan*, May 13, 1902.

30. *Daily Alaskan*, May 13, 1902.

31. *Daily Alaskan*, May 13, 1902.

32. *Daily Alaskan*, May 13, 1902.

33. *Daily Alaskan*, May 13, 1902. William "Red Stocking" Fox was erroneously referred to as Joe Bock in the article.

34. *Daily Alaskan*, May 13, 1902.

35. *Daily Alaskan*, May 9, 1902.

36. "For He's a Jolly Good Fellow," *Daily Alaskan*, May 11, 1902; "A Fitting Tribute to Capt. Hovey," *Daily Alaskan*, May 15, 1902.

37. "Complete Report of the Speech Delivered by R.W. Jennings Saturday," *Daily Alaskan*, May 15, 1902, 3.

38. "Complete Report of the Speech."

39. "Complete Report of the Speech."

40. "Complete Report of the Speech."

41. *Daily Alaskan*, May 15, 1902.

42. Camp Skagway Post Return, May 1902.

43. Camp Skagway Post Return, April–August 1902; *Daily Alaskan*, May 9, 1902, 1.

44. *Daily Alaskan*, May 13, 1902.

45. *Daily Alaskan*, May 13, 1902.

10. Aftermath

1. Convention between Great Britain and the United States of America for the Adjustment of the Boundary between the Dominion of Canada and the Territory of Alaska, Signed at Washington, January 24, 1903; Munro, "English-Canadianism," 189–203. This was the chief impetus for Canada's establishing its Department of Foreign Affairs in 1909 and assuming responsibility for its own dealings with the United States.

2. *Daily Alaskan*, May 18 and 20, 1902. The lineup for the firemen was as follows: Harry St. Clair, manager; H. D. Kirmse, captain; Will Cleveland, catcher; McConnelly, pitcher; Barry, shortstop; Keating, first base; Moore, second base; Frank Peterson, third base; Broemser, left field; T. Cleveland, center field; and Barnes, right field.

3. *Daily Alaskan*, May 24, 1902.

4. *Daily Alaskan*, May 27, 1902.

5. *Daily Alaskan*, May 27, 1902.

6. *Daily Alaskan*, May 27, 1902.

7. *Daily Alaskan*, July 8, 1902.

8. *Daily Alaskan*, May 15, 1902, 3.

9. *Daily Alaskan,* May 15, 1902, 3; see appendix B.

10. *Daily Alaskan,* May 15, 1902.

11. *Fort Wrangel News,* August 10, 1898, 1, as quoted in Levi, *Boom and Bust,* 121.

12. *Daily Alaskan,* May 15, 1902.

13. *Daily Alaskan,* July 12, 1902. The article misidentified the ex-soldier as Ernest C. Morrice.

14. *Daily Alaskan,* July 12, 1902.

15. *Daily Alaskan,* July 12, 1902.

16. *Daily Alaskan,* July 13, 1902.

17. *Daily Alaskan,* July 13, 1902; Spude, *Saloons, Prostitutes, and Temperance,* 78.

18. *Daily Alaskan,* July 13, 1902.

19. *Daily Alaskan,* October 4, 9, 1902.

20. *Daily Alaskan,* October 14, 1902.

21. *Daily Alaskan,* October 14, 1902.

22. Spude, *Saloons, Prostitutes, and Temperance,* 118–20.

23. Spude, *Saloons, Prostitutes, and Temperance,* 120.

24. *Daily Alaskan,* October 17, 1902; Spude, *Saloons, Prostitutes, and Temperance,* 122–23.

25. *Daily Alaskan,* January 26, 1905; Spude, *Saloons, Prostitutes, and Temperance,* 148–49.

26. *Daily Alaskan,* January 26, 1905; Spude, *Saloons, Prostitutes, and Temperance,* 148–49.

27. *Daily Alaskan,* February 16, 1905; Spude, *Saloons, Prostitutes, and Temperance,* 122–49.

28. Spude, *Saloons, Prostitutes, and Temperance,* 148–53; Census, 1910, Skagway, Alaska, Thirteenth Census of the United States, T624, NARA.

Postscript

1. Officers were better educated, more likely to have families, and part of an officer management system that was far more complicated than that of enlisted men. This resulted in alumni records, letters between family members, and a more extensive records collection on each officer at the Department of the Army. For example, I found extensive obituaries on Jenks at West Point and Hovey at Norwich. I also found a descendant of Jenks still possessing his letter, papers, and photos. Both officers had more records preserved in their officer records files.

2. "Major H. W. Hovey Dead," *Northfield Times,* November 17, 1908.

3. "Major H. W. Hovey Dead."

4. "Major H. W. Hovey Dead"; Dodge, *Norwich University, 1819-1911*, 81–82.

5. Summary of the military record of Isaac Colburn Jenks, Adjutant General, U.S. Army, undated, Jenks Papers; "Cropper Has Record as Military Man," undated newspaper clipping, Jenks Papers; *Sixty-Second Annual Report*, 282–95. See biographical entry on Cropper in appendix A.

6. Summary of the military record of Isaac Colburn Jenks; *Sixty-Second Annual Report*, 282–95.

7. Bailey to Adjutant General, May 2, 1902, with 14 Endorsements, Camp Skagway Letters Sent.

8. Camp Skagway Post Return, June 1902.

9. Fort Lawton Post Return, September 1902, Returns from U.S. Military Posts, 1800–1916, M617, RG 94, NARA.

10. *United States Army and Navy Journal* 46 (1908-9): 397; Twentieth Infantry Regimental Return, December 1908-March 1909, Returns from Regular Army Infantry Regiments, June 1821-December 1916, Microfilm M665, RG 94, NARA; U.S. Census, 1920, Rains Precinct, Carbon County, Utah, Fourteenth Census of the United States, T625, NARA.

11. *United States Army and Navy Journal* 46 (1908-9): 397; Twentieth Infantry Regimental Return, December 1908-March 1909; Census, 1920, Rains Precinct, Carbon County, Utah.

12. Enlistment of James Washington, September 2, 1902, September 2, 1905, September 2, 1908, September 2, 1911, Register of Enlistments.

13. Enlistment of Henry C. Robinson, December 18, 1903, November 23, 1905, November 11, 1908, November 11, 1911, Register of Enlistments.

14. Enlistment of Register of Robert O'Connor, December 3, 1904, November 16, 1905, Register of Enlistments; Twenty-Fourth Infantry Regimental Return, June 1907.

15. Stockton Hospital Commitment Registers, 1856–1934, MF8:10, 34 volumes, Dept. of Mental Hygiene—Hospitals, California State Archives, Sacramento.

16. See individual biographies in appendix B for detailed information on the service of the named individuals in this and the preceding five paragraphs.

17. At the time Company L served in Alaska, only three African American officers held commissions in the Regular Army: Captain Charles Young, Second Lieutenant Benjamin O. Davis Sr., and Second Lieutenant John E. Green.

18. Enlistment of Landon Jackson, January 18, 1899, February 12, 1902, February 6, 1907, February 6, 1910, Register of Enlistments; Scott, *Scott's Official History*, 475.

19. Enlistment of Chester Sanders, March 9, 1899, March 9, 1902, March 9, 1905, November 23, 1908, November 23, 1911; Scott, *Scott's Official History*, 220, 479. Sanders's father, also named Chester Sanders, served in Company F, Second Tennessee Colored Infantry, and Company F, Sixty-First U.S. Colored Infantry, during the Civil War and filed for a pension in 1891.
20. U.S. Census, 1910, Juneau, Alaska, Thirteenth Census of the United States, T624, NARA, hereafter Census, Juneau, 1910.
21. Census, Juneau, 1910.
22. Census, Juneau, 1910. Oby was listed in the 1910 census as William Oby. He had enlisted in the army as John W. Oby, so William was probably his middle name.
23. Census, Juneau, 1910.
24. Register of Voters in Fresno County, California, 1888, Ancestry.com; Census, Juneau, 1900, 1910. Waddleton represented white clients in mainly legal cases involving land rights. He was sentenced to six months in federal jail in 1912 for providing whiskey to an Indian. *Douglas Island News*, March 13, 1912. He died and was buried in Juneau in 1938.
25. Company L, Twenty-Fourth Infantry Return, January 1902.
26. Certificate of Registration of American Citizen, George Levi Wilson, U.S. Consulate Dawson, Canada, November 21, 1908, November 20, 1909, April 28, 1910, Ancestry.com; U.S. Census, 1930, Fairbanks, Alaska, Fifteenth Census of the United States, T626, NARA, hereafter Census, Fairbanks, 1930.
27. *Fairbanks Daily News-Miner*, January 11, 1940.
28. Enlistment of Benjamin Green, March 22, 1899, Register of Enlistments.
29. U.S. Census, 1910, Tanana, Alaska, Thirteenth Census of the United States, T624, NARA; Census, Fairbanks, 1930.
30. *Fairbanks Daily News-Miner*, September 23, 1939, 1, and March 18, 1940, 7.
31. *Fairbanks Daily News-Miner*, March 19, 1940, 8.
32. Enlistment of Eugene Swanson, April 10, 1899, Register of Enlistments.
33. *Fairbanks Daily News-Miner*, March 7, 1942, 1. The author could find no record of his enlistment in the Ninth Cavalry. When he enlisted in the army on April 10, 1899, he reported no prior service to the enlistment officer.
34. *Fairbanks Daily News-Miner*, March 7, 1942, 1.
35. U.S. Census, 1920, Rampart, Alaska, Fourteenth Census of the United States, T625, NARA; Swanson Pension Application, July 17, 1926, Ancestry.com; Joan Skilbred, "Eugene E. Swanson," 2018, Alaska Hall of Fame Foundation, alaskamininghalloffame.org. Swanson applied in 1926 for a pension as an invalid based on his military service.

36. U.S. Census, 1930, Rampart, Alaska, Fifteenth Census of the United States, T626, NARA; *Fairbanks Daily News-Miner*, June 12, 1939.

37. U.S. Census, 1940, Tolovana District, Alaska, Sixteenth Census of the United States, T627, NARA; *Fairbanks Daily News-Miner*, December 9, 1938, and March 5, 1941; Thomas K. Bundtzen and Charles C. Hawkey, "Ernest Bilbe Collins," 2008, Alaska Hall of Fame Foundation, alaskamininghalloffame .org. Collins was an ex-miner, former mayor of Fairbanks, and speaker of the house of the First Territorial Legislature of Alaska in 1913.

38. *Fairbanks Daily News-Miner*, March 7, October 24, and December 31, 1942.

39. *Fairbanks Daily News-Miner*, March 7, October 24, and December 31, 1942; Skilbred, "Eugene E. Swanson."

40. This is the motto of the Twenty-Fourth Infantry Regiment and means "Always Prepared."

Appendix B

1. Dyer, *Compendium of the War of the Rebellion*, 11–12 (of 36,847: 2,894 were killed or mortally wounded, 29,658 died of disease, 98 died as prisoners of war, 596 died in accidents, 3,621 died of all other non-battle causes); Schubert, *Black Valor*, 2–4. Sixteen Blacks in the U.S. Navy were awarded the Medal of Honor.

2. Leckie, *Buffalo Soldiers*, 25–26.

3. Leckie, *Buffalo Soldiers*, 25–26.

4. General Order No. 56, August 1, 1866, and General Order No. 92, November 23, 1866, General Orders and Circulars, 1797–1910, Records of the Adjutant General's Office, 1780–1917, RG 94, NARA; Coffman, *The Old Army*, 218–20.

5. Coffman, *The Old Army*, 218–20.

6. Adjutant General's Office, *Army Register for January 1880*, 280–83; Dobak and Phillips, *Black Regulars*, xii–xiii.

7. Kenner, *Buffalo Soldiers and Officers*, 27.

8. Dobak and Phillips, *Black Regulars*, 267–73.

9. Schubert, *Black Valor*, xi.

10. Dobak and Phillips, *Black Regulars*, 265–66; Kenner, *Buffalo Soldiers and Officers*, 23–26.

11. General Order No. 56 and General Order No. 92.

12. *Army and Navy Journal*, February 19, 1887 (italics in the original); Kenner, *Buffalo Soldiers and Officers*, 25.

13. Heitman, *Historical Register of the U.S. Army*, 1:850; Kenner, *Buffalo Soldiers and Officers*, 26; Shellum, *Black Officer in a Buffalo Soldier Regiment*, 34–47.

14. Ninth Cavalry Regimental Return, November 1889–September 1890; Kenner, *Buffalo Soldiers and Officers*, 113–14; Coffman, *The Old Army*, 221.

15. Shellum, *Black Cadet in a White Bastion*, 42–47.

16. Coffman, *The Old Army*, 228–29; Leckie, *Buffalo Soldiers*, 238; Jackson et al., "Bending toward Justice: The Posthumous Pardon of Lieutenant Henry O. Flipper." The U.S. Army Board for the Corrections of Military Records concluded that the conviction and punishment were "unduly harsh and thus unjust" and issued Flipper an honorable discharge posthumously in 1976.

17. Gatewood, "John Hanks Alexander," 124–25.

18. Shellum, *Black Officer in a Buffalo Soldier Regiment*, 9–47.

19. Utley, *Frontier Regulars*, 399–400.

20. Rodenbough and Haskin, *Army of the United States*, 695–96; Schubert, *Black Valor*, xi.

BIBLIOGRAPHY

Archives and Manuscript Materials

Alaska State Library, Juneau.

Frank B. Bourn Collection

California State Archives, Sacramento.

Isaac C. Jenks Collection, private collection, Hanover NH.

Isaac C. Jenks Papers.

Library and Archives Canada, Ottawa.

National Archives and Records Administration, Washington DC.

Annual Reports of the War Department.

Bureau of the Census, Census of the United States, 1870, 1880, 1900,
1910, 1920, 1930, 1940.

Camp Skagway Letters and Telegrams and Endorsements Received,
1898–1904, Records of U.S. Army Commands, 1821–1920, Entry 435-4,
Volume 4, RG 393.

Camp Skagway Letters Sent, 1899–1904, Records of U.S. Army Commands, 1821–1920, Entry 435-5, Volume 1, RG 393.

Congressional Documents.

General Index to Compiled Service Records of Volunteer Soldiers Who
Served during the War with Spain, Records of the Adjutant General's
Office, 1780–1917, M871, RG 94.

General Orders and Circulars, 1797–1910, Records of the Adjutant General's Office, 1780–1917, RG 94.

Letters Received by the Appointment, Commission, and Personnel
Branch, Adjutant General's Office, RG 94.

Register of Enlistments in the U.S. Army, 1798–1914, M233, RG 94.

Returns from Regular Army Cavalry Regiments, 1833–1916, M744, RG 391.

Returns from Regular Army Infantry Regiments, June 1821–December
1916, M665, RG 94.

Returns from U.S. Military Posts, 1800–1916, M617, RG 94.
New York State Archives, Albany.

Published Works

Adjutant General's Office. *Army Register for January, 1880.* Washington DC: Government Printing Office, 1880.

Annual Report of the Chief Signal Officer, U.S.A. for the Fiscal Year Ending June 30, 1901. Washington DC: Government Printing Office, 1901.

Annual Report of the Department of the Interior, Miscellaneous Reports, Part II, 1903. Washington DC: Government Printing Office, 1903.

Annual Report of the War Department, 1894. Washington DC: Government Printing Office, 1894.

Annual Report of the War Department, 1896. Washington DC: Government Printing Office, 1896.

Annual Report of the War Department, 1898. Part 2. Washington DC: Government Printing Office, 1898.

Annual Report of the War Department, 1899. Part 2. Washington DC: Government Printing Office, 1899.

Annual Report of the War Department, 1899/1900. Part 1. Washington DC: Government Printing Office, 1900.

Annual Report of the War Department, 1900. Washington DC: Government Printing Office, 1900.

Annual Report of the War Department, 1901. Vol. 1, Part 2. Washington DC: Government Printing Office, 1901.

Annual Report of the War Department, 1902. Vol. 9. Washington DC: Government Printing Office, 1902.

Annual Report of the War Department, 1908. Vol. 2. Washington DC: Government Printing Office, 1908.

Ashburn, Percy M. *A History of the Medical Department of the United States Army.* New York: Houghton Mifflin, 1929.

Association of Graduates. *Register of Graduates and Former Cadets of the United States Military Academy.* West Point: Association of Graduates, 2000.

Bearss, Edwin C. "Proposed Klondike Gold Rush National Historical Park: Historic Resource Study." Washington DC: National Park Service, 1970.

Bielakowski, Alexander M. *U.S. Cavalryman, 1891–1920.* Oxford: Osprey, 2004.

Bowman, Ashley. *The Arctic Brotherhood: The Story of Alaska-Yukon's Most Influential Order*. Skagway AK: Lynn Canal, 2014.

Brady, William J. *Skagway: City of the New Century*. Skagway AK: Lynn Canal, 2013.

Brands, Benjamin D. "'Unsatisfactory and Futile': The Officers' Lyceum Program and U.S. Army Reform." *Journal of Military History* 83 (October 2019): 1067–94.

Brunet-Jailly, Emmanuel. *Border Disputes: A Global Encyclopedia*. 3 vols. Santa Barbara: ABC-CLIO, 2015.

Cirillo, Vincent J. *Bullets and Bacilli: The Spanish-American War and Military Medicine*. Rutgers NJ: Rutgers University Press, 2003.

Coffman, Edward M. *The Old Army: Portrait of the American Army in Peacetime, 1784–1898*. New York: Oxford University Press, 1986.

——. *The Regulars: The American Army, 1898–1941*. Cambridge MA: Belknap Press of Harvard University Press, 2004.

Cole, David. "Survey of U.S. Army Uniforms, Weapons, and Accoutrements." Center for Military History. https://history.army.mil/html/museums/uniforms/survey.html.

Cole, George. *Record of Service of Connecticut Men in the Spanish-American War*. Whitefish MT: Kessinger Press, 2007.

Coleman, E. C. *Pig War: The Most Perfect War in History*. Stroud, UK: The History Press, 2009.

Conner, Glen. "History of Weather Observations: Fort Huachuca, Arizona, 1886–1948." Midwestern Climate Center, NOAA, December 2006.

Coumbe, Arthur T. *A History of the U.S. Army Officer Corps, 1900–1990*. Carlisle PA: U.S. Army War College Press, 2014.

Cullum, George W. *Biographical Register of the Officers and Graduates of the U.S. Military Academy, Volume IV, 1890–1900*. Cambridge MA: Riverside Press, 1901.

Cunningham, Roger D. "'We Are an Orderly Body of Men': Virginia's Black 'Immunes' in the Spanish-American War." *Historic Alexandria Quarterly*, Summer 2001.

DeArmond, R. N. *Klondike Newsman: "Stroller" White*. Skagway AK: Lynn Canal, 1990.

Demerjian, Bonnie. *Wrangell*. Charleston SC: Arcadia, 2011.

Dobak, William A., and Thomas D. Phillips. *Black Regulars, 1866–1898*. Norman: University of Oklahoma Press, 2001.

Dodge, Grenville M. *Norwich University, 1819-1911: Her History, Her Graduates, Her Role of Honor.* Vol. 3. Compiled and edited by William A. Ellis. Montpelier VT: Capital City Press, 1911.

Dumonceaux, Scott. "The Conspiracy: The Canadian Response to the Order of the Midnight Sun and the Alaska Boundary Dispute." Master's thesis, University of Saskatchewan, 2013.

Dyer, Frederick H. *Compendium of the War of the Rebellion.* Des Moines IA: Dyer, 1908.

Elihu Root Collection of United States Documents. Series A–F. Washington DC: Government Printing Office, 1904.

Emerson, William K. *Encyclopedia of United States Army Insignia and Uniforms.* Norman: University of Oklahoma Press, 1966.

Gatewood, Willard B., Jr. "John Hanks Alexander of Arkansas: Second Black Graduate of West Point." *Arkansas Historical Quarterly* 41 (Summer 1982): 103–28.

Gestner, Donald A. *Skagway in Days Primeval: The Writings of J. Bernard Moore.* Skagway AK: Lynn Canal, 1997.

Glasrud, Bruce A., and Michael N. Searles, eds. *Buffalo Soldiers in the West: A Black Soldiers Anthology.* College Station: Texas A&M University Press, 2007.

Glass, Edward L. N. *The History of the Tenth Cavalry, 1866–1921.* Fort Collins CO: Old Army Press, 1972.

Graves, Samuel H. *On the "White Pass" Pay-Roll.* Chicago: Paladin Press, 1908.

Gurcke, Karl. "Company L, 24th Infantry (Colored) in Skagway, Alaska: A Historic Photo Essay (Draft)." Klondike Gold Rush National Monument, Skagway AK.

———. "Lynch and Kennedy Dry Goods and Haberdashery (1900/1908) A Historic Photo Essay (Draft)." Klondike Gold Rush National Monument, Skagway AK.

Harring, Sidney L. "The Incorporation of Alaska Natives under American Law: The United States and Tlingit Sovereignty, 1867–1900." *Arizona Law Review* 31 (1989): 279–327.

Hartman, Ian C. *Black History in the Last Frontier.* Anchorage: University of Alaska, 2018.

Haycox, Stephen. *Alaska: An American Colony.* Seattle: University of Washington Press, 2002.

Heitman, Francis B. *Historical Register and Dictionary of the U.S. Army.* Vols. 1 and 2. Washington DC: Government Printing Office, 1903.

Hunt, William R. *Alaska: A Bicentennial History.* New York: W. W. Norton, 1976.

Jackson, Darryl W., Jeffery H. Smith, Edward H. Sisson, and Helene T. Krasnoff. "Bending toward Justice: The Posthumous Pardon of Lieutenant Henry O. Flipper." *Indiana Law Journal* 74, no. 1251 (1999): 1252–96.

James, Carolyn C. "Canada, Sovereignty and the Alaska Boundary Dispute." Prepared for presentation at the Canadian Political Science Association Annual Meeting, May 30–June 1, 2017, Toronto, Ontario.

Jarvis, William H. P. *The Great Gold Rush: A Tale of the Klondike.* Toronto: Mamillan, 1913.

Johnson, Alan I. "In Search of Freedom: African Americans and the Massachusetts' Militia from 1852–1917." Master's thesis, Brandeis University, 2017.

Johnson, Charles, Jr. *African American Soldiers in the National Guard.* Westport CT: Praeger, 1992.

Keller, Julia. *Mr. Gatling's Terrible Marvel.* New York: Penguin, 2008.

Kenner, Charles L. *Buffalo Soldiers and Officers of the Ninth Cavalry, 1867–1898: Black and White Together.* Norman: University of Oklahoma Press, 2014.

Langellier, John P. *Fighting for Uncle Sam: Buffalo Soldiers in the Frontier Army.* Atglen PA: Schiffer, 2016.

Laurie, Clayton D., and Ronald H. Cole. *The Role of Federal Military Forces in Domestic Disorders, 1877–1945.* Washington DC: Government Printing Office, 1997.

Leckie, William H. *The Buffalo Soldiers.* Norman: University of Oklahoma Press, 1999.

Levi, Steven C. *Boom and Bust in the Alaska Goldfields: A Multicultural Adventure.* Westport CT: Praeger, 2008.

Lieber, G. Norman. *Use of the Army in Aid of the Civil Power.* Washington DC: Government Printing Office, 1898.

Manual for Army Cooks. Washington DC: Government Printing Office, 1896.

A Manual for Courts-Martial and of Procedure under Military Law. Washington DC: Government Printing Office, 1898.

McQuiston, James A. *Captain Jack: Father of the Yukon.* Denver: Outskirts Press, 2017.

Mielke, Coleen. "Newlyweds Murdered in Chilkat Territory, 1899 (A True Story)." 2021. http://freepages.rootsweb.com/~coleen/genealogy/horton.html.

Military Laws of the United States, 1901. 4th ed. Washington DC: Government Printing Office, 1901.

Miller, Carman. *The Canadian Career of the Fourth Earl of Minto: The Education of a Viceroy.* Waterloo, Canada: Wilfrid Laurier University Press, 1980.

Morgan, H. Wayne. *William McKinley and His America.* Syracuse NY: Syracuse University Press, 1963.

Moss, James A. *Officers' Manual.* 5th ed. Menasha WI: George Banta, 1917.

Muir, John. *Travels in Alaska.* Boston: Houghton Mifflin, 1915. https://vault.sierraclub.org/john_muir_exhibit/writings/travels_in_alaska/.

Muller, William G. *The Twenty-Fourth Infantry: Past and Present.* Fort Collins CO: Old Army Press, 1972.

Munro, John A. "English-Canadianism and the Demand for Canadian Autonomy: Ontario's Response to the Alaska Boundary Decision, 1903." *Ontario History* 57, no. 4 (1965): 189–203.

National Park Service. *Chilkoot Trail: Cultural Landscape Report for the Chilkoot Trail Historic Corridor, Part 1: History, Existing Conditions, and Analysis.* National Park Service, 2011.

Neal, Patricia A. *Stikeen River Journal: Early Days on the Stikine River.* Self-published, 2012.

Neufeld, David. *Chilkoot Trail: Heritage Route to the Klondike.* Madeira Park, Canada: Lost Moose, 2005.

Official Register of the United States, Containing a List of Officers and Employees in the Civil, Military, and Naval Service. Vol. 1. Washington DC: Government Printing Office, 1901.

Orth, Donald J. *Dictionary of Alaska Place Names.* Washington DC: Government Printing Office, 1971.

Peterson, Harold L. *The American Sword, 1775–1945.* Mineola NY: Dover, 1954.

Population of the United States and Counties of the United States. U.S. Department of Commerce, Bureau of Statistics. Washington DC: Government Printing Office, March 1996.

Proceedings of the Alaskan Boundary Tribunal: Convened at London, under the Treaty between the United States of America and Great Britain, Concluded at Washington, January 24, 1903, for the Settlement of Questions with Respect to the Boundary Line between the Territory of Alaska and the British Possessions in North America. Washington DC: Government Printing Office, 1903.

Record of Service of Connecticut Men in the Army, Navy, and Marine Corps of the United States in the Spanish-American War, Philippine Insurrection and China Relief Expedition from April 21, 1898 to July 4, 1904. Connecticut Adjutant General. Hartford CT: Press of the Case, Lockwood, and Brainard Co., 1919.

Regulations and Decisions Pertaining to the Uniform of the Army of the United States. Washington DC: Government Printing Office, 1897.

Regulations for the Army of the United States, 1895, with Appendix Showing Changes to January 1, 1899. Washington DC: Government Printing Office, 1899.

Regulations for the United States Army, 1901. Washington DC: Government Printing Office, 1902.

Rodenbough, Theodore F., and William L. Haskin. *Army of the United States.* New York: Argonaut Press, 1966.

Roosevelt, Theodore. "The Rough Riders." *Scribner's Magazine* 25, no. 4 (1899): 420–40.

Sawyer, Charles W. *Our Rifles, Volume III.* Boston: Cornhill, 1920.

Sawyer, Lemuel K. *A Biography of John Randolph, of Roanoke.* New York: William Robinson, 1884.

Schubert, Frank N. *Black Valor: Buffalo Soldiers and the Medal of Honor, 1870–1890.* Wilmington DE: Scholarly Resources, 1997.

———. *Voices of the Buffalo Soldier.* Albuquerque: University of New Mexico Press, 2003.

Scidmore, Eliza R. "The Stikine River in 1898." *National Geographic Magazine* 10, no. 1 (1899): 1–15.

Scott, Edward Van Zile. *The Unwept: Black American Soldiers and the Spanish-American War.* Montgomery AL: River City, 1996.

Scott, Emmett J. *Scott's Official History of the American Negro in the World War.* Scott, 1919.

Shellum, Brian G. *Black Cadet in a White Bastion: Charles Young at West Point.* Lincoln: University of Nebraska Press, 2006.

———. *Black Officer in a Buffalo Soldier Regiment: The Military Career of Charles Young.* Lincoln: University of Nebraska Press, 2010.

Sixty-Second Annual Report of the Association of Graduates of the United States Military Academy at West Point, June 10, 1932. Chicago: Lakeside Press, 1931.

Skirbunt, Peter. "From Commissary Sergeant to U.S. President." Defense Commissary Agency. www.commissaries.com.

Smith, Bolling W., and William C. Gaines. "Coast Artillery Organization: A Brief Overview." Coast Defense Study Group. cdsg.org.

Smith, Jeff. *Alias Soapy Smith: The Life and Death of a Scoundrel.* Juneau: Klondike Research, 2009.

Soldier's Handbook for Use in the Army of the United States. Washington DC: Government Printing Office, 1902.

Spude, Catherine Holder. *Saloons, Prostitutes and Temperance in Alaska Territory.* Norman: University of Oklahoma Press, 2015.

———. *"That Fiend in Hell": Soapy Smith in Legend.* Norman: University of Oklahoma Press, 2012.

Steward, Theophilus G. *The Colored Regulars in the United States Army.* Philadelphia: A. M. E. Book Concern, 1904.

United States Congressional Serial Set. Serial Set Vol. 4155, Vol. 81, Document 258. Washington DC: Government Printing Office, 1900.

U.S. Ordnance Department. *Handbook of the Gatling Gun, Caliber .30 Models of 1895, 1900, and 1903.* Washington DC: Government Printing Office, 1905.

Utley, Robert M. *Frontier Regulars: The United States Army and the Indian, 1866-1891.* New York: Macmillan, 1973.

Warrington, Bob. "The Fight for Sunday Baseball in Philadelphia." Philadelphia Athletics Historical Society. www.philadelphiaathlectics.org/history.

Weigley, Russell F. *The History of the United States Army.* New York: Macmillan, 1967.

Whitehorne, Joseph W. A. *The Inspector Generals of the United States Army, 1903-1939.* Washington DC: Government Printing Office, 1998.

Winthrop, William. *Military Law and Precedents.* Washington DC: Government Printing Office, 1920.

Woll, Allen. *Black Musical Theatre: From Coontown to Dreamgirls.* Baton Rouge: Louisiana State University Press, 1989.

Zang, David W. *Fleet Walker's Divided Heart: The Life of Baseball's First Black Major Leaguer.* Lincoln: University of Nebraska Press, 1995.

INDEX

Barry, Edward, 3, 136, 179, 184–85, 288n19
baseball, xx, xxi, 2–3, 10, 20, 43, 94–99, 106, 121, 122, 133–37, 138, 139, 141, 149, 158, 168, 173, 178–80, 182–85, 188, 189, 190–93, 198, 207, 209, 269n6, 288n19, 288n25, 301n9
Bayard, Levi H., 214–15
Belcher, Thomas A., 215, 300n52
Belcher, Walter, 24, 103, 215, 300n52
Belmont, Frankie, 196–97
Belmont, Ollie, 197
Bennett City BC, xx, 30, 43, 45, 69
Black community, 78, 139–44, 174, 181, 188, 189, 193–98, 206–8, 209, 212
blackface, 49, 148–53
Blanchard, William C., 3, 136
Board of Trade saloon, xxi, 72, 106, 116, 118
Boer War, 123, 131
Bogardus, Eldridge, 49
Bordinghammer, Edward, 18–19, 27, 43, 101, 120, 215–16
Bourn, Frank B., 38–39
Brackett, A. H., 186, 295n26
Bracy, George, 98–99, 137, 179, 216, 300n49
Brady, John G., 113
Brainard, David L., 34
Breckinridge, Joseph C., Sr., 80–81, 285n47
Brereton, John J., 12
British soldiers, 31–32, 56, 107–8
Brown, Frank, 216
Brown, George A., 17
Brown, Melville C., 103–4, 113, 169, 197

Brown, Peter, 207
Brown, Phil, 102
Brown, Ruth, 143, 164, 196–98
Bullitte, Marion P., 161–62, 216
Burns, Frank, 3, 136
Busby, I. W., 124–25

Callahan, Tim, 52–53, 194
Callaway, Andy, 216, 300n52
Camp Alger VA, 23
Camp Grant IL, 205
Camp Thomas GA, 129
Camp Wikoff (Montauk Point) NY, 13, 17
Canadian Pacific Railway, 43
Caribou Crossing (Carcross), Yukon Territory, xx, 108–9, 134
Case, William, 145
Casselle, Nelson A., 137, 149, 151, 217, 259–60
Caughman, David, 149, 151, 217, 259, 261, 300n49
Causten, J. C., 52
cavalry: First U.S. Cavalry, 11, 77, 78; First U.S. Volunteer Cavalry, 154; Fourth U.S. Cavalry, 34, 279n16; Sixth U.S. Cavalry, 155; Ninth U.S. Cavalry, 21, 34–35, 174, 210–11, 250–51, 254, 255, 256, 270n18, 272n48, 275n16, 306n33; Tenth U.S. Cavalry, 10, 14, 250–51, 255, 271n34, 291n71
Census of 1900, U.S., 99–102
Ceovich, Louis, 157
Chappelear, Louis S., 177, 181, 187
Cheyenne Indians, 8, 250
children, 55, 62, 83, 100, 135, 200, 202, 209
Chilkat River, 29, 117, 123, 147–48

Chilkat Tribe (Jilḵáat Ḵwáan), 33, 38–39, 42, 102, 118, 276n30, 277n31, 290n42
Chilkoot Pass, 30, 31, 37, 128
Chilkoot Trail, 30, 45, 147
Chilkoot Tribe (Jilḵoot Ḵwáan), 33, 196
Circle City AK, 35, 64
civil court, 38, 53, 57, 58, 77, 79, 103, 117, 141, 142, 181, 186, 189, 164, 194, 195–98, 279n18, 301n55
Civil War, 15, 17, 18, 101, 120, 127, 132, 135, 153, 155, 174, 211, 249, 250–54, 258, 269n6, 275n16, 276n28, 282n62, 283n8, 285n47, 295n15, 299n20, 306n19
Clancy's Theater, 77–78
Clarkson, Charles, 83–84, 187
Cleveland, Tom, 96, 288n19, 303n2
Cleveland, William, 96, 288n19, 303n2
Clevenger, G. S., 193
Coast Artillery Corps: Thirty-Second Company, 177–78, 180–81; 106th Company, xx, 177–78, 187, 191
Coats, Lafayette, 103, 217, 270n6, 300n48
Cole, Robert A., 152, 296n45
Coleman Hotel barracks, 38, 39
Collier, Emery, 60, 93, 119, 217
Collier, Frank, 217–18, 300n49
Collins, Edward J., 53–54, 149, 151, 218, 259–60, 300n49
Collins, Nathan A. See Casselle, Nelson A.
color line, 72–73, 116, 150, 166–67, 176
Columbus Barracks OH, 8, 16, 20, 270n10
Comanche Indians, 8, 18, 19, 250

Commerce saloon, 180
company clerks, 36, 50
confinement, civil, 59, 76, 77, 137, 142, 162, 175, 181, 206, 282n66
confinement, military, 7, 57, 75, 76, 77, 78, 79, 93, 117, 270n6
cooks, military, 26, 27, 36, 43, 50, 57, 59, 90, 92, 145, 147, 173, 175, 207, 289n35
Corrigan, James, 169
Cottage (brothel), 196–97
Cotton, Robert, 172, 205, 218
court martial, general, 11, 47, 57–58, 79, 117, 175, 203, 251, 254, 255, 279n18
court martial, summary, 57, 76, 77, 79, 117, 181, 302n15
Crompton, John, 50, 65
Cropper, Samuel, 201, 219
Cuba, 6, 9, 12–13, 14–15, 17, 19, 21, 25, 50, 64, 79, 81, 154, 172, 257–58, 285n47
Curtis, Edward C., 55
Cushman, Gabriel, 85–86, 92–93, 286n67

Daily, William, 219, 300n49
Dalton, Kitt, 220, 300n48
Daniels, George B., 136, 179, 184
Davids Island NY, 60, 270n10
Davidson, Edward G., 180–81, 302n15
Davis, A. H., 70
Davis, Benjamin O., 291n71, 305n17
Davis, John E., 173, 220
Davis, Reid W., 137, 220, 300n52
Dawson, Junius, 205, 220–21, 300n52
Dawson City, Yukon Territory, 30, 76, 110, 114, 127, 143, 164, 169, 179, 208, 210

unteer Infantry, 23; Forty-Ninth U.S. Volunteer Infantry, 183–84
inspector general, 80–81, 133, 285n47

Jackson, Landon, 172, 205, 227–28, 270n6, 300n48
Jenks, Alice G. (Girard), 12, 13, 62–64, 93, 107, 145–46, 158, 228
Jenks, Dorothy, 13, 63, 145, 158, 228
Jenks, Isaac C.: early life of, 10; at West Point, 10; army career of, 10–15, 26, 28, 228; at Fort Wrangel, xix, xx, 7, 29, 35–36, 46–66, 67, 87–89, 100; at Skagway Barracks, 90–92, 94–95, 101, 107, 109–10, 111, 113–14, 115, 124–25, 131; promotion and temporary command of, 131–39, 145, 147, 148–49, 156, 160, 186; departure of, 157–58; Alaska accomplishments of, 160, 186, 189, 190, 199–200; after Alaska, 200–201; death of, 201
Jenks, Marion, 63, 146, 158
Jennings, R. W., 186–87, 263–67
Jennings, William, 3, 98–99, 136, 179, 228, 300n49
Johnson, Albert L., 228–29
Johnson, Charles S. (district judge), 38
Johnson, Charles S. (soldier), 57, 229
Johnson, Ernest L., 98–99, 136, 229, 300n52
Johnson, George, 163
Johnson, Green, 142
Johnson, John J., 229
Johnson, Samuel, 229
Johnston, Henry, 175, 229
Joiner, Fred, 24, 58–59, 78, 229–30, 280n42
Jones, Minnie, 52, 194

Jones, Thomas J., 57, 230, 300n52
Jordan, Harry V., 53–54, 57, 115, 119, 230
Jordan, Robert W., 58, 230
Juneau AK, 125–26, 147, 153, 155, 198, 206–8, 212, 290n44, 306n24

Kake AK, 33, 39, 56
Kane, Henry G., 86
Keating, Slim, 184–85, 303n1
Kelly, J. H., 187
Kennedy, Thomas, 183–84, 185, 230, 302n28
Kenny, Fred, 96, 288n19
Kern, P. E., 168, 295n26
Kimball, A. E., 137
Kimball, John, 86, 230, 300n52
Kincaid, Orestus J., 24, 173, 230–31
King, Robert, 231, 300n52
Kiowa Indians, 8, 18, 19
Kipling, Rudyard, 56
Kirmse, H. D., 179, 180, 303n1
Kirmse Cup, 180, 182–85, 191–92
Klondike gold rush, 2, 30–33, 48, 51, 67–68, 100, 104–5, 207
Klukwan AK, 117–19
Knox, Elijah H., 23, 120, 231
Kostrometinoff, George, 38–39
Krag-Jørgensen rifle, 41, 115, 127, 168
Ku Klux Klan Act, 114

Lake Bennett, Yukon Territory, 31, 43
Landers, John, 68
Last Chance saloon, 72, 143, 161–62
Laumeister, John L., 104–5
laundresses, 63, 102, 140–41, 152, 193, 281n57
law enforcement, 31, 102, 103, 112–14, 122, 186, 190

Norwich University (Northfield VT), 5, 9, 26, 83, 200

Oakford, Charles R., 86
Oby, John W., 98–99, 136, 141, 168, 173, 179, 207–8, 236, 306n22
O'Connor, Louisa "Sussie" (Withers), 15, 84, 93, 101, 151–52, 203, 236
O'Connor, Robert: early life of, 14; army career of, 14–15, 18, 27, 28, 236–37; at Dyea Barracks, 36, 42, 277n33; at Skagway Barracks, 67, 75, 76–77, 84, 89, 92, 93, 101, 103, 136, 139, 171–72, 187; after Alaska, 203
Olsen, Clarence, 136, 179, 182–83, 184–85, 192, 299n34
Order of the Midnight Sun, 169–71

Pacific & Arctic Railway & Navigation Company, 71, 126
Pack Train Restaurant, 157, 297n64
Pare, L. A., 108
Parkin, Robert M., 157
Pate, William, 23, 53–54, 136, 148–49, 151–52, 179, 237, 259–61, 300n48
pay, military, 19, 26, 72, 73–75, 78, 80, 81–82, 86, 120, 171, 202, 252, 258, 283n22
Payne, George M., 53–54, 106, 115–16, 120, 237
Peniel Mission, 143, 197
Peoples, Edgar R., 104–5, 129
Perkins, John A., 174, 180–82, 206–8, 237, 270n6, 300n52, 302n15
Perry, Joseph, 237
Phelps, John C., 2, 96, 136, 183–85, 192, 288n19
Phelps, Mark, 178

Philippine Islands, 5–6, 28, 31, 48, 111, 122, 131, 136, 158, 164, 177, 184, 200, 203, 204, 291n71
Pig War, 32, 275n9
Pon, Jacob A., 173, 237–38
Poole, Fran, 150, 259
Pope, E. T., 97–98
Porcupine City AK, 109, 122–23, 124, 148
Portland OR, 7, 59, 74, 137, 288n25
Posse Comitatus Act, 32, 113
Presbyterian church, 145
Presidio (San Francisco CA), 6, 36, 63, 75–76, 181
Preston, Guy H., 34–35
Price, John G., 104
Primrose, Philip C. H., 108, 169–70
Principal Barbershop, 141
promotion, 8, 10, 15, 84, 86, 92, 93, 111, 130, 131–32, 202, 254, 275n16, 287n5
prostitution, 2, 76, 78, 100, 102, 140, 142–43, 162–64, 193, 195, 196–98
Puerto Rico, 28
Pullen House, 186, 295n24
Pyramid Harbor AK, 118–19, 123

Rains, Edward L.: early life of, 111; army career of, 111–12; at Skagway Barracks, 112–14, 117–19, 131, 135, 141, 146–47, 152, 159, 167–68, 184, 186, 187–88, 199, 238; after Alaska, 201–2; death of, 202
Rains, Ella Burns (Hayes), 147, 238
Rains, James K., 111
Rampart AK, 64, 199, 210, 212
Randall (baseball player), 96, 288n19
Randall, Ernest C., 24, 238, 300n45

Randall, George M., 64–65, 88–89, 90, 114, 159–61, 171, 204, 282n62, 282n64, 286n77, 298n6
Randolph, John, 20
Rare, James, 76, 77, 78, 238
Ray, Charles F., 238, 300n52
Reed, Charles, 173, 204, 238–39
Reed, James E. B., 165–66, 167, 172, 239
Reid, Frank H., 68
Reid, W. A., 166
religion, 96, 132, 164–65, 299n20
replacements, 27, 119, 175, 183
restricted district, 143, 195–97
Richards, Charles D., 239, 300n49
Roberts, Wilkins G., 239
Robinson, Henry C.: in Alaska, 74–75, 84, 93, 101, 139, 148; after Alaska, 203, 239–40
Robinson, Sarah M. (Clemons), 84, 86, 93, 101, 139, 203, 240
Rogers, James P., 145, 297n63
Rogers, J. J., 180, 181, 195–96
Rollins, William, 136–37, 240
Roosevelt, Theodore, xx, 154
Root, Elihu, 112, 165
Rounds, Jessie, 163
Rucker, Edward, 240
Rucker, John, 240
Rucker, Louis H., 34–35, 254, 275n16
Rudisell, William, 240–41, 300n52
Russia, xix, 46–47, 85
Russian American Company, 46
Ryan, James A., 34–35
Ryan, Richard, 143–44

Saint Michael AK, 30, 64–65, 159, 298n6

Salt Lake City UT, 5, 6, 12, 13, 15, 63, 84, 94, 202
Salvation Army, 102, 103
Sanders, Chester, 205–6, 241, 300n52, 306n19
San Juan Hill, Cuba, 12–13, 14–15, 17, 18, 19, 21, 79, 128, 143, 210–11, 257, 285n47
Schofield, John M., 256
Seattle WA, xix, 7, 21, 32, 38, 49, 52, 63, 64–65, 68, 75, 80, 93, 105, 112, 127, 132, 154, 158, 169–70, 179, 193, 201, 208, 210, 288n25
Seely, J. H., 169–70
Sehlbrede, Charles A., 102, 104, 113, 116, 141, 142–43, 301n55
Senate saloon, 116
Shannon, Huston, 59, 241, 281n43
Shoup, James M., 169
Siboney, Cuba, 12, 13, 15, 17, 19, 25
sickness, 7, 8–9, 17, 25, 27, 36, 43, 44, 60, 76, 81, 84–87, 120, 128–29, 132, 137, 160, 154, 175, 176, 194
Simmons, Esaw, 128–29, 241
Sims, William, 3, 98–99, 136, 179, 183, 241–42, 300n52
Sitka AK, 38, 102, 147, 153, 264, 290n42
Sitka Prison, 53, 58, 59, 66, 77, 78–79, 80, 93, 103, 116, 137, 142, 162–63, 175, 181, 206, 282n66, 301n55
Skagway fire companies, 42, 69, 70, 106, 156–57
Skagway Rifle Club, 168, 299n34
Slone, Leroy H., 242, 300n48
Smith, David, 242
Smith, James, 242
Smith, Jefferson R. "Soapy," 2, 33, 68, 105, 190, 282n3

Smith, M. E., 115
Smith, Viola, 142–43
Smith, Walter, 141–42
Snook, J. W., 142, 162, 168, 170, 195, 299n34
Snoten, Augustus: early life of, 17; army career of, 17–18, 27, 242–43, 272n48; in Alaska, 101, 140, 174; after Alaska, 204
Snoten, Cora (Smith), 140
Snoten, Peter, 17, 272n48
Snoten, William W., 140
Snyder, Philip W., 71, 91, 145
Spanish-American War, xix, 9, 18, 19, 21–22, 24–28, 41, 51, 61, 68, 76, 86, 99, 111, 112, 128, 129, 132, 153, 154, 163, 173, 194, 205, 208, 210, 211, 257, 280n42, 285n47
ss *Alert*, 118–19
ss *Amur*, 108
ss *City of Seattle*, xxi, 97, 102, 133, 187–88
ss *Cottage City*, 78, 173
ss *Dirigo*, 57
ss *George W. Elder*, 34, 55
ss *Humboldt*, xx, 7, 29, 35, 46, 49, 65, 90, 129
ss *Oregon*, 34
ss *South Portland*, 112–14
ss *Topeka*, 184
Stanish, Anton, 157
Starkey, Benjamin F., 52–53, 194
St. Clair, Harry, 179, 303n2
Sterling, Develor, 243–44
Sterly, Henry, 86, 286n67
Stewart, Harry, 75–76, 181, 243, 270n6, 300n52
Stewart, John D., 68
Stokes, Edward, 243–44, 300n52

strikers, 36, 50, 279n14
Summerall, Charles P., 187, 189, 191
Swanson, Alice (Graves), 210–11, 244
Swanson, Amelia (Beckwith), 151–52, 174, 244
Swanson, Eugene: early life of, 20–21; army career of, 21; in Alaska, 152, 174, 199, 210–11, 244, 306n35; death of, 211
Swanson, Gracie, 210
Sylvester, E. O., 104–5

Tagish, Yukon Territory, 127
Tanana AK, 64, 209, 210
Tanner, Josias M., 43, 68, 102–3, 104, 197–98
Taylor, Frank B., 254
Taylor, John, 244, 300n52
telegraph, xx, 9, 12, 29, 64, 65, 127, 154–55, 251, 256
telephone, 71, 127
Terrell, Robert, 244
Tharlson (baseball player), 96, 288n19
Tholin, Edward J., 136, 179, 183–85
Thornell, George, 195–96, 244, 300n49
Thwing, Clarence, 55
Tlingit Indians, 30, 33, 38, 46, 47, 52, 59, 63, 66, 81, 97, 100, 102–4, 117–19, 121, 128, 137, 147–48, 158, 163, 190, 278n4, 289n42
Toledo Blue Stockings, 20
Tolovana AK, 210
Trice, Benton, 24, 244–45, 270n7, 300n52
Trip to Coon Town, 152–53
Troy, John W., 97–98, 105, 112–13, 114, 116, 118, 136, 142–43, 162–63, 169–70

Truax, Jesse P., 201
Turner, Ellis, 103, 120, 245
Tustin, Fred P., 49, 52, 281n59
Tutherly, Herbert E., 80, 133
Tweedale, John, 38–40, 42, 276n28, 277n42
typewriters, 126–27

uniforms, baseball, 94, 96, 179
uniforms, military, 3, 26, 40–42, 61, 80, 81, 135, 140, 168, 258
United Kingdom, 31–32, 47, 66, 107–10, 122–25, 142, 170, 189–90, 289n31
U.S. Army Engineer School of Application (Willets Point NY), 11, 26, 125
U.S. Army Quartermaster Department, 26, 37, 50, 65, 70, 83–84, 91, 173, 200, 204, 252, 254, 298n2
U.S. Army School of Application for Infantry and Cavalry (Fort Leavenworth KS), 130
U.S. Army Transport *McDowell*, 7
U.S. Army Transport *Seward*, 160
U.S. Military Academy (West Point NY), 10, 11, 23, 64, 94, 111, 125, 145, 253, 255, 258, 270n18, 304n1
U.S. Navy, 33, 94, 137, 163–64, 175, 307n1
U.S. Revenue Cutter *McCulloch*, 55
U.S. Revenue Cutter *Parry*, 113
U.S. Revenue Service, 33, 47, 119

Valdez AK, 64
Van Brocklin (baseball player), 136, 179
Vancouver Barracks WA, 7, 29, 35, 36, 45, 46, 57–58, 64, 81, 86, 93, 117, 120, 159, 171, 175, 201

Van Zant (baseball player), 96, 288n19
Veterans of Foreign Wars, 211
von Wrangel, Ferdinand, 47

Waddleton, William N. C., 207–8, 306n24
Walker, Moses F., 20
Walker, Weldy, 20
Washington, Alice (Cooper), 63, 93, 101, 245
Washington, Booker T., 154
Washington, James: early life of, 15; army career of, 15–17, 27–28, 245–46; at Fort Wrangel, 35–36, 50–51, 58–60, 63, 280n42; at Skagway Barracks, 92–93, 101, 129–30, 139, 187–88; after Alaska, 202–3
Washington, Maggie, 63, 101
Washington DC, 15, 38, 44, 80, 124, 126, 129–30, 154–55, 276n28
Waters, James A., 246, 270n6, 300n49
Watkins, Leonard, 103, 246, 300n49
Watson, Frank W., 151, 246, 261, 300n52
Wesley, Maris P., 246, 300n49
West Point. *See* U.S. Military Academy (West Point NY)
wharfs, 37, 39–41, 44–45, 65, 67–70, 83, 89, 90–91, 105, 110, 112–13, 177, 188, 276n28, 277n33, 277n42
Wheeler, Arthur, 175, 246
Wheeler, Earnest S., 177, 187
White, Charlie J., 151, 246
White, William H., 119, 247
Whitehorse, Yukon Territory, 43, 108–10, 133–35, 169, 189, 191
White Pass, 30, 51, 114, 145, 190

White Pass & Yukon Route, xx, 2, 30, 43, 45, 66, 68–69, 82, 85, 88, 96, 104, 107–10, 127, 145, 150, 194, 289n30

White Pass baseball club, xx, xxi, 3, 134, 135–36, 178–80, 182–85, 191–92

White Pass Quartet, 145

Williams, Edward, 247

Williams, Edward (musician), 151, 247, 260–61

Williams, George H., 149–50, 152–53, 259, 296n44

Williams, Herbert, 139, 173, 247

Williams, Laura, 207

Williams, Thomas, 142, 175, 247, 301n55

Willson, T. A., 55

Wilson, George L.: early life of, 21; army career of, 21–22, 23, 27, 28; in Alaska, 103, 173, 208, 211, 248, 300n48; death of, 208

Wood, George W., 77, 78

Wood, Z. T., 169

Yeatman, Richard T., 33–34, 37

yellow fever, 13, 17, 257

YMCA (Young Men's Christian Association), 149–50, 165–67, 172, 176

Young, Charles, 23, 174, 254–56, 305n17

Yukon Field Force, 31, 34, 108

CPSIA information can be obtained
at www.ICGtesting.com
Printed in the USA
LVHW110413120921
697632LV00004BA/11